NUMBER 63

Yale French Studies

The Pedagogical Imperative:
Teaching as a Literary Genre

D0107928

Yale French Studies

Barbara Johnson, *Special editor for this issue*

Liliane Greene, *Managing editor*

Editorial board: Charles Porter (Chairman), Peter Brooks, Paul de Man, Karen Erickson, Shoshana Felman, John Gallucci, Richard Goodkin, Fredric Jameson, Roddey Reid

Editorial office: 315 William L. Harkness Hall.

Mailing address: 2504A Yale Station, New Haven, Connecticut 06520.

Sales and subscription office: Yale University Press, 92A Yale Station, New Haven, Connecticut 06520.

Published twice annually by Yale University Press.

Printed in the United States of America by The Vail-Ballou Press, Binghamton, N.Y.

ISSN 0044–0078

ISBN for this issue 0–300–02856–3

Teaching as a Literary Genre

This collection of essays is designed to probe the theory and practice of teaching in an unusual way. While discussions of pedagogy generally deal with classroom procedures for the teaching of texts, this volume studies the ways in which the texts themselves dramatize the problematics of teaching. From Plato's Socrates to Nietzsche's Zarathustra, from Rousseau's *Nouvelle Héloïse* to Sade's *Immoral teachers*, the figure of the teacher and the question of pedagogy have indeed been fundamental topoi throughout the history of Western philosophy and literature. Basing itself on such texts, this volume asks not: how should *we* teach literature? but rather: what does literature have to teach *us* about the act of teaching?

Focusing on a wide variety of works by such authors as Balzac, Molière, Diderot, Maupassant, Laclos, and Flaubert as well as Freud, Lacan, Barthes, Nietzsche, and even the Cornell English Department, these articles elaborate a rich, provocative series of analyses of the nature and functioning, within the pedagogical arena, of authority, seduction, judgment, resistance, desire, mystification, narrative, ignorance, and the relations between the sexes. This collection thus provides a many-faceted opportunity for teachers to reflect on the nature of their profession and to examine the dynamics of their own language—indeed, of language itself—in relation both to the play of power and to the process of understanding.

The fact that most of the essays collected here deal with literary works that represent the pedagogical situation is not, however, the only way of understanding the notion of "teaching as a literary genre." For just as Socrates, in the *Phaedrus*, sees teaching as an attempt to reach the truths that are already "*inscribed* in the soul" (278a), so, it seems, is there always a "written" dimension to the learning process. In suggesting that teaching as such is somehow "literary," I do not mean to estheticize pedagogy into a form of art, but rather to attempt to analyze how and what the literarity of literature itself "teaches." In an effort to do this, I would like to turn briefly to a text in which the moral "lesson" is explicitly glossed as such: Coleridge's "Rime of the Ancient Mariner." The pedagogical dimensions of this text are, in fact, double: not only does the mariner conclude his tale by describing himself as a teacher, but the poetic text is itself accompanied by a running prose gloss designed to "teach" the poem to the reader. By studying these two juxtaposed modes of didactic self-reflection, we may be able to glimpse some of the ways in which literature can dramatize the fundamental literarity of teaching.

"The Rime of the Ancient Mariner" is the story of an old seaman who "stoppeth one of three"—in this case a young Wedding Guest—in order to tell the tale of an uncanny ocean voyage during which he shot an albatross, witnessed the death of the rest of the ship's crew, encountered angels and phantoms, curses and blessings, agony and relief, until he finally returned to his native land. At the conclusion of the mariner's tale, the young listener turns away from the festival toward which he was heading and disappears, arising the next morning "a sadder and a wiser man."

What has the Wedding Guest learned? The mariner's last words seem to sum up the tale's moral lesson:

> He prayeth best, who loveth best
> All things both great and small;
> For the dear God who loveth us,
> He made and loveth all.

But is this innocuous moral enough to explain the tale's haunting effect on the Guest, who goes out "like one that hath been stunned"? How can this Sunday School quatrain leave a lusty young reveler "of sense forlorn"? Something has clearly gone on in the tale that is not accounted for by its explicit moral. The tale's pedagogical dimension would seem to be somehow at odds with itself.

This difficulty in fitting the moral to the tale has been noted by more than one reader. Take, for example, the oft-cited remark of Mrs. Barbauld, and Coleridge's response to it:

Mrs. Barbauld once told me that she admired the Ancient Mariner very much, but that there were two faults in it,—it was improbable, and had no moral. As for the probability, I owned that that might admit some question; but as to the want of a moral, I told her that in my own judgment the poem had too much; and that the only or chief fault, if I might say so, was the obtrusion of the moral sentiment so openly on the reader as a principle or cause of action in a work of such pure imagination.[1]

Coleridge is here suggesting that the didactic impulse has overrun the bounds proper to it in a work of pure literature. Yet if the pedagogical dimension of a poem ought, according to Coleridge, to be kept to a minimum, why has he added to his text a gloss designed to be even more "obtrusive" than the original poem? It is perhaps precisely in this split between too much and too little moral, between obtrusiveness and purity, that the literarity of the teaching process here resides.

---

1. Quoted in James D. Boulger, *Twentieth Century Interpretations of "The Rime of the Ancient Mariner"* (Englewood Cliffs, N.J.: Prentice-Hall, Inc., 1969), p. 116.

Let us now look more closely at the pedagogical climax of the poem, in which the mariner and the gloss both explain the tale's moral:

And ever and anon throughout his future life an agony constraineth him to travel from land to land;

"Since then, at an uncertain hour,
That agony returns:
And till my ghastly tale is told,
This heart within me burns.

I pass, like night, from land to land;
I have strange powers of speech;
That moment that his face I see,
I know the man that must hear me:
To him my tale I teach.

. . . .

And to teach, by his own example, love and reverence to all things that God made and loveth.

Farewell, farewell! but this I tell
To thee, thou Wedding-Guest!
He prayeth well, who loveth well
Both man and bird and beast.

He prayeth best, who loveth best
All things both great and small;
For the dear God who loveth us,
He made and loveth all."

The poem and the gloss disagree slightly over the nature of the act of teaching they describe. While in the gloss the mariner "teaches . . . love and reverence," in the poem he teaches only his "tale." While in the gloss love is taught by *example*, in the poem love is described as the highest form of *prayer*. In other words, the gloss consistently transforms acts of speech (telling, praying) into ways of living (setting an example of love and reverence). If the move from text to gloss is a move from the more literary to the more didactic, then the gloss's omission of the linguistic dimension is symptomatic of pedagogy's anxiousness *not* to be a literary genre.

But if, as both poem and gloss insist, the mariner *is* a teacher, what and how does he teach? It appears that teaching here occurs as a compulsion to repeat a tale. Interestingly, in the *Phaedrus*, Socrates too teaches through a kind of compulsion to speak: "As the speech proceeds, I often seem to be in a frenzy. . . . I'll cross the stream and go away before you put any greater compulsion on me" (238c, 242a). In the mariner's case, the purpose of storytelling is to relieve the agony of the compulsion to tell the story. The story, it turns out, is itself a series of agonies and compulsions: the mariner kills the albatross for no apparent reason and afterward lives through agonies of repentance that alternate with unwilled moments of release. The most effective relief seems to come from the telling of the tale. What is the lesson in all this?

The poem has often been criticized for its repetitiveness, for the wanton-
ness or arbitrariness of its events, for the monstrous disproportion between the
punishment and the crime, and for the mariner's apparent passivity. The
mariner's entire life seems to be dictated by the guilt arising out of a
completely unmotivated act. But all these "flaws" can of course be read as
signs that the poem obeys a logic different from the "rational."

The discontinuity in rational logic represented by the bird's murder is
textually evoked as a break in the mariner's tale. The Wedding Guest
interrupts the mariner precisely at the point where the motivation for the act
ought to have been given:

> "In mist or cloud, on mast or shroud,
> It perched for vespers nine;
> Whiles all the night, through fog-smoke white,
> Glimmered the white Moon-shine."

> "God save thee, ancient Mariner!
> From the fiends, that plague thee thus!—
> Why look'st thou so?"—"With my cross-bow
> I shot the ALBATROSS."

The gloss, perfectly dramatizing the pedagogical inability to leave any gap
unfilled, rushes in with an arsenal of adjectives:

The ancient Mariner
inhospitably killeth
the pious bird
of good omen.

The ship's crew, too, attempts to subsume the mariner's act under the rational
categories of right and wrong, first by berating the mariner for killing the bird
of good luck, then by agreeing that it was right to slay the bird that brought the
fog and mist. The mariner himself, however, never reaches a stable judgment
or explanation for his act; on the contrary, the rest of his life is but a repetition
of the question. It would seem that what he has to teach is merely his own
particular experience of not knowing. An experience that cannot, however,
simply be called "irrational," since it partakes of a different kind of rationality,
an *other* logic.

Coleridge has thus given us two views of pedagogy in this poem. On the
one hand, the gloss represents the desire to transform linguistic knowledge
into existential knowledge and to fill gaps and discontinuities with causal
explanations, moral judgments, or, at the very least, evaluative descriptions.
The gloss, in other words, stands for a pedagogy that would repress the very
stuff that literature is made of. But on the other hand, a reading of the mariner

himself would suggest that teaching is a compulsion: a compulsion to repeat[2] what one has not yet understood. The locus of that non-understanding, the point at which rational continuity is eclipsed, is transmitted by the very punctuation of the poem:

> "Why look'st thou so?"—"With my cross-bow
> I shot the albatross."

It is in the break between the Wedding Guest's stunned question and the mariner's resumption of his tale that the pedagogical moment is represented as inherently and constitutively missed—represented by the dash that marks the place where what is not known is evoked as the blank that makes the story go on forever. That blank is precisely what must—and cannot—be taught. And literature is the means by which such a blank—the very agony of teaching— can somehow, nevertheless, be captured.

BARBARA JOHNSON

---

2. The idea that this poem is, among other things, a dramatization of the Freudian repetition compulsion receives unexpected confirmation in the enigmatic second line, "And he stoppeth one of three." The fact that the mariner's *first* telling of the tale was precisely to one of the *three* people that rescued him would dictate that henceforth he would unconsciously always seek to recreate the exact conditions of his first experience of relief. The unexplained generality of that "one of three" would thus make profound psychoanalytic sense.

The Lesson of Teaching

PAUL DE MAN

The Resistance to Theory

This essay was not originally intended to address the question of teaching directly, although it was supposed to have a didactic and an educational function—which it failed to achieve. It was written at the request of the Committee on the Research Activities of the Modern Language Association as a contribution to a collective volume entitled *Introduction to Scholarship in Modern Languages and Literatures.* I was asked to write the section on literary theory. Such essays are expected to follow a clearly determined program: they are supposed to provide the reader with a select but comprehensive list of the main trends and publications in the field, to synthesize and classify the main problematic areas and to lay out a critical and programmatic projection of the solutions which can be expected in the foreseeable future. All this with a keen awareness that, ten years later, someone will be asked to repeat the same exercise.

I found it difficult to live up, in minimal good faith, to the requirements of this program and could only try to explain, as concisely as possible, why the main theoretical interest of literary theory consists in the impossibility of its definition. The Committee rightly judged that this was an inauspicious way to achieve the pedagogical objectives of the volume and commissioned another article. I thought their decision altogether justified, as well as interesting in its implications for the teaching of literature.

I tell this for two reasons. First, to explain the traces in the article of the original assignment which account for the awkwardness of trying to be more retrospective and more general than one can legitimately hope to be. But secondly, because the predicament also reveals a question of general interest: that of the relationship between the scholarship (the key word in the title of the MLA volume), the theory, and the teaching of literature.

Overfacile opinion notwithstanding, teaching is not primarily an inter-subjective relationship between people but a cognitive process in which self and other are only tangentially and contiguously involved. The only teaching worthy of the name is scholarly, not personal; analogies between teaching and various aspects of show business or guidance counseling are more often than not excuses for having abdicated the task. Scholarship has, in principle, to be eminently teachable. In the case of literature, such scholarship involves at least two complementary areas: historical and philological facts as the preparatory condition for understanding, and methods of reading or interpreta-

3

tion. The latter is admittedly an open discipline, which can, however, hope to evolve by rational means, despite internal crises, controversies and polemics. As a controlled reflection on the formation of method, theory rightly proves to be entirely compatible with teaching, and one can think of numerous important theoreticians who are or were also prominent scholars. A question arises only if a tension develops between methods of understanding and the knowledge which those methods allow one to reach. If there is indeed something about literature, as such, which allows for a discrepancy between truth and method, between *Wahrheit* and *Methode,* then scholarship and theory are no longer necessarily compatible; as a first casualty of this complication, the notion of "literature as such" as well as the clear distinction between history and interpretation can no longer be taken for granted. For a method that cannot be made to suit the "truth" of its object can only teach delusion. Various developments, not only in the contemporary scene but in the long and complicated history of literary and linguistic instruction, reveal symptoms that suggest that such a difficulty is an inherent focus of the discourse about literature. These uncertainties are manifest in the hostility directed at theory in the name of ethical and aesthetic values, as well as in the recuperative attempts of theoreticians to reassert their own subservience to these values. The most effective of these attacks will denounce theory as an obstacle to scholarship and, consequently, to teaching. It is worth examining whether, and why, this is the case. For if this is indeed so, then it is better to fail in teaching what should not be taught than to succeed in teaching what is not true.

A general statement about literary theory should not, in theory, start from pragmatic considerations. It should address such questions as the definition of literature (what is literature?) and discuss the distinction between literary and non-literary uses of language, as well as between literary and non-verbal forms of art. It should then proceed to the descriptive taxonomy of the various aspects and species of the literary genus and to the normative rules that are bound to follow from such a classification. Or, if one rejects a scholastic for a phenomenological model, one should attempt a phenomenology of the literary activity as writing, reading or both, or of the literary work as the product, the correlate of such an activity. Whatever the approach taken (and several other theoretically justifiable starting-points can be imagined) it is certain that considerable difficulties will arise at once, difficulties that cut so deep that even the most elementary task of scholarship, the delimitation of the corpus and the *état présent* of the question, is bound to end in confusion, not necessarily because the bibliography is so large but because it is impossible to fix its borderlines. Such predictable difficulties have not prevented many writers on literature from proceeding along theoretical rather than pragmatic lines, often with considerable success. It can be shown however that, in all cases, this success depends on the power of a system (philosophical, religious or ideological) that may well remain implicit but that determines an *a priori* conception of what is "literary" by starting out from the premises of the system rather than from the literary thing itself—if such a "thing" indeed exists. This last qualification is of course a real question which in fact accounts for the predictability of the difficulties just alluded to: if the condition of existence of an entity is itself particularly critical, then the theory of this entity is bound to fall back into the pragmatic. The difficult and inconclusive history of literary theory indicates that this is indeed the case for literature in an even more manifest manner than for other verbalized occurrences such as jokes, for example, or even dreams. The attempt to treat literature theoretically may as well resign itself to the fact that is has to start out from empirical considerations.

Pragmatically speaking, then, we know that there has been, over the last fifteen to twenty years, a strong interest in something called literary theory and that, in the United States, this interest has at times coincided with the importation and reception of foreign, mostly but not always continental influences. We also know that this wave of interest now seems to be receding as some satiation or disappointment sets in after the initial enthusiasm. Such an ebb and flow is natural enough, but it remains interesting, in this case, because it makes the depth of the resistance to literary theory so manifest. It is a recurrent strategy of any anxiety to defuse what it considers threatening by magnification or minimization, by attributing to it claims to power of which it is bound to fall short. If a cat is called a tiger it can easily be dismissed as a paper tiger; the question remains however why one was so scared of the cat in the first place. The same tactic works in reverse: calling the cat a mouse and then deriding it for its pretense to be mighty. Rather than being drawn into this polemical whirlpool, it might be better to try to call the cat a cat and to document, however briefly, the contemporary version of the resistance to theory in this country.

The predominant trends in North American literary criticism, before the nineteen sixties, were certainly not averse to theory, if by theory one understands the rooting of literary exegesis and of critical evaluation in a system of some conceptual generality. Even the most intuitive, empirical and theoretically low-key writers on literature made use of a minimal set of concepts (tone, organic form, allusion, tradition, historical situation, etc.) of at least some general import. In several other cases, the interest in theory was publicly asserted and practised. A broadly shared methodology, more or less overtly proclaimed, links together such influential text books of the era as *Understanding Poetry* (Brooks and Warren), *Theory of Literature* (Wellek and

Warren) and *The Fields of Light* (Reuben Brower) or such theoretically oriented works as *The Mirror and the Lamp, Language as Gesture,* and *The Verbal Icon.*

Yet, with the possible exception of Kenneth Burke and, in some respects, Northrop Frye, none of these authors would have considered themselves theoreticians in the post-1960 sense of the term, nor did their work provoke as strong reactions, positive or negative, as that of later theoreticians. There were polemics, no doubt, and differences in approach that cover a wide spectrum of divergencies, yet the fundamental curriculum of literary studies as well as the talent and training expected for them were not being seriously challenged. New Critical approaches experienced no difficulty fitting into the academic establishments without their practitioners having to betray their literary sensibilities in any way; several of its representatives pursued successful parallel careers as poets or novelists next to their academic functions. Nor did they experience difficulties with regard to a national tradition which, though certainly less tyrannical than its European counterparts, is nevertheless far from powerless. The perfect embodiment of the New Criticism remains, in many respects, the personality and the ideology of T.S. Eliot, a combination of original talent, traditional learning, verbal wit and moral earnestness, an Anglo-American blend of intellectual gentility not so repressed as not to afford tantalizing glimpses of darker psychic and political depths, but without breaking the surface of an ambivalent decorum that has its own complacencies and seductions. The normative principles of such a literary ambiance are cultural and ideological rather than theoretical, oriented towards the integrity of a social and historical self rather than towards the impersonal consistency that theory requires. Culture allows for, indeed advocates, a degree of cosmopolitanism, and the literary spirit of the American Academy of the fifties was anything but provincial. It had no difficulty appreciating and assimilating outstanding products of a kindred spirit that originated in Europe: Curtius, Auerbach, Croce, Spitzer, Alonso, Valéry and also, with the exception of some of his works, J.P. Sartre. The inclusion of Sartre in this list is important, for it indicates that the dominant cultural code we are trying to evoke cannot simply be assimilated to a political polarity of the left and the right, of the academic and the non-academic, of Greenwich Village and Gambier, Ohio. Politically oriented and predominently non-academic jour-nals, of which the *Partisan Review* of the fifties remains the best example, did not (after due allowance is made for all proper reservations and distinctions) stand in any genuine opposition to the New Critical approaches. The broad, though negative, consensus that brings these extremely diverse trends and individuals together is their shared resistance to theory. This diagnosis is borne out by the arguments and complicities that have since come to light in a more articulate opposition to the common opponent.

The interest of these considerations would be at most anecdotal (the historical impact of twentieth-century literary discussion being so slight) if it were not for the theoretical implications of the resistance to theory. The local manifestations of this resistance are themselves systematic enough to warrant one's interest.

What is it that is being threatened by the approaches to literature that developed during the sixties and that now, under a variety of designations, make up the ill-defined and somewhat chaotic field of literary theory? These approaches cannot be simply equated with any particular method or country. Structuralism was not the only trend to dominate the stage, not even in France, and structuralism as well as semiology are inseparable from prior tendencies in the Slavic domain. In Germany, the main impulses have come from other directions, from the Frankfurt school and more orthodox Marxists, from post-Husserlian phenomenology and post-Heideggerian hermeneutics, with only minor inroads made by structural analysis. All these trends have had their share of influence in the United States, in more or less productive combinations with nationally rooted concerns. Only a nationally or personally competitive view of history would wish to hierarchize such hard-to-label movements. The possibility of doing literary theory, which is by no means to be taken for granted, has itself become a consciously reflected-upon question and those who have progressed furthest in this question are the most controversial but also the best sources of information. This certainly includes several of the names loosely connected with structuralism, broadly enough defined to include Saussure, Jakobson and Barthes as well as Greimas and Althusser, that is to say, so broadly defined as to be no longer of use as a meaningful historical term.

Literary theory can be said to come into being when the approach to literary texts is no longer based on non-linguistic, that is to say historical and aesthetic, considerations or, to put it somewhat less crudely, when the object of discussion is no longer the meaning or the value but the modalities of production and of reception of meaning and of value prior to their establishment—the implication being that this establishment is problematic enough to require an autonomous discipline of critical investigation to consider its possibility and its status. Literary history, even when considered at the furthest remove from the platitudes of positivistic historicism, is still the history of an understanding of which the possibility is taken for granted. The question of the relationship between aesthetics and meaning is more complex, since aesthetics apparently has to do with the *effect* of meaning rather than with its content *per se*. But aesthetics is in fact, ever since its development just before and with Kant, a phenomenalism of a process of meaning and understanding, and it may be naive in that it postulates (as its name indicates) a phenomenology of art and of literature which may well be what is at issue.

Aesthetics is part of a universal system of philosophy rather than a specific theory. In the nineteenth-century philosophical tradition, Nietzsche's challenge of the system erected by Kant, Hegel and their successors, is a version of the general question of philosophy. Nietzsche's critique of metaphysics includes, or starts out from, the aesthetic, and the same could be argued for Heidegger. The invocation of prestigious philosophical names does not intimate that the present-day development of literary theory is a by-product of larger philosophical speculations. In some rare cases, a direct link may exist between philosophy and literary theory. More frequently, however, contemporary literary theory is a relatively autonomous version of questions that also surface, in a different context, in philosophy, though not necessarily in a clearer and more rigorous form. Philosophy, in England as well as on the Continent, is less freed from traditional patterns than it sometimes pretends to believe and the prominent, though never dominant, place of aesthetics among the main components of the system is a constitutive part of this system. It is therefore not surprising that contemporary literary theory came into being from outside philosophy and sometimes in conscious rebellion against the weight of its tradition. Literary theory may now well have become a legitimate concern of philosophy but it cannot be assimilated to it, either factually or theoretically. It contains a necessarily pragmatic moment that certainly weakens it as theory but that adds a subversive element of unpredictability and makes it something of a wild card in the serious game of the theoretical disciplines.

The advent of theory, the break that is now so often being deplored and that sets it aside from literary history and from literary criticism, occurs with the introduction of linguistic terminology in the metalanguage about literature. By linguistic terminology is meant a terminology that designates reference prior to designating the referent and takes into account, in the consideration of the world, the referential function of language or, to be somewhat more specific, that considers reference as a function of language and not necessarily as an intuition. Intuition implies perception, consciousness, experience, and leads at once into the world of logic and of understanding with all its correlatives, among which aesthetics occupies a prominent place. The assumption that there can be a science of language which is not necessarily a logic leads to the development of a terminology which is not necessarily aesthetic. Contemporary literary theory comes into its own in such events as the application of Saussurian linguistics to literary texts.

The affinity between structural linguistics and literary texts is not as obvious as, with the hindsight of history, it now may seem. Peirce, Saussure, Sapir and Bloomfield were not originally concerned with literature at all but with the scientific foundations of linguistics. But the interest of philologists such as Roman Jakobson or literary critics such as Roland Barthes in semiology reveals the natural attraction of literature to a theory of linguistic signs. By considering language as a system of signs and of signification rather than as an established pattern of meanings, one displaces or even suspends the traditional barriers between literary and presumably non-literary uses of language and liberates the corpus from the secular weight of textual canonization. The results of the encounter between semiology and literature went considerably further than those of many other theoretical models—philological, psychological or classically epistemological—which writers on literature in quest of such models had tried out before. The responsiveness of literary texts to semiotic analysis is visible in that, whereas other approaches were unable to reach beyond observations that could be paraphrased or translated in terms of common knowledge, these analyses revealed patterns that could only be described in terms of their own, specifically linguistic, aspects. The linguistics of semiology and of literature apparently have something in common that only their shared perspective can detect and that pertains distinctively to them. The definition of this something, often referred to as literariness, has become the object of literary theory.

Literariness, however, is often misunderstood in a way that has provoked much of the confusion which dominates today's polemics. It is frequently assumed, for instance, that literariness is another word for, or another mode of, aesthetic response. The use, in conjunction with literariness, of such terms as style and stylistics, form or even "poetry" (as in "the poetry of grammar"), all of which carry strong aesthetic connotations, helps to foster this confusion, even among those who first put the term in circulation. Roland Barthes, for example, in an essay properly and revealingly dedicated to Roman Jakobson, speaks eloquently of the writer's quest for a perfect coincidence of the phonic properties of a word with its signifying function. "We would also wish to insist on the Cratylism of the name (and of the sign) in Proust . . . Proust sees the relationship between signifier and signified as motivated, the one copying the other and representing in its material form the signified essence of the thing (and not the thing itself) . . . This realism (in the scholastic sense of the word), which conceives of names as the 'copy' of the ideas, has taken, in Proust, a radical form. But one may well ask whether it is not more or less consciously present in all writing and whether it is possible to be a writer without some sort of belief in the natural relationship between names and essences. The poetic function, in the widest sense of the word, would thus be defined by a Cratylian awareness of the sign, and the writer would be the conveyor of this secular myth which wants language to imitate the idea and which, contrary to the teachings of linguistic science, thinks of signs as motivated signs."[1] To the extent that Cratylism assumes a convergence of the phenomenal aspects of

1. "Gérard Genette, "Proust et les noms" in To honor Roman Jakobson (The Hague, 1967) part I, pp. 157ff.

language, as sound, with its signifying function as referent, it is an aesthetically oriented conception; one could, in fact, without distortion, consider
aesthetic theory, including its most systematic formulation in Hegel, as the
complete unfolding of the model of which the Cratylian conception of
language is a version. Hegel's somewhat cryptic reference to Plato, in the
Aesthetics, may well be interpreted in this sense. Barthes and Jakobson often
seem to invite a purely aesthetic reading, yet there is a part of their statement
that moves in the opposite direction. For the convergence of sound and
meaning celebrated by Barthes in Proust and, as Gérard Genette has decisively
shown,[2] later dismantled by Proust himself as a seductive temptation to
mystified minds, is also considered here to be a mere *effect* which language can
perfectly well achieve, but which bears no substantial relationship, by analogy
or by ontologically grounded imitation, to anything beyond that particular
effect. It is a rhetorical rather than an aesthetic function of language, an
identifiable trope (paranomasis) that operates on the level of the signifier and
contains no responsible pronouncement on the nature of the world—despite
its powerful potential to create the opposite illusion. The phenomenality of
the signifier, as sound, is unquestionably involved in the correspondence
between the name and the thing named, but the link, the relationship between
word and thing is not phenomenal but conventional.

This gives the language considerable freedom from referential restraint,
but it makes it epistemologically highly suspect and volatile, since its use can
no longer be said to be determined by considerations of truth and falsehood,
good and evil, beauty and ugliness, or pleasure and pain. Whenever this
autonomous potential of language can be revealed by analysis, we are dealing
with literariness and, in fact, with literature as the place where this negative
knowledge about the reliability of linguistic utterance is made available. The
ensuing foregrounding of material, phenomenal aspects of the signifier creates
a strong illusion of aesthetic seduction at the very moment when the actual
aesthetic function has been, at the very least, suspended. It is inevitable that
semiology or similarly oriented methods be considered formalistic, in the
sense of being aesthetically rather than semantically valorized, but the
inevitability of such an interpretation does not make it less aberrant. Literature involves the voiding, rather than the affirmation, of aesthetic categories.
One of the consequences of this is that, whereas we have traditionally been
accustomed to reading literature by analogy with the plastic arts and with
music, we now have to recognize the necessity of a non-perceptual, linguistic
moment in painting and in music, and learn to *read* pictures rather than to
imagine meaning.

If literariness is not an aesthetic quality, it is also not primarily mimetic.
Mimesis becomes one trope among others, language choosing to imitate a

2. "Proust et le langage indirect" in *Figures II* (Paris, 1969).

non-verbal entity just as paranomasis "imitates" a sound without any claim to identity (or reflection on difference) between the verbal and non-verbal elements. The most misleading representation of literariness, and also the most recurrent objection to contemporary literary theory, considers it as pure verbalism, as a denial of the reality principle in the name of absolute fictions, and for reasons that are said to be ethically and politically shameful. The attack reflects the anxiety of the aggressors rather than the guilt of the accused. By allowing for the necessity of a non-phenomenal linguistics, one frees the discourse on literature from naive oppositions between fiction and reality, which are themselves an offspring of an uncritically mimetic conception of art. In a genuine semiology as well as in other linguistically oriented theories, the referential function of language is not being denied—far from it; what is in question is its authority as a model for natural or phenomenal cognition. Literature is fiction not because it somehow refuses to acknowledge "reality," but because it is not *a priori* certain that language functions according to principles which are those, or which are *like* those, of the phenomenal world. It is therefore not *a priori* certain that literature is a reliable source of information about anything but its own language.

It would be unfortunate, for example, to confuse the materiality of the signifier with the materiality of what it signifies. This may seem obvious enough on the level of light and sound, but it is less so with regard to the more general phenomenality of space, time or especially of the self: no one in his right mind will try to grow grapes by the luminosity of the word "day," but it is very difficult not to conceive the pattern of one's past and future existence as in accordance with temporal and spatial schemes that belong to fictional narratives and not to the world. This does not mean that fictional narratives are not part of the world and of reality; their impact upon the world may well be all too strong for comfort. What we call ideology is precisely the confusion of linguistic with natural reality, of reference with phenomenalism. It follows that, more than any other mode of inquiry, including economics, the linguistics of literariness is a powerful and indispensable tool in the unmasking of ideological aberrations, as well as a determining factor in accounting for their occurrence. Those who reproach literary theory for being oblivious to social and historical (that is to say ideological) reality are merely stating their fear at having their own ideological mystifications exposed by the tool they are trying to discredit. They are, in short, very poor readers of Marx's *German Ideology*.

In these all too summary evocations of arguments that have been much more extensively and convincingly made by others, we begin to perceive some of the answers to the initial question: what is it about literary theory that is so threatening that it provokes such strong resistances and attacks? It upsets rooted ideologies by revealing the mechanics of their workings; it goes against a powerful philosophical tradition of which aesthetics is a prominent part; it upsets the established canon of literary works and blurs the borderlines between literary and non-literary discourse. By implication, it may also reveal the links between ideologies and philosophy. All this is ample enough reason for suspicion, but not a satisfying answer to the question. For it makes the tension between contemporary literary theory and the tradition of literary studies appear as a mere historical conflict between two modes of thought that happen to hold the stage at the same time. If the conflict is merely historical, in the literal sense, it is of limited theoretical interest, a passing squall in the intellectual weather of the world. As a matter of fact, the arguments in favor of the legitimacy of literary theory are so compelling that it seems useless to concern oneself with the conflict at all. Certainly, none of the objections to theory, presented again and again, always misinformed or based on crude misunderstandings of such terms as mimesis, fiction, reality, ideology, reference and, for that matter, relevance, can be said to be of genuine rhetorical interest.

It may well be, however, that the development of literary theory is itself overdetermined by complications inherent in its very project and unsettling with regard to its status as a scientific discipline. Resistance may be a built-in constituent of its discourse, in a manner that would be inconceivable in the natural sciences and unmentionable in the social sciences. It may well be, in other words, that the polemical opposition, the systematic non-understanding and misrepresentation, the unsubstantial but eternally recurrent objections, are the displaced symptoms of a resistance inherent in the theoretical enterprise itself. To claim that this would be a sufficient reason not to envisage doing literary theory would be like rejecting anatomy because it has failed to cure mortality. The real debate of literary theory is not with its polemical opponents but rather with its own methodological assumptions and possibilities. Rather than asking why literary theory is threatening, we should perhaps ask why it has such difficulty going about its business and why it lapses so readily either into the language of self-justification and self-defense or else into the overcompensation of a programmatically euphoric utopianism. Such insecurity about its own project calls for self-analysis, if one is to understand the frustrations that attend upon its practitioners, even when they seem to dwell in serene methodological self-assurance. And if these difficulties are indeed an integral part of the problem, then they will have to be, to some extent, a-historical in the temporal sense of the term. The way in which they are encountered on the present local literary scene as a resistance to the introduction of linguistic terminology in aesthetic and historical discourse about literature is only one particular version of a question that cannot be reduced to a specific historical situation and called modern, post-modern, post-classical or romantic (not even in Hegel's sense of the term), although its compulsive way of forcing itself upon us in the guise of a system of historical periodization is certainly part of its problematic nature. Such difficulties can be read in the text of literary theory at all times, at whatever historical moment one wishes to select. One of the main achievements of the present theoretical trends is to have restored some awareness of this fact. Classical, medieval and Renaissance literary theory is now often being read in a way that knows enough about what it is doing not to wish to call itself "modern."

We return, then, to the original question in an attempt to broaden the discussion enough to inscribe the polemics inside the question rather than having them determine it. The resistance to theory is a resistance to the use of language about language. It is therefore a resistance to language itself or to the possibility that language contains factors or functions that cannot be reduced to intuition. But we seem to assume all too readily that, when we refer to something called "language," we know what it is we are talking about, although there is probably no word to be found in the language that is as overdetermined, self-evasive, disfigured and disfiguring as "language." Even if we choose to consider it at a safe remove from any theoretical model, in the pragmatic history of "language," not as a concept, but as a didactic assignment that no human being can bypass, we soon find ourselves confronted by theoretical enigmas. The most familiar and general of all linguistic models, the classical *trivium*, which considers the sciences of language as consisting of grammar, rhetoric and logic (or dialectics), is in fact a set of unresolved tensions powerful enough to have generated an infinitely prolonged discourse of endless frustration of which contemporary literary theory, even at its most self-assured, is one more chapter. The difficulties extend to the internal articulations between the constituent parts as well as to the articulation of the field of language with the knowledge of the world in general, the link between the *trivium* and the *quadrivium*, which covers the non-verbal sciences of number (arithmetic), of space (geometry), of motion (astronomy) and of time (music). In the history of philosophy, this link is traditionally, as well as substantially, accomplished by way of logic, the area where the rigor of the linguistic discourse about itself matches up with the rigor of the mathematical discourse about the world. Seventeenth-century epistemology, for instance, at the moment when the relationship between philosophy and mathematics is particularly close, holds up the language of what it calls geometry *(mos geometricus)*, and which in fact includes the homogeneous concatenation between space, time and number, as the sole model of coherence and economy. Reasoning *more geometrico* is said to be "almost the only mode of reasoning that is infallible, because it is the only one to adhere to the true method, whereas all other ones are by natural necessity in a degree of confusion of which only geometrical minds can be aware."[3] This is a clear instance of the

3. Pascal, "De l'esprit géométrique et de l'art de persuader," in *Oeuvres complètes* presented by L. Lafuma (Paris: Editions du Seuil, 1963) pp. 349ff.

interconnection between a science of the phenomenal world and a science of language conceived as definitional logic, the pre-condition for a correct axiomatic-deductive, synthetic reasoning. The possibility of thus circulating freely between logic and mathematics has its own complex and problematic history as well as its contemporary equivalences with a different logic and a different mathematics. What matters for our present argument is that this articulation of the sciences of language with the mathematical sciences represents a particularly compelling version of a continuity between a theory of language, as logic, and the knowledge of the phenomenal world to which mathematics gives access. In such a system, the place of aesthetics is preordained and by no means alien, provided the priority of logic, in the model of the *trivium*, is not being questioned. For even if one assumes, for the sake of argument and against a great deal of historical evidence, that the link between logic and the natural sciences is secure, this leaves open the question, within the confines of the *trivium* itself, of the relationship between grammar, rhetoric and logic. And this is the point at which literariness, the use of language that foregrounds the rhetorical over the grammatical and the logical function, intervenes as a decisive but unsettling element which, in a variety of modes and aspects, disrupts the inner balance of the model and, consequently, its outward extension to the non-verbal world as well.

Logic and grammar seem to have a natural enough affinity for each other and, in the tradition of Cartesian linguistics, the grammarians of Port-Royal experienced little difficulty at being logicians as well. The same claim persists today in very different methods and terminologies that nevertheless maintain the same orientation toward the universality that logic shares with science. Replying to those who oppose the singularity of specific texts to the scientific generality of the semiotic project, A.J. Greimas disputes the right to use the dignity of "grammar" to describe a reading that would not be committed to universality. Those who have doubts about the semiotic method, he writes, "postulate the necessity of constructing a grammar for each particular text. But the essence *(le propre)* of a grammar is its ability to account for a large number of texts, and the metaphorical use of the term . . . fails to hide the fact that one has, in fact, given up on the semiotic project."[4] There is no doubt that what is here prudently called "a large number" implies the hope at least of a future model that would in fact be applicable to the generation of all texts. Again, it is not our present purpose to discuss the validity of this methodological optimism, but merely to offer it as an instance of the persistent symbiosis between grammar and logic. It is clear that, for Greimas as for the entire tradition to which he belongs, the grammatical and the logical function of language are co-extensive. Grammar is an isotope of logic.

It follows that, as long as it remains grounded in grammar, any theory of

4. A.G. Greimas, *Du Sens* (Paris: Editions du Seuil, 1970), p. 13.

language, including a literary one, does not threaten what we hold to be the underlying principle of all cognitive and aesthetic linguistic systems. Grammar stands in the service of logic which, in turn, allows for the passage to the knowledge of the world. The study of grammar, the first of the *artes liberales*, is the necessary pre-condition for scientific and humanistic knowledge. As long as it leaves this principle intact, there is nothing threatening about literary theory. The continuity between theory and phenomenalism is asserted and preserved by the system itself. Difficulties occur only when it is no longer possible to ignore the epistemological thrust of the rhetorical dimension of discourse, that is, when it is no longer possible to keep it in its place as a mere adjunct, a mere ornament within the semantic function.

The uncertain relationship between grammar and rhetoric (as opposed to that between grammar and logic) is apparent, in the history of the *trivium*, in the uncertain status of figures of speech or tropes, a component of language that straddles the disputed borderlines between the two areas. Tropes used to be part of the study of grammar but were also considered to be the semantic agent of the specific function (or effect) that rhetoric performs as persuasion as well as meaning. Tropes, unlike grammar, pertain primordially to language. They are text-producing functions that are not necessarily patterned on a non-verbal entity, whereas grammar is by definition capable of extra-linguistic generalization. The latent tension between rhetoric and grammar precipitates out in the problem of reading, the process that necessarily partakes of both. It turns out that the resistance to theory is in fact a resistance to reading, a resistance that is perhaps at its most effective, in contemporary studies, in the methodologies that call themselves theories of reading but nevertheless avoid the function they claim as their object.

What is meant when we assert that the study of literary texts is necessarily dependent on an act of reading, or when we claim that this act is being systematically avoided? Certainly more than the tautology that one has to have read at least some parts, however small, of a text (or read some part, however small, of a text about this text) in order to be able to make a statement about it. Common as it may be, criticism by hearsay is only rarely held up as exemplary. To stress the by no means self-evident necessity of reading implies at least two things. First of all, it implies that literature is not a transparent message in which it can be taken for granted that the distinction between the message and the means of communication is clearly established. Second, and more problematically, it implies that the grammatical decoding of a text leaves a residue of indetermination that has to be, but cannot be, resolved by grammatical means, however extensively conceived. The extension of grammar to include para-figural dimensions is in fact the most remarkable and debatable strategy of contemporary semiology, especially in the study of syntagmatic and narrative structures. The codification of contextual elements well beyond the syntactical limits of the sentence leads to the systematic study of metaphrastic dimensions and has considerably refined and expanded the knowledge of textual codes. It is equally clear, however, that this extension is always strategically directed towards the replacement of rhetorical figures by grammatical codes. The tendency to replace a rhetorical by a grammatical terminology (to speak of hypotaxis, for instance, to designate anamorphic or metonymic tropes) is part of an explicit program, a program that is entirely admirable in its intent since it tends towards the mastering and the clarification of meaning. The replacement of a hermeneutic by a semiotic model, of interpretation by decoding, would represent, in view of the baffling historical instability of textual meanings (including, of course, those of canonical texts) a considerable progress. Much of the hesitation associated with "reading" could thus be dispelled.

The argument can be made, however, that no grammatical decoding, however refined, could claim to reach the determining figural dimensions of a text. There are elements in all texts that are by no means ungrammatical, but whose semantic function is not grammatically definable, neither in themselves nor in context. Do we have to interpret the genitive in the title of Keats' unfinished epic *The Fall of Hyperion* as meaning "Hyperion's fall," the case story of the defeat of an older by a newer power, the very recognizable story from which Keats indeed started out but from which he increasingly strayed away, or as "Hyperion falling," the much less specific but more disquieting evocation of an actual process of falling, regardless of its beginning, its end or the identity of the entity to whom it befalls to be falling. This story is indeed told in the later fragment entitled *The Fall of Hyperion*, but it is told about a character who resembles Apollo rather than Hyperion, the same Apollo who, in the first version (called *Hyperion*), should definitely be triumphantly standing rather than falling if Keats had not been compelled to interrupt, for no apparent reason, the story of Apollo's triumph. Does the title tell us that Hyperion is fallen and that Apollo stands, or does it tell us that Hyperion and Apollo (and Keats, whom it is hard to distinguish, at times, from Apollo) are interchangeable in that all of them are necessarily and constantly falling? Both readings are grammatically correct, but it is impossible to decide from the context (the ensuing narrative) which version is the right one. The narrative context suits neither and both at the same time, and one is tempted to suggest that the fact that Keats was unable to complete either version manifests the impossibility, for him as for us, of reading his own title. One could then read the word "Hyperion" in the title *The Fall of Hyperion* figurally, or, if one wishes, intertextually, as referring not to the historical or mythological character but as referring to the title of Keats' own earlier text *(Hyperion)*. But are we then telling the story of the failure of the first text as the success of the second, the Fall of *Hyperion* as the Triumph of *The Fall of Hyperion?*

Manifestly yes, but not quite, since the second text also fails to be concluded. Or are we telling the story of why all texts, as texts, can always be said to be falling? Manifestly yes, but not quite, either, since the story of the fall of the first version, as told in the second, applies to the first version only and could not legitimately be read as meaning also the fall of *The Fall of Hyperion*. The undecidability involves the figural or literal status of the proper name Hyperion as well as of the verb falling, and is thus a matter of figuration and not of grammar. In "Hyperion's Fall," the word "fall" is plainly figural, the representation of a figural fall, and we, as readers, read this fall standing up. But in "Hyperion falling," this is not so clearly the case, for if Hyperion can be Apollo and Apollo can be Keats, then he can also be us and his figural (or symbolic) fall becomes his and our literal falling as well. The difference between the two readings is itself structured as a trope. And it matters a great deal how we read the title, as an exercise not only in semantics, but in what the text actually does to us. Faced with the ineluctable necessity to come to a decision, no grammatical or logical analysis can help us out. Just as Keats had to break off his narrative, the reader has to break off his understanding at the very moment when he is most directly engaged and summoned by the text. One could hardly expect to find solace in this "fearful symmetry" between the author's and the reader's plight since, at this point, the symmetry is no longer a formal but an actual trap, and the question no longer "merely" theoretical.

This undoing of theory, this disturbance of the stable cognitive field that extends from grammar to logic to a general science of man and of the phenomenal world, can in its turn be made into a theoretical project of rhetorical analysis that will reveal the inadequacy of grammatical models of non-reading. Rhetoric, by its actively negative relationship to grammar and to logic, certainly undoes the claims of the *trivium* (and by extension, of language) to be an epistemologically stable construct. The resistance to theory is a resistance to the rhetorical or tropological dimension of language, a dimension which is perhaps more explicitly in the foreground in literature (broadly conceived) than in other verbal manifestations or—to be somewhat less vague—which can be revealed in any verbal event when it is read textually. Since grammar as well as figuration is an integral part of reading, it follows that reading will be a negative process in which the grammatical cognition is undone, at all times, by its rhetorical displacement. The model of the *trivium* contains within itself the pseudo-dialectic of its own undoing and its history tells the story of this dialectic.

This conclusion allows for a somewhat more systematic description of the contemporary theoretical scene. This scene is dominated by an increased stress on reading as a theoretical problem or, as it is sometimes erroneously phrased, by an increased stress on the reception rather than on the production of texts. It is in this area that the most fruitful exchanges have come about

between writers and journals of various countries and that the most interesting dialogue has developed between literary theory and other disciplines, in
the arts as well as in linguistics, philosophy and the social sciences. A
straightforward *report* on the present state of literary theory in the United
States would have to stress the emphasis on reading, a direction which is
already present, moreover, in the New Critical tradition of the forties and the
fifties. The methods are now more technical, but the contemporary interest in
a poetics of literature is clearly linked, traditionally enough, to the problems of
reading. And since the models that are being used certainly are no longer
simply intentional and centered on an identifiable self, nor *simply* hermeneutic in the postulation of a single originary, pre-figural and absolute text, it
would appear that this concentration on reading would lead to the rediscovery
of the theoretical difficulties associated with rhetoric. This is indeed the case,
to some extent; but not quite. Perhaps the most instructive aspect of
contemporary theory is the refinement of the techniques by which the threat
inherent in rhetorical analysis is being avoided at the very moment when the
efficacy of these techniques has progressed so far that the rhetorical obstacles
to understanding can no longer be mistranslated in thematic and phenomenal
commonplaces. The resistance to theory which, as we saw, is a resistance to
reading, appears in its most rigorous and theoretically elaborated form among
the theoreticians of reading who dominate the contemporary theoretical
scene.

It would be a relatively easy, though lengthy, process to show that this is
so for theoreticians of reading who, like Greimas or, on a more refined level,
Riffaterre or, in a very different mode, H.R. Jauss or Wolfgang Iser—all of whom
have a definite, though sometimes occult, influence on literary theory in this
country—are committed to the use of grammatical models or, in the case of
Rezeptionsaesthetik, to traditional hermeneutic models that do not allow for
the problematization of the phenomenalism of reading and therefore remain
uncritically confined within a theory of literature rooted in aesthetics. Such an
argument would be easy to make because, once a reader has become aware of
the rhetorical dimensions of a text, he will not be amiss in finding textual
instances that are irreduceable to grammar or to historically determined
meaning, provided only he is willing to acknowledge what he is bound to
notice. The problem quickly becomes the more baffling one of having to
account for the shared reluctance to acknowledge the obvious. But the
argument would be lengthy because it has to involve a textual analysis that
cannot avoid being somewhat elaborate; one can succinctly suggest the
grammatical indetermination of a title such as *The Fall of Hyperion*, but to
confront such an undecideable enigma with the critical reception and reading
of Keats' text requires some space.

The demonstration is less easy (though perhaps less ponderous) in the case of theoreticians of reading whose avoidance of rhetoric takes another turn. We have witnessed, in recent years, a strong interest in certain elements in language whose function is not only not dependent on any form of phenomenalism but on any form of cognition as well, and which thus excludes, or postpones, the consideration of tropes, ideologies, etc., from a reading that would be primarily performative. In some cases, a link is reintroduced between performance, grammar, logic, and stable referential meaning, and the resulting theories (as in the case of Ohman) are not in essence distinct from those of avowed grammarians or semioticians. But the most astute practitioners of a speech act theory of reading avoid this relapse and rightly insist on the necessity to keep the actual performance of speech acts, which is conventional rather than cognitive, separate from its causes and effects—to keep, in their terminology, the illocutionary force separate from its perlocutionary function. Rhetoric, understood as persuasion, is forcefully banished (like Coriolanus) from the performative moment and exiled in the affective area of perlocution. Stanley Fish, in a masterful essay, convincingly makes this point.[5] What awakens one's suspicion about this conclusion is that it relegates persuasion, which is indeed inseparable from rhetoric, to a purely affective and intentional realm and makes no allowance for modes of persuasion which are no less rhetorical and no less at work in literary texts, but which are of the order of persuasion by *proof* rather than persuasion by seduction. Thus to empty rhetoric of its epistemological impact is possible only because its tropological, figural functions are being bypassed. It is as if, to return for a moment to the model of the *trivium*, rhetoric could be isolated from the generality that grammar and logic have in common and considered as a mere correlative of an illocutionary power. The equation of rhetoric with psychology rather than with epistemology opens up dreary prospects of pragmatic banality, all the drearier if compared to the brilliance of the performative analysis. Speech act theories of reading in fact repeat, in a much more effective way, the grammatization of the *trivium* at the expense of rhetoric. For the characterization of the performative as sheer convention reduces it in effect to a grammatical code among others. The relationship between trope and performance is actually closer but more disruptive than what is here being proposed. Nor is this relationship properly captured by reference to a supposedly "creative" aspect of performance, a notion with which Fish rightly takes issue. The performative power of language can be called positional, which differs considerably from conventional as well as from "creatively" (or, in the technical sense, intentionally) constitutive. Speech act oriented theories of reading read only to the extent that they prepare the way for the rhetorical reading they avoid.

5. Stanley Fish, "How to do things with Austin and Searle: Speech Act Theory and Literary Criticism," in *MLN* 91 (1976), pp. 983–1025. See especially p. 1008.

But the same is still true even if a "truly" rhetorical reading that would stay clear of any undue phenomenalization or of any undue grammatical or performative codification of the text could be conceived—something which is not necessarily impossible and for which the aims and methods of literary theory should certainly strive. Such a reading would indeed appear as the methodical undoing of the grammatical construct and, in its systematic disarticulation of the *trivium*, will be theoretically sound as well as effective. Technically correct rhetorical readings may be boring, monotonous, predictable and unpleasant, but they are irrefutable. They are also totalizing (and potentially totalitarian) for since the structures and functions they expose do not lead to the knowledge of an entity (such as language) but are an unreliable process of knowledge production that prevents all entities, including linguistic entities, from coming into discourse as such, they are indeed universals, consistently defective models of language's impossibility to be a model language. They are, always in theory, the most elastic theoretical and dialectical model to end all models and they can rightly claim to contain within their own defective selves all the other defective models of reading-avoidance, referential, semiological, grammatical, performative, logical, or whatever. They are theory and not theory at the same time, the universal theory of the impossibility of theory. To the extent however that they are theory, that is to say teachable, generalizable and highly responsive to systematization, rhetorical readings, like the other kinds, still avoid and resist the reading they advocate. Nothing can overcome the resistance to theory since theory *is* itself this resistance. The loftier the aims and the better the methods of literary theory, the less possible it becomes. Yet literary theory is not in danger of going under; it cannot help but flourish, and the more it is resisted, the more it flourishes, since the language it speaks is the language of self-resistance. What remains impossible to decide is whether this flourishing is a triumph or a fall.

SHOSHANA FELMAN

Psychoanalysis and Education:
Teaching Terminable and Interminable

In memory of Jacques Lacan

> *Meno:* Can you tell me, Socrates, if virtue can be taught?
> Or is it not teachable but the result of practice, or is it nei-
> ther of these, but men possess it by nature?
> *Socrates:* ... You must think me happy indeed if you
> think I know whether virtue can be taught ... I am so far
> from knowing whether virtue can be taught or not that I do
> not even have any knowledge of what virtue itself is.
>
> ....
>
> *Meno:* Yes, Socrates, but how do you mean that we do
> not learn, but that what we call learning is recollection? Can
> you teach me how this is so?
> *Socrates:* ... Meno, you are a rascal. Here you are asking
> me to give you my "teaching", I who claim that there is no
> such thing as teaching, only recollection.
>
> —Plato, *Meno*[1]

THE MEASURE OF A TASK

Socrates, that extraordinary teacher who taught humanity what pedagogy is,
and whose name personifies the birth of pedagogics as a science, inaugurates
his teaching practice, paradoxically enough, by asserting not just his own
ignorance, but the radical impossibility of teaching.

Another extraordinarily effective pedagogue, another one of humanity's
great teachers, Freud, repeats, in his own way, the same conviction that
teaching is a fundamentally impossible profession. "None of the applications
of psychoanalysis," he writes, "has excited so much interest and aroused so
many hopes ... as its use in the theory and practice of education ...":

My personal share in this application of psychoanalysis has been very slight. At an
early stage I had accepted the *bon mot* which lays it down that there are three
impossible professions—educating, healing, governing—and I was already fully occupied with the second of them.[2]

---

1. Plato, *Meno*, 70 a, 71 a, 82 a. Translated by G.M.A. Grube (Indianapolis: Hackett Publishing
Company, 1980), pp. 3, 14 (translation modified).
2. *The Complete Psychological Works of Sigmund Freud*, translated from the German under
the general editorship of James Strachey (London: The Hogarth Press and the Institute of
Psychoanalysis), volume XIX, p. 273. Hereafter, this edition will be referred to as "Standard,"
followed by volume number (in roman numerals) and page number (in arabic numerals).

In a later text—indeed the very last one that he wrote—Freud recapitulates this paradoxical conviction which time and experience seem to have only reinforced, confirmed:

It almost looks as if analysis were the third of those 'impossible' professions in which one can be sure beforehand of achieving unsatisfying results. The other two, which have been known much longer, are education and government. [Standard, XXIII, 248]

If teaching is impossible—as Freud and Socrates both point out—what are we teachers doing? How should we understand—and carry out—our task? And why is it precisely two of the most effective teachers ever to appear in the intellectual history of mankind, who regard the task of teaching as impossible? Indeed, is not their radical enunciation of the impossibility of teaching itself actively engaged in teaching, itself part of the lesson they bequeath us? And if so, what can be learnt from the fact that it is impossible to teach? What can the impossibility of teaching teach us?

As much as Socrates, Freud has instituted, among other things, a revolutionary pedagogy. It is my contention—which I will here attempt to elucidate and demonstrate—that it is precisely in giving us unprecedented insight into the impossibility of teaching, that psychoanalysis has opened up unprecedented teaching possibilities, renewing both the questions and the practice of education.

This pedagogical renewal was not, however, systematically thought out by Freud himself, or systematically articulated by any of his followers; nor have its thrust and scope been to date fully assimilated or fully grasped, let alone utilized, exploited in the classroom. The only truly different pedagogy to have practically emerged from what might be called the psychoanalytic lesson is the thoroughly original teaching-style of Jacques Lacan, Freud's French disciple and interpreter. If Lacan is, as I would argue, Freud's best student— that is, the most radical effect of the insights of Freud's teaching—perhaps his teaching practice might give us a clue to the newness of the psychoanalytic lesson about lessons, and help us thus define both the actual and, more importantly, the potential contribution of psychoanalysis to pedagogy.

WHAT IS A CRITIQUE OF PEDAGOGY?

Lacan's relationship with pedagogy has, however, been itself—like that of Freud—mostly oversimplified, misunderstood, reduced. The reason for the usual misinterpretations of both Lacan's and Freud's pedagogical contribution lies in a misunderstanding of the critical position taken by psychoanalysis with respect to traditional methods and assumptions of education. Lacan's well-known critique of what he has pejoratively termed "academic discourse" *(le discours universitaire)* situates "the radical vice" in "the transmission of knowledge." "A Master of Arts," writes Lacan ironically, "as well as other titles, protect the secret of a substantialized knowledge."[3] Lacan thus blames "the narrow-minded horizon of pedagogues" for having "reduced" the "strong notion" of "teaching"[4] to a "functional apprenticeship" (E 445).

Whereas Lacan's pedagogical critique is focused on grown-up training—on academic education and the ways it handles and structures knowledge, Freud's pedagogical critique is mainly concerned with children's education and the ways it handles and structures repression. "Let us make ourselves clear," writes Freud, "as to what the first task of education is":

The child must learn to control his instincts. It is impossible to give him liberty to carry out all his impulses without restriction . . . Accordingly, *education must inhibit, forbid and suppress*[5] and this is abundantly seen in all periods of history. But we have learnt from analysis that precisely this suppression of instincts involves the risk of neurotic illness. . . . Thus education has to find its way between the Scylla of non-interference and the Charybdis of frustration. . . . An optimum must be discovered which will enable education to achieve the most and damage the least. . . . A moment's reflection tells us that hitherto education has fulfilled its task very badly and has done children great damage. [Standard, XXII, 149]

Thus, in its most massive statements and in its polemical pronouncements, psychoanalysis, in Freud as well as in Lacan—although with different emphases—is first and foremost *a critique of pedagogy.* The legacy of this critique has been, however, misconstrued and greatly oversimplified, in that the critical stance has been understood—in both Lacan's and Freud's case—as a desire to escape the pedagogical imperative: a desire—whether possible or impossible—to do away with pedagogy altogether. "Psychoanalysis," writes Anna Freud, "whenever it has come into contact with pedagogy, has always expressed the wish to *limit education.* Psychoanalysis has brought before us the quite definite danger arising from education."[6]

The illocutionary force of the psychoanalytical (pedagogical) critique of pedagogy has thus been reduced, either to a simple negativity, or to a simple positivity, of that critique. Those who, in an oversimplification of the Freudian lesson, equate the psychoanalytic critical stance with a simple positivity, give

3. Jacques Lacan, *Ecrits* (Paris: Seuil, 1966), p. 233, my translation. Henceforth I will be using the abbreviations: "E" (followed by page number)—for this original French edition of the *Ecrits*, and "N" (followed by page number) for the corresponding Norton edition of the English translation (*Ecrits: A Selection*, translated by Alan Sheridan, New York: Norton, 1977). When the reference to the French edition of the *Ecrits* (E) is not followed by a reference to the Norton English edition (N), the passage quoted (as in this case) is in my translation and has not been included in the "Selection" of the Norton edition.

4. Which for Lacan involves "the relationship of the individual to language": E 445.

5. Italics mine. As a rule, in the quoted passages, italics are mine unless otherwise indicated.

6. Anna Freud, *Psychoanalysis for Teachers and Parents,* translated by Barbara Low (Boston: Beacon Press, 1960), pp. 95–6.

consequently positive advice to educators, in an attempt to conceive of more liberal methods for raising children—methods allowing "to each stage in the child's life the right proportion of instinct-gratification and instinct-restriction."[7] Those who, on the other hand, in an oversimplification of the Lacanian lesson, equate the psychoanalytical critical stance with a simple negativity, see in psychoanalysis "literally an inverse pedagogy": "the analytic process is in effect a kind of reverse pedagogy, which aims at undoing what has been established by education."[8] In the title of a recent book on the relationship of Freud to pedagogy, Freud is thus defined as "The Anti-Pedagogue."[9] This one-sidedly negative interpretation of the relation of psychoanalysis to pedagogy fails to see that every true pedagogue is in effect an anti-pedagogue, not just because every pedagogy has historically emerged as a critique of pedagogy (Socrates: "There's a chance, Meno, that we, you as well as me . . . have been inadequately educated, you by Gorgias, I by Prodicus"[10]), but because, in one way or another, every pedagogy stems from its confrontation with the impossibility of teaching (Socrates: "You see, Meno, that I am not teaching . . . anything, but all I do is question . . ."[11]). The reductive conception of "Freud: The Anti-Pedagogue" thus fails to see that there is no such thing as an anti-pedagogue: an anti-pedagogue is *the* pedagogue par excellence. Such a conception overlooks, indeed, and fails to reckon with, Freud's own stupendous pedagogical performance, and its relevance to his declarations about pedagogy.

The trouble, both with the positivistic and with the negativistic misinterpretations of the psychoanalytical critique of pedagogy, is that they refer exclusively to Lacan's or Freud's explicit *statements* about pedagogy, and thus fail to see the illocutionary force, the didactic function of the *utterance* as opposed to the mere content of the statement. They fail to see, in other words, the pedagogical situation—the pedagogical dynamic in which statements function not as simple truths but as performative speech-*acts*. Invariably, all existing psychoanalytically-inspired theories of pedagogy fail to address the question of the pedagogical speech-act of Freud himself, or of Lacan himself: what can be learnt about pedagogy not just from their theories (which only fragmentarily and indirectly deal with the issue of education) but from their way of *teaching* it, from their own practice as teachers, from their own pedagogical performance.

Lacan refers explicitly to what he calls the psychoanalyst's "mission of

7. Ibid., p. 105.
8. Catherine Millot, interview in *l'Âne, le magasine freudien*, N° 1, April–May 1981, p. 19.
9. Catherine Millot, *Freud Anti-Pedagogue* (Paris: Bibliothèque d'Ornicar?, 1979).
10. Plato, *Meno*, 96 d, op. cit., p. 28 (translation modified).
11. Ibid., 82 e, p. 15.

teaching" (E 241, N 34 TM[12]), and speaks of his own teaching—the bi-monthly seminar he gave for forty years—as a vocation, "a function . . . to which I have truly devoted my entire life" (S-XI, 7, N 1)[13]. Unlike Lacan, Freud addresses the issue of teaching more indirectly, rather by refusing to associate his person with it:

But there is one topic which I cannot pass over so easily—*not, however, because I understand particularly much about it* or have contributed very much to it. Quite the contrary: *I have scarcely concerned myself with it at all.* I must mention it because it is so exceedingly important, so rich in hopes for the future, perhaps the most important of all the activities of analysis. What I am thinking of is the application of psychoanalysis to education. [Standard, XXII, 146]

This statement thus promotes pedagogy to the rank of "perhaps the most important of all the activities of analysis" only on the basis of Freud's denial of his own personal involvement with it. However, this very statement, this very denial is itself engaged in a dramatic pedagogical performance; it itself is part of an imaginary "lecture," significantly written in the form of an academic public address and of a dialogue with students—a pedagogic dialogue imaginarily conducted by a Freud who, in reality terminally ill and having undergone an operation for mouth-cancer, is no longer capable of speech:

My *Introductory Lectures on Psychoanalysis* were delivered . . . in a lecture room of the Vienna Psychiatric Clinic before an audience gathered from all the Faculties of the University. . . .

These new lectures, unlike the former ones, have never been delivered. My age had in the meantime absolved me from the obligation of giving expression to my membership in the University (which was in any case a peripheral one) by delivering lectures; and a surgical operation had made speaking in public impossible for me. If, therefore, I once more take my place in the lecture room during the remarks that follow, it is only by an artifice of the imagination; it may help me not to forget to bear the reader in mind as I

12. The abbreviation "TM"—"translation modified"—will signal my alterations of the official English translation of the work in question.

13. The abbreviation S-XI (followed by page number) refers to Jacques Lacan, *Le Séminaire, livre XI, Les Quatre concepts fondamentaux de la psychanalyse* (Paris: Seuil, 1973). The following abbreviation "N" (followed by page number) refers to the corresponding English edition: *The Four Fundamental Concepts of Psychoanalysis,* edited by Jacques-Alain Miller, translated by Alan Sheridan (New York: Norton, 1978).

As for the rest of Lacan's Seminars which have appeared in book form, the following abbreviations will be used:

S-I (followed by page number), for: J. Lacan, *Le Séminaire, livre I: Les Ecrits techniques de Freud* (Paris: Seuil, 1975);

S-II (followed by page number), for: J. Lacan, *Le Séminaire, livre II: le Moi dans la théorie de Freud et dans la technique de la psychanalyse* (Paris: Seuil, 1978);

S-XX (followed by page number), for: J. Lacan, *Le Séminaire, livre XX: Encore* (Paris: Seuil, 1975).

All quoted passages from these (as yet untranslated) Seminars are here in my translation.

enter more deeply into my subject. . . . Like their predecessors, [these lectures] are addressed to the multitude of educated people to whom we may perhaps attribute a benevolent, even though cautious, interest in the characteristics and discoveries of the young science. This time once again it has been my chief aim to make no sacrifice to an appearance of being simple, complete or rounded-off, not to disguise problems and not to deny the existence of gaps and uncertainties. [Standard, XXII, 5–6]

No other such coincidence of fiction and reality, biography and theory, could better dramatize Freud's absolutely fundamental pedagogic gesture. What better image could there be for the pedagogue in spite of himself, the pedagogue in spite of everything—the dying teacher whose imminent death, like that of Socrates, only confirms that he is a born teacher—than this pathetic figure, this living allegory of the speechless speaker, of the teacher's teaching out of—through—the very radical impossibility of teaching?

Pedagogy in psychoanalysis is thus not just a theme: it is a rhetoric. It is not just a statement: it is an utterance. It is not just a meaning: it is action; an action which itself may very well, at times, belie the stated meaning, the didactic *thesis*, the theoretical assertion. It is essential to become aware of this complexity of the relationship of pedagogy and psychoanalysis, in order to begin to think out what the psychoanalytic teaching about teaching might well be.

Discussing "The Teaching of Psychoanalysis in Universities," Freud writes: "it will be enough if [the student] learns something *about* psychoanalysis and something *from* it" (Standard, XVII, 173). To learn "something *from* psychoanalysis" is a very different thing than to learn "something *about* it:" it means that psychoanalysis is not a simple *object* of the teaching, but its *subject*. In his essay, "Psychoanalysis and its Teaching," Lacan underlines the same ambiguity, the same dynamic complexity, indicating that the true object of psychoanalysis, the object of his teaching, can only be that mode of learning which institutes psychoanalysis itself as subject—as the purveyor of the act of teaching. "How can what psychoanalysis teaches us be taught?," he asks (E 439).

As myself both a student of psychoanalysis and a teacher, I would here like to suggest that the lesson to be learnt about pedagogy from psychoanalysis is less that of "the *application* of psychoanalysis to pedagogy" than that of the *implication* of psychoanalysis in pedagogy and of pedagogy in psychoanalysis. Attentive, thus, both to the pedagogical speech-act of Freud and to the teaching-practice of Lacan, I would like to address the question of teaching as itself a psychoanalytic question. Reckoning not just with the pedagogical thematics *in* psychoanalysis, but with the pedagogical rhetoric *of* psychoanalysis, not just with what psychoanalysis says *about* teachers but with psychoanalysis *itself as teacher*, I will attempt to analyze the ways in which—modifying the conception of what *learning* is and of what *teaching* is—psychoanalysis has shifted pedagogy by radically displacing our very modes of intelligibility.

ANALYTICAL APPRENTICESHIP

Freud conceives of the process of a psychoanalytic therapy as a learning process—an apprenticeship whose epistemological validity far exceeds the contingent singularity of the therapeutic situation:

> Psychoanalysis sets out to explain ... uncanny disorders; it engages in careful and laborious investigations ... until at length it can speak thus to the ego:
>
> "... A part of the activity of your own mind has been withdrawn from your knowledge and from the command of your will ... you are using one part of your force to fight the other part ... A great deal more must constantly be going on in your mind than can be known to your consciousness. Come, *let yourself be taught* ...! What is in your mind does not coincide with what you are conscious of; whether something is going on in your mind and whether you hear of it, are two different things. In the ordinary way, I will admit, the intelligence which reaches your consciousness is enough for your needs; and *you may cherish the illusion that you learn of all the more important things.* But in some cases, as in that of an instinctual conflict ... your intelligence service breaks down ... In every case, the news that reaches your consciousness is incomplete and often not to be relied on.... Turn your eyes inward, ... *learn first to know yourself!* ...
>
> It is thus that *psychoanalysis has sought to educate the ego.* [Standard, XVII, 142–143]

Psychoanalysis is thus a pedagogical experience: as a process which gives access to new knowledge hitherto denied to consciousness, it affords what might be called a lesson in cognition (and in miscognition), an epistemological instruction.

Psychoanalysis institutes, in this way, a unique and radically original mode of learning: original not just in its procedures, but in the fact that it gives access to information unavailable through any other mode of learning—unprecedented information, hitherto *unlearnable.* "We learnt", writes Freud, "a quantity of things which could not have been learnt except through analysis" (Standard, XXII, 147).

This new mode of investigation and of learning has, however, a very different temporality than the conventional linear—cumulative and progressive—temporality of learning, as it has traditionally been conceived by pedagogical theory and practice. Proceeding not through linear progression, but through breakthroughs, leaps, discontinuities, regressions, and deferred action, the analytic learning-process puts indeed in question the traditional pedagogical belief in intellectual perfectibility, the progressistic view of learning as a simple one-way road from ignorance to knowledge.

It is in effect the very concept of both ignorance and knowledge—the understanding of what "to know" and "not to know" may really mean—that psychoanalysis has modified, renewed. And it is precisely the originality of this renewal which is central to Lacan's thought, to Lacan's specific way of understanding the cultural, pedagogical and epistemological revolution implied by the discovery of the unconscious.

KNOWLEDGE

Western pedagogy can be said to culminate in Hegel's philosophical didacticism: the Hegelian concept of "absolute knowledge"—which for Hegel defines at once the potential aim and the actual end of dialectics, of philosophy—is in effect what pedagogy has always aimed at as its ideal: the exhaustion—through methodical investigation—of all there is to know; the absolute completion—termination—of apprenticeship. Complete and totally appropriated knowledge will become—in all senses of the word—a *mastery.* "In the Hegelian perspective," writes Lacan, "the completed discourse" is "an instrument of power, the scepter and the property of those who know" (S-II, 91). "What is at stake in absolute knowledge is the fact that discourse closes back upon itself, that it is entirely in agreement with itself." (S-II, 91).

But the unconscious, in Lacan's conception, is precisely the discovery that human discourse can by definition never be entirely in agreement with itself, entirely identical to its knowledge of itself, since, as the vehicle of unconscious knowledge, it is constitutively the material locus of a signifying difference from itself.

What, indeed, is the unconscious, if not a kind of *unmeant knowledge* which escapes intentionality and meaning, a knowledge which is spoken by the language of the subject (spoken, for instance, by his "slips" or by his dreams), but which the subject cannot recognize, assume as *his,* appropriate; a speaking knowledge which is nonetheless denied to the speaker's knowledge? In Lacan's own terms, the unconscious is "knowledge which can't tolerate one's knowing that one knows" (Seminar, Feb. 19, 1974; unpublished). "Analysis appears on the scene to announce that there is *knowledge which does not know itself,* knowledge which is supported by the signifier as such" (S-XX, 88). "It is from a place which differs from any capture by a subject that a knowledge is surrendered, since that knowledge offers itself only to the subject's slips—to his misprision" (*Scilicet* I, 38)[14]. "The discovery of the unconscious . . . is that the implications of meaning infinitely exceed the signs manipulated by the individual" (S-II, 150). "As far as signs are concerned, man is always mobilizing many more of them than he knows" (S-II, 150).

---

14. Abbreviated for Lacan's texts published in *Scilicet: Tu peux savoir ce qu'en pense l'école freudienne de Paris* (Paris: Seuil). The roman numeral stands for the issue number (followed by page number). Number I appeared in 1968.

If this is so, there can constitutively be no such thing as absolute knowledge: absolute knowledge is knowledge that has exhausted its own articulation; but articulated knowledge is by definition what cannot exhaust its own self-knowledge. For knowledge to be spoken, linguistically articulated, it would constitutively have to be supported by the ignorance carried by language, the ignorance of the *excess of signs* that of necessity its language—its articulation—"mobilizes". Thus, human knowledge is, by definition, that *NB* which is *untotalizable*, that which rules out any possibility of totalizing what it knows or of eradicating its own ignorance.

The epistemological principle of the irreducibility of ignorance which stems from the unconscious, receives an unexpected confirmation from modern science, to which Lacan is equally attentive in his attempt to give the theory of the unconscious its contemporary scientific measure. The scientific a-totality of knowledge is acknowledged by modern mathematics, in set theory (Cantor: "the set of all sets in a universe does not constitute a set"); in contemporary physics, it is the crux of what is known as "the uncertainty principle" of Heisenberg:

This is what the Heisenberg principle amounts to. When it is possible to locate, to define precisely one of the points of the system, it is impossible to formulate the others. When the place of electrons is discussed . . . it is no longer possible to know anything about . . . their speed. And inversely . . . [S-II, 281]

From the striking and instructive coincidence between the revolutionary findings of psychoanalysis and the new theoretical orientation of modern physics, Lacan derives the following epistemological insight—the following pathbreaking pedagogical principle:

Until further notice, we can say that *the elements do not answer in the place where they are interrogated*. Or more exactly, as soon as they are interrogated somewhere, it is impossible to grasp them in their totality. [S-II, 281]

IGNORANCE

Ignorance is thus no longer simply *opposed* to knowledge: it is itself a radical condition, an integral part of the very *structure* of knowledge. But what does ignorance consist of, in this new epistemological and pedagogical conception?

If ignorance is to be equated with the a-totality of the unconscious, it can be said to be a kind of forgetting—of forgetfulness: while learning is obviously, among other things, remembering and memorizing ("all learning is recollection," says Socrates), ignorance is linked to what is *not remembered*, what will not be memorized. But what will not be memorized is tied up with repression, with the imperative to forget—the imperative to exclude from consciousness, to not admit to knowledge. Ignorance, in other words, is not a passive state of absence—a simple lack of information: it is an active dynamic of negation, an active refusal of information. Freud writes:

> It is a long superseded idea . . . that the patient suffers from a sort of ignorance, and that if one removes this ignorance by giving him information (about the causal connection of his illness with his life, about his experiences in childhood, and so on) he is bound to recover. The pathological factor is not his ignorance in itself, but the root of this ignorance in his *inner resistances;* it was they who first called this ignorance into being, and they still maintain it now. The task of the treatment lies in combating these resistances. [Standard, XI, 225]

Teaching, like analysis, has to deal not so much with *lack* of knowledge as with *resistances* to knowledge. Ignorance, suggests Lacan, is a "passion." Inasmuch as traditional pedagogy postulated a desire for knowledge, an analytically informed pedagogy has to reckon with "the passion for ignorance" (S-XX, 110). Ignorance, in other words is nothing other than a *desire to ignore:* its nature is less cognitive than performative; as in the case of Sophocles' nuanced representation of the ignorance of Oedipus, it is not a simple lack of information but the incapacity—or the refusal—to acknowledge *one's own implication* in the information.

The new pedagogical lesson of psychoanalysis is not subsumed, however, by the revelation of the dynamic nature—and of the irreducibility—of ignorance. The truly revolutionary insight—the truly revolutionary *pedagogy* discovered by Freud—consists in showing the ways in which, however irreducible, *ignorance itself can teach us something*—become itself *instructive*. This is, indeed, the crucial lesson that Lacan has learnt from Freud:

> It is necessary, says Freud, to interpret the phenomenon of doubt as an integral part of the message. [S-II, 155]

> The forgetting of the dream is . . . itself part of the dream. [S-II, 154]

> The message is not forgotten in just any manner. . . . A censorship is an intention. Freud's argumentation properly reverses the burden of the proof—"In these elements that you cite in objection to me, the memory lapses and the various degradations of the dream, I continue to see a meaning, and even an additional meaning. When the phenomenon of forgetting intervenes, it interests me all the more . . . *These negative phenomena, I add them to the interpretation of the meaning, I recognize that they too have the function of a message.* Freud discovers this dimension . . . What interests Freud . . . [is] *the message as an interrupted discourse,* and which insists. [S-II, 153]

The pedagogical question crucial to Lacan's own teaching will thus be: *Where does it resist?* Where does a text (or a signifier in a patient's conduct) precisely make no sense, that is, *resist interpretation?* Where does what I see—and what I read—resist my understanding? Where is the *ignorance*—the resistance to knowledge—located? And what can I thus *learn* from the locus of that ignorance? How can I interpret *out of* the dynamic ignorance I analytically encounter, both in others and in myself? How can I turn ignorance into an instrument of teaching?

. . . Teaching—says Lacan—is something rather problematic. . . . As an American poet has pointed out, no one has ever seen a professor who has fallen short of the task because of ignorance . . .

One always knows enough in order to occupy the minutes during which one exposes oneself in the position of the one who knows. . . .

This makes me think that there is no true teaching other than the teaching which succeeds in provoking in those who listen an insistence—this desire to know which can only emerge when they themselves have *taken the measure of ignorance as such*—of ignorance inasmuch as it is, as such, fertile—in the one who teaches as well. [S-II, 242]

THE USE OF THAT WHICH CANNOT BE EXCHANGED

Teaching, thus, is not the transmission of ready-made knowledge, it is rather the creation of a new *condition* of knowledge—the creation of an original learning-disposition. "What I teach you", says Lacan, "does nothing other than express the *condition* thanks to which what Freud says is possible" (S-II, 368). The lesson, then, does not "teach" Freud: it teaches the "condition" which make it *possible to learn* Freud—the condition which makes possible Freud's teaching. What is this condition?

In analysis, what sets in motion the psychoanalytical apprenticeship is the peculiar pedagogical structure of the analytic situation. The analysand speaks to the analyst, whom he endows with the authority of the one who possesses knowledge—knowledge of what is precisely lacking in the analysand's own knowledge. The analyst, however, knows nothing of the sort. His only competence, insists Lacan, lies in "what I would call *textual knowledge,* so as to oppose it to the referential notion which only masks it" (*Scilicet* I, 21). Textual knowledge—the very stuff the literature teacher is supposed to deal in—is knowledge of the functioning of language, of symbolic structures, of the signifier, knowledge at once derived from—and directed towards—interpretation.

But such knowledge cannot be acquired (or possessed) once and for all: each case, each text, has its own specific, singular symbolic functioning, and requires thus a different—an original—interpretation. The analysts, says Lacan, are "those who share this knowledge only at the price, on the condition of their *not being able to exchange it*" (*Scilicet* I, 59). Analytic (textual) knowledge cannot be *exchanged,* it has to be *used*—and used in each case differently, according to the singularity of the case, according to the specificity of the text. Textual (or analytic) knowledge is, in other words, that peculiarly specific knowledge which, unlike any commodity, is subsumed by its *use* value, having no exchange value whatsoever[15]. Analysis has thus no use for ready-made interpretations, for knowledge given in advance. Lacan insists on "the insistence with which Freud recommends to us to approach each new case as if we had never learnt anything from his first interpretations" (*Scilicet*, I, 20). "What the analyst must know," concludes Lacan, "is how to ignore what he knows."

DIALOGIC LEARNING, OR
THE ANALYTICAL STRUCTURE OF INSIGHT

Each case is thus, for the analyst as well as for the patient, a new apprenticeship. "If it's true that our knowledge comes to the rescue of the patient's ignorance, it is not less true that, for our part, we, too, are plunged in ignorance" (S-I, 78). While the analysand is obviously ignorant of his own unconscious, the analyst is doubly ignorant: pedagogically ignorant of his suspended (given) knowledge; actually ignorant of the very knowledge the analysand presumes him to possess of his own (the analysand's) unconscious: knowledge of the very knowledge he—the patient—lacks. In what way does knowledge, then, emerge in and from the analytic situation?

Through the analytic dialogue the analyst, indeed, has first to learn where to situate the ignorance: where his own textual knowledge is *resisted*. It is, however, out of this resistance, out of the patient's active ignorance, out of the patient's speech which says much more than it itself knows, that the analyst will come to *learn* the *patient's own* unconscious *knowledge*, that knowledge which is inaccessible to itself because it cannot tolerate knowing that it knows; and it is the signifiers of this constitutively a-reflexive knowledge coming from the patient that the analyst *returns* to the patient from his different vantage point, from his non-reflexive, asymmetrical position as an Other. Contrary to the traditional pedagogical dynamic, in which the teacher's question is addressed to an answer from the other—from the student—which is totally reflexive, and expected, "the true Other" says Lacan, "is the Other who gives the answer one does not expect" (S-II, 288). Coming from the Other, knowledge is, by definition, that which comes as a surprise, that which is constitutively the return of a difference:

Teiresias: . . . You are the land's pollution.
Oedipus: How shamelessly you started up this taunt! How do you think you will escape?

15. As soon as analytic knowledge *is* exchanged, it ceases to be knowledge and becomes opinion, prejudice, presumption: "the sum of prejudices that every knowledge contains, and that each of us transports . . . . Knowledge is always, somewhere, only one's belief that one knows" (S-II, 56).

Teiresias: . . . I have escaped; the truth is what I cherish and that's my strength.
Oedipus: And *who has taught you* truth? Not your profession surely!
Teiresias: You have taught me, for you have made me speak against my will.
Oedipus: Speak what? Tell me again that I may *learn* it better.
Teiresias: Did you not understand before or would you provoke me into speaking?
Oedipus: I did not grasp it, not so to call it known. Say it again.
Teiresias: I say you are the murderer of the king whose murderer you seek.[16]

As Teiresias—so as to be able to articulate the truth—must have been *"taught"* not by "his profession" but *by Oedipus,* so the analyst precisely must be *taught* by the analysand's unconscious. It is by structurally occupying the position of the analysand's unconscious, and by thus making himself a *student of the patient's knowledge,* that the analyst becomes the patient's teacher—makes the patient learn what would otherwise remain forever inaccessible to him.

For teaching to be realized, for knowledge to be learnt, the position of alterity is therefore indispensable: knowledge is what is already there, but always in the Other. Knowledge, in other words, is not a substance but a structural dynamic: it is not *contained* by any individual but comes about out of the mutual apprenticeship between two partially unconscious speeches which both say more than they know. Dialogue is thus the radical condition of learning and of knowledge, the analytically constitutive condition through which ignorance becomes structually informative; knowledge is essentially, irreducibly dialogic. "No knowledge," writes Lacan, "can be supported or transported by one alone" (*Scilicet* I, 59).

Like the analyst, the teacher, in Lacan's eyes, cannot in turn be, alone, a *master* of the knowledge which he teaches. Lacan transposes the radicality of analytic dialogue—as a newly understood structure of insight—into the pedagogical situation. This is not simply to say that he encourages "exchange" and calls for students' interventions—as many other teachers do. Much more profoundly and radically, he attempts to *learn from the students his own knowledge.* It is the following original pedagogical appeal that he can thus address to the audience of his seminar:

It seems to me I should quite naturally be the point of convergence of the questions that may occur to you.

Let everybody tell me, in his own way, *his idea of what I am driving at.* How, for him, is opened up—or closed—or how already he resists, the question as I pose it . . . (S-II, 242)

16. Sophocles, *Oedipus the King,* translated by David Grene, in *Sophocles I,* (Chicago & London: The University of Chicago Press, 1954), pp. 25–6.

THE SUBJECT PRESUMED TO KNOW

This pedagogical approach, which makes no claim to total knowledge, which does not even claim to be in possession of its own knowledge, is, of course, quite different from the usual pedagogical pose of mastery, different from the image of the self-sufficient, self-possessed proprietor of knowledge, in which pedagogy has traditionally featured the authoritative figure of the teacher. This figure of infallible human authority implicitly likened to a God, that is, both modeled on and guaranteed by divine *omniscience*, is based on an illusion: the illusion of a consciousness transparent to itself. "It is the case of the unconscious," writes Lacan, "that it abolishes the postulate of the subject presumed to know" (*Scilicet* I, 46).

Abolishing a postulate, however, doesn't mean abolishing an illusion: while psychoanalysis uncovers the mirage inherent in the function of the subject presumed to know, it also shows the prestige and the affective charge of that mirage to be constitutively irreducible, to be indeed most crucial to, determinant of, the emotional dynamic of all discursive human interactions, of all human relationships founded on sustained interlocution. The psychoanalytical account of the functioning of this dynamic is the most directly palpable, the most explicit lesson psychoanalysis has taught us about teaching.

In a brief and peculiarly introspective essay called "Some Reflections on Schoolboy Psychology," the already aging Freud nostalgically probes into his own "schoolboy psychology," the affect of which even time and intellectual achievements have not entirely extinguished. "As little as ten years ago," writes Freud, "you may have had moments at which you suddenly felt quite young again":

As you walked through the streets of Vienna—already a grey-beard and weighed down by all the cares of family life—you might come unexpectedly on some well-preserved, elderly gentleman, and would greet him humbly almost, because you had recognized him as one of your former schoolmasters. But afterwards, you would stop and reflect: 'Was that really he? or only someone deceptively like him? How youthful he looks! And how old you yourself have grown! . . . *Can it be possible that the men who used to stand for us as types of adulthood were so little older than we were?*' [Standard, XIII, 241]

Commenting on "my emotion at meeting my old schoolmaster," Freud goes on to give an analytical account of the emotional dynamic of the pedagogical situation:

It is hard to decide whether what affected us more . . . was our concern with the sciences that we were taught or with . . . our teachers . . . In many of us *the path to the sciences led only through our teachers. . . .*

We courted them and turned our backs on them, we imagined sympathies and antipathies which probably had no existence . . .

> . . . *psychoanalysis has taught us* that the individual's emotional attitudes to other
> people . . . are . . . established at an unexpectedly early age . . . The people to whom [the
> child] is in this way fixed are his parents . . . His later acquaintances are . . . obliged to
> *take over a kind of emotional heritage;* they encounter sympathies and antipathies to
> the production of which they themselves have contributed little . . .
>
> These men [the teachers] became our *substitute fathers.* That was why, even
> though they were still quite young, *they struck us as so mature and so unattainably*
> *adult.* We *transferred* to them *the respect and expectations attaching to the omniscient*
> *father of our childhood,* and then we began to treat them as we treated our own fathers at
> home. We confronted them with the *ambivalence* that we had acquired in our own
> families and with its help we struggled with them as we had been in the habit of
> struggling with our fathers . . . [Standard, XIII, 242–44]

This phenomenon of the compulsive unconscious reproduction of an
archaic emotional pattern, which Freud called "transference" and which he
saw both as the energetic spring and as the interpretive key to the psychoanalytic situation, is further thought out by Lacan as what accounts for the
functioning of authority in general: as essential, thus, not just to any pedagogic
situation but to the problematics of knowledge as such. "As soon as there is
somewhere a subject presumed to know, there is transference," writes Lacan
(S-XI, 210).

Since "transference is the acting out of the reality of the unconscious"
(S-XI, 150, 240, N 174, 267), teaching is not a purely cognitive, informative
experience, it is also an emotional, erotical experience. "I deemed it necessary," insists Lacan, "to support the idea of transference, as indistinguishable
from love, with the formula of the subject presumed to know. I cannot fail to
underline the new resonance with which this notion of knowledge is endowed.
The person in whom I presume knowledge to exist, thereby acquires my love"
(S-XX, 64). "The question of love is thus linked to the question of knowledge"
(S-XX, 84). "Transference *is* love . . . I insist: it is love directed toward,
addressed to, knowledge" (*Scilicet* V, 16).

"Of this subject presumed to know, who," asks Lacan, "can believe
himself to be entirely invested?—That is not the question. The question, first
and foremost, for each subject, is how to situate *the place from which he*
himself addresses the subject presumed to know?" (S-XX, 211) Insofar as
knowledge is itself *a structure of address,* cognition is always both motivated
and obscured by love; theory, both guided and misguided by an implicit
transferential structure.

ANALYTIC PEDAGOGY, OR DIDACTIC
PSYCHOANALYSIS: THE INTERMINABLE TASK

In human relationships, sympathies and antipathies usually provoke—and
call for—a similar emotional response in the person they are addressed to.

Transference on "the subject presumed to know"—the analyst or the teacher—may provoke a counter-transference on the latter's part. The analytic or the pedagogical situation may thus degenerate into an imaginary mirror-game of love and hate, where each of the participants would unconsciously enact past conflicts and emotions, unwarranted by the current situation and disruptive with respect to the real issues, unsettling the topical stakes of analysis or education.

In order to avoid this typical degeneration, Freud conceived of the necessity of a preliminary psychoanalytic training of "the subjects presumed to know," a practical didactic training through their own analysis which, giving them insight into their own transferential structure, would later help them understand the students' or the patients' transferential mechanisms and, more importantly, keep under control their own—avoid being entrapped in counter-transference. "The only appropriate preparation for the profession of educator," suggests Freud, "is a thorough psycho-analytic training . . . The analysis of teachers and educators seems to be a more efficacious prophylactic measure than the analysis of children themselves" (Standard, XXII, 150).

While this preliminary training (which has come to be known as "didactic psychoanalysis") is, however, only a recommendation on Freud's part as far as teachers are concerned, it is an absolute requirement and precondition for the habilitation—and qualification—of the psychoanalyst. In his last and there-fore, in a sense, testamentary essay, "Analysis Terminable and Interminable," Freud writes:

Among the factors which influence the prospects of analytic treatment and add to its difficulties in the same manner as the resistances, must be reckoned not only the nature of the patient's ego but the individuality of the analyst.

It cannot be disputed that *analysts . . . have not invariably come up to the standard* of psychical normality *to which they wish to educate their patients.* Opponents of analysis often point to this fact with scorn and use it as an argument to show the uselessness of analytic exertions. We might reject this criticism as making unjustifiable demands. *Analysts are people who have learnt to practice a particular art;* alongside of this, they may be allowed to be *human beings like anyone else.* After all, nobody maintains that a physician is incapable of treating internal diseases if his own internal organs are not sound; on the contrary, it may be argued that there are certain advantages in a man who is himself threatened with tuberculosis specializing in the treatment of persons suffering from that disease. . . .

It is reasonable, [however,] . . . to expect of an analyst, as part of his qualifications, a considerable degree of mental normality and correctness. In addition, he must possess some kind of superiority, so that in certain analytic situations he can *act as a model for his patient* and in others *as a teacher.* And finally, we must not forget that the analytic relationship is based on a love of truth—that is, on a recognition of reality—and that it precludes any kind of sham or deceit. . . .

It almost looks as if analysis were the third of those 'impossible' professions . . .

Where is the poor wretch to acquire the ideal qualifications which he will need in his profession? *The answer is, in an analysis of himself,* with which his preparation for his future activity begins. For practical reasons this analysis can only be short and incomplete. . . . It has accomplished its purpose if it gives *the learner* a firm conviction of the existence of the unconscious, if it enables him . . . to perceive in himself things which would otherwise be incredible to him, and if it shows him a first example of the technique . . . in analytic work. *This alone would not suffice for his instruction; but we reckon on the stimuli he has received in his own analysis not ceasing when it ends* and *on the process of remodelling the ego continuing* spontaneously in the analysed subject and making use of all subsequent experiences in this newly-acquired sense. This does in fact happen, and *in so far as it happens, it makes the analysed subject qualified to be an analyst.* [Standard, XXIII, 247–49]

Nowhere else does Freud describe as keenly *the revolutionary radicality of the very nature of the teaching* to be (practically and theoretically) derived from the originality of the psychoanalytical experience. The analysand is qualified to be an analyst as of the point at which he understands his own analysis to be inherently unfinished, incomplete, as of the point, that is, at which he settles into his own didactic analysis—or his own analytical apprenticeship—as fundamentally interminable. It is, in other words, as of the moment the student recognizes that *learning has no term,* that he can himself become a teacher, assume the position of the teacher. But the position of the teacher is itself the position of *the one who learns,* of the one who *teaches* nothing other than *the way he learns.* The subject of teaching is interminably—a student; the subject of teaching is interminably—a learning. This is the most radical, perhaps the most far-reaching insight psychoanalysis can give us into pedagogy.

   Freud pushes this original understanding of what pedagogy is to its logical limit. Speaking of the "defensive" tendency of psychoanalysts "to divert the implications and demands of analysis from themselves (probably by directing them on to other people)"—of the analysts' tendency, that is, "to *withdraw from the critical and corrective influence of analysis,*" as well as of the temptation of power threatening them in the very exercise of their profession, Freud enjoins:

   Every analyst should periodically—at intervals of five years or so—submit himself to analysis once more, without feeling ashamed of taking this step. This would mean, then, that not only the therapeutic analysis of patients[17] but *his own analysis would change from a terminable into an interminable task.* [Standard, XXIII, 249]

   17. The therapeutic analysis of patients is "interminable" to the extent that repression can never be totally lifted, only displaced. Cf. Freud's letter to Fliess, dated April 16, 1900: " 'E's career as a patient has at last come to an end . . . His riddle is *almost* completely solved, his condition is excellent . . . At the moment a residue of his symptoms remains. I am beginning to understand that the apparently interminable nature of the treatment is something determined by law and is dependent on the transference." Hence, Freud speaks of "the asymptotic termination of treatment." (Standard, XXIII, 215) Freud's italics.

Of all Freud's followers, Lacan alone has picked up on the radicality of Freud's pedagogical concern with didactic psychoanalysis, not just as a subsidiary technical, pragmatic question (how should analysts be trained?), but as a major theoretical concern, as a major pedagogical investigation crucial to the very innovation, to the very revolutionary core of psychoanalytic insight. The highly peculiar and surprising style of Lacan's own teaching-practice is, indeed, an answer to, a follow-up on, Freud's ultimate suggestion—in Lacan's words—"to make psychoanalysis and education (training) collapse into each other" (E 459).

This is the thrust of Lacan's original endeavor both as psychoanalyst and as teacher: "in the field of psychoanalysis," he writes, "what is necessary is the restoration of the identical status of didactic psychoanalysis and of the teaching of psychoanalysis, in their common scientific opening" (E 236).

As a result of this conception, Lacan considers not just the practical analyses which he—as analyst—directs, but his own public teaching, his own seminar—primarily directed towards the (psychoanalytical) training of analysts—as partaking of didactic psychoanalysis, as itself, thus, analytically didactic and didactically analytical, in a new and radical way.

"How can what psychoanalysis teaches us be taught?" (E 439)—Only by continuing, in one's own teaching, one's own interminable didactic analysis. Lacan has willingly transformed himself into the *analysand* of his Seminar[18] so as to teach, precisely, psychoanalysis *as* teaching, and teaching *as* psychoanalysis.

Psychoanalysis as teaching, and teaching as psychoanalysis, radically subvert the demarcation-line, the clear-cut opposition between the analyst and the analysand, between the teacher and the student (or the learner)—showing that what counts, in both cases, is precisely the transition, the struggle-filled *passage* from one position to the other. But the passage is itself interminable; it can never be crossed once and for all: "The psychoanalytic act has but to falter slightly, and it is the analyst who becomes the analysand" (*Scilicet* I, 47). Lacan denounces, thus, "the reactionary principle" of the professional belief in "the duality of the one who suffers and the one who cures," in "the opposition between the one who knows and the one who does not know. . . . The most corrupting of comforts is intellectual comfort, just as one's *worst* corruption is the belief that one is *better*" (E 403).

Lacan's well-known polemical and controversial stance—his *critique of psychoanalysis*—itself partakes, then, of his understanding of the pedagogical imperative of didactic psychoanalysis. Lacan's original endeavor is to submit *the whole discipline of psychoanalysis* to what Freud called "the critical and corrective influence of analysis" (Standard, XXIII, 249). Lacan, in other words,

18. The occasional master's pose—however mystifying to the audience—invariably exhibits itself as a parodic symptom of the analysand.

is the first to understand that the psychoanalytic discipline is an unprecedented one in that its *teaching* does not just reflect upon itself, but turns back upon itself so as to *subvert itself,* and truly *teaches* only insofar as it subverts itself. Psychoanalytic teaching is pedagogically unique in that it is inherently, interminably, self-critical. Lacan's amazing pedagogical performance thus sets forth the unparalleled example of a teaching whose fecundity is tied up, paradoxically enough, with the inexhaustibility—the interminability—of its *self-critical potential.*

From didactic analysis, Lacan derives, indeed, a whole new theoretical (didactic) mode of *self-subversive self-reflection.*

A question suddenly arises . . . : in the case of the knowledge yielded solely to the subject's mistake, what kind of subject could ever be in a position to know it in advance? (Scilicet I, 38)

Retain at least what this text, which I have tossed out in your direction, bears witness to: my enterprise does not go beyond the act in which it is caught, and, therefore, its only chance lies in its being mistaken. (*Scilicet* I, 41)

This lesson seems to be one that should not have been forgotten, had not psychoanalysis precisely taught us that it is, as such, forgettable. [E 232]

Always submitting analysis itself to the instruction of an unexpected analytic turn of the screw, to the surprise of an additional reflexive turn, of an additional self-subversive ironic twist, didactic analysis becomes for Lacan what might be called a *style:* a teaching style which has become at once a life-style and a writing-style: "the ironic style of calling into question the very foundations of the discipline" (E 238).

Any return to Freud founding a teaching worthy of the name will occur only on that pathway where truth . . . becomes manifest in the revolutions of culture. That pathway is the only training we can claim to transmit to those who follow us. It is called—a style. (E 458)

Didactic analysis is thus invested by Lacan not simply with the practical, pragmatic value, but with the theoretical significance—the allegorical instruction—of a paradigm: a paradigm, precisely, of the interminability, not just of teaching (learning) and of analyzing (being analyzed), but of the very act of thinking, theorizing: of teaching, analyzing, thinking, theorizing, in such a way as to make of psychoanalysis "what it has never ceased to be: an act that is yet to come" (*Scilicet* I, 9).

TEACHING AS A LITERARY GENRE

Among so many other things, Lacan and Freud thus teach us teaching, teach us—in a radically new way—what it might mean to teach. Their lesson, and their pedagogical performance, profoundly renew at once the meaning and the status of the very act of teaching.

If they are both such extraordinary teachers, it is—I would suggest—because they both are, above all, quite extraordinary learners. In Freud's case, I would argue, the extraordinary teaching stems from Freud's original—unique—position as a student; in Lacan's case, the extraordinary teaching stems from Lacan's original—unique—position as disciple.

"One might feel tempted," writes Freud, "to agree with the philosophers and the psychiatrists and like them, rule out the problem of dream-interpretation as a purely fanciful task. *But I have been taught better"* (Standard, IV, 100).

By whom has Freud been taught—taught better than by "the judgement of the prevalent science of today," better than by the established scholarly authorities of philosophy and psychiatry? Freud has been taught *by dreams* themselves: his own, and those of others; Freud has been taught by his own patients: *"My patients* . . . told me their dreams and so *taught me* . . .——" (Standard, VI, 100–101).

Having thus been taught by dreams, as well as by his patients, that—contrary to the established scholarly opinion—dreams do have meaning, Freud is further taught by a literary text:

> This discovery is confirmed by a legend that has come down to us from antiquity. . . .
>
> While the poet . . . brings to light the guilt of Oedipus, he is at the same time compelling us to recognize our own inner minds . . .
>
> Like Oedipus, we live in ignorance of these wishes. . . . and after their revelation, we may all of us well seek to close our eyes to the scenes of our childhood. [Standard, VI, 261–263]

"But I have been taught better." What is unique about Freud's position as a student—as a learner—is that he learns from, or puts in the position of his teacher, the least authoritative sources of information that can be imagined: that he knows how to derive a teaching, or a lesson, from the very unreliability—the very *non-authority*—of literature, of dreams, of patients. For the first time in the history of learning, Freud, in other words, has recourse—scientific recourse—to a knowledge which is not authoritative, which is not that of a master, a knowledge which does not know what it knows, and is thus *not in possession of itself.*

Such, precisely, is the very essence of literary knowledge. "I went to the poets," says Socrates; ". . . I took them some of the most elaborate passages in their own writings, and asked them what was the meaning of them—thinking that they would teach me something. Will you believe me? I am almost ashamed to confess the truth, but I must say that there is hardly a person present who would not have talked better about their poetry than they did themselves. Then I knew that *not by wisdom do poets write poetry, but by a sort of genius or inspiration;* they are like diviners or soothsayers who also *say many fine things, but do not understand the meaning of them.* The poets appeared to me to be much in the same case."[19] From a philosophical perspective, knowledge is mastery—that which is in mastery of its own meaning. Unlike Hegelian philosophy, which *believes it knows all that there is to know;* unlike Socratic (or contemporary post-Nietzschean) philosophy, which *believes it knows it does not know*—literature, for its part, *knows it knows, but does not know the meaning of its knowledge*—does not know *what* it knows.

For the first time, then, Freud gives authority to the instruction—to the teaching—of a knowledge which does not know its own meaning, to a knowledge (that of dreams, of patients, of Greek tragedy) which we might define as literary: knowledge that is not in mastery of itself.

Of all Freud's students and disciples, Lacan alone has understood and emphasized the *radical* significance of Freud's indebtedness to literature: the role played by *literary knowledge* not just in the historical constitution of psychoanalysis, but in the very actuality of the psychoanalytic act, of the psychoanalytic (ongoing) *work* of learning and of teaching. Lacan alone has understood and pointed out the ways in which Freud's teaching—in all senses of the word—is not accidentally, but radically and fundamentally, a *literary* teaching. Speaking of "the training of the analysts of the future," Lacan thus writes:

> One has only to turn the pages of his works for it to become abundantly clear that Freud regarded a study . . . of the resonances . . . of literature and of the significations involved in works of art as necessary to an understanding of the text of our experience. Indeed, Freud himself is a striking instance of his own belief: he derived his inspiration, his ways of thinking and his technical weapons, from just such a study. But he also regarded it as a necessary condition in any teaching of psychoanalysis. [E 435, N 144]

> This [new] technique [of interpretation] would require for its teaching as well as for its learning a profound assimilation of the resources of a language, and especially of those that are concretely realized in its poetic texts. It is well known that Freud was in this position in relation to German literature, which, by virtue of an incomparable translation, can be said to include Shakespeare's plays. Every one of his works bears witness to this, and to the continual recourse he had to it, no less in his technique than in his discovery. [E 295, N 83]

> The psychoanalytic experience has rediscovered in man the imperative of the Word as the law that has formed him in its image. It manipulates the poetic function of language to give to his desire its symbolic mediation. [E 322, N 106]

19. Plato, *Apology,* 22 a–c, in *Dialogues of Plato,* Jowett translation, edited by J. D. Kaplan (New York: Washington Square Press, Pocket Books, 1973), p. 12.

Freud had, eminently, this feel for meaning, which accounts for the fact that any of his works, *The Three Caskets,* for instance, gives the reader the impression that it is written by a soothsayer, that it is guided by that kind of meaning which is of the order of poetic inspiration. [S-II, 353]

It is in this sense, among others, that Lacan can be regarded as Freud's best student: Lacan is the sole Freudian who has sought to learn from Freud how to learn Freud: Lacan is "taught" by Freud in much the same way Freud is "taught" by dreams; Lacan reads Freud in much the same way Freud reads *Oedipus the King,* specifically seeking in the text its *literary knowledge.* From Freud as teacher, suggests Lacan, we should learn to derive that kind of *literary teaching* he himself derived in an unprecedented way from literary texts. Freud's text should thus itself be read as a poetic text:

. . . the notion of the death instinct involves a basic irony, since its meaning has to be sought in the conjunction of two contrary terms: instinct . . . being the law that governs . . . a cycle of behavior whose goal is the accomplishment of a vital function; and death appearing first of all as the destruction of life. . . .

This notion must be approached through its resonances in what I shall call *the poetics of the Freudian corpus,* the first way of access to the penetration of its meaning, and the essential dimension, from the origins of the work to the apogee marked in it by this notion, for an understanding of its dialectical repercussions. [E 316–17, N 101–02]

It is here, in conjunction with Lacan's way of relating to Freud's literary teaching and of learning from Freud's literary knowledge, that we touch upon the historical uniqueness of Lacan's position as disciple, and can thus attempt to understand the way in which this pedagogically unique discipleship accounts for Lacan's astounding originality as a teacher.

"As Plato pointed out long ago," says Lacan, "it is not at all necessary that the poet know what he is doing, in fact, it is preferable that he not know. That is what gives a primordial value to what he does. We can only bow our heads before it" (Seminar, April 9, 1974, unpublished). Although apparently Lacan seems to espouse Plato's position, his real pedagogical stance is, in more than one way, at the antipodes of that of Plato; and not just because he bows his head to poets, whereas Plato casts them out of the Republic. If Freud himself, indeed, bears witness, in his text, to some poetic—literary—knowledge, it is to the extent that, like the poets, he, too, cannot exhaust the meaning of his text—he too partakes of the poetic ignorance of his own knowledge. Unlike Plato who, from his position as an admiring disciple, reports Socrates' assertion of his ignorance without—it might be assumed—really believing in the *non-ironic truth* of that assertion ("For the hearers," says Socrates, "always imagine that I myself possess the wisdom I find wanting in others"[20]), Lacan can be said to be the first disciple in the whole history of pedagogy and of

20. Plato, *Apology,* 22 a–c, op. cit., p. 12.

culture who *does indeed believe in the ignorance of his teacher—of his master.* Paradoxically enough, this is why he can be said to be, precisely, Freud's best student: a student of Freud's own revolutionary way of learning, of Freud's own unique position as the unprecedented student of unauthorized, unmastered knowledge. "The truth of the subject," says Lacan, "even when he is the position of a master, is not in himself" (S-XI, 10).

[Freud's] texts, to which for the past . . . years I have devoted a two-hour seminar every Wednesday . . . without having covered a quarter of the total, . . . , have given me, and those who have attended my seminars, the surprise of genuine discoveries. These discoveries, which range from concepts that have remained unused to clinical details uncovered by our exploration, demonstrate *how far the field investigated by Freud extended beyond the avenues that he left us to tend,* and how little his observation, which sometimes gives an impression of exhaustiveness, was the slave of what he had to demonstrate. Who . . . has not been moved by this research in action, whether in 'The Interpretation of Dreams,' 'The Wolf Man,' or 'Beyond the Pleasure Principle?' [E 404, N 117, TM]

Commenting *The Interpretation of Dreams,* Lacan situates in Freud's text the discoverer's own transferential structure—Freud's own unconscious structure of address:

What polarizes at that moment Freud's discourse, what organizes the whole of Freud's existence, is the conversation with Fliess. . . . It is in this dialogue that Freud's self-analysis is realized . . . This vast speech addressed to Fliess will later become the whole written work of Freud.

The conversation of Freud with Fliess, this fundamental discourse, which at that moment is unconscious, is the essential dynamic element [of *The Interpretation of Dreams*]. Why is it unconscious at that moment? Because its significance goes far beyond what both of them, as individuals, can consciously apprehend or understand of it at the moment. As individuals, they are nothing other, after all, than two little erudites, who are in the process of exchanging rather weird ideas.

The discovery of the unconscious, in the full dimension with which it is revealed at the very moment of its historical emergence, is that the scope, the implications of meaning go far beyond the signs manipulated by the individual. As far as signs are concerned, man is always mobilizing many more of them than he knows. [S-II, 150]

It is to the extent that Lacan precisely teaches us to read in Freud's text (in its textual excess) the signifiers of Freud's ignorance—his ignorance of his own knowledge—that Lacan can be considered Freud's best reader, as well as the most compelling teacher of the Freudian pedagogical imperative: the imperative to learn from and through the insight which does not know its own meaning, from and through the knowledge which is not entirely in mastery—in possession—of itself.

This unprecedented *literary* lesson, which Lacan derives from Freud's revolutionary way of learning and in the light of which he learns Freud, is transformed, in Lacan's own work, into a deliberately literary style of teaching. While—as a subject of praise or controversy—the originality of Lacan's eminently literary, eminently "poetic" style has become a stylistic *cause célèbre* often commented upon, what has not been understood is the extent to which this style—this poetic theory or theoretical poetry—is *pedagogically* poetic: poetic in such a way as to raise, through every answer that it gives, the literary question of its non-mastery of itself. In pushing its own thought beyond the limit of its self-possession, beyond the limitations of its own capacity for mastery; in passing on understanding which does not fully understand what it understands; in *teaching*, thus, *with blindness*—with and through the very blindness of its literary knowledge, of insights not entirely transparent to themselves—Lacan's unprecedented theoretically *poetic pedagogy* always implicitly opens up onto the infinitely literary, infinitely *teaching* question: What is the "navel"[21] of my own theoretical dream of understanding? What is the specificity of my incomprehension? What is the riddle which I in effect here pose under the guise of knowledge?

"But what was it that Zarathustra once said to you? That poets lie too much? But Zarathustra too is a poet. Do you believe that in saying this he spoke the truth? Why do you believe that?"

The disciple answered, "I believe in Zarathustra." But Zarathustra shook his head and smiled.[22]

Any return to Freud founding a teaching worthy of the name will occur only on that pathway where truth . . . becomes manifest in the revolutions of culture. That pathway is the only training we can claim to transmit to those who follow us. It is called—a style. [E 458][23]

21. "There is," writes Freud, "at least one spot in every dream at which it is unplumbable—a navel, as it were, that is its point of contact with the unknown" (Standard, IV, 111).

22. Nietzsche, *Thus Spoke Zarathustra*, translated by Walter Kaufmann (TM), in *The Portable Nietzsche* (New York: the Viking Press, 1971), p. 239, "On Poets."

23. The present essay is a chapter from my forthcoming book: *Psychoanalysis in Contemporary Culture: Jacques Lacan and the Adventure of Insight.*

The news of Lacan's death (on September 9, 1981) reached me as I was writing the section here entitled "The Interminable Task." The sadness caused by the cessation of a life as rich in insight and as generous in instruction, was thus accompanied by an ironic twist which itself felt like a typical Lacanian turn, one of the ironies of his teaching: teaching terminable and interminable . . . Few deaths, indeed, have been as deeply inscribed as a lesson in a teaching, as Lacan's, who always taught the implications of the Master's death. "Were I to go away," he said, some time ago, "tell yourselves that it is in order to at last be truly Other."

I have deliberately chosen not to change, and to pursue, the grammatical present tense which I was using to describe Lacan's teaching: since his life has ceased to be, his teaching is, indeed, all the more present, all the more alive, all the more interminably "what it has never ceased to be: an act that is yet to come."

MICHAEL RYAN

Deconstruction and Radical Teaching

> Culturally, the greatest interest of powerful Texans has been in
> higher education. Of prime importance has been the direction
> of the state's two land-grant colleges, the University of Texas
> and Texas A & M. Through the years, the University of Texas
> at Austin has provided a disproportionate number of the state's
> most powerful men and at times has possessed a virtual stran-
> glehold on the state's political officeholders. But all of Texas'
> diverse galaxy of educational institutions derive considerable
> financial support from members of the business community; an
> examination of the boards of regents and large donors usually
> will provide a guide to the names of the powerful who've taken
> on the task of shaping the future through education.
>
> —*Texas Business*

> One of the problems of communism is that it is a dictatorship of
> intellectuals and professors.
>
> —S. I. Hayakawa

Two opposed groups—radical teachers and business technocrats—hold the
same view of the university, but for different reasons. Radicals argue that the
university services capitalism by providing it with trained manpower, technology, and new knowledge. Business technocrats essentially agree, but
whereas the radicals deplore this situation, business people recognize its
importance, and they do all they can to foster it.

In the years to come, the two groups will clash over the issue of whether or
not the classroom should have walls, that is, be immune to manipulation by
business, as well as maintain a liberal neutrality in regard to external politics.
Given that these days, the most crucial politics on the agenda of radical
teachers are the politics of business, business people are likely to be tempted to
seek more of a say than they already have in university affairs, partly as a
defense against irrefutable attacks by academics on their hegemony, partly as a
guard against the "false" education of their trained manpower. The fiscal crisis
of the university and the necessity of seeking external funding (one million
from South Korea, as the USC dean admitted my first day on the job; later in
the year the controversial source would be Saudi Arabia) will enable this
breaking down of the walls of the classroom from without.

Radical teachers are equally unconvinced by the liberal ideology of
academic neutrality. They break down the walls of the classroom from within,

45

opening intellectual discussion out upon a public sphere. The traditional academic enterprise of stockpiling and communicating knowledge is replaced by a politicized concern for social issues, the most pressing of which is the power of capitalist business in structuring and controlling the economic, political, and cultural life of the U.S. and much of the world.

The direct presence of business (and of business related government enterprises—defense, research & development, etc.) in the university has been amply documented.[1] When a major private university, upon whose board sit representatives of several major pharmaceutical firms, has some of its sizeable investments in those same companies, and when one of those companies, the major manufacturer of valium, funds a new department of therapy at the university in which the only method promoted is valium-treatment, then one has reason to suspect that phrases like "academic neutrality" and "conflict of interest" have lost all critical significance. Business schools offer a more striking example of an institutionalized service performed by universities for capital. To put the matter deconstructively, the walls of the business school classroom are not so much lines of strict demarcation between a pure outside and an inside which is self-sufficient and autarchic, as they are margins where inside and outside become interchangeable. Each is structurally dependent on the other. Business could not survive without business schools which teach not only technical knowledge, but also the "self-evident," "natural," and "good" character of capitalism. And business schools depend on business for endowments and for indirect, retroactive financing in the form of guaranteed jobs.

Business is aware that its profitable relationship to the universities could be disturbed by the presence of radical teachers on campuses. In *The Crisis of Democracy*, a Trilateral Commission book, Samuel Huntington has expressed concern over an excessively democratic left intelligensia in the U.S. A few years ago, William Simon, a government businessman, suggested that corporations avoid giving money to those universities that do not promote the conservative interests of business.[2] More recently, *Business Week* published an article on Marxists on campus in which fear was expressed that business might wake up too late to the possibility that American universities were going the way of West European universities—with disastrous consequences for business. In April, 1979, a line-up of conservative ideologues from the American Assembly met at Arden House in Harriman (as in Averell), New York, to discuss the "disorders of the university." The meeting was made

1. The business version is provided by K. Patrick and R. Eells, *Education and the Business Dollar* (London: Macmillan, 1969); the radical view by David Smith, *Who Rules the University?* (New York, 1974). See also James Ridgway, *The Closed Corporation* (New York, 1968), and Samuel Bowles and Herbert Gintis, *Schooling in Capitalist America* (New York: Basic Books, 1976).

2. "Angry Tigers; campaigning to withhold contributions because of faculty political views," *Newsweek* (March 29, 1976).

possible by "generous support" from parties who may have reason to worry about leftwing critics of rightwing business "order"—"The Ford Foundation, Exxon Education Foundation, IBM and AT&T." The shared term in their discussion was "integrity." "Disorders" threaten the "moral and intellectual *integrity* of our colleges and universities."[3] "Integrity" usually implies wholeness, purity, and uprightness. According to the American Heritage Dictionary, the first meaning of "integrity" is "rigid adherence to a code of behavior," and it is this more sinister definition that the American Assembly seems really to have in mind. In order to assure "integrity," the Arden House conservatives conclude that "our institutions of higher education will do well to rid themselves of unbecoming conduct." As the code word integrity probably refers to the way the academy has traditionally served the interests of business, the code words "unbecoming conduct" seem a disguised reference to the Marxist presence on the campuses. The message hardly needs to be expounded, although it is couched in the contradictory logic of conservative ideology. The academy must repress "disorderly" internal elements, or else, it is implied, external "government regulations" might be imposed. It never seems to occur to conservatives that they themselves advocate what they ostensibly resist from government—repressive regulation.

Business ideologists conceal the fact that their worries about resistance to government regulation actually serve specific business interests by fabricating general concepts which make their interests seem universal. If they were sincere in their concern for autonomy and self-regulation, then they would not make pronouncements about how academics should behave. Frederick Bohm, the director of the Exxon Education Foundation, for example, describes the university's "cohesion of purpose" in terms of a "new allegiance to the acquisition of knowledge and to new openness to those able to follow." "Naturally," he goes on, "this leaves out any moral perspective." He criticizes the "irrationalism" and "ambiguity" of the 60s, when "democratic values and rational authority" were "confused" (p. 6). But Bohm seems confident that order and reason can be restored. Another participant in the conference supplies the probable cause for such confidence: "As money gets tighter, institutions will pressure faculty, and faculty themselves may scurry to do whatever is necessary to get external funds. Outside pressures will accordingly be harder to resist. . . . The balance of influences is clearly tipping toward the donor" (pp. 122–3).

A deconstructive analysis of the concepts and values which inform this discourse would focus on words like "integrity" and "cohesion of purpose." They suggest an institutional identity of being and of will which seems to incarnate the metaphysical model of the logos. The university is given out to

---

3. The American Assembly, *Disorders in Higher Education* (Englewood Cliffs: Prentice Hall, 1979), p. vii. I am indebted to Gayatri Chakravorty Spivak for bringing this book to my attention.

be integral and selfsame, proper to itself. This assumption predicates two others: that the university has an essence—knowledge-gathering—and that this essence is defined by a norm—"becoming" or proper conduct. The attribution of an essence ("integrity") necessarily precipitates a norm which defines the exclusion of an outside—"unbecoming conduct." Anti-business politics will be kept out of the classroom, in other words. As is usually the case in such ideological rationalizations of institutions, the value of reason is claimed as the norm of the institution, and deviation from that norm is characterized as "irrationalism." The political and institutional corollary of the metaphysical postulates of conscious intention is the cohesive purpose which would eliminate all "ambiguity," that is, all that troubles the normative ratio of the institution. Such characteristics of metaphysics as an unproblematic ontology ("integrity"), teleology ("cohesive purpose"), and logocentrism ("rationalism," no "ambiguity," clear and determinable meaning) are summoned as modes of institutional legitimation.

These theoretical rationalizations of the university institution are of course undone by the practice of the university. Universities are fields of conflict and force, not integrated wholes with cohesive intentions. Their "reasonableness" is simply the benign face of power, coercion, and the everyday brutality of patriarchal capitalism in America. A professor cited in the American Assembly book as someone who attempts to elevate the "souls" of his students was also recently cited in a university scandal for soliciting sex from female graduate students just prior to their exams. Cornell University (where this essay was written) itself engages in unbecoming political conduct when it engages in union busting tactics to counter the UAW's attempt to organize the employees. And without the infrastructure provided by those workers, the neutral gathering of academic knowledge could not continue. The microstructures of university life are crosshatched with political and economic forces. The suggestion that this heteronymous arena is cohesive or integral is mystifying. Universities like Cornell do indeed cohesively service business. However, the point of ideological generalizations like "integrity" is not to name that purpose. Rather, it is to provide a justification for countering any move to introduce "irrationalism" or "ambiguity" into that rationally functioning, cohesively purposeful system. In other words, to counter radicalism which becomes "irrational" and "ambiguous" by a circular argument. By assigning "integrity" to the university, conservatives define their own project as an effort to maintain or restore a spuriously natural condition of purity or wholeness. The postulation of a normative attribute like integrity permits any radical attempt at modification to be characterized as a disintegrative degradation, a falling off from nature. Restoration of "integrity" will consist of curtailing that new development.

From the perspective of both Marxism and deconstruction, the notion of integrity is idealist. A Marxist analysis would point to the ideological function of the concept, the way it enables the exercise of power through a misrepresentation of the realities of the academic situation. A deconstructive analysis would show how what the conservatives call integrity is itself a form of dis-integrity; it would question the conservative habit of thinking in terms of such binaries which make a norm of some ideal model of self-possessed self-identity ("integrity") and treat anything which doesn't cohere with the model as a derivative deviation or degradation. If integrity names the service universities provide for business, then, simply by shifting criteria, one can say that the business-university channels people into narrow economic functions which are scarcely integrative for them. A different criterion of integrity, a Marxist one, for instance, which would demand the full development of all human faculties, makes the business criterion appear obscenely impoverished. In terms of the status of the institution, the deconstructive and Marxist arguments intersect in criticizing the "propriety" (selfsameness, wholeness, integrity) of the university. The Marxist argument states that the university is bound by social relations to supposedly extraneous instances such as politics and economics. It cannot be isolated as a thing-in-itself from those relations. The deconstructive argument uses the concept of a force field. The university is a locus of forces which constitute the university as a point of intersection in a broad field which defies any single or ultimate determination. The interior or essence of the university is constitutively impugned by what supposedly is "exterior" to it.

The university is an historical product; it reflects and reproduces social stratification by rationing knowledge according to class; it trains "leaders," thus preserving external structures of political authority; it embodies conservative business ideology in its institutional structure by segmenting and instrumentalizing knowledge; it promotes a monopoly of scarce scientific knowledge and technology by business; it trains social agents in the norms and mores of the dominant culture; and so on.

Deconstructive analysis would consider the incredible multiplicity of universities, from the elite country club campuses of the Ivy League leadership factories, with a paradoxical monopoly on elite left culture as well, to the low prestige two-year community colleges which track the working class away from liberatory culture and into job-training. What is integrative about all this is quite simply the integration of new generations into a business world where their roles will be determined, all apologies for "equality of opportunity" notwithstanding, by wealth and privilege at one end, and by the imposition of wage labor at the other. In the name of "integrity," then, what the business leaders of the American Assembly are actually defending is the dis-integrity of the university, its specific supportive function in capitalist America.

As far back as 1973, radical educators would have seen the American

Assembly-led conservative backlash coming. The Carnegie Commission Report on Higher Education doesn't bother to camouflage the link between education and business behind a benign vocabulary. "Education," it states, "is the main instrument of opportunity in an industrial society requiring a high level of employment skills from many of its citizens."[4] The commissioners point to academic freedom as the crucial issue for an "industrial society" (read business community) desirous of maintaining unimpeded access to a supply of university skilled labor. It was the duty of the "independent" Commission to issue a warning to the academic left on behalf of business. It takes the form of an indirect threat: "Left faculty members, in particular, may have generally decided, as have several of their most prominent leaders, that campus political neutrality is the best protection of their own individual right to dissent" (p. 55). They go on, with characteristic flair for self-contradiction, to claim that "the price of academic freedom is eternal vigilance." Vigilance is necessary because those who exercise too much academic freedom are its greatest enemy:

Academic freedom is now threatened internally as well as externally—by some ideological adherents within as well as by some holders of power without. Thus it becomes more important than ever before that judicial processes on the campus are fully independent of improper internal processes and biases. Processes of faculty hearing established, in part, to protect faculty members from attacks by external powers must now also be capable of protecting the integrity of the campus against those who undertake internal attacks on academic freedom; they must be able to convict internal enemies of freedom. . . .

And they conclude:

Faculty members, concomitantly, should not be able to plead that their civil liberties as citizens are a basis for not meeting academic standards of conduct on campus. "Free speech" is not an excuse for inaccuracy as a scholar or misuse of the classroom as a teacher. . . . As citizens, scholars should be held to the standards of citizenship, and as scholars, to the standards of scholarship.

Students are also warned that they "need to be guided by reasonable outer boundaries on what they can and cannot do" (p. 61).

The Carnegie Commission raises two questions which will become increasingly more important to radical teachers as the conservative program for the academy is applied: the question of boundaries and of bias. Radicals, of course, already have answers to those questions, but I want to formulate them in deconstructive terms, since I think deconstructive analysis provides a stronger basis than simple assertion upon which to base a defense of the radical position.

The norm of propriety which defines the boundaries of academic freedom is similar to the concept of integrity, in that it establishes a set of actions

4. *Priorities for Action:* final report (New York: McGraw Hill, 1973), p. 39.

integral to the norm, while it excludes a body of actions considered external or improper. A deconstruction of this discursive institution points out that the principle of exclusion used assumes a "nature" free from bias. If bias is to be excluded, then what remains is a pure, unbiased position which functions as the norm defining exclusion. Carnegie seems to define bias in terms of "ideological adherents" and "internal enemies of freedom." I assume that in order to deduce a definition of Carnegie's unstated norm of unbiased teaching, all I need do is generate the opposites of the characteristics of bias: "ideological non-adherents" or "non-ideological adherents" or perhaps "non-ideological non-adherents," and, of course, "friends of freedom." Now, the defining terms for Carnegie's unbiased natural norm must also be natural and unbiased, and given the terms deduced, that cannot be the case. In the ideological lexicon, "ideological" refers to radicals, socialists, progressives, and Marxists. And "to adhere," when subtended to "ideological," means to associate oneself with a worked-out, systematic critique of capitalism. A non-ideological non-adherent, then, would be someone who dissociates himself from the critique of capitalism. Put differently, a liberal pluralist. If I use "anti" instead of "non" to indicate the opposition, his position becomes more markedly conservative— an anti-progressive pro-capitalist opponent of critics of capitalism. Hardly an unbiased position, let alone grounds for establishing a natural norm in relation to which a concept of "bias" could be defined.

The term "friend of freedom" implies a similar pro-business bias. "Freedom" is not a neutral term, and its abstractness conceals a specific history which detracts from its apparent naturalness ("all men are born free" and so on). The word-idea "free" was first used by the thirteenth-century Celts to name members of a household who related to the head or master by family ties rather than as slaves. Its first meaning was economic, and freedom came to be defined negatively as exemption from slavery or bondage, as well as from autocratic control. It wasn't until the fourteenth century that it was applied to civil liberties and individual rights. The first meaning of "free" as free labor indicates how the concept was bound up with the onset of small capitalist production. The emergent capitalists first needed unbonded labor "free" from feudal obligation and, later, legal freedom from the power of the feudal lords. More recently, freedom has become almost equatable with pro-capitalism; freedom means free enterprise. Children are taught that the opposite of "free" is "communist." To be a "friend of freedom," then, is to be a friend of capitalism. Again, hardly an unbiased position, unless you accept a definition of capitalist free enterprise as natural, acquiescence to which is itself so natural that it defines the norm beyond all bias, all adherence, and all ideology which permits condemnation of the "ideological" radical anti-capitalist position. The Carnegie position, then, seems to rest on a norm of a natural acquiescence to capitalism, one that would be so spontaneous it would transcend all ideological or systematically formulated adherence. The pure state prior to all bias turns out to be a state of pure bias, that is, of unquestioned, precritical belief.

Carnegie claims a questionable norm of a self-identical, self-possessed nature as the basis for determining the boundaries of academic freedom. The unbiased, natural attitude they propose is itself a form of bias. They are, to a limited extent, aware of this but they would prefer to have their economic and ideological interests prevail by persuasion rather than force, although a rather frightful subdued violence underlies their discourse. In fact, it is ideological coercion which distinguishes highly developed American capitalism from underdeveloped forms which still require physical force. In one way, they (I use "they" for the singular Carnegie, since it is a corporation) are faithful to Aristotle's argument that what "contributes most to preserve the state is . . . to educate children with respect to the state."[5] One should not expect people interested (by self-definition) in conserving things, especially things which serve their own material interests, to argue otherwise. "Power within the university," as Edgar Fiedenberg remarks, "aligns itself with power outside it."[6]

The American Assembly uses the word "loyalty" rather than "academic freedom" to describe academic life. It is interesting that the concept of freedom, which originally was used as an ideological instrument against kings demanding loyalty, has with time come to be used as an instrument for enforcing economic fealty. What both Carnegie and the American Assembly demand is that academics be loyal to standards of propriety which are supportive of business property and the business ideology of free enterprise. At the same time, they remove the radical academic defense of its position in terms of academic freedom by branding radicals as "internal enemies of freedom," that is, of free enterprise. And the conservative offensive against government regulation in the name of freedom is used to justify "self-regulation" on the part of university administrators, who, of course, are owned and operated by business trustees. Ideologically and rhetorically, the academic left is cornered. If they choose to defend themselves on the basis of the liberal concept of academic freedom, they become their own judges, since the word "freedom" has been appropriated by business ideologues to name precisely that against which the left defines itself—free enterprise, non-ideological non-adherence, freedom fighting, and so on. The Carnegie commissioners make the point with great clarity: academic leftists will retain their right to freedom only as long as they are loyal to the principles of citizenship which identify civic freedom with the economic model of free enterprise. If you like free enterprise, you're free; if not, you're not.

5. Aristotle, *Politics*, tr. E. Walford (London, 1908), p. 194.
6. *Power and Empowerment in Higher Education* (Louisville, 1978), p. 16.

I'll now argue for an alternate principle to the liberal concept of academic freedom as a support for the position of radical teachers in the academy.

I'll begin with a generalized version of the deconstructive argument concerning boundaries and biases: no boundary is possible which would rigorously distinguish a natural, pedagogic attitude, one that would be unbiased, neutral, and disinterested, from an external arena of unnatural bias. The purity of the internal arena is always already contaminated by what it seeks to exclude, because the act of exclusion itself signifies a bias. Self-identity wrested from heterogeneous relations by an exclusivist reduction immediately ceases to be self-identical. The logical practice which establishes the theoretical possibility of an unbiased natural attitude in teaching at once makes such a thing impossible.

All knowledge operates through acts of exclusion and marginalization similar to the ones which define the proper arena of supposedly unbiased teaching. Rational demarcation bears a resemblance to institutional demarcation. The production of theoretical concepts entails judgments which delimit a field of study and exclude certain unrelated or irrelevant factors. An institutional version of this operation of division by exclusion is the academic disciplines and the professions.

The institutional divisions between disciplines reflect metaphysical conceptual divisions (between the Business School and the study of the uses of language, politics and economics, or sociology and formal law) and promote an ideological structuring of the social world. Perhaps the most significant case of such structuring is the separation of economics as an isolated domain of free human activity—business—from politics, which is the area marked off for the struggle for power between various interest groups. That the political struggle is motivated by economic interest and that the economy is structured by political classes puts the conceptual, institutional, and "real" division in question and shows it to serve an ideological function. Certain determinable economic and political interests are served by the maintenance of the division both conceptually and institutionally (in the academic disciplines as well as in the "world"). As long as people think of economics as an isolated instance which entails no force or coercion, where workers and capitalists exchange "freely," which therefore is free from "politics," then it is unlikely they will make the connection between their own economic position and political processes. As long as "politics" means elections and government, then people are unlikely to see it at work in the marketplace—as economics. The intellectual division of labor in the disciplines reflects and reproduces institutional divisions which make economics and politics seem to be autonomous and independent instances. These divisions conceal the relationality of these instances, that they are nothing "in themselves" and that they constitute each other as mutually interdependent determinations or differentiations of a complex system of heterogeneous forces. And they thus prevent the making of the kind of effective connections between "economic" and "political" events which might put an end to apathy and lead to a revolutionary consciousness.

Metaphysical categories are institutionalized by the disciplinary divisions of the academy. To study business instead of, say, language or politics is to assume implicitly that the latter have nothing to do with business, which is an independent, isolatable realm, as the singularity of the word suggests. But business could not be carried on if words like "demand," "free enterprise," "labor market," "equilibrium," and "investment climate" were not available to enable the operations of business. Such words are effective in lending conceptual coherence and legitimacy to the "business world." They also function ideologically by occluding real relations of contradiction, power, coercion, and struggle. Their simplicity, their singularity, and their benign character make a world of incessant battle and suffering seem orderly, non-contradictory, natural, self-evident.

They also effectively inscribe a disposition in the agents of business to expect the world to be so ordered and to behave accordingly. The vocabulary of business contains embedded in it a theory of the world which, once absorbed by social agents through education, helps produce certain practices which reproduce the objective conditions—the business world—which give rise to that vocabulary. Language, then, is a material force in the reproduction of capitalism, more specifically, of the conceptual system which necessarily accompanies the structuring of the real world in a way which serves the ends of capital.

The phrase "stable investment climate" imparts a sense of teleology, of a goal to be reached and of the necessity of attaining it. The model of equilibrium embedded in the phrase accounts for the placing of ends over means which ensues from it. What matters is the goal—stability. The phrase thus helps guide (and also overlook) such actions as the military terror against the left in the southern cone of Latin America. The phrase/concept enables political action, while also concealing an act of political repression under a seemingly innocuous term that limits the description of the situation to purely economic matters. The political function of the language of business is in part the concealment of the politics of business.

The division of the academy into disciplines, then, might not be as apolitical or unbiased an affair as it gives itself out to be. It reflects a metaphysical conceptuality which would classify a world that denies the possibility of such classificatory divisions. In the world, politics, economics, and language overlap; they exist differentially. That is, one can be distinguished only by marginalizing the others and subtracting something from the one distinguished such that it could never be complete "in itself." It is impossible to analyze politics without taking language and economics into account. One cannot determine the function of language in literature and in society without taking into account the political and economic functions and uses of language.

The operations of rational conceptualization—division, exclusion, isolation, concentration, identification, and so on—are institutionalized in the academic disciplines. They help to structure the social world by instituting "rational" dispositions in social agents.[7] It is a commonplace that one's conception of the world is in part determined by one's practice. Academics, for example, tend to see the world according to their disciplinary training—historians as history, economists as economy, etc. The same can be said for an entire society which has attained a high level of educational homogeneity. From grade school to university, the institutional form and practice of education by rational categorical divisions determines how agents think about the world and how they act in it. Disciplinary teaching imparts to students an attitude of rationalization, the tendency to think of the world in terms of discrete sectors of analysis. This tendency is enforced by the direct linkage between education and employment; there are no jobs for generalists.

The act of knowledge is not spontaneous; it is something instituted through training and practice. From the point of view of education itself, then, there can be no natural knowledge which would serve as the basis for distinguishing an unbiased teaching from an external political arena. The practice of knowing is itself already a form of bias, since it entails selecting and excluding, more often than not, according to historically determined institutional norms of what *should* be studied and known. Literary critics, for example, are supposed to know certain things, and not others—good style, for example, but never economic theory. The disciplinary segmentation of the

---

7. In capitalist management, the analog of rational conceptual determination is called "specification" (of tasks, variables, environment problems, etc.); its practical form is organizational division: "Let us assume a rational owner, that is, one who will attempt to achieve his goals in an efficient manner. Given high visibility of consequences, the owner will be able to specify those procedures which will maximize efficiency and eliminate inappropriate procedures . . ." (S. W. Becker and D. Neuhauser, *The Efficient Organization* (New York: Elsevier, 1975), p. 94). These procedures are what I mean by rational exclusion, isolation, division, etc. Efficiency maximization can be described as an essentialist "rational" operation because, like reason itself, it must eliminate the "inappropriate" in order to achieve "property" or selfsameness—the point where inefficient complexity and marginal elements are entirely purged. For a description of a similar process of structuration along the lines of rational concept formation, see Magali Sarfatti Larson, *The Rise of Professionalism* (Berkeley, 1977), pp. 40, 55: "What makes the codification of knowledge so important from the point of view of the professional project is that it depersonalizes the ideas held about professional practice and its products. It sets up a transcendent cognitive and normative framework within which, ideally, differences in the interpretation of practice and in the definition of the 'commodity' can be reconciled. . . . The more formalized the cognitive basis, the more the profession's language and knowledge appear to be connotation-free and 'objective.' . . . Professional identity is experienced as shared expertise and therefore involves a sense of at least cognitive superiority. . . . The whole process of setting up a monopolistic market of services [is] based . . . on articulating and enforcing principles of inclusion and exclusion."

world implies imperatives that govern the limits of what can, legitimately, be known.

The liberal notion of neutral pedagogy, as grounds for granting academic freedom, requires a model of natural knowledge which exists prior to bias. But if all knowledge is educated or formed, and if that formation occurs through disciplinary institutions, then it is highly unlikely that an unbiased knowledge will be found in the world, even if it were theoretically possible. Education (whether formal or informal, that is, education carried on through the practices of habituation and socialization in the community, the family, the media, etc.) enables knowledge, and education, both in the formal and the informal sense, necessarily produces bias. Formal education does so through a disciplinary division which skews knowledge away from an ideal absolute, that would mark the end to partiality and the attainment of impartial neutrality—a positionedness without position. Informal education does so according to a principle of political non-contradiction: if the system is to retain legitimacy and survive, the consciousness of social agents must not contradict the presuppositions of the economy, the social network, and the state. This principle explains the programmatic exclusion of the possibility of a general radical culture in the U.S. Informal education is biased by the requirements of social cohesion and political economic legitimation. "Natural" knowledge, then, the normative basis of a disinterested scholarly education, is itself produced and conditioned by an irreducibly biased education. The outside of the university, especially the political outside, is always already internal to the university, in the form of the social and institutional knowledge the university occludes.

The cohabitation of education and economics is not an altogether recent discovery. Aristotle, in the *Economics*, writes: "Since we see that modes of education form the characters of the young, it is necessary when you have procured them to rear up those to whose care liberal offices are to be committed."[8] Capitalist planners began to notice in the 60s that economic growth required educational planning. "Human capital investment" was seen to be a necessary factor of capital costs, costs which, for the most part, were shunted onto the public. It was found that education raised the average quality of labor, the amount of qualified manpower, entrepreneurial ability, the marginal productivity of real capital, general economic activity, as well as the gross national product. Education, clearly, was a factor of economic growth.[9]

The business scientists discovered a truth Marx outlined in the past

8. Aristotle, *Economics*, tr. E. Walford (London, 1908), p. 243.
9. M. Blaug, *The Economics of Education* (New York, 1968); George Kneller, *Education and Economic Thought* (New York: Wiley, 1968); Herbert Parnes, *Forecasting Educational Needs for Economic and Social Development* (Paris, 1962); *The Economics of Education*, ed. E. A. G. Robinson and J. E. Vaizey (New York, 1966).

century—the social world is the product of human labor. The economy is not an objective machine; it requires subjective manual and mental inputs. The human mind provides needed technological inventiveness, an instrument of economic calculation, a ready-made machine for decision and management, as well as marketing inspiration. As capitalism becomes more technologically and logistically complex, more dependent on technology, marketing, calculation, planning, and management, industrial production will itself become increasingly more dependent on the production of knowledge.

I'd argue, then, that the notion of boundary (between unbiased scholarship and biased world politics) should be replaced by a concept of *economy*—of reciprocal exchange between two instances that have no existence outside of that exchange. The social world "outside" the university permits the university to work by providing the ground for education, both formal and informal. Similarly, that social world would collapse without an educational process of some sort (be it formal or informal) which trains social agents in the skills necessary for the reproduction of that society. The social world is constructed by intellectual labor and rationally guided technology. Given the high degree of technology required to maintain U.S. capitalist society, one could say with confidence that the dependence of the university on the social world is matched by a reciprocal dependence of the social world on university education. Business, for one thing, has reached such a high stage of refinement that it could not reproduce itself without business schools. And business, by creating an artificial environment of scarcity, exerts indirect economic pressure on schools to turn out more employable M.B.A.s than unemployment-bound Ph.D.s in other disciplines.

The problem of bias, which governs the question of academic freedom, leads, by way of a radical deconstructive analysis, to the problem of social construction, and it is in terms of this problem that academic Marxists can begin to formulate an alternate principle to that of academic freedom as a basis for arguing their case.

If radical teachers accept the Marxist and the deconstructive arguments—that the mind is a mode of technology which is instrumental in the construction of the world and that knowledge, because synoptic representation is always partial, a theory which can never by definition fully account for practice, never has a "natural" form which is exempt from bias—then they acquire grounds for claiming that the walls of the classroom never strictly demarcate an outside from an inside, "interested" activism from "disinterested" scholarship, or an objective, social world from the constructive, subjective activities of the working mind. The liberal argument for "academic freedom," which assumes the classroom is an enclave where an unbiased and disinterested activity—the compilation of truth and the communication of technical or rational skills—goes on, loses all relevance. The Marxist and the deconstructive positions claim there is never a teaching whose natural, unbiased status could be restored by an elimination of all bias. Indeed, each school of thought would claim that the fiction of an unbiased position is perhaps the most ideologically biased of all the possible positions. Neither, they would claim, is there an isolatable realm of "freedom" or self-sufficient autonomy which academics can claim. The academy is constitutively extraverted in that it forms and is formed by the world in contradistinction to which its autonomy is supposedly defined.

Radical teachers, I suggest, might base their arguments for their activities in the academy on a less defensive principle than that of "academic freedom." To accept academic freedom as a rallying cry is tantamount to accepting a definition of the academy as a separable realm from the social world. The clear link between intellectual technology and capitalist business is denied. Instead of emphasizing the fact that the social world is constructed and that therefore it could be constructed in a different form, the liberal philosophy of academic freedom would make that world appear natural, an independent object to be contemplated studiously by the non-activist, disinterested liberal academic. Liberal academic ideology makes the radical position of pedagogic activism for the sake of an alternate social construction seem a deviation in relation to its apolitical norm. Nevertheless, upholders of the norm are themselves unconscious participants in the structuring of the world by intellectual labor—either as technology or ideology. All pedagogy is a form of activism; and the radical teacher's activism is therefore second degree. It reflects upon the existing activism of the schools in maintaining the mind-patterns and the technical levels needed by capitalism, and it engages in its work not in terms of a deviation from a norm, but as an alternative to another "deviation." In order to mark a break with the liberal ideology which promotes academic isolation, scholarly theory, and academic freedom, radical teachers engage increasingly in popular education. Teaching beyond the walls of the classroom can take place in counter-institutions (NAM's socialist schools, U Mass' Center for Popular Economics, the New York Marxist School, Cornell City and Regional Planning's technical assistance center), or through the media (Doug Kellner's public access program in Austin) or through direct participation in urban affairs of the sort Al Watkins and Dave Perry engage in.[10] Whatever the form, the important thing in a very literal sense (and it is this perhaps which has the conservatives worried) is to get the word *out* (of the classroom and the scholarly journals). As Bill Tabb pointed out at the Marxist Union conference (New York University, June 20, 1980), the time is come when the economic crisis will permit the word of socialism to fall on receptive ears. And Barbara Ehrenreich on the same occasion: the academicization of Marxism in the 70s has run its course.

10. See, for example, A. Watkins and D. Perry, "Giving Cities the Business," *The Nation*, March 1, 1980.

NEIL HERTZ

Two Extravagant Teachings

For many years, students entering Cornell have been handed a pamphlet, prepared by the English Department, entitled "A Writer's Responsibilities." The plural is slightly misleading: the pamphlet addresses itself to only one "responsibility," the student's "responsibility always to demonstrate the extent to which he is master of what he is learning." And, lest this seem too massive, too unbearable a charge, the next sentences go on to specify it somewhat: "He must make clear what is his and what is someone else's. His teacher must know whose words he is reading or listening to." The pamphlet, in other words, is about plagiarism, and it contains the usual mixture of sensible advice (about paraphrasing, quoting, footnoting, etc.) and ill-assured moral exhortation. For our purposes its interest lies in its ill-assurance, in a rhetoric that wavers in its address to its student-readers in a predictable and symptomatic fashion. Here, for example, are the pamphlet's opening words:

Education at its best, whether conducted in seminar, laboratory, or lecture hall, is essentially a dialogue between teacher and pupil in which questions and answers can be explored, arguments can be posed and resolved, data can be sought and evaluated. From the time of Socrates and his disciples to that of the nightly discussion on the corridor, this dialogue has been the mark and delight of the intellectual life.

The allusion to Socrates may not be obligatory, but it is characteristic of this earnest moment in teachers' imaginings of themselves, their students and what passes between them. Equally characteristic of the complementary cynical moment is the note of tight-lipped institutional fussiness struck on the pamphlet's last page:

The Policy of the English Department

For the first instance of plagiarism or of any other kind of academic dishonesty or irresponsibility, the student will immediately receive a failing grade in the course and be reported to the appropriate department, division or college for whatever further action may be in order.

The lineaments of an American Scene of Instruction are sketched in these passages. The student might be Alcibiades, but then again he might be Al Capone; his teacher is either a master of instructive dialogue or a disciplinarian, and the whole operation can feel like "the intellectual life" one moment, the next like a low budget cops-and-robbers routine. Or so it would appear from language of this sort: I don't think I'm describing higher education in America so much as calling attention to some common teacherly fantasies about it, fantasies largely ignored by serious writers engaging the sociology or the economics of universities, or else alluded to obliquely under some more general rubric, like professorial "conservatism". Yet the fantasies I propose to dwell on seem pervasive, sluggishly unresponsive to changes in the system of higher education, and distributed across generational and political lines. You don't have to be over thirty or a bourgeois humanist, for example, to find yourself beside yourself about a paper you suspect was plagiarized.

I have picked two documents to examine which embody such fantasies, characterizations of the relations between teachers and students that take the form of images or, sometimes, of tendentious implicit narratives. Each seems to have been elaborated by a teacher in response to a perceived threat. I shall be arguing that in each case that threat has been misperceived, that indeed the function of the characterization would seem to be first to misrepresent a threat and then to respond, more or less aggressively, to that misrepresentation. The extravagance of these teachings, then, lies both in the misrepresentation and in the vehemence of the response.

I. PUNISHING PLAGIARISTS

The pamphlet "A Writer's Responsibilities" is not wholly the work of the Cornell English Department. About half of it is excerpted (with appropriate acknowledgement) from what was, in the 1960s, a popular freshman textbook, Harold C. Martin's *The Logic and Rhetoric of Exposition*.[1] In these pages, entitled "A Definition of Plagiarism," Martin leads his readers through the variety of forms—some bald-faced, some more subtle and devious, some conscious, some inadvertent—of what he calls, in ironic quotation marks, "borrowing," then ends his discussion with this untypically intense paragraph:

Since one of the principal aims of a college education is the development of intellectual honesty, it is obvious that plagiarism is a particularly serious offense and the punishment for it is commensurately severe. What a penalized student suffers can never really be known by anyone but himself; what the student who plagiarizes and "gets away with it" suffers is less public and probably less acute, but the corruptness of his act, the disloyalty and baseness it entails, must inevitably leave an ineradicable mark upon him as well as on the institution of which he is privileged to be a member.

A strange paragraph, urgent in its wish to stigmatize the crime it knows it can't be sure won't be committed, can't be sure won't go undetected, no matter what one says. Hence the rising rhythms of the last sentence ("the corruptness of his

---

1. Harold C. Martin, *The Logic and Rhetoric of Exposition* (New York: Holt, 1958).

act, the disloyalty and baseness it entails . . ."), the echoing absolutes ("inevitably," "ineradicable"), the huff and puff of its concluding phrase. And what are we to make of "gets away with it" in quotation marks? Does that mean "he only thinks he gets away with it—we know better"? Or is it perhaps mimicking student diction and presenting the difference between the vulnerable institution and its disloyal member as though it were also a difference in verbal refinement: *we* are polysyllabic, *they* are slobs?

More intriguing are the paragraph's speculations about the consequences of plagiarism, not its explicit consequences but its ideal or imagined ones, some odd combination of interior suffering (which "can never really be known by anyone but" the sufferer) and an ineradicable mark which, if not literally exterior must at least be conceived as somehow legible, if only to the eye of God. For this is pure fantasy, compensatory in its function and moral-theological in its form. The inevitable, ineradicable mark is a lineal descendant of the Mark of Cain, like the Scarlet Letter or the inscription on the body of the criminal in Kafka's penal colony. It is "inevitable" in this brief fiction because it is anything but inevitable in fact: plagiarists do, we all know, get away with it. And they get away with it because it is always possible for profiteers of difference to take advantage of the distance between legitimate authors and the sheets of paper on which their words are registered and distributed. The fantasy, then, is constructed so as to produce the sense of satisfaction that comes with contemplating a punishment so aptly fitted to its crime: the "author" of *this* mark, at least, will be inseparable from it; here, for once—so the wish would have it—mark, paper and author will be fused. For this is, among other things, a fantasy of integration, of the overcoming of difference.

We may still wonder why the paragraph dwells on the student's "suffering"; is it because a *soupçon* of sadism clings to all such dreams of punishment? Perhaps; but notice that this is at once a dream of punishment and a dream of interpretation: what is at issue is not just suffering but the extent to which it can be known, and by whom. The paragraph moves from the apparent unknowability of the penalized student's suffering to the wished-for legibility of the ineradicable mark. Private pain is conjured up not to be gloated over but rather because it indicates a region where it may be thought to exist, an interior space about whose contents we outsiders may make some guesses— gravely weighing the pains, deciding that one is "probably less acute" than another—but about which we "can never really know" as much as the sufferer himself.

Here again we can see the teacher's fantasy blending the student and his paper, or rather substituting the student for his paper as an object of interpretation. And, of course, that is what usually goes on in "cases" of plagiarism. Recall the scenario: you have either found yourself caught up in the process or listened as some colleague eagerly recited the details of his own involvement.

There is, first, the moment of suspicion, reading along in a student's paper; then the verification of the hunch, the tracking-down of the theft, most exhilarating when it involves a search through the library stacks, then the moment of "confrontation" when the accusation is made and it is no longer the student's paper but this face which is read for signs of guilt, moral anguish, contrition, whatever. The most telling account of such a moment comes from George Orwell's recollections of school-days in England[2]:

> Another boy, Beacham, whom I have mentioned already, was similarly over-whelmed with shame by the accusation that he "had black rings round his eyes."
> "Have you looked in the glass lately, Beacham?" said Bingo. "Aren't you ashamed to go about with a face like that? Do you think everyone doesn't know what it means when a boy has black rings round his eyes?"
> Once again the load of guilt and fear seemed to settle down upon me. Had *I* got black rings round my eyes? A couple of years later I realised that these were supposed to be a symptom by which masturbators could be detected. But already, without knowing this, I accepted the black rings as a sure sign of depravity. And many times, even before I grasped the supposed meaning, I have gazed anxiously into the glass, looking for the first hint of that dreaded stigma, the confession which the secret sinner writes upon his own face.

Which is more dismaying to the secret sinner: to have sinned or to have written out his confession on his own face? Which is more rewarding to his judge: to have saved a boy from masturbation or to have accurately read the signs of his depravity? These are not rhetorical questions to the extent that neither sinner nor judge can be sure of the answers to them. Indeed the aim of such fantasies of moral legibility, whether they are elaborated by sinners or judges, is precisely that exciting confusion of ethical and hermeneutical motifs; for fantasies are compromise-formations, they seek to have things both ways. Our paragraph about plagiarism offers just such a compromise: the ineradicable mark is there to satisfy the interpreter's wish to read stable and undeceptive signs, while the unknowable suffering is there to satisfy the teacher's wish to be something other than a reader—it serves as an acknowledgement of an interiority opaque enough to baffle his hermeneutical skills, a residual *je-ne-sais-quoi* that is there to remind him of (and, specularly, to confirm him in) his own private humanity.

So much for the terms of the fantasy; what of its motivation? We might attribute it to justifiable moral indignation, the righteous contempt of the honest for the dishonest, but that wouldn't quite account for either the intensity of this rhetoric or its peculiar figuration—or for the strong fascination that student plagiarism generally seems to hold for academics. Here again

2. "Such, such were the joys . . .", in George Orwell, *A Collection of Essays* (Garden City: Doubleday, 1954), p. 37.

the passage from Orwell may be of some help: just as the masturbation of children can serve to focus the anxieties of their elders about sexuality in general, so the plagiarizing of students can focus their teachers' anxieties about writing in general, more particularly about the kind of "writing" involved in teaching—the inscription of a culture's heritage on the minds of its young. A teacher's uncertainty about (to cite the pamphlet again) "whose words he is reading or listening to" begins, in the classroom, with his own words—and this would be true not merely for those colleagues we think of complacently as less original than ourselves. The recurrent touting of originality—in letters of recommendation, reports of *ad hoc* committees, etc.—is no doubt a sign of the same uneasiness that produces the ritual condemnation of student plagiarists when they are unlucky enough to be caught. The paragraph we have been considering is an imagined version of such a scapegoating. Its structure is that of projection. A troublesome interior difference—the sense of self-division implicit in all linguistic activity, sometimes more pronounced, sometimes less so, depending on the social context in which speech or writing is produced—that difference is exteriorized as the difference between the offended institution and its delinquent member. And, in one of those nicely economical turns that characterize powerful fantasies, the delinquent member is himself made to unwillingly represent an emblem of integrity, of the binding of the self and its signs.

II. WOOING NARCISSISTS

What can be made of the gestures by which a teacher places himself somewhere between his subject and his students? I have a very specific gesture in mind—Earl Wasserman, conducting a seminar on *The Rape of the Lock*, leaning forward across the table and asking his audience, a group of young men and women, graduate students and junior faculty, in a tone that was at once pugnacious and coy, "How far can I go?" I recall it as a nicely appropriate question, not just because it seemed obscurely in touch with all the erotic aggression and coquetry in Pope's poem, but because it was so much the interpreter's question par excellence, whether you took it straight or rhetorically. If it called for an answer, that answer would bear on the theoretical limits of interpretation—was it a terminable or an interminable activity? If, instead, the question was rhetorical, it could be heard as a sort of teasing cry for help, like those phone calls police stations receive from time to time: "Stop me before I strike again! I can't help it!", and then the phone goes dead, the Mad Rapist having hung up without giving his name or address. There is something obsessive about interpretation; there is something flirtatious about teaching: both impulses seemed at work in Wasserman's question in ways that invited one to reflect on the relation between them.

The material of the seminar was later published in a paper called "The Limits of Allusion in *The Rape of the Lock*,"[3] so it was possible to review its argument in detail, and to notice another scene framing Wasserman's interpretive gestures, this one not of instruction but of professional polemic. Though he had mentioned no names at the seminar, and included no footnotes in its published version to anything more recent than *Tristram Shandy*, it was clear that Wasserman was out to counter what had become, by the 1960s, the current informed reading of *The Rape of the Lock*. It was also clear that a quarrel about how to read that poem was part of a larger argument, that between interpreters associated more or less closely with the New Criticism and those who accused the New Critics of ignoring literary and intellectual history. During the 1930s critics like Empson and Leavis and Tillotson had redirected attention to Pope's remarkable verbal control and a series of acute and tactful readings had appeared praising Pope for his acuteness and tact. When these critics turned to *The Rape of the Lock* what they found was a poem which, if not the highpoint of Pope's art was at least an epitome of his talents, a poem to which words like tact, balance or control could be easily applied.

But what exactly was it that Pope was so tactfully balancing? For critics like Tillotson, Brooks, Wimsatt or Brower, one answer was "his attitudes towards poetry." The particular finesse with which Pope wrote mock heroic couplets could be read as simultaneously parodying the language and apparatus of major epic, invoking epic values to sustain a satiric attack on a decidedly unheroic contemporary scene and, still further, conferring poignancy and charm on that same scene. More intriguing was the fact that, within the poem itself, that balancing act was doubled by another: the presentation of Pope's heroine, Belinda, who was rendered—and this was the point of Brooks' essay in *The Well-Wrought Urn*—as both a goddess and a "frivolous tease." These two balancings were easily analogized: Belinda became, in the discourse of these critics, a synecdoche for the poem—for, as the phrase went, "the poem itself." Both were objects of fascination, diminutive, perhaps trivial, but highly desirable; like frail china, bound to be handled but requiring of their admirers a lightness of touch mimicking that of their creator. The metaphor of tactful balancing easily slid into one of controlled erotic involvement. Tillotson could say:

The poem provides a picture, rather than a criticism; or, rather, the poem is so elaborate, shifting, constellated, that the intellect is baffled and demoralized by the emotions. One is left looking at the face of the poem, as at Belinda's.[4]

3. In *JEGP* 65 (1966), pp. 422–44. Pages references to this article will be given parenthetically.
4. "Introduction" to Geoffrey Tillotson, ed., *The Rape of the Lock and Other Poems*, Vol. II of *The Twickenham Edition of the Poems of Alexander Pope* (London, 1962).

And Wimsatt could add:

The sophistication of the poem lies in its being no less affectionate than critical. . . . The critic's difficulty with *The Rape of the Lock* is to find words not too heavy to praise the intricacies of its radiant sense.[5]

Earl Wasserman's arrival on this scene of admiration—of critics admiring Pope who is himself admiring Belinda who is, of course, admiring herself—is something like the arrival of the bull at the china shop. He argues carefully but he is not excessively tactful and, though he admires Pope, he does not admire Belinda, does not think Pope really does either, and is, in general, all for disrupting what he refers to as "the sheltered Petit Trianon world of conventionalized manners that the . . . poem constructs" (427).

Wasserman's strategy is two-fold: he attacks the insularity implicit in a New Critical reading of the poem by insisting on the range and importance of Pope's allusions to traditional motifs and *topoi*, and—it is, structurally, the same move—he attacks Belinda as a "narcissistic coquette" (430), or, more accurately, he takes Pope to be himself elaborating and criticizing "the prideful image of Belinda as an independent world and female society as a self-sufficient scheme" (434). I shall trace these lines of attack one at a time, then consider the links between them and suggest how they bear on the relations of poems, teachers and students.

Wasserman begins by posing the question of what he calls the limits of allusion: granting the steady allusiveness of Pope's verse—to Dryden and Milton and Shakespeare, but more especially to Virgil and Homer and the Bible—how did these allusions function? How far was one entitled to go in interpreting them? If a phrase of Pope's turned out to be a literal translation of a phrase in the *Aeneid*, how much of the context of that fragment of Virgil's poem was drawn along with it into Pope's? As you might guess, the answer to the theoretical question of the limits of allusion is that no theoretical limits can be set at all: Pope's interpreter is entitled, Wasserman argues—and not only entitled but positively encouraged by Pope—to go as far as he can; he is, Wasserman concludes, "actively invited by (the allusions) to exercise, within poetic reason, his own invention by contemplating the relevances of the entire allusive context and its received interpretation" (443). It would seem that some principles of limitation are implicit in expressions like "within poetic reason" or "received interpretation" but what is principally interesting about them is their vagueness. They gesture in the direction of the reader who would adequately embody them, for the question of how far an interpreter should go is obviously inseparable from the question of the interpreter's own erudition:

5. "Introduction" to William K. Wimsatt, Jr., ed., *Alexander Pope: Selected Poetry and Prose* (New York: Rinehart, 1951), pp. xxxvi f.

one needs to know the texts Pope was alluding to in order to spot an allusion in the first place, and one needs to know enough about neo-classical practice to know when to stop interpreting. Both the occasion that initiates an interpretive process and the restraints regulating it are functions of one's learning. And Wasserman makes it clear that while we might—with an effort, perhaps a lifetime's effort—familiarize ourselves with the range of Pope's reading, we could never possess that knowledge with the same degree of easy authenticity as did Pope or his ideal contemporary reader:

The mind that composed *The Rape of the Lock* was less an English one hearkening back to the classics for witty references than one applying itself to an English social situation from the viewpoint of a deeply ingrained classicism. Classical literature and its manners, together with Scripture and its exegetical tradition, are not merely Pope's acquired learning; they shaped the character and processes of his thought. Correspondingly, his poems consistently ask for a reader who is equally native to the whole classical-Scriptural world, a Christian Greco-Roman scrutinizing eighteenth-century English culture. [426–27]

Confronted with a statement of this sort, one might want to say "Of course Wasserman is being hyperbolical, but you know what he means." Suppose, instead, one were to reverse the weightings of that response and say "Of course we know what he means, but why should he put it so hyperbolically?" Why this fiction of a transhistorical meeting of minds—the "mind that composed *The Rape of the Lock*" and that of his perfect reader, someone "equally native to the whole classical-Scriptural world?" Is this merely a heuristic fiction, an ideal totalization posited to urge us on to some serious, if only approximating, interpretive activity? Perhaps; but it is also a figure of perfect communication, suitable for framing and display in the classroom, where it might function rather like an allusion to the conversations of Socrates and his disciples.

Now Wasserman also suggests a related figure for what goes on in the classroom, not that of a closed-circuit of ideal communication, but rather that of a controlled linearity, a graded series: at the head of the line is "the mind that composed *The Rape of the Lock*," a mind whose learning is not something acquired but rather something "deeply ingrained" or—as he says elsewhere— "deeply embedded." Next in line, in a middleman's position, is the teacher, whose knowledge *is* acquired. Finally there are the students, presumably there to acquire the erudition their teacher already possesses in part. This is a familiar enough account of academic lineage, and it might be that at moments literary education comes to feel like that. But more often what happens is that—by a trick of the mind, call it a deeply embedded inclination to convert series into binary oppositions—the teacher's position is experienced (by the teacher as well as by his class) not as a middle ground somewhere between his author and his students, but as a dramatic occupation, more or less earned, of the position of authority itself. The series becomes a proportion: Wasserman is to his seminar as Pope is to Wasserman. When that happens the teacher-interpreter's mind stands in for "the mind that composed *The Rape of the Lock*" and the distinction between knowledge that is deeply ingrained and knowledge that is merely acquired starts to fade. One sentence of Wasserman's article begins "Disinherited as we are from (Pope's) referential systems . . ." (425): the classroom becomes the place where the teacher-scholar, at least, can appear to reclaim his inheritance.

I offer this not as a description of classroom teaching so much as a readily available possible mystification, a common and reassuring way of bringing the activity of reading into touch with that of teaching. The relation of teacher to student, figured as a descent, a lineage, reinforces and sustains the fiction of the perfect play between the mind of the poet and that of his ideal reader. Both figures—that of lineage and that of the closed circuit—depend for their intelligibility on a radical reduction of what is in fact plural (a certain number of students in a class, many of them unresponsive; a still greater number of texts in the tradition, many of them at odds with one another, many of them unread, even by Wasserman, even by Pope)—a reduction of these plurals to an imagined interplay of paired elements: poet and tradition, poet and reader, teacher and student. The power such figures exert over readers is in proportion to the reduction they promise to perform.

Turning to Belinda, Wasserman rejects the notion that Pope's attitude towards her was "no less affectionate than critical" and instead proposes another way of dealing with the subtleties of her presentation: he would see Pope superficially praising his heroine but systematically undercutting that praise with ironic allusions to Christian and classical texts. Pope, in this reading, mobilizes his allusions to break the fragile construct Wasserman calls "the beau monde, made of conventional signs, decorative and playful, that substitute for flesh-and-blood reality." And "flesh-and-blood reality," as Wasserman's analysis makes clear, is primarily sexual. Citing the words Belinda's guardian sylph whispers in her ear as the poem begins ("Hear and believe! thy own importance know, / Nor bound thy narrow views to things below" I 35–36), Wasserman writes

As Plutarch wrote in one of the major *loci* of the doctrine, to "know thyself" means to "use one's self for that one thing for which Nature has fitted one"; and exactly what Belinda is most fitted for and what is radical for Pope in the carnal world that Belinda ought to accept is intimated by "Things below", a term we may let Swift explicate for us. [432]

The passage Wasserman takes from Swift is his retelling of the old tale of the philosopher Thales who, while looking at the stars, found himself, in Swift's words, "seduced by his *lower parts* into a *Ditch*." Wasserman remarks:

No one who had read at least his Juvenal—to say nothing of the Priapeia—would have failed to understand the real meaning of *fossa,* or ditch, any more than he would have failed to understand Pope's "Things below." [432]

And, lest we fail to understand, a footnote delicately spells it out:

For this sense of *res,* see Martial, XI, 44. In his "Sober Advice from Horace," Pope translated Horace's "magno prognatum deposco consule CUNNUM" as "A Thing descended from the Conqueror". [432 n. 16]

Disinherited though he may be, Wasserman's acquired learning seems to have put him in a position to know "exactly what Belinda is most fitted for": what this girl needs is a good Judeo-Christian Greco-Roman husband.

Wasserman's *paideia* seems to be advancing under a pedagogical banner with a familiar enough device: "I'll teach you a thing or two" is the motto. But it would be a mistake to assume that the aggressive misogyny here is all the critic's, that he is simply seeing things in an innocuous text. The bawdy and misogyny are there—in Swift most obviously but in Pope as well. Wasserman's assertive proclamation of this element in the poem can be taken as corrective of the rhetoric of delicacy and tact preferred by the New Critics, a readjustment that has the virtue of reminding us that *The Rape of the Lock* is not least of all about a struggle for power. Moreover, Wasserman's own rhetoric—its stridency and its implicit thematic linkings—can give us a better idea of what the elements of that struggle might be. For it is not simply a struggle between men and women, any more than Western misogyny is the simple antagonism of one group of people to another. If we follow Wasserman's polemic we shall see that what he is attacking in Belinda is what he takes to be her imaginary relation to herself, her narcissism, which Wasserman treats as a perverse upsetting of the proper hierarchical relation of "conventional signs" to "flesh-and-blood reality" (429). Tracing the motif of the shearing of the lock back to Apollonius and, along with him, to "Euripides, Herodotus, Callimachus, Valerius Flaccus, Pausanias, and Lucian, among others" (423–29), Wasserman reminds us of the tradition of offering up a lock of a maiden's hair as a nuptial rite. "What the Baron has raped," he comments, "is not Belinda's virginity but . . . the ritualistic sign of it." And Belinda's distress is a function of her commitment to a world of signs, "in which a rouged cheek surpasses a real blush, . . . a card game takes the place of the contest of the sexes, China jars stand for virginity, and a mirror reflection transcends the viewer" (429). Wasserman's misogyny here is hard to distinguish from what seems like a more general semiotic uneasiness: what troubles him about Belinda is not that, being a woman, she is different, but that, being a woman she has somehow been beguiled by "conventional signs" into a confusing self-alienation. She is both different and self-divided: hence the prurient allusions to flaws, cracks, ditches, etc. It isn't clear from Wasserman's account why this confusion should be limited to Belinda—or to women; we know that some distinguished formalist critics (all male) have been equally beguiled by the delicacy and glitter of Belinda's world of signs. What is clear however is that Wasserman would like so to limit it, to focus his uneasiness on *one* form of the relation of signs and reality, the beautiful woman's fascination with her reflected image. Our earlier glance at Orwell might lead us to expect—in this region where semiotic and sexual questions seem to be converging—some further fine-tuning of the notion of narcissism in the form of a denunciation of auto-erotic behavior, and indeed in Wasserman's account that is one of the forms Belinda's self-sufficiency is made to take: we are told that "she is wedded to and sexually gratified by her own virginity" (430).

But just as we watched Harold Martin simultaneously stigmatize the plagiarist and confer on him a poignantly unknowable interior life, so we can follow a movement in some ways similar in Wasserman's dealings with Belinda. There are depths behind all that surface, it turns out. And the last pages of Wasserman's paper are devoted to the discovery, within those depths, of the heterosexual desire that Belinda cannot consciously acknowledge, a secret passion for the Baron, a wish to marry, to perform what Wasserman describes as "the heroic sacrifice that makes female life meaningful and glorious" (436). Teasing out the signs of that desire involves Wasserman in his most elaborate effort at documenting and interpreting Pope's allusions to the classics, and it produces a strong case for their importance in the poem. At a series of points Wasserman can show that when Belinda is heard complaining about the loss of her lock, her language—or the poet's language about her—echoes passages in Virgil, in Catullus and in Martial which, read in context, bear a meaning at cross-purposes to Belinda's: "Pope's words and their allusive context contradict each other," Wasserman comments, "and if we take the contradiction as the conflict between Belinda's conscious and subconscious mind, it only confirms Pope's psychoanalysis of her elsewhere." There is after all, as Pope had made explicit earlier in the poem, "an Earthly Lover lurking at her Heart" (440–41).

But it's worth noting that Pope *had* made that explicit earlier in the poem, just as he had placed in the mouth of one of his characters, Belinda's sensible friend Clarissa, a long speech advising her to marry. Wasserman's tracing of Pope's allusions in order to explore Belinda's unconscious desires discovers nothing that he didn't already know; in fact it is because of what he already knew from more explicit passages in the poem that he could decide how much of the original context of each allusion was pertinent. Wasserman isn't mistaken about either the presence or the meaning of these allusions, but he has organized his account of them so as to introduce an element of hermeneutic suspense that is absent from the poem. What Pope offers in a variety of forms—explicit statement, hint, coded allusion—in the course of a narrative which unfolds in accordance with its own plotting, Wasserman presents as an *inquest:* he marshals his evidence sequentially, as though preparing for the moment when he can confront Belinda with the unacknowledged signs of her desire: "Perhaps this will refresh your memory!" What comes through in the tone of his article—and was conspicuous in the seminar as I recall it—is the intellectual energy and muted glee of a particularly zealous *juge d'instruction.* It is not unlike the tone of the teacher confronting the plagiarist, nor is it entirely out of touch with the tone of a teacher teasing his seminar: "How far can I go? Tell me when to stop!" Let me pursue these analogies.

What is sought in each case is an end to an ongoing interpretive process, and what makes the end feel like an end in each case is not that the interpreter runs out of signs to interpret, but that he achieves a state of equilibrium with another person. When the teacher gets the plagiarist to admit that he copied something from one book, he doesn't have to return to the stacks to see how many other books his student cribbed: the process comes to an end with the acknowledgement of guilt. When Wasserman can produce enough evidence so that he can say that "despite the conscious social artfulness of her mind, Belinda is flesh and blood," he can put aside his Virgil, his Catullus, his Martial, his Juvenal, his Euripides, his Herodotus, his Callimachus . . . *ad* (no longer) *infinitum:* his hermeneutical task is done.

The instances I just cited suggest that it may be worth distinguishing two different aspects of this achieved equilibrium. When the tracking-down of a plagiarist is over, we can say it is over because we know the rules of such procedures: a more or less explicit code governs criminal investigations and stipulates what counts as a satisfactory conclusion—for example, a confession. But there is also an element of fantasy that frequently enters into the structure of such moments: I suggested as much in discussing Martin's language about the plagiarist, where the concern with unknowable suffering is there, oddly enough, to establish a rapport between the teacher and the guilty student. They meet—so the fantasy would have it—not simply as role-occupying figures in a codified investigative scenario, but as fellow-possessors of distinct but resonantly analogous interior lives. This is even more obvious in the case of Wasserman's tracking-down of Belinda's secret desire: it is what allows him to use the phrase "flesh and blood" to describe what he has discovered her to be. She has crossed over from her position under the sign of "conventional signs" to join Wasserman where he has all along imagined himself to stand, in the world of "flesh-and-blood reality." It is as if he had bullied and wooed her into acknowledging that she, just like himself, is heterosexual.

In both Martin's text and Wasserman's it is that establishment of a fancied consubstantiality with the offending party—the student plagiarist, the female narcissist—that allows the gesture of scapegoating to take place. Anxiety about the relation of authors to their words, anxiety about the relation of flesh-and-blood reality to conventional signs—these may be exorcised if they can be laid on the head of a figure not wholly unlike the fantasist. We can see this most clearly when we think of the most benign encounter of the ones we've been considering, the humorous gesture of a scholar to a room full of graduate students, asking "How far can I go?" In that gentle parody of anxiety, the obsessive interpreter becomes the flirtatious teacher, entering into a mildly erotic intersubjective relation, fully within his control (for who, after all, around that table, could have told Èarl Wasserman how far he could or couldn't go?), an equilibrium that replaces the scholar's prior set of dealings with a long list of texts, each made up of many conventional signs.

JEAN-FRANÇOIS LYOTARD

Endurance and the Profession

It has become an enviable rarity these days to obtain a salary in exchange for the kind of discourse that is commonly called philosophy. As the twentieth century draws to a close, the statesmen and families who run the French secondary school system seem to want to have nothing to do with it. For according to the spirit of the times, which is theirs, to do is to produce; that is, to reproduce with a surplus value. Those who teach philosophy are thus condemned to decimation or worse, while those who have studied it remain unemployed or give themselves up as hostages to other professions. Here, we will turn our attention to a minor but unexpected consequence: despite the adverse pressures in the socio-professional context, and at a time when the Philosophy Department at Vincennes (University of Paris VII) has been stripped of its right to grant those degrees and research diplomas that it is a University Department's duty to issue, the rate of attendance in philosophy courses has, little by little, been on the rise.

Why do they come? One day you asked this question solemnly during class. They told you it was their business, not yours.

A public institution of higher learning is by law an organ by which a nation insures the education of its children. The State is the guardian of such institutions. When the State removes all credibility from the Department of Philosophy at Vincennes, one expects it to die out. But the nation's children— grown-up children at that, and even foreigners—persist in attending the courses in large numbers. Would you conclude that the mere existence of this Department refutes the ideas of the State and of its educational guardians?

You enter; they are waiting for you. You have nothing in particular, nothing set to say, which is the general condition of philosophical discourse. But here, in addition, you have no long or short-range aim set by an institutional function (to prepare degrees, monitor competitions, follow programs and syllabi, and keep track of things through examinations). There you are, given over to indeterminate requirements. (Generally a few readings ahead of them, but in any case readings done with the frightful and shameful disorder of the philosopher.)

Does that mean that each teacher in your Department speaks of what he or she likes?—No, it means that no one is protected, and above all in his or her own eyes, by prescribed rules. And everyone must give his or her name to what he or she says, without pleading necessity; and everyone, like a stutterer, must head towards what he or she wants in order to say it. —You're exaggerating. —Don't forget they wait for you every week, and without telling you what they're expecting. —All the same, you know what you are driving at . . . —For the day's session, yes, very precisely: for example, demonstrating the machinery of an "antistrephon" put in the mouth of Protagoras by Diogenes Laertes. —So, you really did have an idea in the back of your mind!

Is it an idea, this strength or weakness which, from year to year, makes you believe that with the analysis of this or that fragment of Diels and Kranz, and with many others like it, some in the discernable framework of the week's thought, others at the horizon, for later on, two months, a semester from now, eventually you'll succeed?

—Succeed at what? At holding on for another year? —It's not to be laughed at. You're in free-fall in the atmosphere and it's a matter of not landing too hard. So you're crafty, you stall. So, this slow-down, due to an institutional void, which is the opposite of the feverishness experienced by a teacher anxious to cover coursework in a limited time, creates or presupposes a soft and gentle "tempo." —That of research? —No, you've known researchers in the exact sciences. Their rhythm is one of athletic, economic, bureaucratic competition. More like the rhythm of study. But not of studies. Studies are something you work at, you pursue. In these classes, study goes along in its own way. You announce that you will study Thucydides, and three years later you still haven't begun.

—But yet, you, too, want something. —When one was younger, one might have wanted to please, or help, or lead by argument or revelation. Now, it's all over. You no longer know exactly what's wanted. How can you make others understand what you haven't really understood? But when the course works out well, you also know that since you made them understand what you didn't, it didn't really work out. The anguish, when you enter the classroom, especially at the beginning of the year, is not the stage fright of the actor or the orator (although it can be), the feeling of claustrophobia (all of us will burn in here), or the predicament of not knowing everything (rather reassuring). It is the sovereign pressure of an imbecilic "You must go there," which does not say where.

Just two years ago, this or that leftist commando was bursting in, denouncing the magisterial function, the star-system, alienation, apathy, cutting the electricity, raising his clubs, locking up the teacher awhile, and abusing the students. In their eyes, our palaver, our readings, our reffinnements [Translators' note: The misspelling is present in the French text, (raffinnement) as a comment on the notion] are gimmicks at best, and at worst treasons; for them, it's a state of war, an emergency. To ponder a metalepsis in the narration of Book 9 of The Laws is not futile, it's criminal. They know where to go.

We used to fight a bit. Only once did it lead to something worthwhile. It was on the day of an active strike. What could we do? At the time we were working on the operators in persuasive discourse, making use of Plato's dialogues and Aristotle's *Rhetoric* and *Sophistic Refutation*. We subjected the statements relative to the strike to the same analysis. Once again we were speaking of Platonic pragmatics. Enter the commando unit armed with clubs, shouting that we were breaking the strike—a fight starts, quickly followed by palavers between the two groups, the besiegers and the besieged. The latter argue as follows: on the one hand, our "normal" activity is to study persuasive discourse, especially political discourse. On the other hand, to participate in an active strike is to occupy the workplace and to think together about the discourses which persuade or dissuade us from striking. The difference between these two activities is not distinguishable. You demand that it be, and you think it could be if we used certain words (*exploitation, alienation* . . .), a certain syntax ("it is not by chance that . . ."), certain names (*Marx* . . .). Question: In your eyes how many "Marxes" per sentence would it take for our discourse to become one of active strikers? Most of the assaillants backed off, admitting that we were as much "out of it" as they were.

The rhythm of work in progress seems tentative and peaceful. But on the occasion of each of these pointless classes, it becomes asceticism, impatience, and fear. You get up well before dawn and tell yourself: this particular part of the current work has to be done for tonight. For example: express the temporal logic of Protagoras' antistrephon before midnight. Because the day after tomorrow, you must explain it to those who are waiting for you. By looking straight at them, and not at your notes. And, as you aren't protected by an institution, make them furthermore understand that it's opportune or bearable to speak about such things.

So you sit down at your desk, and nothing has ever assured you that, by midnight, you will have understood. What if you didn't understand? Or what if it were to take longer than anticipated? What if you were extremely tired? Or what if you entertained the idea that, after all, the antistrephon of Protagoras or another, who gives a damn? Or else, what if you got your hands on a good Italian or American article supplying the interpretation you had imagined yourself giving?

In this last case, you're happy, you'll be able to do your course with this article. But at the same time, you're annoyed: there's something you have received and transmitted without transformation, without being transformed by it. This isn't work. You put it off till next week. What are you thus putting off? Confrontation, challenge and the judgment of God. This is why you can wade through the antistrepha; I mean, dabble around them for six months. Audiences are surprising.

Sometimes you allow yourself to think that your working notes keep accumulating, you're making progress. But, with age, you know the opposite is true, that you hoard waste, scraps, that the thing to be thought slips away from you, as in interminable evasions and metastases.

As for making this mortification the substance of what you have to say, this seems henceforth a paltry resource. For such a solution proceeds only from your memory, allowing you to compare what you wanted to obtain with what you hold, and not from your imagination which is indifferent to your grasp of anything. Moreover, here, amnesia rules. So much so that it's not even true that anything "slips away." Don't be satisfied with this shoddy pessimism. There's nothing to compare.

A few books are written this way out of the weekly rumination. There was a horizon sketched, uncertain. You've made headway here and there for two, three, four years. Sometimes bits of analyses are already published as articles. Nevertheless, you collect all of those attempts and you publish them as a book. Producing such a book means only one thing: that you're fed up with this approach, this horizon, this tone, these readings. Of course, the notes and even the parts already written don't exempt you from writing the book; that is, from re-thinking almost everything. But you do so to get it over with. What makes you happy, the sense of well-being you have with the book, is that you'll be done with the work. Whereas teaching is as endless as study itself.

But in order to finish and thus write the book, you must reach a certain satisfaction with what you thought, or believed you thought. And this is so to speak a grace momentarily granted, and you're truly unfortunate if you don't jump to exploit it. But also unfortunate if it stays with you.

The media have the truly unintelligible habit of making you speak about your latest book. How do you convince the *mediators* that, obviously, you wrote it to be done with it, and that once done, it is really finished? They believe it is false modesty. And they say they're doing you a favor. You become proud, you forget about this sort of publicity, you rely on another kind of distribution, osmosis or capillary action. After a little while, you no longer have a choice.

You aren't cut out for thinking; you're a philosopher. You believe it's not natural to think. You're envious of—but after all you disdain—your colleagues and friends who work in the human sciences, who seem to be in symbiosis with their work, who have a corpus, a method, a bibliography, a strategy, exchanges. That's what makes you different even from those close to you, like historians of philosophy, whom you admire nonetheless. You like what is unfinished. Nothing of what you write will be authoritative. You lend yourself willingly to this prescription: "to go there, without knowing where." You're certain that nobody can do it, least of all yourself. You know you're doing what you're not cut out to do. You're an impostor. You hate all this. Little by little you cease to draw any vanity from it. And this Department at Vincennes, if it's pleasant, it's because its total lack of aims and imposed airs lends itself to surprisingly few bursts of vanity: impostors cannot be convicted here, the mask holds, and so does honor. You don't edit a journal, you're not a school.

The media and the worldly wise smile in vain at your humility, insinuating that many paths lead to importance, and that to vegetate in your prefab bungalow in "the sticks" is one way to acquire it—but you know this isn't true. In better established professorships you become tempted to say what should be thought. Here, in Vincennes, this infatuation is not protected.

This doesn't at all prevent this pitiful state of affairs from trading on its misery and catching the eye of a few cynics. You fight it, eliminating from your discourse most connotations, making yourself, if possible, even more temperate and meticulous. For example, you give up the metaphysical euphoria of energies and convert to logic, especially that of prescriptives, severe and fastidious. Now, this dissuades a few cynics from staying, but not the most cynical.

—They would have a certain function in your economy, as long as they also force you incessantly to take a new line. And after all, how do you know what their cynicism is all about?

Taking a new line: the metaphor is reassuring. What is behind you isn't more certain than what you are facing; in fact, it's more uncertain. To go beyond is an idea that makes you smile. What has been studied energetically for a year, two years, ten years, you've let lie fallow. Study doesn't order; it disorders. They tell you to keep your cool.

Which you wouldn't be doing if you believed that what you have to do is name the unnamable, say the unsayable, conceive the unconceivable, pronounce the unpronounceable, or decide the undecidable—and that this is what it means to philosophize. You leave these poses to others.

Of course, you speak of what you don't comprehend. But it doesn't necessarily follow that it's incomprehensible. You read and give your course to see if others might have understood, by chance. The idea of a mission fades away.

They ask questions. So sometimes questions are posed, and sometimes people are only posing as they question. You're caught between your duty to listen and be patient, and your right to impatience. Others write to you, point to references, share thoughts—and question. A few are or will be your mentors.

You try for two kinds of understanding: first, that which permits you tomorrow, to situate the antistrephon of Protagoras within the writing of temporal logic. A strong understanding, and ultimately useless. The other is totally different: to learn obscurely, after months, years of study, why this bizarre verbal argument interested you. You first included it within a general examination of ruse, for example, and that had attracted you because you saw it as a weapon against the powerful. We're weak, you used to say as a justification. All this seemed directed toward some political end; you were inspecting the available arsenal. You easily refuted those who judged you as too picky, too slow in moving on towards action. You compared the funeral oration of Overney by Geismar with the one Socrates parodies in *De Sophistis Eleuchis*. You analyzed the jail letters and the declarations of the ROTE ARMEE FRAKTION [Red Army Faction] in the file constituted by Klaus Croissant, in the light of the alternative between the non-pedagogical struggle and the Platonic pragmatics of dialogue. The antistrephon found its place naturally in this general strategy and you studied it as such. Now, two and a half years later, you confess the vanity of your manicheism. The antistrephon may very well be a weapon at the disposal of the weak; it is also the strength of philosophical discourse, for this latter is made up of reflexive (or speculative) statements of which it is one type. Your general approach to paradoxes is modified by it, as are your "politics." You say so. Your listeners, especially foreigners from poor countries, believe that with this move you have lost even more pugnacity, that you have become even more of a product of that cold thought and refined style which they call French and which exasperates them. On your side, little by little you stop justifying your interests, your tribulations, giving a good front to your disorder. It can even look like a challenge.

Who's going to follow you if you no longer even say where you want to go? But you take a certain pleasure in this silence. You feel its opacity as an interesting resource against Hegelianism or absolutism in general. You think you're making a contribution, however minute, to the destiny of what you believe philosophy to be: figuring, and not just conceiving. You find yourself in agreement with this Department, which is a figure now more than an organ.

The concessions to what you feel is expected become rarer. You'd like to neglect even what your own mind desires, make it accessible to thoughts it doesn't expect. You don't read anymore to strip authors, but to steal away from yourself. You aim at this deculturation in every direction: science fiction, underground cinema, linguistics and singular logics, monsters of plastic and sound, surprising banalities, oblique re-readings. You are unfaithful in your alliances like the barbarians of Clastres [prisoners who during an escape attempt turned against guards who had previously aided them—Trans.], but for a different reason, opposite at least. You're at war with the institutions of your own mind and with your own identity. And you know that with all this, you're probably only perpetuating Western philosophy, its laborious libertinage, and its obliging equanimity. At least you also know that the only chance (or mischance) to do so lies in setting philosophy beside itself.

Translated by Christophe Gallier, Steven Ungar, and Barbara Johnson

"L'endurance et la profession" first appeared in French in no. 369 of *Critique*, a special issue entitled *La Philosophie malgré tout [Philosophy in spite of everything]*, February 1978. The present translation is printed with the kind permission of the author and Jean Piel, the editor.

What Does a Teacher Want?

Roland Barthes (third from left) with students at the Ecole Pratique des Hautes Etudes, 1974. By permission of the *Editions du Seuil*.

STEVEN UNGAR

The Professor of Desire

I.
To the realists.—You sober people who feel well armed against passion and fantasies and would like to turn your emptiness into a matter of pride and an ornament: you call yourselves realists and hint that the world really is the way it appears to you. As if reality stood unveiled before you only, and you yourselves were perhaps the best part of it.—O you beloved images of Sais! But in your unveiled state are not even you still very passionate and dark creatures compared to fish, and still too similar to an artist in love? And what is "reality" to an artist in love?

—Nietzsche, *The Gay Science* (II, 57)

Readers of the *Roland Barthes* may recall a photograph of Barthes *professeur* surrounded by a dozen or so young men and women. As every picture tells a story, so this informal group portrait commemorates a seminar given by Barthes at the Ecole Pratique des Hautes Etudes. But the documentary function of the image is, as the saying goes, only part of the story as long as it fails to account for the singular nature of the seminar in Barthes's pedagogy:

The space of the seminar is phalansteric, i.e., in a sense, fictive, novelistic. It is only the space of the circulation of subtle desires, mobile desires; it is within the artifice of a sociality whose consistency is miraculously extenuated, according to a phrase of Nietzsche's: 'the tangle of amorous relations.'[1]

As an interplay of word and image, the passage asserts the irreducible difference of the seminar space as a privileged site where eros and knowledge converge. All of which might easily lend itself to a Platonic discussion of souls and truth, were it not for the troublesome presence of "subtle desires, mobile desires," to remind us, as if we did not already know it too well, that teaching can be utterly personal because of the intimacy it can produce: "Teaching is not only very personal, it is also very physical. That teacher there, walking from the library to his office, dispensing smiles and warm greetings to fresh-faced students, is me. I talk a lot about souls—perhaps too much—but no

1. Roland Barthes, *Roland Barthes*, trans. Richard Howard (New York: Hill and Wang, 1977), p. 171.

81

soul have I ever seen that did not come in a body and when I teach somebody I teach some body."[2]

Despite their conceptual density—"phalansteric" connotes the utopian thought of Charles Fourier and "fictive" *The Philosophy of As-If* by Hans Vaihinger—Barthes's comments temper traditional conceptions of how knowledge is transmitted with something bordering on the confessional. A teacher who confesses or professes desire can no longer be scandalous except to those who still believe that the so-called life of the mind has nothing to do with the rest of the body. Barthes's comments also point to the pedagogical dimensions of what has been the thrust of his critical practice over the past decade. Namely, that an affective motivation for theory needs to be recognized in the face of what is otherwise mistaken for an objective or scientific project of critical undertanding. Known primarily as a literary critic, Barthes has taught at various institutions since the 1930's, at the Ecole Pratique des Hautes Etudes since 1961, and at the Collège de France from 1977 to 1980. As his work has moved away from straightforward structural analysis, the role of his annual seminar as a testing-ground for theory has evolved to the point where *S/Z, The Pleasure of the Text,* and *Roland Barthes* are quite openly the products of collective thought and elaboration. On its own, that relationship is the exception in an educational system built on the *cours magistral* and an absolute minimum of verbal exchange. As a result, what most American students take for granted as an institutional right or personal privilege to free expression is only sparingly tolerated in France after the stormy educational reforms enacted in the late 1960's. When this freedom of exchange is understood beyond its institutional function, the pursuit of knowledge can, in turn, be seen as part of a more personal practice and affirmation of values. No longer a simple laboratory for theory, the seminar space has become for Barthes the prime site of inquiry around which any subsequent formulation of theory is but a trace. All of which has given to this space its singularity. To relate this development back to Barthes's critical practice, we might ask exactly what kind of knowledge might be gained from professing desire *in the classroom.* From letters to life, what kind of knowledge does the lover of knowledge seek?

A traditional answer to this question can be organized around the differences between *philias* and *eros,* Greek terms commonly translated as "friendly feeling" and "love." As they appear in the Socratic dialogues, the terms overlap, with the latter distinguished as a desire more intense than affection and more closely tied to the sexual drive than the former.[3] Etymology

2. Werner J. Dannhauser, "On Teaching Politics Today," *Commentary,* 59, no. 3 (March 1975), 74.

3. Gregory Vlastos, "The Individual as Object of Love in Plato," in *Platonic Studies* (Princeton: Princeton University Press, 1973), p. 4. For additional views of Socratic theories of love

suggests that the love of knowledge and concommitant knowledge of love are not what we had believed them to be, but rather (always already) internally divided into a play of difference along the lines of those between *plaisir* and *jouissance* set forth by Barthes in *The Pleasure of the Text.* From letters to life, the concepts of *plaisir* and *jouissance* reappear in the seminar as *philias* and *eros*, less in order to resolve or deconstruct the question of knowledge and pleasure than to give it a living and dramatic expression.

From letters to life, the professor of desire teaches the text of difference and plurality: sex and love, two master *topoi* and two versions of classical and modern knowledge. From the first volume of Michel Foucault's projected history of sexuality, this passage on the author of an underground Victorian classic:

The solitary author of *My Secret Life* often says, in order to justify his describing them, that his stranger practices were shared by thousands of men on the surface of the earth. But the guiding principle, for the strangest of these practices, which was the fact of recounting them all, and in detail, from day to day, had been lodged in the heart of modern man for over two centuries.[4]

From Barthes's *Fragments d'un discours amoureux*, this prefatory remark addressed directly to the reader:

The necessity for this book is to be found in the following consideration: that the lover's discourse is today *of an extreme solitude.* This discourse is spoken, perhaps, by thousands of subjects (who knows?), but warranted by no one; it is completely forsaken by the surrounding languages; ignored, disparaged, or derided by them, severed not only from authority (science, techniques, arts). Once a discourse is driven by its own momentum into the backwater of the "unreal," exiled from all gregarity, it has no recourse but to become the site, however exiguous, of an *affirmation.* That affirmation is, in short, the subject of the book which begins here.[5]

Against Foucault's claim that sexuality has replaced eros with a compulsion to say everything that can be said in the name of an institutional will to truth, Barthes revels in the untimeliness of his reflections. As both writers treat love and sex as discursive objects—as things written or spoken—their

and knowledge, see Paul Friedlander, *Plato: An Introduction*, trans. Hans Meyerhoff (Princeton: Princeton University Press, 1973), I, pp. 32–58, W. K. C. Guthrie, *Socrates* (New York: Cambridge University Press, 1971), pp. 70–77, and Léon Robin, *La Théorie platonicienne de l'amour*, nouvelle édition (Paris: Presses Universitaires de France, 1964). For a materialist reading of *The Symposium*, see John Brenkman, "The Other and the One: Psychoanalysis, Reading, *The Symposium*," *Yale French Studies*, no. 55/56 (1978), pp. 396–456.

4. Michel Foucault, *The History of Sexuality: An Introduction*, trans. Robert Hurley (New York: Pantheon, 1978), p. 12. See also Stephen Heath, "Le Corps victorien, anthologiquement," *Critique*, no. 405–06 (February-March 1981), pp. 152–65.

5. Barthes, *A Lover's Discourse: Fragments*, trans. Richard Howard (New York: Hill and Wang, 1978), p. 1. Future references will cite this translation as *Fragments*.

inquiries focus in large part on questions of method and interpretation pointing to the convergence of doctrine, meaning, and authority. In French and American cultures presently saturated with manuals, studies, and gossip dealing with sex and love, there is something scandalous—either willfully naive or openly backward—in attempting to rethink the ways we think and talk about what is all too evidently present. For Foucault, the questions of method are not merely those of how to talk about sex without hypocrisy, but how to resist a prevailing view of sexuality as the product of a sustained rule of clinical thinking, and thus a privileged secret shared by Western societies since the seventeenth century.

In contrast to Foucault, Barthes concentrates on what he finds repressed by the practices Foucault cites as having led to a middle-class sexuality. As a result, Barthes questions the appropriate ways to write about love at a moment when, from all indications, it is a labor of lust, nothing more than sex. This makes for a willful attempt at untimeliness, an ostensibly unpopular attitude which might be dismissed as quaint or precious except for its unsentimental basis in the critical view of the repressed as that which comes back.

In order for love to return as that which is repressed by a practice of clinical sexuality, it must first do so at the level of discourse from which it has been displaced. Thus, in keeping with the spatial metaphor Foucault uses to talk about the place of discourse, Barthes states that the *Fragments* are constructed less as an analysis than as the staging of an utterance:

Whence the choice of a "dramatic" method which renounces examples and rests on the single action of a primary language (no metalanguage). The description of the lover's discourse has been replaced by its simulation, and to that discourse has been restored its fundamental person, the *I*, in order to stage an utterance, not an analysis. What is proposed, then, is a portrait—but not a psychological portrait; instead a structural one which offers the reader a discursive site: the site of someone speaking within himself, *amorously*, confronting the other, who does not speak. [*Fragments*, p. 3]

While both Foucault and Barthes write about discourse—what they write is also very much within discourse—the above passage from the *Fragments* illustrates a positionality of address much more bound to interpersonal communication than the anonymous and institutional phenomenon studied by Foucault. And although I intend to return to Foucault's comments on the various connections between knowledge, power, and pleasure, the concrete discursivity of dramatic address takes priority in the *Fragments* as part of the pedagogy tied to Barthes's practice of semiology over the past decade.

The amorous discourse—not a discourse *on* love but *in* or *of* love—relates that semiotic practice to a dramatic formulation which derives alternately from the most intimate of pleasure principles and insights into the most institutionalized of social relations. At first glance, a political reading would seem to be incongruous with the artifice of confessional fragments which composes the *Fragments*. But only if we fail to link theory and criticism with the rule of the written or spoken word. Because of the evident physical and cultural differences, American students of French culture and ideas are in a singular position to observe the impact of the importation and exportation of foreign discourse on native institutions. We may read Proust, Colette, Genette, or Cixous as "French," but we do so within cultural institutions which heighten our awareness of the social factors affecting the distribution of French ideas as something other than duty-free import. If we agree with Foucault that all discourse is closed because it is predicated on acts of exclusion and inclusion, the reception of French ideas by American readers needs to be accounted for as something more than the abstract translation from one language or culture to another.

Any general statement about the evolution of Barthes's critical practice during the so-called post-structuralist period since 1968 should address—indeed it should beg—the relations between criticism and teaching. Whenever intellectuals are accused of an unwillingness or an inability to move from word to act, the presence of a pedagogical imperative ought to remind us, via the Kantian connection, of the moral rule known to every fully formed human being. Whatever attitudes we claim to hold about literature and criticism carry with them an implied pedagogy which we experience first-hand in the classroom, seminar, or lecture hall as a lived relation of power and knowledge. Displaced with varying degrees of discretion and subtlety under the guise of authority and doctrine, the Great Books teach a personal experience of institutional power. No one who has been criticized (or reprimanded) as a student for holding ideas or attitudes unacceptable—that is, antagonistic—to those of the teacher or professor will believe in the autonomy of critical exchange from an educational process of indoctrination. If, for example, we cite Althusser's notion of ideology and ramble on about practical relations between the "real" and the "imaginary," we need also to recognize that our will to distinguish between the "real" and the "imaginary" is a cultural expression of what we already know to be predicated on an affective basis. Because Barthes's practice of semiotics acknowledges the emotive structure of cognition in relation to what others might prefer to identify as a less individualized activity and because he has seen critical discourse as a staging of classroom struggles in the space of the seminar, the evolution of his critical attitudes is also exemplary for the clarification of pedagogical problems.

II.   Imagine that I am a teacher: I speak, endlessly, in front of and for someone who remains silent. I am the person who says *I* (the detours of *one*, *we* or impersonal sentence make no difference), I am the person who, under cover of *setting out* a body

of knowledge, *puts out* a discourse, *never knowing how that
discourse is being received* and thus forever forbidden the
reassurance of a definitive image—even if offensive—which
would *constitute me.*
—Barthes, "Writers, Intellectuals, Teachers"

For *Communications*, no. 8 (1966), Barthes wrote an "Introduction to the
Structural Analysis of Narratives" which is still considered a basic text of
literary semiotics. Toward the end of the article, in a passage devoted to
narrative situation, he states the following on the principle of immanence
which maintains the narrational codes as the final level or limit of analysis:

Narration can only receive its meaning from the world which makes use of it; beyond
the narrational level begins the world, other systems (social, economic, ideological)
whose terms are no longer simply narratives but elements of a different substance
(historical facts, determinations, behaviors, etc.). Just as linguistics stops at the
sentence, so narrative analysis stops at discourse—from there it is necessary to shift to
another semiotics.[6]

Personally, I have felt somewhat uncomfortable with the article because I am
unwilling to believe that the operation of reading can be adequately conceptualized as processes of switching, distributing, and integrating, actions
evoking the image of a vast computer terminal with an unlimited potential for
assimilating, processing, and storing data.

The period separating the "Introduction to the Structural Analysis of
Narratives" from the present forms a historical space within which the shift
toward another semiotics has entailed not merely the expansion of the
Parisian Structuralism of the 50's and early 60's practiced by Lévi-Strauss,
Barthes himself, and other contributors to the *Communications* issue, but
what I see as a distinct and substantive break in both the theory and practice of
criticism. For Barthes, the shift appears to be acute and irreversible: less a
gradual progression than an emphatic break. And while it is possible and
perhaps even felicitous to insist on the constant elements in Barthes's career,
to do so is to neglect why *Fragments d'un discours amoureux* is less the
product of a fully articulated semiotics ("Une autre sémiotique") than a
paradoxical or antithetical response to the earlier practice in view of something completely different ("une sémiotique autre") in which Barthes drops
the conventional distinction between theory and practice. The *Fragments*
address problems of analysis and interpretation intelligible as the traditional
concerns of literary critics. At the same time, Barthes's manner of addressing
those problems needs to be confronted in view of what is no longer a mere
revision of the mid-60's practice. Specifically, his choice of *topoi*, as well as the

6. Barthes, "Introduction to the Structural Analysis of Narratives," in *Image, Music, Text*,
trans. Stephen Heath (New York: Hill and Wang, 1977), pp. 115–16. The entire issue of *Communications*, no. 8 has been reissued in book form in 1981 by the Editions du Seuil in Paris.

refusal of a metalanguage, devolve from theoretical considerations which, although pertinent to any reading of the *Fragments,* are secondary to the textual presence of the amorous discourse and the narrative function of the fragments. Thus, Barthes writes that we should resist our will to locate a fixed origin out of which the sequence of fragments might acquire a necessary order, describing that will to order as monstrous. Instead, he adds, we should look for "no more than affirmation" (*Fragments,* p. 8).

Saying yes . . . to systematic discourse or to love, as the case may be, is neither a simple affirmation nor the handle of some pop sentimentality. For even if I persist in taking Barthes at his word, his statement needs to be (re) situated in the context of a discourse which is no longer simply critical, as in a hypothetical discourse *on* love. To affirm love in the name of . . . love? In the name of literary criticism? What is it that can be said today—critically and otherwise—about love without falling into untimeliness or repetition? Whom can Barthes be addressing? And finally, who is (and also, *what* is) the subject of love encountered in this book? To look for no more than the affirmation of love is then not at all a simple task when the very affirmation—in a mode of semantic and textual density which I want to term polymorphic—calls for an attention whose rigor and sensitivity are none other than those of critical reading. To affirm love is thus to concur—tentatively, that is in the spirit of critical thinking—that the subject of love (overdetermined as both discursive voice and humanist *topos*) is perhaps nothing more than (nothing other than) its polymorphous affirmation.

All of which is not at all to suggest that the *Fragments* formulate an idealist theory of love. For what counts in the amorous discourse—what gives it a textual or differential effect—is its repositioning of critical utterance as dramatic address. The lover's monologue is staged (simultaneously set on stage and simulated), addressed to the loved one whose silence appears only to feed the anxieties of the lover/narrator in search of signs of response. For despite prefatory disclaimers, the *Fragments* are a kind of psychological portrait—a playful one at that—of the semiotician in love. Oxymoron? Oxy-moronic, that is, stupid as the lover smitten and stupefied by emotion into sappy *bêtise.* The amorous discourse—the text, not the book—extends what I have noted earlier as another semiotics whose uncanniness derives from the fact that the world of the lover is indistinguishable from the *word* of the lover and thus from the processes of symbolization and verbal production. The word/world of the lover in which universal signification (even silence, especially silence) speaks to his or her personal predicaments to simulate an illusion of systematicity bordering on the paranoid. Faced with a number of possible meanings, the lover's predicament becomes a question of how to choose between a number of conflicting interpretations: "*Everything signifies:* by this proposition, I entrap myself, I bind myself in calculations, I keep myself from enjoyment" (*Fragments*, p. 63; the French version ends, "Je m'empêche de jouir").

The lover on the lookout for signs of love engages in a semiotics in which ambiguity heightens the central function of value. Writing on or about love in order to semiotize it is thus always to locate it this side of the *plaisir* Barthes describes in *The Pleasure of the Text* as a cultural and verbal phenomenon contrasted to the ineffable *jouissance*, commonly translated as "bliss" but more directly rendered by Stephen Heath in terms of orgasm. The bind of the semiotician-in-love—what makes for the oxymoron—is the surfeit or supplement of the body which a conventional semiotics cannot contain without equating *jouissance* and *plaisir*. The excess of signs produces discomfort and arousal, so that the lover turns into a concerned (or "involved") semiotician whose desire to locate and interpret leaves him invariably unsatisfied. Between his desire to find signs of love and his reluctance to accept that such signs are always uncertain, the lover derives a kind of fearful pleasure in the compression or reduction of feeling to concepts. In addition, the very same excess allows the verbal discourse to continue. As in the French expression, *ça laisse à désirer*.

Without wanting to further quantify that excess by suggesting that it can be contained with a concept, I find that the best way to approach it comes from critiques of idealist love found in current psychoanalysis and feminist writing. As characterized by two Frenchmen in a passage echoing the prefatory remarks in the *Fragments*, the rise of sexual liberation and feminism has displaced love both in terms of personal experience and cultural discourse:

If there is a romanticism today, it is libidinal and no longer sentimental. In place of passion, there is desire; in place of the heart, the genitals. The former construct of body and soul has been gotten at by the various ideologies of pleasure, and in order to say the following: (that) there are not two loves, the first spiritual and the other material, one noble, the other vulgar, low—because emotions have but a single fatherland/site: the body.[7]

Barthes's book of love is then very much also a book of the body. That is, a book in which elements of classical rhetoric—*inventio, elocutio, dispositio*—are inscribed within a primary concern with the gestures of the body *(figures)* and the rhetorical term *actio*, equated by Barthes with drama, gymnastics, and choreography. Priority of the body does not, however, exclude the word, body and word interacting in what Lacan describes as the convergence of the Imaginary, the Symbolic, and the Real: "Underneath the figure, there is something of the verbal hallucination (Freud, Lacan)" (*Fragments*, p. 6).

In the *Roland Barthes*, the reader was offered a twenty-five page section of

---

7. Pascal Bruckner and Alain Finkielkraut, *Le Nouveau Désordre amoureux* (Paris: Seuil, 1977), p. 121.

annotated photographs of Barthes's youth. In one shot, the young Roland sits on his mother's lap as she points directly toward the camera. The caption reads: "The mirror stage, that's you," which both acknowledges and retorts to Lacan's theory of the development of identity in the pre-verbal child. In the *Fragments*, Freud and Lacan continue to be reinvoked in order to relate various corporeal figures to contacts with the symbolic, Lacan's narrative of the rocky road toward mastery of language. In *Beyond the Pleasure Principle* (1920), Freud relates the story of the little boy who compensated for his mother's frequent absences by inventing a game in which he could—symbolically—make her return at will. In the *Fragments*, the lover/narrator states: "Absence: any episode of language which stages the absence of the loved object—whatever its cause and its duration—and which tends to transform this absence into an ordeal of banishment" (*Fragments*, p. 13). The lover/narrator invokes the insecurities of the child who stages the events of everyday existence within a highly developed mental life surrounding the interplay between presence and absence: "As a child, I didn't forget: interminable days, abandoned days, when the Mother was working far away; I would go, evenings, to wait for her at the U^{bis} bus stop, Sèvres-Babylone; the buses would pass one after the other, she wasn't in any of them" (*Fragments*, pp. 14–15). The insecure lover revives the figure of the child who waits, not yet completely severed (*sevré* is the past participle of the French verb *sevrer*, "to wean"); that is, not yet detached from the Mother and thus ever a lonely baby at Babylone.[8] From the child's play emerges a model of the symbolic activity later expanded by the adult to cope with feelings of dependency and infrequent abandonment: "There is a scenography of waiting: I organize it, manipulate it, cut out a portion of time in which I shall mime the loss of the loved object and provoke all the effects of a minor mourning. This is then acted out as a play" (*Fragments*, p. 37).

Following little Hans in *Beyond the Pleasure Principle*, the lover/narrator produces a symbolic fiction, a story to compensate for the absence of the loved one, transforming anxiety into a business (*affairement*) where the oscillation of verbal activity—analogous to throwing and retrieving the spool—stages utterance as a fiction with multiple roles (impatience, jealousy, infatuation, inamoration) and figures (doubts, reproaches, desires, depressions).

As much as the lover/narrator might value the ineffable pleasures of *jouissance* over its cultural counterpart, the *discours amoureux* also affirms the specific pleasures of narration and speech. And despite Barthes's stated desire to rethink the logic of binary distinctions formulated and applied in the mid-60's period, the bulk of the *discours amoureux* illustrates verbal pleasures which only approach *jouissance* by insisting on corporeal figuration. In *Critique et vérité* (1966), Barthes had attacked the naive conception which, in his view, the "old" criticism (in the person of Raymond Picard) had held of

8. Randolph Runyon, "Canon in U^{bis}," *Visible Language*, 11 (1977), 407.

psychoanalysis and its perception of the human body: "The man of the old criticism [*l'ancienne critique*] is, in fact, made up of two anatomical regions. The first is, so to speak, superior-external: the head, artistic creation, noble appearance, that which can be shown, which can be seen; the second is inferior-internal: the genitals (which must not be named), instincts, 'summary drives,' the dark world of anarchical tensions."[9] Roland Barthes may know better than to believe in such clearcut distinctions. But the lover/narrator does not, and continues to hold at least a residual fondness for other binaries which point to the ambiguities of his predicament: "I can do everything with my language, *but not with my body*. What I hide by my language, my body utters. I can deliberately mold my message, not my voice. By my voice, whatever it says, the other will recognize 'that something is wrong with me.' I am a liar (by preterition), not an actor. My body is a stubborn child, my language is a very civilized adult" (*Fragments*, p. 45).

For the lover, which is again not at all to equate the narrator-lover with Barthes himself, the binary is a willed construct, a useful fiction by means of which he hopes to maintain the break between his narration—pleasurable on its own account—and the excess of sensations and signs he wants to interpret only up to a point. Caught within the bind of wanting both to semiotize and leave an excess or surplus of signs, the semiotician-in-love adopts an ironic attitude toward his narration, an attitude which makes the *Fragments* something more (and something "other") than an essay of straightforward critical writing.

The frequent invocation of corporeal figures in the *Fragments* needs to be seen in relation to the wider project of undermining the stable and consistent subject which has informed Barthes's practice since *S/Z*. Specifically, that project has been elucidated in two ways: first, by studying the discourses which resist conventions of "classical" and "modern" narration, and subsequently by clarifying the presuppositions at work in those conventions as what allows literary critics to operate as such. All of which has led Barthes away from the applied practice of the mid-60's period toward an extended reflection on the attitudes toward language seldom acknowledged by critics of a pragmatic orientation. Hence Barthes's stated disillusion with the "scientific" Saussure and his more recent allegiance to the "dramatic" views on language set forth by Nietzsche, Freud, and the Saussure of the clandestine study of anagrams seemingly at odds with the posthumous *Cours de linguistique générale* for which he is best known. But where the discussion and practice of figuration in the *Roland Barthes* derives in large part from Nietzsche's lectures and writings on language and rhetoric, the *Fragments* reveal an active practice of figuration in a way which tempers the Nietzschean views on tropes with a psychoanalytic vocabulary and orientation encoun-

9. Barthes, *Critique et vérité* (Paris: Seuil, 1966), p. 25.

tered in the writings of Freud, Lacan, Benveniste, and Kristeva. More point-edly, the elaboration of the amorous discourse within a wider discourse of critical writing locates figuration as the affirmation of personal involvement. As a result, the amorous discourse counteracts illusions of indifference and value-free inquiry while promoting textual effects somewhere between essay, confession, and fictional narrative. As an intertext composed of heterogeneous materials, the *Fragments* complicate attempts to specify their sources by opposing such attempts with a continuous displacement of master tropes. Seeking the sources may be what most readers would consider the normal way to go about understanding the text. In this sense, a pedagogical or analytic situation would have to confront the impulse to seek sources in order to approach the dynamics of displacement which oppose it.

The difficulties encountered by the lover/narrator are a direct result of his attempts to semiotize personal involvement over and above his admitted desire to keep the loved one beyond classification. The lover/narrator who produces as well as interprets signs recalls the bind of *L'Empire des signes*, Barthes's 1970 study of the cultural dimensions of semiosis as a production and analysis of signification. While the lover/narrator of the *Fragments* situates the loved one as unclassifiable, he nonetheless adopts a discursive relationship whose formality (the "I-to-you" in words and power) implies a number of positions. Invoking a passage from Goethe's *Sorrows of Young Werther*, the lover/narrator identifies with the fictional hero who wants to occupy the "place" already taken by Charlotte's fiancé, Albert. To dramatize his isolation, the lover/narrator compares his situation to that of a player in a parlor game: "There are as many chairs as children, minus one; while the children march around, a lady pounded on a piano; when she stopped, everyone dashed for a chair and sat down, except the clumsiest, the least brutal, the unluckiest, who remained standing, stupid, *de trop*: the lover" (*Fragments*, p. 45). The game, yet another evocation of childhood anxiety and vulnerability projected by the civilized adult is known in French as *le jeu du mouchoir*. In English, it is musical chairs, which combines the commonplace game name into a name game in which the English "chair" is written exactly as the French word for flesh. The socialized parlor game reveals a verbal link with the body, exposed or made obscene as the lover's physical desire characterized in the qualities of sexual arousal evident in the enumeration: standing, stupid, *de trop.*

At a later point, the flesh figure returns as that of love's obscenity which, in a disarming gesture of modesty, the lover/narrator tries to displace by means of a mocking deformation of the word "love" into something more affectionate and corny (another case of amorous *bêtise*) such as "luv." (In the French, the transformation is from *amour* to *amur.*) As a verbal sign of naked sentiment, this kind of obscenity produces its own dramatic figure in an imagined scene from the Marx Brothers' "A Night at the Opera" in which an incompetent tenor faces the public as he sings to the woman he loves. The lover/narrator comments: "I am this tenor: like a huge animal, obscene and stupid, brightly lighted as in a show window, I declaim an elaborately coded aria, without looking at the one I love, to whom I am supposed to be addressing myself" (*Fragments*, p. 175). Unable to stop at a single displacement, the lover/narrator adds another image in which the figure of the tenor becomes that of the teacher giving a course on love in the guise of Paul Géraldy, the minor poet whose syrupy *Toi et moi* (1923) has been a perennial bestseller.

III.   The use of language like a lover ... not the language of love,
                  but the love of language, not matter, but meaning, not what
                  the tongue touches, but what it forms, not lips and nipples,
                  but nouns and verbs.
                                      —William H. Gass, *On Being Blue*

The figure of the sentimental lover who reveals desire on stage or in the classroom dramatizes almost to the point of caricature a personal vulnerability so disarming that we might easily forget the critical function of the amorous discourse. The lesson of love cannot merely be its confession or profession unless we maintain the illusory split between public and private acts. My comments on the *Fragments* have tried to integrate the amorous discourse within the evolution of Barthes's practice of semiotics. In view of the dramatization of that practice, I want to trace some of the pedagogical implications of the space of the seminar as part of the shift toward "another semiotics" referred to in the 1966 "Introduction to the Structural Analysis of Narratives."

At a 1969 colloquium on the teaching of literature, Barthes speaks on the presentation of literary history found in standard French manuals. Elucidating the polemical position taken in *Critique et vérité* against Lansonian scholarship, Barthes calls for a rethinking of literary periods similar to what Michel Foucault provides in *Les Mots et les choses*. Characterizing French literary history as a series of institutional exclusions, Barthes foresees a set of counter-histories of the censures against class differences, sexuality, and the concept of literature itself. At first glance, it appears that Barthes has found in Foucault the methodology he might have needed some twenty years earlier to elaborate the project set forth in *Le Degré zéro*. But where Foucault goes on to trace the disappearance of the individual within the impersonality of institutionalized discourse, Barthes seeks to reassert the possibility of individual utterance as an act of resistance against such disappearance. In view of the function and value Barthes ascribes to the seminar space, it is not surprising that literary study is seen in this earlier text as felicitous for that reassertion.

Barthes writes: "In my view, there is a deep and irreducible antinomy between literature as practice and literature as teaching. This antinomy is serious because it is linked to what is perhaps the most serious of today's problems: the transmission of knowledge and the problem of alienation. For if the larger structures of economic alienation have been brought to light, those of the alienation of knowledge have not. I believe that, on this scale, a political conceptualization is insufficient and that a psychoanalytic conceptualization is necessary."[10]

Some eight years later, Barthes returned to reflect on the overlapping of institutional and personal dimensions of teaching on the occasion of his inaugural lecture at the Collège de France. Acknowledging the status afforded by this honorary appointment, he tries to set it within the conflict he sees exerted by society and technocracy on one side and the revolutionary desires of its youth and students on the other. A longtime foe of university critics, Barthes is also a maverick who bucked the system by teaching at one of the elite *Grandes Ecoles* without ever completing the *Doctorat d'Etat* required for a permanent professorship. (The *Système de la mode*, undertaken to fulfill the thesis requirement, was published without any formal defense.) As a result, Barthes's elevation to the Collège de France sets him in somewhat of a delicate situation. For while his election to the first Chair in Literary Semiology carries academic recognition, his acceptance also acquiesces to personal and professional vanity. Sartre, for one, refused the Nobel Prize in 1964.

Barthes attempts to confront the question of vanity when, in his opening remarks, he describes his elevation as culminating his earliest aspirations to a vocation as writer. In the tradition of the inaugural address, the new member of the Collège de France evokes the memory of the predecessor whose passing is the pretext for the new appointment. When, as in this case, a new Chair precludes the homage to a direct predecessor, the inaugural lesson serves to set off the area of inquiry to be pursued from those already occupied within the institution. In this sense, Barthes's appointment to the Collège needs to be seen in conjunction with those of Lévi-Strauss and Foucault; that is, within the appropriation of the "human sciences" and Structuralism by French cultural institutions. So after setting the ritual into motion with nods to

---

10. "Réflexions sur un manuel," in *L'enseignement de la littérature*, ed. Serge Doubrovsky and Tzvetan Todorov (Paris: Plon, 1971), p. 176. Barthes has also commented at length on teaching in "Writers, Intellectuals, Professors," in *Image, Music, Text*, pp. 190–215 and "Littérature/enseignement: entretien avec Roland Barthes," *Pratiques*, no. 5 (February 1975), pp. 15–21. For additional views on Barthes's evolution and its impact on pedagogy, see Fredric Jameson, "The Ideology of the Text," *Salmagundi*, no. 29–30 (1975–76), pp. 202–46; Barbara Johnson, "The Critical Difference," *Diacritics*, 8, no. 2 (summer 1978), 2–9; and Steven Ungar, "Doing and Not Doing Things with Barthes," *Enclitic*, 2, no. 2 (Fall 1978), 86–109.

Michelet, Valéry, Benveniste, Merleau-Ponty, and Foucault, he states that this honor will make it that much easier for him to enlarge the scope of his pedagogy: "To teach or even to speak outside the limits of institutional sanction is certainly not to be rightfully and totally uncorrupted by power: power (the *libido dominandi*) is there, hidden in any discourse, even when uttered in a place outside the bounds of power. Therefore, the freer such teaching, the further we must inquire into the conditions and processes by which discourse can be disengaged from all will-to-possess."[11]

Sensitive to the external pressures which define teaching as a social activity entailing power and possession, Barthes seeks their impact on the individual. He redefines power as a plurality so diffused within our daily life that one is loath to admit its presence in the most delicate of social mechanisms: the language we speak and write. If, as Barthes implies, there is no escape from institutions of power, then what lesson can the professor of Desire teach? To offer a lapidary answer to an equally lapidary question: the lesson is that of resistance and its means are those of literature as Barthes defines it in the following passage:

I mean by *literature* neither a body nor a series of works, nor even a branch of commerce or of teaching, but the complex graph of the traces of a practice, the practice of writing. Hence, it is essentially the text with which I am concerned—the fabric of signifiers which constitute the work. For the text is the very outcropping of speech, and it is within speech that speech must be fought, led astray—not by the message of which it is the instrument, but by the play of words of which it is the theater. Thus I can say without differentiation: literature, writing, or text. The forces of freedom which are in literature depend not on the writer's civil person, nor on his political commitment—for he is, after all, only a man among others—nor do they depend on the doctrinal content of his work, but rather on the displacement he brings to bear upon the language. Seen in this light, Céline is quite as important as Hugo, and Chateaubriand as important as Zola. By this I am trying to address a responsibility of forms; but this responsibility cannot be evaluated in ideological terms—which is why the sciences of ideology have always had so little hold over it. Of these forces of literature, I wish to indicate three, which I shall discuss in terms of three Greek concepts: *Mathesis, Mimesis, Semiosis.* [*Leçon,* p. 6]

Because it stages language as the production of meaning and affirmation of value, literature promotes a reflexivity in which each of us can recognize the discourses of power as we experience them, so to speak, "outside the text." When that staging reveals the censure or displacement of individual utterances in the name of institutions of power and authority, the act of utterance

11. Barthes, "In Inauguration of the Chair of Literary Semiology, Collège de France, January 7, 1977," trans. Richard Howard, *October,* no. 8 (Spring 1979), p. 4. Future references will cite Howard's translation as *Leçon,* title of the French version published in book form in 1978 by the Editions du Seuil.

reasserts a subversive potential Barthes sees as unique. Because utterance also asserts the materiality of language, literature can temper the lofty abstractions of scientism with the irreducible corporality of a speaking subject: "The act of stating, by exposing the subject's place and energy, even his deficiency (which is not his absence), focuses on the very reality of language, acknowledging that language is an immense halo of implications, of effects, of turns, returns, and degrees. It assumes the burden of making understood a subject both insistent and ineffable, unknown and yet recognized by a disturbing familiarity. Words are no longer mistaken for simple instruments; they are cast as projections, explosions, vibrations, devices, flavors. Writing makes knowledge festive" (Leçon, p. 7).

As they are characterized above, the teaching and study of literature are less concerned with ill-fated attempts to pursue a science than with leading the individual to recognize what happens between the signs emitted by a text and those it elicits via reading in a process of what Barthes, following Lacan, terms "the real." Literature and semiology combine to correct each other; today one might more readily refer to intertextuality and a vision of the reading experience as a turn toward other writings as antidote to myths of pure creativity. For Barthes, the knowledge made possible by literary semiology remains limited in so far as it is equated with pragmatic science. In direct antithesis to what he had set forth in the Michelet as an interpretive model imposed by the literary object, Barthes rejects pragmatic interpretation as a prime focus of the reading process: "In other words, semiology is not a grid; it does not permit a direct apprehension of the real through the imposition of a general transparency which would render it intelligible" (Leçon, p. 13). Since semiology is a language about other languages which replaces the attempts to formalize semiosis with a festive knowledge—Nietzsche's gaya scienza?—Barthes's refusal of the metalinguistic function points to the historical determinants affecting the production and interpretation of signs. Where straightforward political or scientific readings would, respectively, demystify or formalize sign production, Barthes once again asserts a utopian function for a literature attuned to the inevitability of power: "Utopia, of course, does not save us from power. The utopia of language is salvaged as the language of utopia—a genre like the rest. We can say that no writer who began in a rather lonely struggle against the power of language could or can avoid being co-opted by it, either in the posthumous form of an inscription within official culture, or in the present form of a mode which imposes its image and forces him to conform to expectation. No way out for this author than to shift ground—or to persist—or both at once" (Leçon, p. 9).

This utopian function extends fully a similar function sketched at the very end of Le Degré zéro, suggesting at the level of concepts a dialectic or spiral of repetition derived from Vico and Hegel. At the level of personal evolution, however, any repetition yields to irreducible historical differences. In 1957, the *Mythologies* provide a first semiology by reading popular culture as a form of mythic writing worked over by capitalist institutions. By 1970, the militancy spawned in France by the events surrounding May '68 lead to a more violent *sémioclastie* where the study of signs imposes their destruction. By 1977, the impasse of semioclastics as an ill-fated attempt to break out from the inevitability of power imposes a final version as abjuration and change. Continuing the Greek paradigm, Barthes terms this final version *sémiotropie,* or "turning-toward-signs." The third version is an attempt to accept the immediacy of signs while accounting for qualities rejected by earlier approaches via science and politics. Barthes notes first of all how the play of signification relates to its apophatic nature; that is, its dependence on verisimilitude and the uncertainty such verisimilitude implies. After the earlier versions derived from scientific and political projects, the final version of semiology as *sémiotropie* is an attempt to adjust theory and practice to account for the ongoing semiotic process within history. In the terms of Saussurian linguistics, Barthes appears to support the notion that *langue* needs to be understood as a methodological convenience, an illusion of fixity opposed to the plurality of utterances. Only a semiology which affirms the uncertainty of signs can trace within history the differences on which later scientific or political projects are formulated.

In what amounts to a final testament or statement of faith to his generation and those of his students, Barthes defends *sémiotropie* as a direct result of historical change and its impact on his practice as literary critic:

The pleasure of the imaginary sign is conceivable now due to certain recent mutations, which effect culture more than society itself: the use we can make of the forces of literature I have mentioned is modified by a new situation. On the one hand and first of all, the myth of the great French writer, the sacred depositary of all higher values, has crumbled since the Liberation; it has dwindled and died gradually with each of the last survivors of the *entre-deux-guerres*; a new *type* has appeared, and we no longer know—or do not yet know—what to call him: writer? intellectual? scribe? In any case, literary mastery is vanishing; the writer is no longer center stage. On the other hand and subsequently, May '68 has revealed the crisis in our teaching. The old values are no longer transmitted, no longer circulate, no longer impress; literature is desacralized, institutions are impotent to defend and impose it as the model of the human. It is not, if you like, that literature is destroyed; rather it is no longer *protected,* so that this is the moment to deal with it. Literary semiology is, as it were, that journey which lands us in a country free by default; angels and dragons are no longer there to defend it. Our gaze can fall, not without perversity, upon certain old and lovely things, whose signified is abstract, out of date. It is a moment at once decadent and prophetic, a moment of gentle apocalypse, a historical moment of the greatest possible pleasure. (*Leçon,* p. 14)

It is unlikely that anyone reads these lines today—in early 1981—without noting their inadvertent prophecies. Having recognized the decline of traditional values and the illusions of mastery, Barthes seems to have projected into his teaching the lessons of his own evolution. As a professor of Desire, he has demonstrated that while it is unrealistic to compete against institutions of power and authority, teaching can loosen their discourses by revealing their tendentiousness and artifice. For each of us, the study of signs and meaning needs to be recognized as dependent on value and primal scenes of recognition relating knowledge and pleasure. By dramatizing discourse, Barthes can lighten its impact and demonstrate its ties to symbolic processes, a "loosening" by means of fragment, digression, and *excursus* described in the very terms of the primal scene recounted in the *Fragments:* "I should therefore like the speaking and the listening that will be interwoven here to resemble the comings and goings of a child playing beside his mother, leaving her to bring a pebble, a piece of string, and thereby tracing around a calm center a whole locus of play within which the pebble, the string come to matter less than the enthusiastic giving of them" (*Leçon*, p. 15).

When, in the *Symposium,* Socrates states that love is the one thing in the world he understands, he is immediately desired by those who believe mistakenly that to possess the Master physically would be somehow to possess the knowledge to which he claims. What Alcibiades takes to be a jilting by Socrates is also the only way to assure that he might eventually proceed toward self-knowledge. Only by refusing Alcibiades can Socrates prevent him from accepting a subservient role in a social hierarchy of marked class differences. The final entry in the *Fragments* invokes a similar act of refusal which, following Socrates, is less a simple refusal than an apophasis: "So desire still irrigates the non-will-to-possess by this perilous movement: *I love you* in my head, but I imprison it behind my lips. I do not divulge. I say silently to who is no longer or is not yet the other: *I keep myself from loving you*" *(Fragments*, p. 234). Only by acknowledging desire in the very moment of denying it can the professor of Desire teach the knowledge of love and love of knowledge, thus fulfilling the nurturing function essential to the learning process as a continuous affirmation of joyful wisdom.

JOAN DE JEAN

La Nouvelle Héloïse, or the Case for Pedagogical Deviation

On demande s'il faut aux filles des maîtres ou des maîtresses?
Je ne sais. . .

—Rousseau, *Emile*

Observers and practitioners of the pedagogical act have always been aware of its seductive potential. In history and literary history, one of the classic student-teacher relationships is an association through seduction. The archetype of such a relationship could well be the seduction of Eve by the serpent, who, like all the corrupt teachers who follow in its wake, gets the woman to do what it wants by offering her knowledge. Pedagogical corruption can thus be situated at the origin of original sin.

La Nouvelle Héloïse may be the archetypal teaching novel. Its very title serves to inscribe it immediately into a literary-historical tradition in which the act of teaching brings about the disgrace of both teacher and student. Like his predecessor Abelard, Saint-Preux makes a carefully calculated use of his pedagogical authority to seduce his pupil. The similarity between the Saint-Preux/Julie (teaching) relationship and that of their predecessors, Abelard and Heloise, has been noted by Pierre Burgelin.[1] It seems, at least according to the teachers' accounts, that not much teaching took place during their lessons. In his *Historia calamitatum,* Abelard describes the context of his Heloise's education:

With our books open before us, more words of love than of our reading passed between us, and more kissing than teaching . . . love drew our eyes to look on each other more than reading kept them on our texts.[2]

Some of Saint-Preux's earliest letters tell what is essentially the same (old) story: "Les yeux étoient mal fixés sur le livre, la bouche en prononçoit les

1. In a note to the Pléiade edition of *Emile,* Burgelin also extends the comparison to include the pedagogical relationship between Emile and Sophie (Paris: Gallimard, 1962), IV, 791, note 2. Future references to the Pléiade edition of any of Rousseau's works will be indicated in parentheses in the text. References to *Julie* will contain, rather than the volume number (II), the number of the part, the number of the letter, and the page reference to the Pléiade edition.

I will provide English translations for the most problematic passages. All translations will be from the 1761 English edition of *Julie* (2 vols.; London: R. Griffiths) which I will occasionally modify. I have translated all other passages quoted in the article from the French editions cited in footnotes.

2. In *The Letters of Abelard and Heloise* (Penguin Books, 1974), p. 67.

mots, l'attention manquoit toujours" (I, xii, 57). Saint-Preux may condemn Abelard as vigorously as he pleases,[3] but for all intents and purposes he begins his career in Rousseau's novel by retracing the logician's road to calamity. In the early stages of La Nouvelle Héloïse, the teacher is a corrupt figure, condemned by all participants in the drama of seduction, including Julie, who calls him a "vil séducteur" (I, iv, 39), and Rousseau himself, who describes his hero as falling just short of being a "scélérat" (I, xxiv, 85).

Of course, this rather banal[4] vision of the pedagogue's powers of corruption is quickly dissolved. After the scene of Julie's conversion, the teacher reappears, this time endowed with new powers and a new image. During Saint-Preux's reign as teacher, teaching serves almost exclusively as a metaphor for seduction. We never hear of the classroom being used as anything but a pretext for the young lovers' forbidden games. In fact, the only time Saint-Preux really sounds like a teacher is when he gives a brief presentation of his pedagogical system for his "écolière" (I, xii, 57–61), but the passage seems so out of character that it enjoys a marginal status at best. After the fall, however, La Nouvelle Héloïse becomes what Burgelin has called a "practical treatise of education" (IV, cvii). Lessons of all kinds take place all day long, and the educational system that counterbalances Saint-Preux's teaching is laid out at much greater length (V, iii, 561–85) and far more convincingly. (Credit for the development of this system is given to Wolmar, but it is explained by Julie, and the scene of her explanation is transcribed by Saint-Preux in a letter to Milord Edouard, so this might be termed a collective educational vision).

Saint-Preux is the novel's first, and its only "professional" figure of intellectual authority, but the later parts of La Nouvelle Héloïse present the reader with a proliferation of pedagogical characters in search of a student: Julie turns into "la prêcheuse;"[5] Claire for once manages to upstage her cousin, as she indulges in an occasional round of "prêcher la prêcheuse" (IV, xiii, 506); and Wolmar, with his non-stop lessons in generosity, becomes one of the most powerful influences on the once corrupt pedagogue, Saint-Preux: "[il] commençoit à prendre une si grande autorité sur moi. . ." (IV, vi, 425). Julie "la prêcheuse" is a model for the new type of pedagogue in the novel—she teaches ethical values rather than facts, and she does so in a self-effacing gesture for

3. "Quand les lettres d'Héloise et d'Abelard tomberent entre vos mains, vous savez ce que je vous dis de cette lecture et de la conduite du Théologien. J'ai toujours plaint Héloise; elle avoit un coeur fait pour aimer: mais Abelard ne m'a jamais paru qu'un misérable digne de son sort, et connoissant aussi peu l'amour que la vertu" (I, xxiv, 85).

4. In Rousseau's day, the seduction of a student by a teacher was common enough, as either an occurrence or an obsession, for there to be a law condemning the guilty teacher to hanging. Correspondance littéraire, 22, t. IV, p. 347. Quoted in Daniel Mornet's introduction to his edition of Julie (Paris: Hachette, 1925), I, 252.

5. After her own fall, Heloise, like Julie, becomes herself a teacher. She was prioress at the convent of Argenteuil, and so one of her duties was the education of the nuns, novices and children brought up there.

general moral betterment. Teaching as preaching apparently leads to the reversal of pedagogy's movement toward corruption and to the eventual redemption of all those involved in the novel's initial pedagogical act. Teaching could be called the unifying factor in the novel, since it is an initially corrupting force whose energies are rechanneled, making possible the great purification of the end. "Après avoir été ce que nous fumes être ce que nous sommes aujourd'hui, voila le vrai triomphe de la vertu" (VI, vi, 664), so Julie sums it up for Claire. The climax of *La Nouvelle Héloïse* is therefore doubly redemptive, and it is fitting that the first subject on which Julie addresses those gathered around her deathbed is education: "Elle nous parla de ses enfans, des soins assidus qu'exigeoit auprès d'eux la forme d'éducation qu'elle avoit prise" (VI, xi, 704).

Of course, many readers do not find the atmosphere of the novel's last pages nearly so pure and unproblematic as Rousseau would like them to. There is indeed, as Christie McDonald Vance affirms, "something confusing about the end of *La Nouvelle Héloïse*."[6] Julie's death could be considered less an apotheosis than simply the only way out of a situation poised on the brink of disaster. According to Jean Starobinski, happiness at Clarens "continues to be threatened by the disastrous return of carnal desire."[7] In effect, all the preaching and all the rigid enforcement of utopian practices do not succeed in eliminating the forces of seduction and corruption from Julie's garden paradise. In Rousseau's terms, however, such an affirmation condemns me as a liar and a hypocrite: "Quiconque dira que ce tableau dans sa totalité est scandaleux et n'est pas utile, est un menteur et un hypocrite" (*Confessions*, p. 435).

If my discourse is mendacious, this could very well be a professional deformation. I would contend, for reasons I will set out in the following pages, that the figure of the teacher remains a disturbing presence throughout *La Nouvelle Héloïse*. It seems to me that the initial placement of the novel's relationship to teaching under the sign of Abelard, and indeed the entire corruption-redemption schema that this placement permits, constitute an elaborate and complex *fausse piste*. Just as Julie's education serves as a smokescreen for the lovers' trysts, so the apparently utilitarian goals of the novel's other acts of teaching distract attention from their far more problematic seductions and power plays. What we learn about the Rousseauian conception of the teacher/student involvement in *La Nouvelle Héloïse* is far less "classic" than the initial relationship between Saint-Preux and Julie allows us to realize. Rousseau revolutionized pedagogical theory, and he broke open the traditional structures of pedagogical seduction as well. The composi-

6. Christie McDonald Vance, *The Extravagant Shepherd: A Study of the Pastoral Vision in Rousseau's "La Nouvelle Héloïse," SVEC,* Vol. CV (1973), p. 179.
7. Jean Starobinski, "L'Ecart romanesque," *Sept essais sur Rousseau,* in *La Transparence et l'obstacle* (Paris: Gallimard, 1971), p. 413.

tion of his educational novel is so closely entwined with that of *Emile*[8] that Rousseau was able to indulge in at least one act of self-citation in the second work,[9] and it may be that the relationship between the two works is deeper than is immediately apparent. If it is true, as Château believes, that "it is *Julie* that makes us realize what must be the real conclusion of *Emile*," then what can be learned about the implications of Rousseau's educational model from *La Nouvelle Héloïse* can be extended to *Emile*—with the unsettling consequences that I will analyse shortly.

It may by now be apparent that when I earlier described *La Nouvelle Héloïse* as the archetypal teaching novel because it foregrounds the Saint-Preux/Julie couple, I was indulging in some rhetorically motivated hypocrisy, a "vice" to which, as I have since acknowledged, teachers may be inclined. *La Nouvelle Héloïse* is much more than a reworking of Heloise's story in "modern" dress, and it is only by looking beyond the directly erotic relationship between student and teacher that we can begin to define the nature of the Rousseauian variant of pedagogical corruption. I would like to initiate a more general discussion of teaching in Rousseau's novel by examining a text composed at the same period and with which it entertains a peculiar thematic and biographical relationship, the *Lettres morales* addressed to Sophie d'Houdetot. Like *La Nouvelle Héloïse*, the *Lettres morales* illustrate the link between what I have referred to as the "classic" erotic relationship in teaching and the pedagogical act: once again, the physical seduction (in this case unsuccessful) is over before the informative correspondence begins. In fact, the first letter opens with an eye-catching denial of any current seductive intentions: "Venez, ma chére et digne amie, écouter la voix de celui qui vous aime; elle n'est point, vous le savez, celle d'un vil séducteur" (IV, 1081). Rousseau explains that this sublimation is made easy by the special rewards to be gained from replacing seduction by teaching. He can lead his student to an apotheosis similar to the one he had in mind for Julie: "Puisse mon zéle aider à vous elever si fort au dessus de moi, que l'amour propre me dédommage en vous de mes humiliations et me console en quelque sorte de n'avoir pu vous atteindre" (1082).

But Rousseau protests too much. In the manuscript the first paragraph contains a strange and revealing lapsus that casts doubt on the purported innocence of the correspondence. Rousseau intended a sentence to read: "c'est maintenant mon tour, ô Sophie, c'est à moi de vous rendre le prix de vos soins,

---

8. Critics are always in agreement on this point, although they have conversely argued that *Julie* leads into *Emile* (Burgelin, introduction *Emile*, IV, cvii), or, somewhat paradoxically, that "*Emile* . . . emerges . . . into *Julie* . . . because it is *Julie* which makes us realize what must be the real conclusion of *Emile*, by the creation of these little social centers to be governed by a wise man" (Jean Château, *Jean-Jacques Rousseau: sa philosophie de l'éducation*, Paris: Vrin, 1962, p. 92).

9. Part of "Julie's" educational system (pp. 580–1) reappears with only small changes in *Emile* (IV, 351).

puisque vous avez conservé mon âme aux vertus qui vous sont chéres," but instead of writing "Sophie," he wrote "sophisme." The new opening phrase, "c'est maintenant mon tour, ô sophisme" suggests that the potential for deceptiveness in this pedagogical act was very much on his mind (pp. 1081 and 1788). This potential is realized at the end of the same letter in the course of an explanation of how teaching can justify the teacher's fall from virtue, his attempted seduction: "Faites qu'on dise un jour en vous voyant et se rappellant ma mémoire: Ah cet homme aimoit la vertu et se connoissoit en mérite" (1086). In other words, Rousseau, the man of virtue, only tried to seduce because he met a woman who was virtue incarnate, and his attempt must be understood as less a fall from grace than an act of homage to her virtue. There is only one problem with this uplifting imaginary scenario: it is "rigged" by Rousseau. The would-be arch-seducer's self-justification takes the form of another (albeit not yet realized) seduction. Rousseau's future judges will see that he loved Sophie d'Houdetot only because of her virtue—but the virtue they recognize will in fact be a product of Rousseau's teaching, and thus posterior to his attempted seduction of her. In the first moral letter, Rousseau shows his hand. Through teaching, he hopes to achieve a possession of Sophie d'Houdetot far more lasting, complete, and, for a literary sensibility, satisfying than any lover's. Teaching is first of all a form of fiction-making: through it, Rousseau is able to recreate, not only Sophie d'Houdetot's present, but also her past, and especially her past with him. And (re)creation is surely the ultimate form of control. At least for the space of these letters, Rousseau finally has his "chère Sophie" just where he wants her. Through teaching, the man who claimed time and again to be a stranger to jealousy in matters of the heart comes to appreciate the need for total and unique possession. Rousseau as teacher demands complete loyalty from his adult "écolières." Thus, in a subsequent and parallel series of teaching letters, the *Lettres sur la botanique*, he explains to his alleged "chère Cousine" that he refuses to allow her to consult other authorities on botany, because "je suis jaloux d'être votre seul guide en cette partie" (IV, 1161).[10]

The addressee of the *Lettres morales* is in a sense doubly Rousseau's creation. His recreation of his past with her in the first letter is a repetition of a previous aesthetic gesture. "Je vis ma Julie en Mad⁼ d'Houdetot, et bientot je ne vis plus que Mad⁼ d'Houdetot" (*Confessions*, p. 440). His "chère Sophie" is his Julie come to life. His teaching gesture in the *Lettres morales* could be

10. The complete passage has a double movement: Rousseau first works to inspire fear and then to assuage the fear he has created: "Mais je vous préviens que si vous voulez prendre des livres et suivre la nomenclature ordinaire, avec beaucoup de noms vous aurez peu d'idées, celles que vous aurez se brouilleront, vous ne suivrez bien ni ma marche, ni celle des autres, et n'aurez tout au plus qu'une connoissance de mots. Chére Cousine, je suis jalous d'être votre seul guide en cette partie. Quand il en sera tems je vous indiquerai les livres que pouvez consulter. En attendant ayez la patience de ne lire que dans celui de la nature, et de vous en tenir à mes lettres."

considered superfluous, for he is (re)creating what is already his creation. The so-called "model" for Julie enters Rousseau's life only after her fictional *sosie*'s existence has begun—Rousseau/Pygmalion simply acknowledges his creation. In the entire Rousseau/Sophie d'Houdetot relationship of which the moral letters serve as an emblem, teaching and fiction-making conspire to control the relationship's outcome and the verdict of history on it. Rousseau attempts to use this conspiracy to manipulate the woman he sees as his heroine incarnate according to the strategies developed in the novel with which she is so closely aligned.

Teaching in *La Nouvelle Héloïse* is first of all a form of determination, the means by which characters try to blind other characters, and Rousseau tries to blind his reader, into accepting their/his moral universe as a beneficent one. The goal of this teaching is to convert the student (reader) by controlling his response. However, that goal of non-erotic seduction is rarely, if ever, reached, since all the acts of teaching in the novel ultimately end in a lack of control, an *écart* veering into madness. *La Nouvelle Héloïse* really becomes a "teaching" novel only when Rousseau either loses or abandons control of his characters to add long passages on subjects to which he has a moral commitment but which are either out-of-character for the characters, or at the very least, inappropriate for the context in which they are inserted. Thus, Saint-Preux, supposedly wild with love, interrupts the accounts he has been giving of his passion in order to show off to his beloved the merits of his pedagogical system, even though he has already admitted that neither of them has been paying much attention to the fine points of classroom instruction. Julie, in a similar state, delivers a long lecture on wine and its virtues (I, iii). At such moments, and these are but two examples of a repeated occurrence, Rousseau the pedagogue deprives Rousseau the novelist of his instincts, alienates him from his fiction. These are truly marginal passages, textual aberrations, moments when *La Nouvelle Héloïse* is a narrative gone mad.

This loss of control or deviation is, I believe, inherent in Rousseau's pedagogical model. The Rousseauian *précepteur* functions, in terms of Lévi-Strauss's distinction in *The Savage Mind*, as a *bricoleur*, rather than a scientist. Lévi-Strauss explains his distinction in this way: the scientist (he uses the example of an engineer) faced with a problem "is always trying to make his way out of and go beyond the constraints imposed by a particular state of civilization while the 'bricoleur' by inclination or necessity always remains within them."[11] The scientist is a man of the future, a proponent of progress, an individual who traffics in abstractions and concepts and who invents new tools for each new job. The *bricoleur*, firmly anchored in origins and the past, is less an inventor than a remodeler. "The rules of his game are always to make do with 'whatever is at hand' that is to say with a set of tools

11. Claude Lévi-Strauss, *The Savage Mind*, (The University of Chicago Press, 1966), p. 19.

and materials which is always finite." From his already formed stock of materials, the *bricoleur* chooses those appropriate for the job at hand. His means are always already there, while the scientist is constantly forced to create his. The *bricoleur* manipulates a stock of second-hand remnants, fragments with a past that he deconstructs, reconstructs, and reshuffles. And even when he shapes these borrowed fragments into new formations, the *bricoleur* does not sever them completely from the context of their origin. This creature of memory never forgets that his reality is shrouded in what Lévi-Strauss terms "a certain amount of human culture" ["Une certaine épaisseur d'humanité"].[12]

Both Rousseau's philosophy of education and the end results he hopes to achieve have marked affinities with the techniques of *bricolage*. The model he terms "éducation négative,"[13] "éducation (or "méthode") inactive," or "éducation solitaire" is clearly past-oriented, profoundly conservative, resolutely unprogressive, and just as resolutely prudent (anti-risk). It is a system that makes wasting time, rather than gaining it, its most important rule. The entire educational process strives to take place in slow motion. Certain forms of ignorance are valorized. Above all, the educator is told to efface himself whenever possible and simply let nature take its course. Less is more: "Peu lire et beaucoup méditer nos lectures," as Saint-Preux suggests to Julie (I, xii, 57). Erudition is less valuable than a well-formed head. Once again according to Saint-Preux: "il vaut toujours mieux trouver de soi-même les choses qu'on trouveroit dans les livres: c'est le vrai secret de les bien mouler à sa tête et de se les approprier" (p. 58). And as Julie, one-upping her former teacher, later points out to Saint-Preux, the well-formed head should be nothing more than a head shaped according to nature's laws and a head made receptive to nature's lessons. A child is impressionable: "pour que toutes les idees . . . qui se rapportent à son bonheur et l'éclairent sur ses devoirs s'y tracent de bonne heure en caracteres inéfaçables, et lui servent à se conduire pendant sa vie d'une maniere convenable à son être et à ses facultés" (V, iii, 580).

Both the Rousseauian educator and the *bricoleur* seem to be paragons of prudence. They proceed slowly and with all due caution, avoid risk, never venture out into the void of the unknown. The *bricoleur* is comfortable in the possession of a finite set of tools, already tried and tested (albeit for other purposes), which can be manipulated to handle any task imaginable. The educator's role seemingly involves even fewer risks: to form a mind, he has only to engrave upon it laws that, because they are natural, must already be there in some pre-formed state. Neither "system" contains provisions for

12. Ibid., pp. 11 and 20.
13. Certainly an appropriate title on the linguistic level, since the incidence of negative constructions and verbs like "supprimer" is remarkable throughout the passages dealing with educational matters.

failure. It is the nature of the *bricoleur*'s genius to be able to fix anything with what is at hand. All of the Rousseauian *précepteur*'s educational experiments are successful: the child, however recalcitrant, never fails to come around in the end, and consequently no provision is made for the possibility of his refusal to "learn." For both of them, patience and repetition are the keys to success.

Yet such fundamental aspects of their common stance as the desire for success without risk, their rejection of failure, and their belief in the existence of a finite number of tools, materials, laws, or possibilities—all these positions are in a sense contrary to the origins of *bricolage*. *Bricolage*, as Lévi-Strauss reminds us, has its roots in deviation and surprise, rather than in predictable success:

> In its old sense the verb "bricoler" applied to ball games and billiards, to hunting, shooting and riding. It was however always used with reference to some extraneous movement: a ball rebounding, a dog straying or a horse swerving from its direct course to avoid an obstacle.

Today, all that remains of the deviousness initially linked to *bricolage* lies in the realm of technique: "And in our own time the 'bricoleur' is still someone who works with his hands and uses devious means compared to those of a craftsman."[14] Lévi-Strauss fails to note, however, a crucial shift in deviousness. Originally, the deviation of *bricolage* seems accidental and unconscious, made by either an animal or an inanimate object. The movement might be self-protective (the horse avoiding the obstacle), and it is always "natural" and beyond the control of either the sportsman riding the horse or the player hitting the ball. In the case of the modern-day *bricoleur*, however, the deviousness is no longer "natural," but rather a conscious choice of technique. Furthermore, it has shifted its association from the so-called object (the horse or the ball) to the subject (the man manipulating the objects). I say "so-called" object, because, in the case of the original meaning of "bricoler," the deviation could be considered a movement toward subjectivization, a form of self-assertion, albeit unconscious or instinctive, on the part of the animal or ball allegedly in the sportsman or gamesman's control. When it swerves, it momentarily escapes the ruling hand and the pre-conceived plan. *(Bricolage could be the essense of sport: without it, perfect control would guarantee victory.)* However, the deviousness of the modern *bricoleur* shows no lack of control, but is simply the code governing his technical arsenal.

Lévi-Strauss explores one technique from this devious arsenal, reduction in size or miniaturization ("le modèle réduit"). He chooses to do so because he is interested in defining the *bricoleur*'s relationship to the artist, and feels that this technique is precisely what the artist has in common with (borrows from?)

14. *The Savage Mind*, p. 16.

the *bricoleur.* ("Now the question arises whether the small-scale model or miniature . . . may not in fact be the universal type of the work of art.") It is Lévi-Strauss's remarks on the psychology of reduction in size that interest me here, because of their relevance for an understanding of the *bricoleur*—and, more importantly, of the Rousseauian teacher:

What is the virtue of reduction. . . ? It seems to result from a sort of reversal in the process of understanding. To understand a real object in its totality we always tend to work from its parts. The resistance it offers us is overcome by dividing it. Reduction in scale reverses this situation. Being smaller, the object as a whole seems less formidable.[15]

Miniaturization, it seems, is adopted as a result of the *bricoleur*/teacher's insecurity and his attempted rejection of risk and failure. Such excessive prudence must stem from a fear that the object being controlled could somehow step out of line (and out of control)— from a fear of the original swerve of *bricoler.* Reduction in size therefore means also reduction in fearfulness: the miniature is more easily knowable, more easily controllable.[16]

The evocation of miniaturization in connection with *La Nouvelle Héloïse* evidently brings the subject of gardening to mind. Reduction in size is the basic technique used in Chinese gardens and such gardens appear at first glance to have a great deal in common with Julie's Elisée. Technically, one of the principal ways in which Chinese gardens are opposed to French and Italian gardens, the enemies of her Elisée, is precisely by their use of miniaturization. As André Haudricourt points out:

If [in Chinese gardens] one wants to have plants with small dimensions, instead of acting directly and pruning them, one acts indirectly to obtain dwarf plants. Direct action thus seems to lead to artifice, indirect action appears to be a return to nature.[17]

A garden with the appearance of a return to nature—what could be more in the spirit of Julie's horticultural goals? However, Saint-Preux's description of the Chinese gardens he visited during his travels works to abolish the possibility of this comparison:

J'ai vu à la Chine des jardins . . . faits avec tant d'art que l'art n'y paroissoit point, mais d'une maniere si dispensieuse et entretenus à si grands frais que cette idée m'ôtoit tout le plaisir que j'aurois pu goûter à les voir . . . On n'y voyoit à la vérité ni belles allées ni compartimens réguliers, mais on y voyoit entassées avec profusion des merveilles qu'on

15. Ibid., p. 23.
16. "And even if this is an illusion, the point of the procedure is to create or sustain the illusion, which gratifies the intelligence and gives rise to a sense of pleasure which can already be called aesthetic," p. 24. Lévi-Strauss's remark could lead to a discussion of the aesthetic function of miniaturization in the Rousseauian educational model.
17. André Haudricourt, "Domestication des animaux, culture des plantes, et traitement d'autrui," *L'Homme*, #2 (1962), 42–3.

ne trouve qu'éparses et séparées. La nature s'y présentoit sous mille aspects divers, et le tout ensemble n'étoit pas naturel. [IV, xi, 484][18]

With the exception of excessive cost and maintenance, which Julie is careful to avoid, all of Saint-Preux's objections could be extended to Julie's garden: it, too, is "fait avec tant d'art que l'art n'y paroissoit point," and, appearances to the contrary, the least that can be said about it is that "le tout ensemble n'étoit pas naturel."

Saint-Preux's principal criticism of the Chinese garden stems from its miniaturization of nature: all the natural beauties it contains could not be found naturally in one place. Yet even he is surprised by the number and the variety of plants in Julie's *"prétendu* verger"—and how could he help but be, since he notes in it: "massifs, grands berceaux, touffes pendantes, bosquets bien ombragés . . . serpolet, baume, thim, marjolaine et d'autres herbes odorantes, *mille* fleurs des champs, quelques unes de jardin"—(p. 484; my italics) and the list is far from complete? If the two gardens are indeed created on the same principle, then why does Rousseau have Saint-Preux deny their similarity? Is he blinded to the resemblance, or does he condemn miniaturization out of a fear that his own affinities with it will be uncovered, in this and other domains? In *La Nouvelle Héloïse*, the step from gardening to teaching is a short one: some of the longest informative digressions are consecrated to gardening, and one of the novel's central pedagogical acts takes place in Julie's unnaturally natural garden. Could not the same criticisms reserved by Saint-Preux for Chinese gardens also be applied to the teaching methods favored both by Julie and, more elaborately, by Emile's *précepteur* in dealing with their pupils?

Let me illustrate what I mean here with one example from each work. Julie describes at some length the technique she uses to inspire in her eldest son the desire to read (her formulation is more passive than mine: "comment lui est venu le goût d'apprendre à lire," V, iii, 581). She writes tales especially tailored to his concerns and uses every means possible to heighten his interest in her readings of them. Then: "quand je le voyois le plus avidement attentif, je me souvenois quelquefois d'un ordre à donner, et je le quittois à l'endroit le plus intéressant en laissant négligemment le livre" (p. 582). All those who could have continued the child's pleasure are in on the plot—everyone he turns to has been instructed to refuse to read to him. At last, someone suggests "secretly" that he should learn to read for himself. He likes this idea, and

18. "I have seen gardens in China . . . laid out with so much art that the art was not seen, but in such a costly manner, and kept up at such a vast expense, that the single idea destroyed all the pleasure I had in viewing them . . . It is true, there were no fine walks or regular compartments; but you might see curiosities heaped together with profusion, which in nature are only to be found separate and scattered. Nature was there represented under a thousand various forms, and yet the whole taken together was not natural" (II, 138).

searches for a teacher, but his troubles are not over yet. His search, too, becomes transformed into a "nouvelle difficulté qu'on n'a poussée qu'aussi loin qu'il faloit." In Julie's opinion, this complex scenario serves as an illustration of a purely natural educational model:

C'est ainsi que livrés au penchant de leur coeur, sans que rien le déguise ou l'altere, nos enfans ne reçoivent point une forme extérieure et artificielle, mais conservent exactement celle de leur caractere originel (p. 584).

If the reader realizes that Julie's child is a "captive of a clever plot," as Starobinski phrases it, then he will have difficulty accepting this explanation. Julie's child is educated, just as a Chinese garden is laid out, by means of indirection that masquerades as a return to nature's ways. The child is batted around like the ball in the original *bricolage;* he is a plaything in a so-called "natural" method in which there is so much art and so much artifice that, once again according to Starobinski: "We sense deception in the way in which the masters arrange the objects designed to make an impression on the 'âmes sensibles.' "[19] Or, to borrow Saint-Preux's expression: "le tout ensemble n'étoit pas naturel."

The scenario devised by Julie to "allow" her child to preserve the form of his "caractere originel" is overshadowed by some of the lavish plots concocted by Emile's teacher for his pupil's equally natural education. The most unnatural events are staged with a view to making them appear natural (at least to the child). One of the many pedagogical acts described in *Emile* is aimed at reforming a certain "petit tiran" who tries to manipulate everyone around him. The child allegedly learns his lesson when his temporary *précepteur,* Rousseau, refuses to accompany him on an outing. His teacher describes with evident satisfaction how the headstrong child goes out alone for his walk and walks into, not only a trap, but a play:

Tout étoit preparé d'avance et comme il s'agissoit d'une espéce de scéne publique je m'étois muni du consentement du père. A peine avoit-il fait quelque pas qu'il entend à droite et à gauche différens propos sur son compte. Voisin, le joli Monsieur! où va-t-il ainsi tout seul? Il va se perdre . . . Un peu plus loin il rencontre des poliçons à peu pres de son age, qui l'agacent et se moquent de lui. Plus il avance, plus il trouve d'embarras. Seul et sans protection, il se voit le joüet de tout le monde (IV, 367-8).[20]

He is, of course, just that, the plaything of all the falsely innocent passers-by, and especially of the author and director of this vignette who has the pleasure

19. *La Transparence et l'obstacle,* p. 257.
20. "Everything was prepared in advance and since it involved a kind of public scene, I had protected myself with the father's consentment. He had hardly taken a few steps when he hears all around him different remarks about him. Neighbor, the handsome Gentleman! Where is he going all alone? He'll get lost . . . A little farther he meets some rascals of about his age, who taunt him and make fun of him. The farther he goes, the more trouble he encounters. Alone and without protection, he finds himself everyone's plaything."

of imagining it all and then controlling it from afar. This open-air lesson borrows both its structure and at least part of its inspiration from the theatre. One of Rousseau's friends follows his student providing from time to time commentary on what is happening to him, commentary designed to make him fully appreciate the danger of his actions: "Ce rolle qui étoit à peu prés celui de Sbrigani dans *Pourceaugnac* demandoit un homme d'esprit" (p. 368).

This lesson can be considered "natural," only insofar as theatrical mimesis is natural—and surely Rousseau's views on that subject are not easy to reconcile with Julie's opinion of the teaching method they share. Rousseau's pedagogical lesson has in common with Chinese gardens not only a use of indirect action that mimics natural forces while remaining purely artificial, but also their miniaturization of nature's riches. Saint-Preux attacks the Chinese horticultural method because it assembles a variety of plants that in nature could be found only in separate places. But surely the number of individuals and situations brought together at the "tyrant"'s doorstep to produce this little paranoia play for his "benefit" could not be considered a natural configuration! There is a great deal of art in this teaching,[21] and very little effort to imagine the child's "caractere originel" as anything but what the *précepteur* decides it should be.

This inability to encourage individuality and refusal to view the student/ other as anything but a projection of the teacher and his desires are traits common to various Rousseauian pedagogues. Claire's attempt to make Julie understand her influence on all those around her also helps elucidate the functioning of Julie's pedagogical model:

Voila ce qui doit arriver à toutes les ames d'une certaine trempe; elles transforment pour ainsi dire les autres en elles-mêmes; elles ont une sphere d'activité dans laquelle rien ne leur resiste: on ne peut les connoitre sans les vouloir imiter, et de leur sublime élévation elles attirent à elles tout ce qui les environne. C'est pour cela, ma chere, que ni toi ni ton ami ne connoîtrez peut-être jamais les hommes; car vous les verrez bien plus comme vous les ferez, que comme ils seront d'eux-mêmes. Vous donnerez le ton à tous ceux qui

21. The Rousseauian *précepteur* puts so much art in his own teaching that he comes to suspect it in every pedagogical act. In *Emile,* he explains the source of one of his techniques: "L'idée de rendre Emile amoureux avant de le faire voyager n'est pas de mon invention. Voici le trait qui me l'a suggérée" (IV, 853). He was in Venice "en visite chez le gouverneur d'un jeune Anglois." A letter arrives which the governor reads to his pupil. The letter is in English and Emile's teacher "n'y compris rien; mais durant la lecture je vis le jeune homme déchirer de tres belles manchettes de point qu'il portoit, et les jetter au feu l'une aprés l'autre." He asks the governor what this means, and he explains that his pupil ripped up the cuffs given him by a Venetian lady, because the letter he was reading contained a description of the young English lady to whom M. John is promised, Miss Lucy, working on a pair for him. John leaves the room, and the French teacher, incapable of imagining a lesson that is not the product of artifice, asks the English one if he had set up the whole scene by inventing the letter against the Venetian lady: "Non, me dit-il, la chose est réelle; je n'ai pas mis tant d'art à mes soins, j'y ai mis de la simplicité, . . . et Dieu a béni mon travail" (p. 854). Emile's *précepteur,* of course, fails to heed this call for simplicity. He will make this "natural" lesson "unnatural," when he forces his student's education to follow the model it establishes.

vivront avec vous; ils vous fuiront ou vous deviendront semblables, et tout ce que vous aurez vu n'aura peut-être rien de pareil dans le reste du monde. [II, v, 204][22]

According to the terms of Claire's description, neither Julie nor Saint-Preux could ever be capable of creating an educational system whose goal would be the preservation of the pupil's "caractere originel." They could never know anyone outside themselves to that extent, since all their dealings with outsiders are based on assimilation. They "transform . . . les autres en [eux]-mêmes." All those who do not flee them, become like them. Julie and Saint-Preux control those with whom they come into contact by making them into carbon copies of themselves. And if the outsider to be assimilated happens to be a child, then those copies can only be reductions in size, or miniatures. Julie and Saint-Preux show themselves to be true masters of the art of teaching as *bricolage* whenever they imagine elaborate (pedagogical) scenarios and force their students-become-miniatures to move through them with no more control over what is happening than that possessed by the ball in the original game of *bricolage*.[23]

There is, of course, one major methodological error in their pedagogical system. These modern *bricoleurs* practice their devious methods, oblivious to the swerve of resistance inscribed in the origin of *bricoler*. The deviation that marks the original essence of *bricolage*, the (self-assertive) swerve of the object in motion can be linked to the Lucretian notion of the *clinamen:*

While the first bodies are being carried downwards by their own weight in a straight line through the void, at times quite uncertain and uncertain places [sic], they swerve a little from their course, just so much as you might call a change of motion. For if they were not apt to incline, all would fall downwards like raindrops through the profound void, no collision would take place and no blow would be caused among the first-beginnings: thus nature would never have produced anything.[24]

22. "This is what always will be effected by minds of a certain temper. They transform, in a manner, every other into their own likeness; having a sphere of activity wherein nothing can resist their power. It is impossible to know without imitating them, while from their own sublime elevation they attract all that are about them. It is for this reason, my dear, that neither you nor your friend will perhaps ever know mankind; for you will rather see them such as you model them, than such as they are in themselves. You will lead the way for all those among whom you live; others will either imitate you or leave you; and perhaps you will meet with nothing in the world similar to what you have hitherto seen" (I, 273).

23. The editor of this issue has suggested that Julie and Saint-Preux should be referred to as either "bonzai *bricoleurs*" or "headshrinkers."

24. Lucretius, *De rerum natura*, tr. W.H.D. Rouse, Loeb Classical Library (Cambridge; Harvard, 1975), p. 113.

The Lucretian notion of the *clinamen* has recently been discussed by Michel Serres. See his *La Naissance de la physique dans le texte de Lucrèce* (Paris: Editions de Minuit, 1977). This and other Lucretian notions (via Serres) are used by Jeffrey Mehlman in a reading of Diderot's *Lettre sur les aveugles* and *Lettres sur les sourds et muets.* "Cararact: Diderot's Discursive Politics, 1749–51," *Glyph*, #2 (1977), 37–63.

A final note on the importance of the *clinamen* for Rousseau. Starobinski develops René

Like the swerve in *bricolage*, the *clinamen* describes an object's (an atom's) natural movement. I introduce the Lucretian notion here, because his definition of the *clinamen* suggests that the deviation from a straight course that I have interpreted, in the case of *bricolage*, as a possible movement toward subjectivization is linked to the essence of natural creation. Without the *clinamen*, there would be no progress.[25]

The *clinamen* at the origin of *bricolage* might be attributed to a self-assertive movement or a movement toward subjectivization on the part of the *jouet*, but in the case of a human being become plaything, this interpretation is inevitable. A note by W.H.D. Rouse to his translation of *De Rerum natura* comments on the origin of the *clinamen*. What Lucretius calls the *clinamen* "is no part of the theory of Democritus, but was added by Epicurus in order to use it later in his explanation of human freewill."[26] In the Lucretian system, the *clinamen* is not only the swerve that takes place "at times quite uncertain and uncertain places" during the free fall through the void made by particles of matter. The term also applies to movements of human will, the will Lucretius calls "wrested from the fates.": "Don't we also swerve at no fixed time or place, but where our mind directs us?"[27] The examples he gives of free will portray it as a defensive force used, for instance, to resist a foreign will in conflict with our own. A blow from an external body may force the matter in our bodies in one direction, but that undesired movement lasts only until "our will has curbed it [i.e., the matter of the body] back through the limbs." Our will propels us to swerve and thus defend ourselves against foreign control.

The last and most disturbing pedagogical act in *La Nouvelle Héloïse* provides an unsettling illustration of the *clinamen* as an act of resistance. Claire's daughter, Henriette, makes co-education possible in the novel, and she also exemplifies the pedagogical technique of miniaturization. Claire does not even wait for Julie to carry out her usual assimilation on her, but transfers Henriette completely to her cousin's control: "sois dès aujourd'hui la mere de celle qui doit être ta Bru, et pour me la rendre plus chere encore, fais en s'il se peut une autre Julie. Elle te ressemble déja de visage" (IV, ix, 43). In fact, Henriette resembles Julie so closely that, after the transfer, strangers always

---

Hubert's use of the term to describe what goes wrong when man enters history, when with his work he starts to fight nature. When man leaves the state of nature and his original goodness "something was mysteriously distorted *between* man and the world. An uncoupling (a 'clinamen,' writes René Hubert) took place." *La Transparence et l'obstacle*, p. 346.

25. For the notion of the *clinamen* as progress, Harold Bloom's discussions of "creative revisionism" and (mis)reading as *clinamens* immediately come to mind. I will return to them in my conclusion. "Clinamen or Poetic Misprision," in *The Anxiety of Influence* (Oxford, 1973).

26. Lucretius, p. 112.

27. Ibid., p. 115.

Interestingly enough, the first example Lucretius gives of the effect of free will on movement is that of a race horse, so this description of the *clinamen* could be associated with one of the original swerves of *bricoler*.

take Julie for her mother (V, vi, 601–2). After Julie's death, Wolmar, heretofore the author of a system of child pedagogy, but never an active teacher of children, briefly takes on Henriette's "instruction," and thereby provides evidence to suggest that teaching is a dangerous act in any hands. As he explains to Saint-Preux, he attempts to use her as an instrument in a typical Rousseauian teaching play aimed at consoling Claire:

Vous savez que sa fille ressemble beaucoup à Madame de Wolmar. Elle se plaisoit à marquer cette ressemblance par des robes de même étoffe, et elle leur avoit apporté de Genève plusieurs ajustemens semblables, dont elles se paroient les mêmes jours. Je fis donc habiller Henriette le plus à l'imitation de Julie qu'il fut possible, et après l'avoir bien instruite, je lui fis occuper à table le troisieme couvert (VI, xi, 739).

At first, Henriette responds perfectly to his teaching.

Henriette, fiere de réprésenter sa petite Maman, joua parfaitement son rolle, et si parfaitement que je vis pleurer les domestiques. Cependant elle donnoit toujours à sa mere le nom de Maman, et lui parloit avec le respect convenable.

There is, of course, one important departure from the usual structure in this particular teaching vignette: for once, the child is not a victim, "le joüet de tout le monde," but an actor toying with the sensibilities of an adult victim. Perhaps this explains the conclusion of Wolmar's lesson:

Enhardie par le succès, . . . elle s'avisa de porter la main sur une cuillere et de dire dans une saillie: Claire, veux-tu de cela? Le geste et le ton de voix furent imités au point que sa mere en tresaillit.

Far from consoling Claire, the play drives her to the brink of madness:

. . . elle se mit a manger avec une avidité qui me surprit. En la considérant avec attention, je vis de l'égarement dans ses yeux . . . Je l'empêchai de manger davantage, et je fis bien; car une heure après elle eut une violente indigestion . . . Dès ce moment, je résolus de supprimer ces jeux, qui pouvoient allumer son imagination au point qu'on n'en seroit plus maître. [pp. 739–40][28]

28. "You know how much her daughter resembles Mrs. Wolmar; that she took a pleasure in heightening that resemblance, by dressing her in the same manner, having brought several cloaths for her from Geneva, in which she used to dress her like Eloisa. I ordered Harriet therefore to be dressed as much in imitation of Eloisa as possible, and, after having given her her lesson, placed her at table where Eloisa used to sit . . . Harriet, proud to represent her little mama, played her part extremely well; so well indeed that I observed the servants in waiting shed tears. She nevertheless always gave the name of mama to her mother, and addressed her with proper respect. Encouraged by success and my approbation, she ventured to put her hand to the soup-spoon and cried Clara, my dear, do you chuse any of this? the gesture, tone and manner, in which she spoke this, were so like those of Eloisa, that it made her mother tremble . . . She then began to eat with an eagerness that surprised me. Looking at her with some attention, I saw something wild in her eyes . . . I prevented her from eating any more, and 'twas well I did so; for, an hour after she was taken extremely ill with a violent surfeit . . . From this time I resolved to try no more projects of this kind, as they might affect her imagination too much" (II, 242–43).

This scene is recounted only five pages before the end of Rousseau's immense novel and provides therefore one of its last images, that of teaching gone haywire, out of control. As the originator of Julie's pedagogical system, Wolmar is the archetypal teacher of the "redemptive" part of the novel. He performs, or rather has performed, a corrective lesson whose every aspect is subject to his control, from the costumes ("je fis habiller Henriette le plus à l'imitation de Julie qu'il fut possible") to the acting ("après l'avoir bien instruite"). The central figure in his production, his marionette, is designed to remain completely his creature, for she is a perfect miniature, and therefore both instantly knowable in her totality and "moins redoutable." Julie herself controlled all others, and through her refusal to see others for what they were, transformed them into reductions of herself. After her death, Wolmar attempts to rechannel and contain her formidable powers. For once, it is not Julie who turns the child into a miniature projection of her desires, but an outside will that imitates her technique of reduction in size, and in the process attempts to control, not so much the child miniaturized, as the child's model, the chief proponent of teaching as *bricolage*, Julie. As Lévi-Strauss explains, "a child's doll is no longer . . . a rival."[29]

But here, in *La Nouvelle Héloïse*'s last pedagogical vignette, the devious origin of *bricoler* takes its toll with a double swerve in the planned structure of the lesson. Henriette refuses to be confined to her non-speaking part. She pits her will against Wolmar's, and breaks out of his control, at least momentarily. She refuses to be objectified, and her self-assertion constitutes a swerve beyond the pre-imposed limits. Henriette's imitation of Julie's gesture and speech is a *clinamen*, a self-defensive reaction of her will against the will attempting to impose its control. And in this human billiard game, with her swerve she hits another ball, causing it to swerve in turn. So Claire, too, breaks out of Wolmar's sphere of influence with her own instinctive *clinamen*. Her "violente indigestion" is a concrete sign of the movement, a deviation from physical equilibrium. Wolmar's mastery was designed to relieve her grief; his loss of control brings her, and all involved in the "lesson," to the brink of madness. It is clear from this incident that Wolmar is incapable of the indirect control that can make artifice pass for a return to nature. He is forced to intervene directly to try to stamp out the madness that threatens Clarens: "je résolus de supprimer tous ces jeux."

In Wolmar's account of the scene, there is a curious vagueness in the last sentences. After the phrase "sa mere en tresaillit," he uses no further nouns or proper nouns to help the reader work his way through the maze of "elle" and "la" in his description of feminine "égarement." This results in a certain confusion: at times, it is easy to imagine that the madwoman he is describing is Henriette. Wolmar's suppression of the proper name contributes to a

29. *The Savage Mind*, p. 23.

generalization of feminine madness. It is easy to see why he views the *clinamen* as a form of madness. It is a deviation, a loss of control, and, in the eyes of the *maître* who had gone to extraordinary lengths to put himself in complete control of the situation, it is a break in the fortifications of his universe. As he fights for control, the Rousseauian *précepteur* is always struggling against the potential for deviation, for madness, inherent in the pedagogical act. He shows us teaching as a movement to establish control, but also as a fear of the loss of control. Despite its fear of deviation, the pedagogical act consistently unfolds in its own mad universe. The teacher plays a role, transforms himself into another; he "instructs" his assistants in playing their parts, in becoming other—all for the purpose of altering the student according to the principles of miniaturization. Each lesson is a case of outrageous complexity believing itself to be, or at least calling itself, natural simplicity. According to Rousseau's own definition: "voulant être ce qu'on n'est pas, on parvient à se croire autre chose que ce qu'on est, et voilà comment on devient fou" (*seconde préface*, p. 21.) Small wonder that, in such a system, any deviation, any opposition to the all too carefully established order is perceived as madness.

The *clinamen* is also linked to the reappearance of erotic desire in the pedagogical act. In *La Nouvelle Héloïse,* a highly dogmatic working toward utopia allegedly suppresses and replaces the eroticism of the "classic" teacher/ student relationship. But the innocence of the Clarens community is obtained at a heavy price. *Bricolage*'s principal technique, miniaturization, can be viewed as a denial of adult sexuality. The miniature it creates inspires no fear, because it is either a-sexual or not sexually threatening. Claire describes the results of Julie's teaching on the sexuality at Clarens: "l'ame a-t-elle un sexe? En vérité, je ne le sens guere à la mienne.Je puis avoir des fantaisies, mais fort peu d'amour." (II, v, 206). Through assimilation (miniaturization), Claire is maintained as a child, capable of having, and being the object of, sexual fantasies, but not sexual love. She both perceives herself and is perceived as sexually pre-pubescent. She even denies her past sexual reproduction by giving her child to another mother.

Claire's strange musing on the soul's asexuality could be linked to the madness that the cousins' first teacher, Chaillot, always described as natural to her. It is perhaps because she bears in her origins the mark of difference that the deviating function of miniaturization is realized through her during the scene with Henriette. Claire is not, however, the only adult child at Clarens. In this letter and others, she addresses Julie as "mon enfant," a formula that, in this context, functions as much more than a term of endearment. And the adult most frequently miniaturized is, of course, Saint-Preux. In the flawless "monde à l'envers" situation that Clarens provides, the fallen "maître" becomes the "child" (and therefore the pupil) of his former students. As Claire puts it: "Toute la différence est que je vous aimois comme mon frere, et qu'à présent je vous aime comme mon enfant; car quoique nous soyons toutes deux plus jeunes que vous et même vos disciples, je vous regarde un peu comme le notre." (III, vi, 319). He is in the same position with regard to the father of teaching in Rousseau's "utopian" society, Wolmar, who, as Saint-Preux himself explains, "me parla comme un peu à son enfant" (IV, vi 423). In utopia, just as in Rousseau's own life, jealousy does not exist. How could it, in a world dominated by the desire to teach and be taught and one in which pedagogy is based on a form of miniaturization that represses the menace of adult sexuality? In *La Nouvelle Héloïse*, the "classic" model of pedagogical seduction is ultimately supplanted by a far more subtle variant of erotic manipulation in which the act of teaching works, not only to control, but also to redefine and set limits for the student's sexuality.[30]

Behind all the *clinamens* of my own argument lies a very simple belief: the Rousseauian educator may proclaim himself the champion of nature, but with his teaching he is actually working against nature. He fails to see the ultimate paradox of the *clinamen*—that this deviation, this unbalancing, is actually a progressive force, perhaps the only truly beneficent and progressive force in his, or any, pedagogical system. Lucretius explains that without the *clinamen*, "nature would never have produced anything." Final order can only be attained if there is deviation. The *clinamen*, this deviation from a straight line, is the one means by which order emerges from chaos.[31] The deviating atoms collide with other atoms, and from their collision matter is formed. Natural deviation (madness) is a prelude to creation. But the *précepteur* in Rousseau lives in dread of deviation. The most elaborate pedagogical scenarios are always devised to keep rebellious pupils in line. Perhaps a similar fear was partly responsible for Rousseau's own avoidance of all but long-distance, epistolary teaching, despite the fact that he wrote so often about this profession and claimed to love it. Or his fear of the pedagogical act might have been more complex—Rousseau was, after all, a self-taught man who avoided being a student just as carefully as he avoided being a teacher.[32]

In these pages devoted to the implications of Rousseau's pedagogical system, I find myself in the self-conscious position of being a teacher writing about an educational theorist writing about teachers. Certain generalizations inevitably come to mind. Rousseau's failure to allow for the pedagogical

30. The fetishistic objects in *La Nouvelle Héloïse*, such as Julie's corset, and especially her portrait, could also be considered forms of miniaturization.

31. After writing these lines, I discovered that Shoshana Felman's interpretation of the Lucretian system confirms my own. See her "De la nature des choses ou de l'écart à l'équilibre," *Critique*, January, 1979, pp. 3–15.

32. "Mon esprit veut marcher à son heure, il ne peut se soumettre à celle d'autrui" (*Confessions*, I, 119).

clinamen is certainly an all too common practice. No teacher can predict the moment when a hand will shoot up, signalling a question he or she has never before considered, a question that introduces an entirely new perspective on the material under consideration. The question acts as a *clinamen,* and because of it the class is, at least temporarily, out of the teacher's control. But the *clinamen* is formidable not only because it signals a loss of control. It cuts short what must be every teacher's and critic's dream: to find a reading so perfect that no deviation is necessary or possible, a reading that would not be already a deviation. Perhaps it is because all teachers are of necessity masters of deviation that we dread the supplementary swerve that puts our own *écart* into question, the *clinamen* that makes a teacher of the student. The ultimate Lucretian lesson seems to be this: a teacher always believes that the pedagogical act is his creation, but the students must actually take responsibility for it. Without their *clinamens,* no matter would be created, and classes would be only a perpetual free fall straight down through chaos.

JANE GALLOP

The Immoral Teachers

Aux hommes de trente-six ans

"I'm just wild about fourteen."
—Donovan, "Mellow Yellow"

The Marquis de Sade's *Philosophie dans le boudoir* is a group of dialogues staging the sexual/philosophical initiation of a young girl. Also published under the title "Les Instituteurs immoraux" (The Immoral Teachers), this book can be read as Sade's major consideration of the pleasures and dangers of pedagogy. There are several other instances of immoral instruction in Sade's fiction, and inasmuch as certain structural details repeat across textual boundaries, we will read an enlarged text which I call "The Immoral Teachers," a title traditionally part of the Sadian catalogue, but not actually the proper title of any text by Sade. In fact, there may be some sense in treating the entirety of Sade's writings as a meditation on teaching, in that what is continually, repeatedly represented is a confrontation between ignorance as innocence and knowledge as power—a confrontation constitutive of the classroom dialectic. What insists in Sade's writing is the drive to "teach someone a lesson."

Philosophy in the Bedroom has been the pretext for essays by both Jacques Lacan and Luce Irigaray. These two articles will not be our explicit concern here, but may be considered—to borrow Barbara Johnson's phrase—our "frame of reference."[1] The fact that both the "master" of the Freudian School of Paris and one of the leading French feminist theorists (herself a psychoanalyst and an ex-teacher in the Lacanian department at Vincennes) should write about Sade's pornographic philosophical dialogues serves as documentation that a reading of this text might be situated at the busy intersection of French psychoanalysis and feminism.

The one thing that both Irigaray and Lacan say in common about Sade's dialogues is that they lay bare an institutional structure that is usually covered

1. Jacques Lacan, "Kant avec Sade," originally published in *Critique* 191 (avril, 1963); collected in *Ecrits* (Seuil, 1966). Irigaray, " 'Françaises,' ne faites plus un effort . . .", originally published in *La Quinzaine littéraire* 238 (août, 1976); collected in *Ce Sexe qui n'en est pas un* (Minuit, 1977). These two articles are, in fact, my explicit concern in "Impertinent Questions," *Sub-stance* 26. The term "frame of reference" refers to Barbara Johnson's article by that title in *Yale French Studies* 55/56. Our reference to it here marks our doubts about the present text and its "framing" of literature.

117

over. According to Lacan, Sade exposes the "anal-sadistic" in education; according to Irigaray, what is exhibited is "the sexuality that subtends our social order." Taking our cue from this, we propose an examination of what is laid bare. Such an examination is a classic Sadian scene: the object is stripped and her/his body carefully examined and commented upon before any intercourse with it.

One of Sade's contributions to pedagogical technique may be the institution, alongside the traditional oral examination, of an anal examination. The Sadian libertines have a technical term for such an examination; they use the verb *socratiser* (to socratize), meaning to stick a finger up the anus. This association between the great philosopher/teacher and this form of anal penetration reminds us of the Greek link between pedagogy and pederasty. A quick look at the sexuality Sade exposes behind the pedagogical institution could certainly suggest pederasty. The "master" in *Philosophy in the Bedroom*, Dolmancé, is an advocate of buggery, who indeed refuses on principle "normal" penile-vaginal intercourse. The other schoolmaster in Sade's fiction, Rodin, who appears in *Justine* and *La nouvelle Justine*, likewise will only penetrate asses. Both Rodin and Dolmancé are thirty-six years old[2] and have anal intercourse with their students who are just pubescent, from twelve to sixteen.

Pederasty is undoubtedly a useful paradigm for classic Western pedagogy. A greater man penetrates a lesser man with his knowledge. The student is empty, a receptacle for the phallus; the teacher is the phallic fullness of knowledge. In the classroom the students are many; the teacher unique. Unicity is a primary phallic attribute. The fact that teacher and student are of the same sex but of different ages contributes to the interpretation that the student has no otherness, nothing different than the teacher, simply less.

This structure and its sexual dynamic become explicit in Sade. The student is an innocent, empty receptacle, lacking his own desires, having desires "introduced" into him by the teacher. If the phallus is a sign of desire, then the student has no phallus of his own, no desires, is originally innocent. The loss of innocence, the loss of ignorance, the process of teaching, is the introduction of desire from without into the student, is the "introduction" of the teacher's desire. From the first dialogue of Sade's *Philosophy*: "we will place in this pretty little head all the principles of the most unbridled libertinage, we will inflame it with *our fires* . . . we will inspire in it *our desires*."[3]

2. Actually, it is only in *La nouvelle Justine* that Rodin is 36. In *Justine*, he is 40, and in *Infortunes de la vertu*, he is 35. All of these fall within the same "age group," but the fact that Sade bothered to revise the age with each version points to the puzzle of ages which we take up later in this paper.

3. Sade, *La Philosophie dans le boudoir, Oeuvres complètes* xxv (Pauvert, 1970), p. 19, italics mine. All translations mine.

But, although the pederasty behind pedagogy is exposed in Sade, this very exposure does something to alter its paradigmatic structure. The laying bare entails an exposure of the body with all its material, non-paradigmatic detail. And pederasty is, after all, an ideal, a Platonic structure. Let us reconsider the verb *socratiser*. Rather than the Platonic ideal of pederasty—intercourse between phallus and phallic receptacle—, socratizing is a specific non-phallic act. There is penetration, even anal penetration, but the penetrating agent is not unique (one has ten fingers), nor tied into a structure of specular opposition. There is no digital equivalent to the opposition phallic/castrated.

The discrepancy between the specific meaning of "socratizing" and the paradigmatic structure of pederasty is a discrepancy repeated in other aspects of Sadian education. *Philosophy in the Bedroom* is the education of a young girl, not a young boy, and Dolmancé's application of the pederastic model is somewhat disturbed by the encounter with sexual difference. And, just as the penetrating socratic finger is not unique, the introduction of sexuality into the ingénue in the dialogues is an example of team-teaching.

Eugénie (the ingénue of *Philosophy*) has two teachers, Dolmancé and Mme de Saint-Ange. Although in *Justine* Rodin is the only teacher at his school, in *La nouvelle Justine* he is joined by his sister. The sister's first name is Célestine, which seems to put her in the same orbit as Saint-Ange. Mlle Rodin, we are told, has replaced Rodin's late wife in *all* her wifely duties. A brother-sister incest, thus, underlies this example of team-teaching. Although Dolmancé and Saint-Ange are not related, Domancé is seconded by the Chevalier who *is* Saint-Ange's brother. The two siblings in *Philosophy*, like the two Rodin siblings, have long carried out a pleasurable incest.

The first dialogue of *Philosophy in the Bedroom* is a conversation between Saint-Ange and her brother, in which they set up the whole scene, the whole "education." Saint-Ange (26) supplies the 15-year-old girl; her brother (20) brings the 36-year-old man. In this case, the classic Sadian heterosexual pederastic structure stems from and in a sense replaces brother-sister incest.

It seems worthwhile to examine the relations between these two sexual models. Brother-sister incest plays out in a purified form, the question of sexual difference. Both partners are of the same generation and the same origin, so they can paradigmatically be thought to differ only by sex. The pederastic structure, as I have outlined it, ignores sexual difference and concentrates on age difference, difference of generations. It would seem that the move from brother-sister incest to heterosexual pederasty is a move away from sexual distinction and into classification by age.

The Chevalier, Saint-Ange's brother/lover, prefers vaginal penetration, whereas Dolmancé shuns that feminine orifice. The Chevalier has a larger penis than Dolmancé; but Dolmancé is older and more libertine (that is, less innocent). If phallic power were organized around sexual difference, the

Chevalier would be more phallic. But it is Dolmancé who is more phallic, more powerful, more masterly. He is the schoolmaster and director of the scenes. The Chevalier, when he tries to voice his ideas, is told to shut up and stick to his cocksmanship. He obeys meekly and at the end of the dialogues is dismissed. That Dolmancé should be more phallic with explicitly less penis is the mark that phallic power is attached to questions of knowledge, experience, and age, rather than to the sexual distinction. Thus the move from the brother-sister couple at the beginning of the dialogues to the pederast-ingénue couple is a move away from sexual difference, despite the fact, perhaps intentionally *to spite the fact* that the ingénue is female.

Age difference, in Sade, seems to function as a supplementary form of sexual difference, another mode of the distinction phallus/receptacle. *Philosophy in the Bedroom* begins with the invocation, "Voluptuaries of all ages and of all sexes . . . " Sade meticulously finds a way (even in the dialogues where there is no narrator) to inform the reader of every character's age. This is perhaps best understood in relation to the importance of pedagogy as a structuring model for Sade's fictional world. It is in school where one is classed by age group. The persistence of classification by age group throughout Sade makes even non-pedagogical institutions resemble schools—for example, the convent of Saint Mary of the Woods in the various versions of Justine's story and Silling Castle in *120 Days of Sodom*. As mentioned before, pederasty substitutes age difference for sexual difference, and age becomes the determinant sign for the distinction knowledge/innocence, which is to say phallus/receptacle. When the model of age difference replaces the model of sexual difference, ages come to occupy the place of sex organs. So in the Sadian school, ages fascinate and tantalize; the numbers become erogenous zones.

All these digits strewn through Sade's pages recall the digits that socratize. Those penetrating fingers might seem to be phallic substitutes, but their bodily specificity and marginality as well as their multiplicity deflate the model, belie the phallic expectation. Likewise, if one considers the phallus to be a centrally organized meaningful structure (reproductive genital sexuality rather than polymorphous perversity), the digits always promise some revelation of a centralized meaning, promise the erection of some system; but the promise is merely a tease, is never fulfilled. All the ages in Sade's book seem to be *on the verge* of organizing into a meaningful structure. For example: the fact that Dolmancé and Rodin (as well as Eugénie's father) are both 36; the fact that Eugénie is 15 which would allow her to attend Rodin's school where the pupils are between 12 and 16. But the ages never seem to fall into neat categories, as if the attempt to organize and divide the world scholastically were continually failing. The reader, to the extent that she wants to make sense of this text and its numbers, is drawn into the role of sadistic schoolmaster, trying to whip the unruly objects into shape and order, into neat rows and classes.

In *Justine*, we are told that Rodin has 14 pupils of each sex. He never admits any younger than 12 years old, and he dismisses them at 16. Prompted by a desire for order and symmetry, I at first read that the pupils ranged from 12 to 16. Certainly those are the numbers which appear in the text. This range makes 14 the median age, reinforcing the emphasis on that number, since there are 14 girls and 14 boys. But paying closer attention, I realized my assumption was incorrect. If the students are sent away at 16, there are no 16-year-old students. They range from 12 to 15, and 14 is not the center of the structure. My inattention to this detail, my misreading, was prompted by a desire (a desire solicited by the text) for all these cute little "numbers" to line up.

When Rodin reappears in *La nouvelle Justine*, Sade in fact alters the school's age policy so that in the later version the pupils are sent away at 17. In *La nouvelle Justine*, Rodin's pupils do indeed range from 12 to 16, centering the institution on 14. But it is too late, for in this expanded version of the novel, there are a hundred pupils of each sex, rather than 14. This appearance "too late" of the necessary piece to the pattern seems emblematic of the way Sade's numbers constantly seem about to reveal their significance, but then there is always something else, something new that necessitates another attempt at classification.

A more striking example of the ways Sade's text arouses and frustrates the reader's urge for order can be found in the scene in *Justine* of Rodin's punishing his disobedient pupils. The first student punished is a 14-year-old girl. She is followed by a 15-year-old boy, who is in turn succeeded by a 13-year-old girl. It appears that Rodin is alternating sexes, as well as centering the structure on 14, balancing out the 15 by following it with a 13. The 13-year-old girl is followed by a boy and then another girl. Ages for these two are not specified, but the sexual alternation continues. Rodin whips 9 students altogether, 5 boys and 4 girls, the last victim being a boy of 14. Ending with a 14-year-old boy seems to bear out the importance of 14 and to balance out the fact of beginning with a girl. The alternation of sexes bespeaks an impartiality on Rodin's part, a position of mastery beyond sexual difference, an indifference. Such an alternation thus follows the model of pederastic power, a model that ought to be equally applicable to male or female student, since the student's own sex is unimportant, either is but a blank, empty receptacle for Rodin's phallic mastery.

The reader is led to assume an orderly, elegant alternation of the sexes of Rodin's victims, because those mentioned separately do alternate. But this is a hasty interpretation, a premature presumption of the pederastic paradigm. Only 6 of the 9 victims are listed separately—the first 5 and the last 1. But if Rodin whipped 5 boys and 4 girls and began with a girl and ended with a boy, he must somewhere (in the undisclosed, in the veiled part of the scene) have done two boys in a row. This graphic, detailed text does not list all the victims' sexes separately, does not show the point where the symmetry, the order breaks down. This concealed break in the order marks Rodin's subjectivity, his desire, his loss of mastery. The truly masterful libertine would have no preferences, treat all the objects of his passions equally. Rodin's slight preference for boys—not the preference for boys he expresses in his pederastic discourse, but the one nearly covered over by a narration which gives the reader the quick impression that this is an orderly structure of alternation—is not the ideal, phallic pederasty of the teacher, but his specific, irrational, disorderly desire.

Thus this stock scene of corporal punishment is not reducible to the simple thesis that the teacher gets sadistic, sexual pleasure from his corrections. Not only does Rodin's non-masterful, non-mastered desire leave its mark, but the scene arouses and frustrates (arouses by frustrating?) the reader's drive for mastery. The disorderly detail elicits the reader's urge to reduce that detail to some thesis, some meaningful system, in other words, to class it. Is the reader's desire for orderly classes so different from the impulse behind the teacher's corrections of the disorderly students?

The tension between a desire for neat order and the specific details that seem outside any order enacts one of the central Sadian conflicts: the conflict between rational order, that is, "philosophy" and irrational bodily materiality. Sade's work seems to be a long, concerted effort to subsume the body, sexuality, desire, disorder into the categories of philosophy, of thought. But there is always some disorderly specific which exceeds the systematizing discourse, thus always necessitating another philosophical harangue. This tension also bespeaks a contradiction at the heart of pedagogy. The position of teacher implies a mastery over knowledge, a mastery only possible by mastering desire, by an ascesis transcending one's subjective position. "Sex education," especially one that chooses to join practice to theory, cannot help but make painfully evident the teacher's subjectivity, his desire, his inability to impose an impassive, orderly classification. Yet to exclude sex from education is to leave something outside the teacher's mastery, outside the teacher's knowledge, thus giving him a limited, which is to say a subjective position.

In Sade's text, the teacher's desire is not to be located in the explicit thematics of sex, in the schoolmaster's planned and directed sexual activities with their philosophical justifications and explanations, but in the little details that exceed the vast enterprise of categorization and systematization characteristic of the libertine philosopher. It is those details in Sade that are truly sexy, which is to say disorderly and disconcerting.

With all our philosophizing about classes and specificity, smoothing over the asperities of paragraphs full of digits, a certain number, insistent in its particularity, has been ignored. What of the number 14? What can the reader make of its near centrality? It is in Rodin's school that the number 14 prevails, and Rodin has a 14-year-old daughter named Rosalie, his only child. Perhaps Rosalie is in some way the center of her father's scholastic institution; perhaps the father-daughter relation is the heart, the meaning of this pederastic structure. Almost, but not quite. The relation between Rodin and his daughter is an incest, but one always consummated by anal intercourse. Again we find the structure I have called heterosexual pederasty, a structure situated at the intersection of heterosexuality (privileging sexual difference over other differences) and pederasty (privileging age difference). What results is not heterosexual pederasty as yet a third stable paradigm; rather the full force of this oxymoron persists as a tension, a conflict that never quite stabilizes into either of these two conventional ways of representing, modeling, and thus guaranteeing phallic specular opposition.

Rosalie is 14; her father/lover is 36 (or 35 or 40)[4]. In Sade's short story "Eugénie de Franval," the ingénue Eugénie is 14 when her father becomes her lover. Franval is explicitly his daughter's schoolmaster, having sole control of her education, and designing her curriculum. The name Eugénie suggests analogies with the ingénue heroine of *Philosophy in the Bedroom*. The latter work, of course, does not contain a father-daughter incest. But it is worth noting, on the grounds of digital substitutability, that Eugénie's father M. de Mistival, and her teacher Dolmancé are both 36, would thus both be in the same class. And the father authorizes this education of his daughtr and plans someday to take advantage of it. "I am glad to allow you the first harvest," he writes to her teachers, "but be assured nonetheless that you will have in part been working for me" (p. 291).

Rodin begins his punishment scene with a 14-year-old girl (same category as his daughter), but he and the scene climax with a 14-year-old boy. So it seems that his profession allows him to veer away from his incest with his daughter, in a pederastic direction through digital displacement (Rosalie = 14; 14 = 14, Rosalie's specificity and sexual difference are effaced). In *Philosophy in the Bedroom*, Eugénie's father is replaced by the bugger Dolmancé. Again one finds a displacement of father-daughter incest in the direction of pederasty. It is only in the short story "Eugénie de Franval," from the collection *Crimes de l'amour*, that the pedagogical relation coincides with father-daughter incest. It is also noteworthy that in this story the consummation is not anal intercourse.

How does the ingénue of the *Crimes de l'amour* story, Eugénie de Franval, compare with the pupil of the philosophical dialogues, Eugénie de Mistival? Nominally, the difference between them can be located in the contrast between "fran(c)" and "m(y)sti,"[5] a contrast between two sorts of "vals," two

4. See note 2 above.
5. In French, there is no difference in the pronunciation of "fran" and "franc," nor between "mysti" and "misti."

sorts of vales, of hollows, of receptacles. The vale in *Philosophy in the Bedroom* is misty, mysterious, mystical, from the Greek *mustes,* meaning "initiated." One might think of the anus, preferred receptacle of "the initiated," the knowledgeable, the experienced, the philosophers. In the short story, the vale is *franc,* frank, straightforward, open. If, as Lacan says, "the phallus can only play its role when veiled,"[6] then a misty[7] vale is a better receptacle for the phallus than a frank vale.

And so it would seem. Franval, who had always been libertine and inconstant, falls hopelessly in love with Eugénie. He refuses his patriarchal power which is the power to exchange her: he cannot bear to pass her on to any other man. If he cannot exchange her, he does not really possess her, and instead finds himself possessed by her. The story is a tragedy: this very powerful man loses everything out of passionate love for this eighteenth century Lolita. And in this case, it is not on account of her cruelty, for Eugénie loves her father unreservedly. Tragedy seems to result merely from the father's loss of patriarchal power, loss of the power to exchange his daughter.

No wonder Mistival allows someone else to gather the first harvests. Not only is the initiation to the mysteries displaced from Mistival to Dolmancé, but Dolmancé likewise refuses her *prémices,* her first fruits, her virginity, and hands them over to the Chevalier. This passing from hand to hand, from man to man, protects the phallus, veils it in mystery, vales it in mist. *Philosophy in the Bedroom* has a happy ending.

But there is another difference between the two Eugénies, one more difficult to speculate upon, to arrange neatly into a specular opposition, like frank/mysterious. Eugénie de Franval, like Rosalie Rodin is 14, but Eugénie de Mistival is 15. This digital difference lacks the neat symmetry of the nominal opposition, but it is not without associations, hints, and clues bearing promise of some philosophical explanation in the Sadian context.

In *La nouvelle Justine,* Justine and her sister Juliette are respectively 14 and 15 at the moment that their parents' death sends them out into the world. Justine, like the 14-year-old Eugénie de Franval, lives a tragedy. Juliette, like the 15-year-old Eugénie de Mistival, has a fortunate existence. This story of two sisters so occupied Sade that he wrote it at least three times, the last time covering three thousand pages with it. The fascination of this story of two sisters lies in the puzzling difference between two members of the same sex, with the same origin (from the same parents), of the same generation, and nearly the same age. In the two earlier versions of their story (*Infortunes de la*

6. "La Signification du phallus," *Ecrits,* p. 692.
7. Admittedly, there is no etymological relation between the English word "misty," and words like "mystery," "mystic" etc. But thanks to happenstance, it carries a similar meaning of "obscure, clouded," one that contrasts well with "frank." Oddly enough, in the zone of these two vales, it turns out that "mist" stems from an Indo-European root "meigh" which means "to urinate," and which also produces "micturate" and "mistletoe."

vertu and *Justine*), Justine is 12, not 14, when the story begins. That the difference between 12 and 15 should be reduced to the barely perceptible difference between 14 and 15 in the final, least restrained, most excessive, most violent version of the story implies an attempt to strip their enigmatic difference of any possible garb of rational explanation by categories. That such specularly opposite roles should hang upon the difference between 14 and 15, moves us into a world derisive of structures of meaningful opposition, whether the structure of sexual difference or difference of age group. All the mysterious difference between Juliette's libertinage and Justine's innocence, the entire structure knowledge/innocence—that is, as we have said, phallus/receptacle—hinges upon making a cut between 14 and 15.

It is Rodin who makes that cut. At the end of the Rodin episode in both *Justine* and *La nouvelle Justine*, the daughter Rosalie is locked up in the cellar while Rodin and his friend Rombeau (why all these "ro's"?) plan to do experiments on her in the following terms: "Anatomy, says Rodin, will never reach its final degree of perfection until the examination of the vessels [vaginal canal] is performed on a child of 14 or 15, who expired from a cruel death."[8] Here, at 14 or 15, in the zone between those digits, Sade makes another addition to the pedagogical battery: to complement the oral and anal examination, Rodin adds the vaginal "examination."

Rosalie, who is 14 when Justine first meets her, is 15 by the time of her "examination." Rodin's school, the only actual school visited in all Justine's adventures, is narrated in the space between a 14-year-old daughter and a 15-year-old daughter. The whole process of pedagogy, the confrontation between knowledge and innocence, can be situated in the slice between 14 and 15. In that way Rodin's literal, surgical slice can be read as an emblem of his pedagogical activity.

Rodin has two professions: he is not just a teacher, like so many of us, he also does "research." In his case it is surgical research. That the only teacher Justine meets should also be a surgeon, leads one to ponder the relation between the two professions. One articulation might be the "examination." After all, Dolmancé's socratizing introduction of a finger itself resembles common medical procedure. The academic examination is an effort to discover what the pupil knows: that is, what is inside her head, what of the teacher's discourse has penetrated and made an impression. The medical examination is an attempt to find out what is inside the patient's body. The two examinations have in common the penetration of an interiority (psychi-

---

8. Sade, *Justine ou les malheurs de la vertu, Oeuvres complètes* v. 3 (Cercle du livre précieux, 1966), pp. 150–51. In the original French it is not specified what "vessels" are meant. In Richard Seaver and Austryn Wainhouse's excellent English translation (Grove Press, 1966, p. 551) this is rendered as "vaginal canal," which seems most likely from the context. The same passage occurs in *La nouvelle Justine*, O.c., v. 6 (Cercle du livre précieux), p. 262.

cal/figurative, in one instance; physical/literal, in the other). Sade's pedagogical battery makes physical/literal the exam as a penetration of interiority.
Certainly the easiest path to the inside is through one of the orifices. But
Rodin's double profession carries the penetration one sadistic step further. The
surgeon does not need a natural orifice; he can enter the body wherever he likes
by cutting an opening.

Sadian pedagogy depends upon the pupil's virginity. The two Eugénies are
virgins at the beginning of their educations/initiations, as are all of Rodin's
pupils including his daughter. Rodin's and Domancé's practices even leave the
pupil's virginity intact. If the pupil is virginal, never before penetrated, she is a
blank, empty receptacle, and examination will be exact, revealing nothing but
what the teacher puts there ("We will inspire her with *our desires*").

Rodin's surgical research seems equally concerned with virginity for the
exactitude of the examinations. To Rodin's plan to examine the "vessels" of a
14 or 15 year old, Rombeau adds: "It is the same with the membrane that
assures virginity; a young girl is absolutely necessary for this *examination*.
What can one observe in the age of puberty? nothing; the menses tear the
hymen, and *all research is inexact*" (*Justine*, 152, my italics). Luce Irigaray, in
her reading of *Philosophy in the Bedroom*, suggests that Sadian libertines only
like the blood they cause to flow. Like menstruation, defloration includes
bleeding, but in the latter blood is a sign of some penetration of interiority from
without, while in the former it flows from interior to exterior without the
necessity of a penetrating agent. Just as pedagogical tests seek to draw out from
the student what was implanted there by the teacher; so the Sadian surgeon
wishes to examine an interiority devoid of anything sexual, any carnal
knowledge originating within.

Both "examine" and "exact" come from the same Latin word *exigere*,
itself derived from *ex* (out, from) and *agere* (to lead, to drive). The examination
"leads out," "drives out" what was cloistered within. For the examination to
be exact there must be some external agent, some researcher, some surgeon to
"lead" or "drive" the interior stuff out into the light. Menstrual blood does not
wait for a leader or driver to exact it; so it renders the examination inexact.

Hidden in this supposedly scientific discussion between two surgeons is a
rather unscientific confusion between puberty and defloration. Obviously
both can represent some kind of break between girlhood and womanhood, but
in this discussion puberty is assimilated to the model of defloration. "The
menses tear the hymen," asserts Rombeau. But a surgeon would know that
this is false. Defloration is the tearing of the hymen by a force which goes from
outside to inside. In this mythic model, puberty would consist in a tearing of
the hymen by a force moving from inside to outside. This myth of puberty sets
up a specular opposition between the two different sorts of passages from

innocent child to sexual adult. It works to assimilate both to one model,like Dolmancé/Rodin's attempt to assimilate heterosexuality to pederasty.

In the zone of 14 or 15, in the space between Justine the virgin and Juliette the whore, lies the mysterious break between innocence/ignorance/virginity and experience/knowledge/sexuality. The hymen is the emblematic wall partitioning these two realms. What we have here is the Sadian version of the *coupure épistémologique.* That term from contemporary French philosophy refers to a discontinuity in thought, dividing it into a before and an after, into classification by ages. Prefiguring and deriding *avant la lettre* mid-twentieth century philosophical modes (thus ignoring our historical classing by ages), Rodin enacts a physical/literal epistemological *coupure.*

Rodin's *coupure*, his surgical cut into the virgin, his examination of the hymen, is an examination of the distinction knowledge/innocence, is epistemological research, which is to say research into the origin and nature of knowledge.

Rombeau says of their victim, that although 15, she is not yet *réglée.* "Réglée" can usually be translated as "regulated," but it has a peculiar sense meaning "having begun to menstruate," from *règles*, a usual term for a woman's "period." The pedagogical examination which attempts to regulate the student on the basis of external rules, of the teacher's rules, is messed up by the *règles*, the rules, flowing from within. The bodily, fluid, material, feminine sense of *règles* undermines the Sadian pederastic pedagogue's attempt at exact examination, at subjugation of the pupil to his rational, masterful rules.

Yet, like pederasty, the woman's bloody "rules" suggest numerical regulation. 14 or 15 is not usually considered the age of female puberty. In fact, the first version of Justine's story, *Les Infortunes de la vertu*, places the age of Rombeau-Rodin's victim at 12 or 13. Perhaps 14/15 insists, not because it is the age of puberty, but because those numbers constitute the center of the 28 to 30 day menstrual cycle. The zone between 14 and 15 would thus be the scene, not of the origin of knowledge, but of another mysterious origin.

Having circulated the manuscript of the present text among a small number of readers, I learned—to my surprise—that what I had posited as "the reader's desire" to line the numbers up, to do arithmetic was not shared by many readers. The numbers that fascinate me could leave another reader cold. What I assumed was a general desire, a "normal" attraction to these numbers, turns out to be my peculiar tendency, my perversion. It does not seem infelicitous that I should produce a perverse reading of Sade. My original attraction to Sade is to a site of perversions. Yet Sade's text makes the recognizably perverse readings appropriate and normal. To fix on the numbers is perhaps a way of recovering the thrill originally sought from Sade.

Finally, it does not seem inappropriate that an arithmetic perversion should arise in a discussion of pedagogy. School presents us with a world of numbers: grades, curves, credit hours, course numbers, class hours, and room numbers. I suppose not all teachers experience as I do a diffuse yet unmistakable pleasure when calculating grades at the end of the term.

ANGELA S. MOGER

That Obscure Object of Narrative

Quand on aime l'amour est trop grand pour pouvoir être contenu tout entier en nous; il irradie vers la personne aimée, rencontre en elle une surface qui l'arrête, le force à revenir vers son point de départ et c'est ce choc en retour de notre propre tendresse que nous appelons les sentiments de l'autre et qui nous charme plus qu' à l'aller, parce que nous ne connaissons pas qu'elle vient de nous.

—Marcel Proust

What is the relationship between narrative and pedagogy? A witty and disarming tale by Maupassant might suggest some answers to this question. Like many other Maupassant stories, "Une Ruse" is encompassed by a frame, a secondary tier of narration which then rhetoricizes the "central" story, bringing about a self-conscious reappraisal of its action and consequences. But, in the case of "Une Ruse," the frame is manipulated aggressively enough to confirm what one only suspects in probing the mechanism of most framed stories: to tell a story is to do something to the somebody who listens to it, to affect that listener in ways s/he doesn't anticipate and can't control. It can be a way of taking advantage of someone; in "Une Ruse", the listener has been compromised before she even understands what has happened.

What is more interesting about this story, given the question of the link between narrative and pedagogy, is the choice of thematic elements brought to bear on the particular structural organization referred to above. That is, the tale recounted by the protagonist-narrator—which comprises the story we read except for five short paragraphs at the beginning and five lines at the end—is intended as a "lesson," one imposed on a young bride by an old man. It is an act of persuasion to bring the bride around; it is told with the aim of converting her to a different scheme of beliefs. Furthermore, the storyteller is none other than that supreme figure of disinterested authority, the *physician*. What we have in "Une Ruse," then, is a story about the telling of a story to "teach" someone a lesson about life; and, indeed, the way in which narrational and pedagogical motifs are superimposed in this tale is suggestive of some form of ultimate relationship between the process of narration and the process of instruction. But we have to scrutinize the evidence before elaborating further on the conclusions to which it points.

Our story begins in the bride's boudoir where she, "stretched out on her

129

chaise lounge," is "gossiping" into the night with her doctor. He has been treating her for a malady, says the narrator with a leer, "from which newly married people often suffer when they have made a 'love match'." The young woman is very happy and very much in love and can't imagine, she says, how or why women betray their husbands. One would presumably humor a bride in her smug conviction. But the doctor argues, on the contrary, that marriage is merely a kind of apprenticeship preparing a woman for "real" love and that women are extremely adept at the deception of husbands:

Je suis même certain qu'une femme n'est mure pour l'amour vrai qu'après avoir passé par toutes les promiscuités et tous les dégoûts du mariage, qui n'est, suivant un homme illustre, qu'un échange de mauvaises humeurs pendant le jour et de mauvaises odeurs pendant la nuit. Rien de plus vrai. Une femme ne peut aimer passionnément qu'après avoir été mariée. Si je la pouvais comparer à une maison, je dirais qu'elle n'est habitable que lorsqu'un mari a essuyé les plâtres.

Quant à la dissimulation, toutes les femmes en ont à revendre en ces occasions-là.[1]

[I even feel certain that no woman is ripe for true love until she has passed through all the promiscuousness and all the irksomeness of married life, which, according to an illustrious man, is nothing but an exchange of dreadful words by day and of dreadful odors by night. Nothing is more true, for no woman can love passionately until after she has married. If I might compare her to a house, I would say she isn't habitable until a husband has been the first occupant.

As for dissimulation, all women have plenty of it on hand for such occasions.]

The shocked young woman contests his assertion concerning a woman's capacity for deceit:

. . . on ne s'avise jamais qu'après coup de ce qu'on aurait dû faire dans les occasions périlleuses; et les femmes sont certes encore plus disposées que les hommes à perdre la tête.

[. . . one never thinks until after the fact of what one ought to have done in a dangerous affair, and women are certainly more liable than men to lose their heads on such occasions.]

The cynic retorts by launching rather gratuitously into the story of an illicit liaison in which he became vicariously involved:

Après coup, dites-vous! Nous autres, nous n'avons l'inspiration qu'après coup. Mais vous! . . . Tenez, je vais vous raconter une petite histoire arrivée à une de mes clientes à qui j'aurais donné le bon Dieu sans confession, comme on dit. [98]

After the fact, you say! We men, we are the ones who only have an inspiration after the fact. But you women! . . . Wait, I am going to tell you a little story, something that

1. Guy de Maupassant, *Mademoiselle Fifi*, (Paris: Albin Michel), p. 97–98. All future references to the story are to this edition and appear in parentheses in the text itself. The translations are mine.

happened to one of my female patients to whom I would have given communion without confession, as they say.]

The lover had died in his mistress' bedroom, and the woman turned to her doctor for help in getting the body out of the house. The tale is quite comic and grotesque. The doctor describes how he and the woman and her maid got the underwear on the corpse and then, piece by piece, put on the rest of his clothing (That is, a rather brutal slow motion camera is turned onto each segment of the "beloved"—in this instance, the whole is certainly proven to be more than the sum of its parts!)[2]; how he and the wife carried it off with the cuckold when he returned home to find the lover, much in disarray, lying in his drawing room; how the doctor managed to make it appear that the dead man was actually climbing into his carriage himself, etc. The narrator of this story, being a doctor, has no moral observations to make about adultery, the violation of the sacrament of marriage, the sacrilegious irreverance shown towards the dead; moral judgment is here replaced, in fact, by the doctor's apparent admiration for the wife's cool composure on the arrival of her husband. The bride is to understand that he has no bias in this sort of matter. He is only telling a story in order to *educate* her.

People often tell stories to persuade others of something; narrative and its techniques are constantly used to impart some form of knowledge. But, just as often, the pretext of the transmission of wisdom or information serves to motivate a story. That is, stories rely with arresting frequency on the topos of the instruction of one person by another. This continual reciprocity (mutual dependency?) between the narrative instance and the didactic posture makes us wonder what links them. What is the relationship between teaching and telling? "Une Ruse" represents an answer to the question.

Since it is immediately apparent that a story concerned with illicit sexual love effects a slight semantic displacement (from the language of the discussion above) whereby "education" might be termed, instead, "initiation," the plot alone of "Une Ruse" provokes the association of didactic stance with desire for possession. Furthermore, the structural dynamics of the story, in constituting a kind of exposé of the storyteller's motives, insist on this interpretation; for Maupassant's story does not end with the ruse described above, the deception of the husband by the doctor and Mme. Lelièvre (that other "very young woman" as the doctor expresses it, seeming to insist on a parallelism between the one to whom he is telling and the one told about). That is, *our* narrator returns to close the story with the description of the

2. Je prenais un à un les membres comme ceux d'une énorme poupée, et je les tendais aux vêtements qu'apportaient les femmes. On passa les chaussettes, le caleçon, la culotte, le gilet, puis l'habit ou nous eûmes beaucoup de mal à faire entrer les bras.

Quand il fallut boutonner les bottines, les deux femmes se mirent à genoux, tandis que je les éclairais; mais comme les pieds étaient enflés un peu, ce fut effroyablement difficile. N'ayant pas trouvé le tire-boutons, elles avaient pris leurs épingles à cheveux. (835).

bride's *reaction* to the prurient story, and, more importantly, the doctor's revealing reaction to her reaction.

The prudish young woman is appalled by the story and asks the doctor petulantly why he has told her "cette épouvantable histoire" ["that terrible story"]. The narrator reports that the doctor, "souriant toujours" ["still smiling"] "salua galamment ["bowed gallantly"] (indicating that the tone here is one of insolent impudence), and replied, "Pour vous offrir mes services à l'occasion" (105). ["So that I may offer you my services if necessary"]. It is critical to note that Maupassant's story could have been limited to the doctor's story: the amusing tale of a wife's ability to "jouer la comédie" in dire circumstances. It is the addition of the frame—the doctor and his subsequent patient—and particularly of the question and answer at the end, which makes clear that the author's concern is not so much with seduction and betrayal as with the complicity of pedagogical and narrational postures in bringing about illicit forms of appropriation or dominance.[3] The embedding of one story in the other suggests the nature of the tie which binds narration and education. We come closer to a grasp of the analogy between the two processes implicitly proposed by "Une Ruse", if we review the way in which the doctor exploits his "present" patient, another[4] trick to which the title of the story refers.

Saussure has taught us that the bond between the signifier and the signified is arbitrary. The doctor-storyteller in Maupassant's story seeks to convince his young patient that in sexual intercourse, the link between signifier and signified is as arbitrary as the one which obtains in verbal intercourse.[5] If, in the story the doctor relates, the lover is read as the signifier and love or pleasure as the signified, he seems to be trying to persuade his listener that a woman's choice of sexual partner has no more importance (to the outcome) than would the choice of the sound "paa" over the sound "chaa" to signify "cat" in French. Presumably, while alive, the lover had great significance to that other "very young" wife, Mme Lelièvre; dead, his body has

3. It is, indeed, because of their apparent gratuitousness that we can identify the question and answer at the end as the locus of meaning of the story.

4. Although it lies outside the focus of this discussion, another trick implicit in the title is the one played on the reader. The bride has heard just what the reader has heard, but she doesn't get the joke. She is not yet initiate. The doctor, a man of the world in the fullest sense, knows it is only a matter of time before she will understand his story completely. The larger awareness (a facile cynicism) shared by the author and the reader is demonstrated in the fact that the reader finds his consciousness entirely coincident with that of the author's persona, the doctor. The complicity between the doctor and the reader which is constituted in this coincidence of minds is a snare for the reader who is thus converted unwittingly into the role of voyeur and consumer of prurient stories. In the identification with the suave narrator figure, the reader assures the author a means of exploiting him as well, a control made possible by the multidimensional structure of the framed story.

5. What we have here, in fact, is a kind of comic paradox in that the healer is opting for sickness—the doctor, after all, can't "cure" the young woman of the discomfort which the idea of infidelity causes her except by making her sick, that is, morally diseased.

lost that meaning and has become, instead, a treacherous element which might expose her infidelity to her husband. The signifier has changed its signified—the doctor's account, as we have seen, underlines the fragility of the sign by focusing on the lover as if taking an inventory of moving parts. Indeed, the doctor's tale, or rather, his telling (e.g. the protracted description of the beloved as if he were just a dummy),[6] seems a curious act of aggression and certainly compels the question the young woman poses: "Pourquoi m'avez-vous raconté cette épouvantable histoire?"

On one level, of course, she is merely moving the plot forward with her question, although here we might reiterate that the question is not needed for the story to be a meaningful whole. On another level, the questioner is asking the question put to all storytellers: if you have something to say, why be literary? Why did you tell me a *story* and what is its significance?

The doctor's answer operates on several levels as well. Although on the most literal level he is saying, "If a lover dies in your bed, I will help to remove him," the fact and form of the story suggest another level of message: "If you choose to be unfaithful, and if your lover loses significance, I am available to remove/replace him." On the ultimate level, he is saying with his story what he could not say directly to her: "You will be unfaithful and I am available, for the 'signifié' can be as easily produced by any other 'significant'."[7] Telling a story, then, can be a way of making an indecent proposal, a way of approaching another person about something one could not get away with saying directly. Through the subterfuge of the disinterested wish to convey something—the

6. Cf. Bergson's observations on the nature of the comic: "We laugh every time a person gives us the impression of being a thing" . . . "Any arrangement of acts and events is comic which gives us in a single combination, the illusion of life and the distinct impression of a mechanical arrangement" Henri Bergson, *Laughter*, trans. Cloudesly Brereton and Fred Rothwell (London: Macmillan, 1911), p. 58, p. 69.

7. Bunuel has some fun playing with the same conviction in his "Cet obscur objet de désir," which depicts an aging "hero" madly in love with a virginal young girl who is perpetually inaccessible. Conventional enough as a scenario, except that the girl is played by two different actresses who appear to be randomly interchanged from scene to scene throughout the film. Bunuel seems waggishly persuaded of "l'arbitraire du signe," that is, of the tenuous line between who causes it and the feeling caused, between agent and effect produced by that agent. In view of the point I am trying to make here, it is important to note that Maupassant's story insists, from the beginning, on the arbitrariness of the sign as if to prepare us for the doctor's ultimate innuendo. A brief inventory: the doctor, asleep in his bed mistakes his doorbell for the bells of a fire alarm—the doctor sends word that the other doctor, Monsieur Bonnet, should be "substituted" for himself in this instance—the doctor's servant reports that it is impossible to tell from outward appearances whether the person waiting below is a man or a woman—the woman urges the doctor to use her lover's carriage instead of ordering his own (a first suggestion of the superposition of the roles of doctor and lover?)—The wife steps into the role earlier played by her servant in lighting the staircase—the doctor becomes the vehicle for the bearing away of the dead man: "I got between his two legs as if I had been a horse between the shafts." As soon as one begins thinking along these lines, indeed, one becomes sensitive even to details like the women's substitution of their hair pins for buttonhooks as they try to button the boots on the dead man's feet.

meaning, the lesson, the point, the "story"—to another, one achieves some form of control over that other. The frame surrounding "Une Ruse" permits us to perceive this.

In allowing for the exchange between speakers in reference to the internal story, moreover, the frame enables us to appreciate the vacuity of any message, be it a story or a lesson or a coincidence of the two. The bride does not get the point of the story at all; the short circuit in communication between addressor and addressee which Maupassant takes care to build into his story expresses the awareness that what is dispatched has nothing to do with what is received. Since what is heard may not correspond to what the originator of the message set out to communicate, the tension between the narrator persona and his audience establishes that a message undergoes some form of spontaneous metamorphosis on exposure to a listener and never reaches a "destinataire" intact. The message is fractured in transit and the content reassembled by the beholder according to a design he imposes himself.

But it would be facile to suggest that "Une Ruse" exists to demonstrate only the inability of narratives to impart anything but their failure to impart even the simplest message. The ultimate message of the story is undeniably a message about the message—its complexity, its duplicity, its multiplicity, its ineffectuality, but most of all its insularity, or what we might call its indifference to the question of mimetic accuracy. The function of the frame, then, would be to undercut the framed, to make clear that the central narrative's appearance of substantiality is an optical illusion, and to mock the pretentions of the conventional reading of such a story. A framed story, in other words, takes as its subject the "polysémie" of stories; the tension between teller and listener, offered as the "content" of the story, is the sign of this new optic, this displacement of traditional subject matter (story as imitation of life or nugget of fundamental wisdom).

Parenthetically, if, as indicated above, the telling of a story is often a way of doing something to someone, the choice of calling for the storyteller may here take on heightened significance. In "Une Ruse", the raconteur, as a doctor, has just been concerning himself with the young woman's body—before he launched into his anecdote. The doctor-patient relationship insulates his concern with her body from the suggestion that it is sexual. Yet it is only the sign, the designation of his role as doctor instead of potential lover, which regulated the woman's reading of him.[8] Now he has just given her an

---

8. In *Frame Analysis,* Goffman comments on this particular social situation (doctor-patient) where, as he says, two different perspectives are applicable but only one is meant to apply: . . . "individuals can rather fully constitute what they see in accordance with the framework that officially applies. But there is a limit to this capacity. Certain effects carry over from one perspective in which events could easily be seen to a radically different one, the latter the one which officially applies. The best documented case, perhaps, is the slow development of the easy right of

unspecified medical examination, perhaps some form of treatment or advice—
once she has heard the doctor's prurient story, how is she to "read" what has
preceded?[9] Finally, there may be another level of implication in all of this.
Since the doctor is here acting also as teacher, another suggestion implicit in
the scene is that the pedagogical encounter is the occasion for a similar kind of
exploitation, if only an intellectual molestation of those whose trust in the
role makes them all the more vulnerable to manipulation.

"Une Ruse," then, dramatizes the teaching situation in several ways—old
person/young person; authority (doctor)/layman (patient); precept to impart/
captive audience—and we must not treat the matter of the pedagogical
scenario as arbitrary or innocent. The doctor's ostensible intention to en-
lighten the young woman about life is a thematic choice which represents a
certain bias. Already implicit in the tension between teller and listener is the
conviction that "lessons" have as little to do with truth and falsehood as
stories do. "Une Ruse" suggests that instruction produces no greater awareness of how things "really are," of the actual nature of the world or experience,
than does fiction. The analogy between these two processes is, however, based
on a more active form of resemblance than their *lack* of relevance to the quest
for truth. Actually, pedagogy and narrative are coincident in their reliance on
the mechanism of desire as a modus operandi. Teaching and telling exist,
endure, function, by means of perpetually renewed postponement of
fulfillment. If desire comes into being and is sustained as a result of inaccessi-
bility or otherness of the object which one would like, in principle, to tame or
consume, can't we rightly contend that narrative operations and didactic
operations intersect in their implicit intention to refrain from closing the gap
which is the goal of their explicit *pretentions*? Once the object of desire has
been appropriated, it loses its status as desirable. Now, meaning is to narrative
as fulfillment is to desire; possession means death. Stories work by going
through the motions of imparting information which they only promise but
never really deliver. A story is a question to be pursued; if there is no enigma,
no space to be traversed, there is no story.

Teaching is another such "optical" illusion; it functions by a similar
sleight of hand. The pedagogical stance is a pretext that there is something
substantive to be deciphered and appropriated. But wisdom, like love and the
story, is not found in nature; it has no empirical status. Like the beloved or the
narrative, it exists only in the eye of the beholder; I am a teacher only in the

---

medical people to approach the human naked body with a natural instead of a social
perspective . . . The gynecological examination is even today a matter of some concern, special
effort being taken to infuse the procedure with terms and actions that keep sexual readings in
check" (Erving Goffman, *Frame Analysis: An Essay on the Organization of Experience* (Cambridge,
Mass.: Harvard University Press, 1974), pp. 35–36.

9. On the level of the signifier, indeed, she has perhaps already deceived her husband by
submitting to the physical examination (What was in the doctor's mind during the examination?)

mind of one who thinks I might teach him something he does not know. But since I do not possess the knowledge he desires, to teach is only to continue to generate the desire for wisdom. Pedagogy, like narrative, functions by means of withholding rather than by means of transmission. It works by multiplying the enigmas (obstacles) rather than by eliminating them. Teaching, then, is the subject's telling of the desire for the object rather than the subject's telling of the object. As in fiction, pedagogy's "material" is its own condition; it describes its internal workings rather than an external entity. Neither conveys; both double back on themselves, just as desire is desire only in its recoiling on itself, in its perpetual reaching, and never in its arrival at the proposed destination.

Just as what the lover feels reveals something about him rather than anything about the "real" nature of the beloved—she is "all in his mind"—fiction and instruction are both essentially self-referential. And just as the lover must not realize his dream, the storyteller and the teacher lose their status if they in fact proffer what they presumably exist to yield up. If the immediate goal of teaching is the satisfaction of the quest for knowledge, it can also be said that its fundamental goal is the denial of that satisfaction in favor of the renewal of questing itself.

If it is true that pedagogy and narrative are subject to the same double bind which immobilizes desire—they must not perform the closure which it is definitively their function to perform—we begin to appreciate the performative dynamic of Maupassant's story. If both operate, instead, by telling us something about how they are generated (i.e. why they must not accomplish their announced goal), rather than by naming that other which they dangle before us, we understand the symbolic resonance of Maupassant's choice of seduction as story line. Since, moreover, the framing of a narrative constitutes the explicitation of the self-referential quality of narrative (the frame compels the understanding that the story is *about* the telling of the story), we perceive the complexity of the paradigmatic axis engendered by the interplay of thematic element and structural element. That axis permits us to see not only that fiction and instruction are both grounded in paradox, but also that the paradox of which it is a question is of a particular type. That is, it is in this sense that we are authorized in asserting above that the crucial common element is their mutual reenactment of the mechanism of desire: both proceed by seduction at the same time that they are *predicated on* the nonoccurrence of their announced aims.

But we can submit "Une Ruse" to a kind of proof to verify these conclusions and to see, then, if we are right in attesting the deliberate superposition of the three processes: seduction, narration, education. What if the story had been told the bride by a female friend or by her mother? Or what if the addressee of the story had been presented by the author as a woman more knowing of the ways of the world? It seems obvious that the story would not only be rendered flatly banal and one-dimensional, but also it would, losing all of its performative powers, lapse into mere description—description of a cautionary account of an illicit love affair (Mme de Chartres to her daughter, the Princess of Clèves) or description of the brief entertainment of one person by another. If we consider these alternatives and their potential effects, it should be clear that "Une Ruse" takes on the status of an organism (as opposed to an artifact) where there is a vital and unstable interaction of frame and contained story only when the teller's function is coincident with the role of seducer and when, in turn, that role may be circumstantially confused with the role of pedagogue (age and professional authority). Maupassant's story can only achieve dynamism if it can find a way to act instead of merely describe; if it is to go on detonating, it cannot just deliver itself of some (monovalent) statement. Rather, "Une Ruse" presents itself as a "self-swallowing"[10] construct, escaping the linear reification which menaces narrative by performing what it describes: seduction through instruction. By its very functioning, the reader is forced into the role of the lover and the student;[11] he reaches for the knowledge or control which is always just beyond his grasp. "*Why* did he tell the story?" "How much of it did she really understand?" "What is Maupassant's point?" "Is his irony directed at the doctor, the bride, the reader, or just human/narrative perversity?"

We desire the whole story, then, and we are taught that we're not going to get it; we are taught that telling and teaching are teasing and withholding, that their teasing and withholding are all they can tell if they are to survive. "Une Ruse" teaches by frustrating; it stimulates yearning with denial. Since the story only achieves its highest realization by bringing about a coincidence of the processes of seduction, instruction, and narration, we realize ultimately that this narrative constitutes the proposition (by insisting on desire as the third term of the "trope") that both narration and pedagogy pose, on the

10. I am here adopting the terminology of Douglas Hofstadter in his paraphrase of Bertrand Russell: "Most sets, if would seem, are not members of themselves—for example, the set of walruses is not a walrus, the set containing only Joan of Arc is not Joan of Arc (a set is not a person)—and so on. In this respect, most sets are rather 'run-of-the-mill.' However, some 'self-swallowing' sets *do* contain themselves as members, such as the set of all sets, or the set of all things except Joan of Arc, and so on" (Douglas R. Hofstadter, *Godel, Escher, Bach: an External Golden Braid* (New York: Basic Books, 1979), p. 20).

11. Cf. Shoshana Felman's provocative comment on the link between love and narrative: "Transference, says Lacan, is 'the acting-out of the reality of the unconscious.' On the basis of the literary evidence which we are analyzing, and within the framework of a theory of narrative, we are here prompted to raise the question whether the acting-out of the unconscious is always in effect the acting-out of a *story*, of a narrative; and whether, on the other hand, *all* stories and all narratives imply a transferential structure, that is, a love-relation which both organizes and disguises, deciphers and enciphers them, turning them into their own substitute and their own repetition" (Shoshana Felman, "Turning the Screw of Interpretation," *Yale French Studies*, No. 55/56 (1977), p. 133). Isn't the pedagogical encounter a "transferential structure" in this sense?

constative level, as systems of understanding, and yet engender, on the performative level, only mystification. Given the story's elusiveness, however, we can't be certain of even this, for the readers of a story and the pupils of a classroom are like Proust's lover—we don't know if what we think we experience at the hands of "Une Ruse" comes from it or whether the story's impact is but the ricochet of our own desire.

BARBARA GUETTI

The Old Régime and the Feminist Revolution: Laclos' "De l'Education des Femmes"

It has been known for some time that the author of *Les Liaisons Dangereuses* also wrote a series of texts on the education of women.[1] These were never published in Laclos' lifetime, and all three of them were left unfinished—a sign, perhaps, that we can regard them as false starts on a topic Laclos was unable fully to master. Or it may be that this very busy man, who overextended himself in every phase of the French Revolution, simply had no more time left for theoretical work.[2] Whatever the case, the texts which comprise "On the Education of Women" have been easily available since 1951 in the Pléiade Edition of the *Oeuvres Complètes*—a volume whose tendency to slimness has been further corrected by the inclusion of Laclos' poetry, his correspondence with Mme Riccoboni on the moral import of his novel, his reports for the Jacobin society, his debunking of a respected military strategist, Vauban, and his plan for renumbering the streets of Paris. Specialists on Laclos and the eighteenth century have not failed to take note of these "secondary" texts, and any surprise one might feel upon learning that Laclos devoted a considerable amount of time and energy to the question of women's education—indeed, to the question of women's liberation—ought, by this time, to seem a highly unscholarly emotion.[3]

But old news is often surprising. J. L. Borges, in one of his scholarly improvisations, "The Wall and the Books," offers some reflections on the career of a Chinese emperor that appear relevant to the case in hand:

> I read, some days past, that the man who ordered the creation of the almost infinite wall of China was that first Emperor, Shih Huang Ti, who also decreed that all the books

---

1. Choderlos de Laclos, *Oeuvres Complètes*, ed. Maurice Allem (Paris: Gallimard, 1951). The three manuscripts are presented under the collective title, "De l'Education des Femmes," pp. 406–58.

2. Emile Dard, *Le Général Choderlos de Laclos, auteur des Liaisons Dangereuses* (Paris, 1905).

3. See, for instance, Roger Vailland, *Laclos par lui-même*, (Paris: Le Seuil, 1955) as well as Georges May's discussion of feminism in *Le Dilemme du Roman au XVIIIe siècle* (Paris, 1963). A more recent feminist critic, Nancy K. Miller, does not acknowledge the existence of these texts ("De l'Education des Femmes") in her article, "Female Sexuality and Narrative Structure in *La Nouvelle Héloïse* and *Les Liaisons Dangereuses*," *Signs: A Journal of Women in Culture and Society* (Spring, 1976), vol. 1, number 3, Part 1, pp. 609–38.

139

prior to him be burned. That these two vast operations—the five to six hundred leagues of stone opposing the barbarians, the rigorous abolition of history, that is, of the past—should originate in one person and be in some way his attributes inexplicably satisfied and, at the same time, disturbed me.[4]

Taken as a whole, the Pléiade Edition of Laclos may trouble us in much the same way that Shih Huang Ti's double-play troubled Borges. There is an internal discrepancy at work in this structure, tending to give what ought to be a mere book certain disconcertingly wall-like attributes. Its thickness is, as we say, a dead giveaway. For this volume, with all its amplitude, convenience and stability quite seriously interferes with the kind of attention Laclos' work—by which I mean one very single and singular work, *Les Liaisons Dangereuses*—has always elicited from its most devoted readers.

Included in the Pléiade Edition we find, for example, the reactions of a contemporary, Tilly, who depicts this novel as an essentially solitary and essentially momentary phenomenon, despite his efforts to relate it to the actual history of the revolutionary period. It was, he says, "One of those revolutionary waves amid the ocean which submerged the court . . . one of those disastrous meteors which appeared in a fiery sky at the end of the eighteenth century."[5] These remarks are, we should note, the result of a disappointing interview in which Tilly asked Laclos for further explanations of the novel but was offered instead only enigmatic oratory.[6] Having been brought up short like Borges before the Great Wall of China, Tilly wisely adopts a classic and elegant solution to this problem—reminiscent, in fact, of Valmont's approach to Tourvel in the novel. If Laclos' book remains inaccessible to the frontal attack of direct inquiry, its hidden treasures can be appropriated by means of a different strategy. No longer able to disregard the wall between himself and this book, Tilly treats it with a new respect. He does not attempt to scale it; he does not lie down in front of it and die of despair; he simply takes a long detour around it, thus leaving both himself and the wall intact. Even better, he helps build it. The entire procedure is expressed, oratorically, in the following passages:

It is then one of those thunderous flashes, suspected by no one at the time and which readers now will find exaggerated, perhaps ridiculous; what the author didn't tell me but what a deep plotter like himself must have known amid that vast conspiracy in which, in advance, each person had taken up his role: at court, in the town, in the provinces, and in the army.

4. J. L. Borges, *Labyrinths* (New York: A New Directions Book, 1962), pp. 204–6.
5. Included in Laclos, op. cit., pp. 707–10. This and all translations from the French in this essay are mine unless otherwise noted.
6. Tilly cites Laclos: "I resolved to produce a work that would depart from the ordinary path, create a sensation, and which would still make itself heard on this earth after I had passed on." Tilly comments, "These somewhat oratorical expressions impressed me all the more since his cold and methodical conversation was not otherwise so highly-colored." Laclos, op. cit., p. 708.

One good work (*Les Liaisons Dangereuses*) gets the other it deserves: from the outside, Tilly builds up his own historical fiction of a "vast conspiracy" while safely admiring the structure and contours of the work Laclos is doing from within:

All the parts of the intrigue fit closely together, with a facility that hides the labor involved. These are monstrous vices upon reflection, which appear quite simple as one reads. The author leads you on, and one does not become detached from this collaboration and agreement with him until, after running the whole course, the end appears in view.

This collaboration between author and reader ends, however, when the wicked purpose of the book finally becomes clear: "In a word, it is the work of a mind of the first order, of a rotten heart and an evil genius." But Tilly's text makes this moment of understanding coincide with the passing of the old régime: "In the new order of things, this book has lost all its interest; nevertheless, it will last as long as the language." The result of all this labor is a monumental edifice; we are invited to accept its permanence in compensation for the impermanence of the forces which produced it. It appears that books difficult of access—dangerous books—may inevitably elicit such extravagant defenses from their readers. Even Borges, after struggling to reopen old questions about the past, finds himself succumbing to "The tenacious wall which at this moment and at all moments casts its shadow over lands I shall never see . . ."[7]

Such elegant detours as Tilly's and Borges'—exemplary exercises in cautious reading—may, however, be luxuries we must deny ourselves if we are indeed determined, after all this, to go ahead and read Laclos' texts about women. If I have lingered somewhat indecisively on the threshold of the Pléiade Edition—where, it seems, Laclos' revolutionary wave has washed up just about everything, including the kitchen sink—it is because I feel impelled at the outset to point out the rashness of this possibly disappointing and no doubt thankless project. For our purposes, the Pléiade Edition looks less like a wall than like an abandoned lumber-yard, or a do-it-yourself kit without the instructions. It's not clear how the parts fit, or exactly what we are putting together. Far from resolving the problems which provoked Tilly's initial questions to Laclos, the Pléiade Edition exemplifies them: how are we to reconcile *Les Liaisons Dangereuses* with its historical "context" or, for that matter, with our own? Far from having "lost all interest," as Tilly insisted it had, the book might acquire new relevance if read with these "secondary" texts. Yet it is clear that we wouldn't be reading these treatises on women without the novel, whose previous and more authoritative existence is, after all, what makes them available to us now. How will a double reading enrich or diminish either text? ("Perhaps," muses Borges, "the burning of the library and

7. Borges, op. cit. p. 206.

the erection of the wall are operations which in some secret way cancel each other out.") Do the scholarly accretions presented in the Pléiade Edition as "De l'Education des Femmes" shed new light on the novel, making its author a misread precursor of the women's movement? Or are these texts, after all, only so much *débris* left behind by a literary meteor whose force can't be dissociated from the finality of the burnout? "This book, if it burns, can only burn in the manner of ice," said another prudent reader, Baudelaire. "History book."[8]

A rapid glance at the first of the three texts on women may, nonetheless, give us the impression that our history has only recently begun to repeat what Laclos was already saying in 1783:

Oh! women, approach and hear what I have to say. May your curiosity, at last directed to useful objects, contemplate the advantages that nature gave you, and that society has rudely snatched away [*ravis*]. Come and learn how, born man's companion, you have become his slave; how, fallen to this subject state, you gradually came to enjoy it, to see it as your natural condition; how, finally, degraded more and more by your long habit of slavery, you have preferred disgusting but comfortable vices to the more painful virtues of a free being worthy of respect. If this faithfully drawn picture leaves you cold, if you can look on without emotion, go back to your futile occupations . . . But if on hearing this tale of your suffering and loss, you blush in shame and anger, if you burn with a noble desire to regain your advantages, to repossess the fullness of your being [*rentrer dans la plénitude de votre être*], don't let yourselves be fooled by false promises, don't wait for the help of the men who have authored your troubles: they have neither the will, nor the power to end them, and how could they wish to bring forth [*former*] women before whom they would be impelled to blush? Learn that one only escapes slavery by means of a great revolution.[9]

These are inflammatory words—though the question immediately arises whether they are not too inflammatory to be taken entirely seriously. In its very extravagance the text at once calls to mind the well-known remarks of Alexis de Tocqueville about the prevalence, in the pre-revolutionary period, of abstract treatises recommending sweeping reforms in every area of life by writers who had no actual experience of political freedom.[10] To Tocqueville, the French Revolution is a sinister anomaly: an event which, despite its apparent practical effectiveness (which Tocqueville calls into question) and its unquestionable violence, remains purely literary: "Thus the philosopher's cloak provided safe cover for the passions of the day and the political ferment was canalized into literature, the result being that our writers now became the leaders of public opinion and played for a while the part that normally, in free

8. Baudelaire's notes on the novel are included in Laclos, op. cit. pp. 712–21.

9. Laclos, pp. 404–05. All subsequent citations from Laclos are to this edition; page numbers hereafter will be given in the body of the text.

10. Alexis de Tocqueville, *The Old Régime and the French Revolution*, trans. Stuart Gilbert (New York: Doubleday Anchor Books, 1955), Part 3, Chapter One, pp. 138–48.

countries, falls to the professional politician."[11] Though "the possibility of a violent upheaval never crossed our parents' minds," their literature unleashed the "catastrophe" of the revolution, and this same literature has persisted into the period in which Tocqueville writes, outlasting the aristocracy which fostered it, and the writers who dreamed it up. In fact this "literature" has even outlasted books and literacy:

> What seems particularly odd is that while retaining habits thus derived from books, we have almost completely lost our former love of literature. In the course of my public career I have often been struck by the fact that those who reproduce some of the chief defects of the literary style prevailing in the previous generations are men who rarely, if ever, read our eighteenth-century books or, for that matter, any books at all.[12]

To say that Tocqueville condemns the period in which Laclos wrote for "empty revolutionary rhetoric" is not quite accurate; in fact, Tocqueville himself deliberately empties this literary material of any specific identity or content, disdaining to call any of the actual authors by name, or to single out notable literary works as having been decisively influential. Two rather different responses to this strategy are possible. On the one hand, it is evident that Tocqueville violates elementary rules of scholarly accuracy and fair play, deploying "literature" as a purely accusatory and indeed slanderous term to cover all revolutionary utterances of whatever relative insight or complexity. On the other hand, we may say that this method enables Tocqueville to describe a verbal process in which the normal priorities of authorship and authority are strangely reversed. The phantom "literature" that Tocqueville manages so effectively to conjure up is not in fact so different from the notorious "Spectre" said to be haunting Europe in the opening sentence of Marx and Engels' *Communist Manifesto*. In the conservative rhetoric of Tocqueville, no less than in the radical rhetoric of Marx and Engels, we find delineated the same peculiar process by which a bodiless, bloodless spook—at first a mere figment of the old régime's fevered imagination—at last acquires an inexorable density of its own. Whether this apparition is labeled "literature" or "Communism" (and whether it is celebrated or deplored), the pattern is the same: in these two texts, as in all ghost stories, the most casually uttered words acquire in retrospect a starkly literal accuracy, coming back to haunt those who thoughtlessly launched them (as games, jokes or insults) and brutally imposing meanings that were never intentionally authorized.[13]

11. Ibid. p. 142. Writers are also accused of "usurping" the place left empty by a powerless aristocracy.

12. Ibid. p. 148.

13. Marx and Engels deliberately exploit the provocative overtones of the label, "Communist": they choose to apply a bourgeois term of abuse to their revolutionary program, and then proceed to demonstrate that it will, indeed, confirm the very worst fears of the bourgeoisie. *The Communist Manifesto* (New York: International Publishers, 1948); see especially Engels' preface to the German Edition of 1890 (pp. 14–15) and Chapter II.

If we re-examine Laclos' initial revolutionary appeal to women, we may find much to confirm such a jaundiced Tocquevillian view. For in the first of these three texts, Laclos' logic is indeed dominated by a rhetoric which empties his argument of any utilitarian content, and in this rhetoric we can discern what appears to be a mechanical and perhaps unavoidable repetition of two previous literary texts. Viewed as an excercise in logic, the text is clearly and quite deliberately self-defeating. Laclos takes pains to demonstrate that he cannot make sense of the idea of women's education in the light of his own premises:

Either the word education makes no sense, or one must understand it to mean the development of the faculties of the individual one is bringing up and the direction of these faculties toward social utility . . . In the particular instance which concerns us, woman is the individual, society is the species. [P. 404]

This effort to apply general social axioms to the "case" of women quickly leads to insoluble difficulties:

Where there is slavery, there cannot be education; in all societies, women are slaves; thus social woman is not susceptible of being educated. If the principles of this syllogism are proved, one cannot deny the consequence . . . One would only seek uselessly to invent further distinctions and divisions. One can't escape the general principle that without liberty there is no morality and without morality no education . . . [P. 405]

The treatise comes to an abrupt halt at this point; the ellipses (Laclos') mark the faltering of a discourse that knows itself doomed to repeat further useless subdivisions of its own initial first premises. We are left with a fragment, abandoned by its author, which occupies only three pages in the Pléiade Edition of his works, and which accomplishes virtually nothing more than this initial gesture of self-refutation.

Viewed as rhetoric, however, the text takes on quite a different aspect, achieving finality of a kind that we could hardly avoid attributing to any well-made explosive device.[14] For in the brief span of this fragmentary utterance, Laclos performs a rhetorical gesture that derives its force from the very futility of his argument. A question posed by the Academy at Châlons-sur-Marne— "what are the best means of improving the education of women?"—activates this turn, by which power is transferred from an apparently neutralized and self-sufficient logic to an explicitly gender-determined rhetoric. Laclos' manner of responding to the Academy's question undermines the authority which he must claim, as a man, if he wishes to answer it.

We can see this shift of power occurring especially clearly in the one

14. Biographers such as Dard, op. cit. and Vailland, op. cit., point out that Laclos invented a hollow bullet, which exploded with greater impact than the ones previously used by the French army. The texts we are discussing operate in much the same way.

oblique reference Laclos makes to his own novel. As long as he speaks directly to the Academy (that is, to an allegedly impersonal, but in fact exclusively masculine, institution), Laclos can only advise them that any project for improving the education of women is a can of worms they had better not open. At this point he asks some questions to which his novel may already have provided the answer: "The question is . . . whether in the current state of society a woman such as one might imagine her formed by a good education wouldn't be very unhappy if she kept her place, and extremely dangerous if she tried to step out of it" (404). The contrast between the unhappy, obedient Tourvel and the dangerous, manipulative Merteuil immediately comes to mind: Laclos is alluding to a story he has already told, and reading *Les Liaisons Dangereuses* as a cautionary tale in defense of the *status quo*. The only conclusion he can now draw, as a citizen, from this story is that women should, after all, be kept in their place. But if he seriously urges his audience to accept this conclusion, Laclos must place himself in a strangely divided position; he must in effect sign over the authority to determine the meaning of his book to his masculine peers; it is no longer "his" book, but the collective property of the dominant male establishment. There is, however, an alternate route open to Laclos, which he takes by turning the entire problem of women over to the opposition—that is, to the women themselves—inviting them to reactivate the meaning of his novel, and of the very speech he is now making, as best they can. Still speaking exclusively within the limits of his authority as a member of the masculine social order, Laclos cannot pretend to offer guarantees of any sort to these women, even while he urges them to initiate their own revolution: "Don't let yourselves be fooled by false promises; don't expect help from the men who are the authors of your troubles." He can only recite, *ad infinitum*, the same monotonous admonitory moral with which he began his treatise:

Is this revolution possible? It is up to you [women] to say since it depends on your courage. Is it likely? I keep silent on this question; but until the day it comes, and as long as men continue to decide your fate, I will be authorized to say, *and it will be easy for me to prove that there is no method of improving the education of women.* [405: Laclos' emphases]

The trajectory followed in the course of this piece is especially evident here as Laclos stubbornly cites himself, repeating verbatim the statement he made at the beginning of his address when he first reverently approached the Academy:

I approach this respectable assembly in order to lend to an even more respectable truth a weak but constant voice which won't be influenced either by the fear of displeasing or by the hope of success. Such is the contract I make today. The first duty it imposes on me is to offer a severe truth in place of a seductive error. One must dare to speak it aloud: there is no method of improving the education of women. [P. 403]

Laclos attempts to distinguish himself from the "crowd of orators" competing for a "literary crown;" it is his sacred duty to speak of the truth entirely didactically and logically. But what in fact happens in the course of this address is that without switching his allegiance to the "truth," he is nevertheless forced to convey that truth exclusively as rhetoric; he is not so much delivering a message as he is searching (unsuccessfully) for an audience who can receive it. As a teacher he has virtually nothing to say, either to the men in the Academy (who have simply asked the wrong question) or to the women outside. But even as a rhetorician, he seems to be performing to an empty house. All he can say to the Academy is that they should instantly call a halt to any project for educating women, but he can only repeat, redundantly, to the women what he has been saying to the men all along: *there is no means of improving the education of women.* At this point Laclos is in effect not "speaking" at all, so much as he is quoting himself: citing, as much in parody as in reaffirmation, his original negative response to the Academy's misguided and pointless question. The magnificence of the gesture can hardly be disentangled from its futility: having emptied his discourse of any effective content, he passes it along to the women, much as one might send an elaborately addressed envelope containing no legible message whatever.

As it happens, an extremely crucial and remarkably cruel letter in *Les Liaisons Dangereuses* contains a message which appears to summarize what is actually being said in this abortive treatise on women's education: *Ce n'est pas ma faute.*[15] It is easy enough to translate this message into English: "It's not my fault" or "Don't blame *me*." But despite the facility with which the message can be transmitted—in translation, or in the numerous copies that circulate in the novel—its legibility remains seriously open to question. Indeed Valmont, after sending the letter to Tourvel, admits to Merteuil "I am not sure I know how to read [it]." By his own account he has merely copied, unthinkingly, a previous text: "What I can say is that I found the letter original, and likely to make an impression: so I simply copied it out and, just as simply, sent it on to the heavenly Présidente" (339). It appears that one must keep sending this letter on in order not to have to read it; like a hissing bomb, it is tossed from hand to hand until it finally detonates. When the letter at last reaches Tourvel, she goes mad and dies, and in the aftermath of this event, Valmont and Merteuil become involved in open warfare, leading to his death and to her exposure and banishment.

In order to account for the devastating impact of this message, we must consider its context—or, more precisely, its obstinate refusal to acquire a context, to be traceable to any particular source. Merteuil, who originally provided this "little epistolary model" for Valmont to copy, disavows responsi-

15. This message circulates in Part IV of *Les Liaisons Dangereuses*, Letters CXXXVIII–CXLV, and letter CLXI.

bility for it by inventing the transparent fiction of "a man I know" who lacked the courage to break with a woman: "He passed his life that way, never ceasing to do stupid things, and always saying afterwards, 'It's not my fault' " (337). Merteuil's anecdote extends the chain of disavowal; the man she knew knew a woman, who copied his complaint in a letter, and gave it to him to send on—as she, Merteuil, now gives it to Valmont, to use as he sees fit (338). It appears that Valmont does something extraordinarily stupid when he passes the letter on to Tourvel; later, Merteuil will castigate him for this mistake, reveling nastily in her triumph over him ("She's not the one I've beaten on this round: it's you"), while at the same time taking credit for the vengeance she has successfully practised on her rival: "Ah, Vicomte, when one woman strikes at the heart of another, she rarely fails to find the tender spot, and the wound is incurable" (343–4). But instead of accusing Valmont of blindness, we might just as well congratulate him for adopting a remarkably astute policy in regard to this letter. In passing it on to Tourvel he refuses, in the full diplomatic sense of the term, to "recognize" himself in Merteuil's little story, refuses to hear, in the refrain *Ce n'est pas ma faute*, his own perpetual deferral of erotic commitment in the game he has been playing all along with these two women and any others who care to join. Valmont is nothing if not generous, and the gift he sends to Tourvel is an amply open invitation to remain within this circuit of exchange: "Goodbye, my Angel. I took you with pleasure, I leave you without regret: perhaps I'll come back. So goes the world. It's not my fault" (338). As long as the letter remains in circulation, passing through Valmont's lax and careless hands, it is as innocuous as it says it is; it succeeds, triumphantly, not only in meaning what it says but in doing exactly as it says it means—endlessly shifting the burden of authorship and interpretation down the line in a perpetual chain reaction of disavowals: *Ce n'est pas ma faute* ("Here: catch").

Men do not have to know how to read such letters: they would have to be crazy (like Tourvel) or wicked (like Merteuil) even to try. As we read Tourvel's last letter we discover that it is, literally, folly to try to make sense of this message: she can only lend it meanings that refuse to coalesce: "Come and punish an unfaithful woman. Let me finally suffer the torture I deserve. I would have submitted already to your vengeance, but I lacked the courage to tell you your shame. This was not dissimulation: it was respect" (379). Tourvel struggles to accept this letter, to assume or assign the blame of its transmission, but she no longer knows who she is, or to whom she is writing: "Haven't you made it impossible for me to listen to you, or to answer?" By this time the letter means what it says with a vengeance—and not even Merteuil, as it turns out, can appropriate that vengeance, or that meaning, as being, properly, hers. When she discovers that Valmont still refuses to understand what he has done, Merteuil contemptuously turns her back on the matter: "If I've been deceived in my vengeance, I agree to accept the blame . . . I'm so calm on this score that I don't want to be bothered any longer. Let's speak of other things" (345). As Merteuil well knows, and as the sheer imbecilic obstinacy of its re-citation indicates, the letter is best left to make its rounds without a sponsor: what makes it work so well is the fact that it belongs to no-one, and is intended for no one in particular.[16] *Ce n'est pas ma faute* is meaning perpetually bestowed and endlessly retracted. What gives the message its potency is its capacity to circulate; what keeps it in circulation is the danger that it might, if the circuit is broken, go off, causing the destruction of anyone who would presume to claim it: to take it or to mean it seriously.

If we return, now, to Laclos' first educational treatise, we may begin to suspect that it is, indeed, a sequel to his novel, if only in the most literal sense. For we find Laclos, in effect, still trying to post the entire packet of letters to the correct address—although this time around, unlike Valmont in the book, he appears to acknowledge the severe restrictions he must impose on the message he sends, in speaking as an authoritative member of the male establishment. Men are given a simple message to read here: Don't educate women. But while the text, with its obvious irony, encourages us to suspect that this is not precisely what Laclos means to say, the irony makes itself felt only through this gesture, by which he simultaneously assumes, and casts off, the mask of masculine authority—if it is a mask, and if it can, after all, be so easily discarded.[17] When, in the novel, all the masks at last come off, what lies behind them is the face of a woman (Merteuil), but it is half-blind and hideously disfigured. It remains to be seen whether, in his subsequent educational project, Laclos was able to do more than repeat a no doubt entirely earnest and unwitting version of the same cruel practical joke that Merteuil played in the novel, with such dire consequences to herself and to everyone else.

One guarantee, perhaps, of Laclos' earnestness is that he is not merely repeating himself in these three treatises on women. He is also diligently copying and re-copying a series of messages that quite obviously come from another source: that is, from Rousseau. If the first of Laclos' treatises consists of virtually nothing more than the gesture of turning an academy question against itself, that gesture (apart from its feminist revolutionary sequel) exactly copies one performed by Rousseau in his *First Discourse*—"the unhappy work," he said later, "to which I owe my celebrity."[18] Rousseau won

16. The critical controversy over the destination of Edgar Allan Poe's *Purloined Letter* is clearly relevant to this discussion. See Jacques Lacan, *"Seminar on 'the Purloined Letter,'"* trans. Jeffrey Mehlman, YFS 48, *French Freud*, 1973; Jacques Derrida, "The Purveyor of Truth," YFS 52, *Graphesis*, 1975; Barbara Johnson, "The Frame of Reference," YFS 55/56, *Literature and Psychoanalysis*, 1977.

17. Roland Barthes asserts that the irony of all narration produced by our culture is summed up in this formula, *Larvatus prodeo: Writing Degree Zero*, trans. Annette Lavers and Colin Smith (Boston, 1967), pp. 29–40.

18. In Rousseau, *Du Contrat Social* (Paris: Garnier, 1960), p. 1.

the prize and launched his own public career by giving a negative answer to the question set by the Academy of Dijon: "Whether the sciences and arts have contributed to the purification of social customs *(moeurs)*." This notoriously successful affront to established cultural institutions seems to have acquired an irresistible appeal, of exactly the sort noted darkly by de Tocqueville: one would think that the academies might have become wary of proposing any improvements whatever, since the dire possibility suggests itself of hundreds of would-be Rousseaus eagerly at work to disappoint them. But we have seen that Laclos, even though he may have set out to improve on Rousseau by inserting the question of women into the critique of learning established in the *First Discourse*, is unable to finish successfully what Rousseau started.[19] And this pattern repeats itself in Laclos' second treatise—the longest and most ambitious of the three—in which he continues to follow a well-trodden path, along strictly Rousseauian lines, moving from the questions about culture raised in the first treatise to the questions about nature that Rousseau raised in the *Second Discourse* ("On the Origins of Inequality among Men"). Here Laclos sets out to explore woman, "not . . . disfigured by our institutions, but such as she is emerging from the hands of nature" (406). Scrupulously citing Rousseau's disclaimer of literal historical accuracy, he nevertheless attempts to re-imagine woman as a "free and powerful" being (407), in the same way that Rousseau sought to imagine natural man.[20] This feminized repetition of Rousseau is also highly eroticized—as we see in the following passage, where Laclos' nature-girl *(fille naturelle)* at last meets her mate:

Victim of a need she does not perceive, a secret ardor consumes her; restless days are followed by even more troubled nights; the first dawn no longer finds her in the arms of sleep, she no longer finds the cooling repose of morning; everything sleeps around her, she alone is awake in nature; no sooner does a faint light enable her to distinguish objects than she begins to roam about anxiously; she runs to the nearest stream, seeking to quench the fire that torments her in the waters, the first rays of the sun light her way to the bath. Vain remedy! she climbs out and burns again. She looks around with anxious eagerness; her eyes are fixed with enchantment on the spectacle of the morning; she has felt the first heat of love; nature has just become animate for her; the sweet scent of the flowers prepares her for pleasure; the song of the birds is no longer an empty sound, but a touching harmony which responds to her heart; their repeated caresses affect her even more strongly. Hands raised, mouth half-open, she looks on with wet eyes and fears to disturb them; her short and rapid breathing, the rapid

19. Laclos' remarks on women's willing submission to social slavery (cited above in this text, p. 5) exactly echo Rousseau's account of the insidious effects of culture on human freedom in general: "While government and law ensure the safety and well-being of human assemblies, sciences, letters and the arts, perhaps less despotic but more powerful, cast garlands of flowers over the chains that weigh men down, stifling their sense of the original freedom for which they were born, and making them love their slavery . . ." Rousseau, op. cit. pp. 3–4.

20. Laclos quotes directly from Rousseau, who described his own method as being "more suited to clarify the nature of things than to demonstrate their actual origin." Laclos, p. 407.

movement of her breast, reveal all too clearly the disturbance within her. Then, at a distance, she sees a man; a powerful instinct, an involuntary movement, makes her run towards him; closer, she becomes timid, and stops; then, carried on again, she closes in and presses him in her arms . . . delicious rapture *(jouissance)*: who, ever, would dare describe you? [415]

In this text, as in the previous one, Laclos disconcertingly repeats himself and Rousseau simultaneously. For a reader of *Les Liaisons Dangereuses* might well suspect that Laclos' primary motive in writing this passage was to enjoy at last the indefinitely postponed climax to the prolonged strip-tease offered in the novel. It is all too evident that this lavishly evoked moment (carefully prepared in the first five chapters of the essay) is the focus of all the desires expressed in *Les Liaisons Dangereuses:* this is what Valmont wants from Tourvel, what Merteuil imitates, with consummate skill, in her encounters with Belleroche and Prévan, and what is automatically expected of Cécile—adding to the enormous cash value she has on the marriage market and making her such delectable prey to the machinations of Valmont and Merteuil. The entire society depicted in the novel seems to have been arranged around this primal scene of surprised rapture, which it continually seeks to recapture or to exploit. It is difficult, therefore, to read this passage with an entirely straight face as a healthy "natural" alternative to that diseased culture. And quite apart from the suspicions that Laclos' own novel may cast on this idyllic fantasy, his argument also falls apart in a predictable Rousseauian manner; Laclos is unable to envision a more permanent resolution of natural needs and social passions: "As soon as society, which constantly alters the work of nature, had changed the passing union of the two sexes into a durable *liaison,* voluptuous sensations ceased to be the only tie that united them" (441). For Laclos, as for Rousseau, "nature" and "culture" remain irreparably opposed concepts that can hardly be defined except by being placed in antithesis to one another.[21]

Laclos' second treatise trails off, as did the first, in an inconclusive manner that demonstrates the author's inability to hold to his initial intention of helping women "return to the fullness of [their] being" (405). We leave Laclos caught up in a disapproving but fascinated description of the pains civilized women take to manufacture the naiveté they have lost—much as he himself, in writing this piece, set out to reproduce Rousseau's (already fictional) natural state. At the close of the essay, the unguarded astonishment of the *fille naturelle* upon seeing a man has undergone a significant change:

21. In Rousseau's text, "vice" is the immediate result of the most idyllic social union; although this union is imagined as a dance under the trees, and although Rousseau briefly mentions sexual jealousy, the focus is on more generalized and de-sexualized *liaisons* among humans *(les hommes),* leading to "vanity, mistrust, shame and envy." (Op. cit. p. 71). Instinctual pre-social sexual passion is of no interest at all to Rousseau. Laclos' effort to picture this passion seems prurient precisely because it is irrelevant to the view of culture he shares with Rousseau; he can therefore be accused of a kind of nostalgia that Rousseau never gives in to.

We are all aware that the great movements of the soul and the senses can be discerned in the eyes, surmounting even the obstacles that oppose them. Such is the right of nature; art has tried to imitate it, and has succeeded: the custom is frequent in the theater; this abuse has slipped into society where glances have become false and perfidious. This tendency can be seen in make-up *(parure)*; if one believes the reports of travellers, the ballad-singers of Hindustan know how, with the aid of a powder, to give their looks the expression of pleasure, introducing into their eyes the burning tears of voluptuous-ness—and quite apart from these tales, we can see how the European women around us make their eyes shine with the heat of desire that is reflected from the rouge they put on their cheeks.[448]

This is exactly the kind of deception that is practised from the beginning to the end of *Les Liaisons Dangereuses*, where signs of the utmost spontaneity and frankness become the favored means of concealment. Even Cécile, very early on, is able to observe this: "I noticed that when anyone looked at other women, they didn't blush; or perhaps it's the rouge they wear which prevents you from seeing them grow red with embarrassment" (15). We know that Merteuil and Valmont are experts at the same strategic use of the truth to conceal the truth: often in this novel a carefully regulated self-exposure becomes the surest safeguard of one's most deeply-hidden intentions.[22] After Merteuil is un-masked at the end of the book, Mme de Volange's closing comments indicate the futility of any attempt to isolate or to condemn what is in fact the inescapable and pervasive course of ordinary social existence: "these tardy reflections never come until after the event, and one of the most important truths, perhaps even one most commonly recognized, is uselessly smothered in the whirl of our thoughtless customs *(dans le tourbillon de nos moeurs inconséquents)*" (399). This is a society that manages to tell its lies entirely openly—in its very blushes, as in its most commonly-accepted and self-evident truths.

The question of women can't, it seems, be resolved by investigating a "natural" or pre-social state; it must instead be located in the ambivalent and tricky area of *nos mœurs inconséquents*. At this point the issue of Laclos' indebtedness to Rousseau becomes more complex, for it is only in the *Letter to D'Alembert* that we find any extended discussion of women in the social state, and this text is one Laclos appears to have read, if at all, rather carelessly, as his remarks in the third treatise indicate: "J. J. Rousseau has made us see the danger [of plays], d'Alembert their utility; each of them simply assumes a different point of view" (455). Nevertheless Laclos is forced, in the second treatise, to shift the emphasis of his own argument from the "primary" realm of politics to the "secondary" realm of aesthetics as he seeks to account for the

---

22. See, for example, the touching scene between Valmont and Tourvel: "taking her hands, I bathed them with tears. This was a necessary precaution, for she was so occupied with her own sadness that she would not have noticed mine, if I had not found this means of getting her attention." (53)

central place women occupy in a society which never included them as equals in the initial contractual arrangement.[23] This is exactly the procedure Rousseau follows in the *Letter to D'Alembert*, for his discussion of women arises in the course of his efforts to exclude one institution—the theater—from his native republic of Geneva.[24] Since that text demonstrates so emphatically the core of Rousseau's resistance to women, it is undertandable that Laclos should have sought to brush it aside in his third treatise, where he is attempting to set up an optimistic and practical program of guided instruction for young ladies.[25] Nevertheless we shall have to examine the *Letter to D'Alembert* if we wish to understand why Laclos found it impossible to apply Rousseauian theories of political freedom to the "case" of women.

Women are very much present in this text, not as a subcategory of humanity in general, but as beings who are fundamentally different from men. This difference is discussed in explicitly sexual terms, and in defining it Rousseau firmly distinguishes his own views on the matter from more liberal notions of sexual equality that were, apparently, gaining currency at the time. From Rousseau's own report, his opponents sought to challenge the sexual politics of a patriarchal society by insisting that sexual desire is a morally uncomplicated natural need, which both sexes are equally entitled to express and to gratify.[26] In retaliation Rousseau insists that an innate modesty distinguishes women from men: this *pudeur* is a natural and a God-given instinct that must precede any further social arrangements. At one important moment, Rousseau becomes quite anatomically explicit, although verbal problems immediately arise which tend to mask the point he is making:

23. "When one studies the history of different peoples and examines their laws, one is led to believe that women only conceded, and never consented, to the Social Contract." (Laclos, pp. 443–44) One might say that this is the central paradox around which all major discussions of women center during this period: women don't sign the contract, but they clearly share in the burdens of civilized society, and often appear to exemplify its worst vices. Mary Wollstonecraft is eloquent on this point: see *A Vindication of the Rights of Women* (Penguin Books, 1978), p. 88 and Chapter Four, pp. 141–72.

24. By focussing on this text, I attempt to disclose one particularly significant aspect of the vast and obsessive discussion of women that runs throughout Rousseau's work. My own abbreviated account would have been impossible without the perceptive and exhaustive treatment given this topic by Susan Moller Okin, *Women in Western Political Thought* (Princeton: Princeton U. Press, 1979), whose four chapters on Roussau (pp. 99–194) have been most useful to me.

25. In the third treatise, having argued himself out of his initial revolutionary enthusiasm, Laclos launches into a discussion of reading, "a second education which may supplement the inadequacy of the first" (449). He argues that women may avoid the dangers of fiction under the tutelage of cautious male mentors. Coming from an admirer of *La Nouvelle Héloïse*, this solution suggests an astonishing *naiveté* or a total failure of nerve on Laclos' part; he seems to be trying to forget ever having read Rousseau at all.

26. Rousseau puts very pointed political statements into his opponents' mouths: "modesty . . . is only an invention of social laws designed to conceal the privilege of fathers and husbands, and keep order in families. Why should we blush at needs that nature has given us? Why find a motive for shame in an act as indifferent in itself and as useful in its effects, which leads to the perpetuation of the species?" Rousseau, op. cit. p. 189. Subsequent references to the *Letter to D'Alembert* will be given in the body of the text.

Desires are equal: what a thing to say! Are there, on the one side and the other, the same faculties with which to satisfy them? What would happen to the human race if the order of attack and defense were to change? The [female] assailant would choose, by accident, times when victory would be impossible: the one pursued *(l'assailli)* would be left in peace just when he needed to give himself up, and pursued without mercy when he was too weak to succumb; thus power and will, always in confusion, would never permit desire to be shared; love would no longer be the support of nature, it would become a destructive scourge. [190]

The language of "attack" and "defense" is used with bizarre effect in this passage; it is impossible to distinguish between decorous circumlocution and deliberate irony when Rousseau employs this vocabulary of "victory" and "defeat" with reference to what he is in fact discussing—the possibility of masculine impotence: "the one pursued would be left in peace just when he needed to give himself up, and pursued without mercy when he was *too weak to succumb*" [emphasis mine]. This last ungainly phrase is an important indication of a problem that is simultaneously sexual and verbal. In marked contrast, a few pages later, Rousseau finds a more graceful way of describing the capacities of women, who, he assures us, have been perfectly designed for the role he wishes to assign them. They are at once "strong enough not to succumb unless they want to, and weak enough always to have a good excuse for giving themselves up" (192). Here Rousseau is able to express, with a certain amount of rhetorical control, a truism about female sexual behavior that often found its way into eighteenth-century discourse, and provided occasion for not a few witty remarks—such as Fielding's famous sentence, "[He] would have ravished her, if she had not, by a timely compliance, prevented him."[27] In the case of women, the relationship between deliberate strategy and involuntary instinct always remains undecidable (at least to the male observer), and hence subject to such balanced comic or coquettish reversals. In the case of men, however, there is always the threatening possibility that power and will may, unpredictably, fail to coincide—with the result that instead of a good joke we have an unintelligible *fiasco*, to borrow Stendhal's code phrase for such calamities. Since the language of dominance and subordination to which Rousseau has committed himself can't even handle this discrepancy coherently, the state of affairs that might arise if women were the pursuers and men the pursued must be described, in the conditional, not only as a horrible prospect but as a virtually unthinkable one.

The assertion that men are "naturally" stronger than women is a common way of justifying, biologically, their social and political dominance; this passage, however, betrays a sexual anxiety that may always underlie such arguments. Whatever the case, Rousseau's verbal embarrassment at this point can be traced as well to an important distinction he made himself between two areas: that of natural need or instinct *(besoin)*, and that of art, politics and

27. Henry Fielding, *Jonathan Wild* (New York: New American Library, 1961), p. 132.

culture *(passion)* where signs come into play and games originate.[28] For the problem, here, is not so much which sex is "naturally" weaker or stronger. Instead a purely strategic question must be asked: which sex, given the unpredictable male capacity for sexual performance, can best afford to assume the role of attacker or defender in the erotic cultural game? It seems that women are best qualified to play defense because it is never entirely clear, at a given moment, how willing or needy they are—whereas a sure sign always indicates to the careful observer if a man, as Rousseau puts it, "needs to give himself up." Thus Laclos' Merteuil, in a moment of consummate gamesmanship, plays her prescribed role of *pudeur* to the hilt, as she gazes with becomingly downcast eyes at Prévan's erection:

You may well imagine that my timid eyes hardly dared meet those of my vanquisher: but directed downward in a more humble fashion, they quickly let me see that I was obtaining the effect I wanted to produce. [193]

Men must take—or be given—the initiative in the sexual act, not because they are "naturally" stronger, but because otherwise it might become all too clear that the decision of when to start and stop is, in fact, beyond their control. Woman must always be available because man can't be; yet her resistance is also necessary in order to conceal (perhaps from both of them) the actual difficulties of getting the process under way. In the passage just cited, Merteuil applies these lessons with all the docility of a star pupil.

The passage under discussion may have enabled us to see how deeply women become implicated in specifically verbal problems that arise, throughout Rousseau's work, whenever he seeks to articulate the transition from nature to culture. In our own analysis of the passage, we have been forced to adopt a vocabulary of artifice (game-playing) even though Rousseau pretends to be discussing a "natural" process. In his *Essay on the Origins of Language,* Rousseau diagnosed an unavoidable retroactive drift by which language perpetually invents figures in order to portray its own dubious origins. The same process is operative here: Rousseau discusses what is essentially a cultural, verbal arrangement as if it were a natural condition; what is in fact an examination of the capacity of human beings to formulate meanings in terms of sexual difference is presented in the guise of an authoritative explanation of the "natural" causes of that difference. When Rousseau asks, "What would become of the human race *(l'espèce humaine)* if the order of attack and defense were changed?" he is not, like his liberal opponents, thinking of the perpetuation of the species, but of the capacity to conceive an entity that can be called *l'espèce humaine.* He wants to make sense (not babies) out of human beings

28. Rousseau, *Essai sur l'Origine des Langues* (Paris, le Graphe, supplément au No. 8 des *Cahiers pour l'Analyse).* For an account of the distinction between *passion* and *besoin* in the essay, see Paul de Man, *Blindness and Insight* (New York: Oxford Press, 1971), pp. 133–35.

marked as essentially (sexually) different, and what he fears is not the literal end of the human race but disorganized, unplayable nonsense: "love would no longer be the support of nature; it would become a destructive scourge." There is always, in nature, an alternative to what is intelligibly human, and that alternative must be avoided at all costs. Indeed, in the *Essay on the Origins of Language,* the emergence of intelligible speech (in the word, "man"—Rousseau's example) is explicitly linked to the rejection of such alternatives ("giants"). Men agree to speak together by agreeing to regard their initial differences as mistakes, fictions, figures of speech.[29] Temporal priority is assigned to the difference (the fiction, "giants"); logical priority is assigned to the similarity, viewed as truth ("man"). But these priorities refuse to fall so happily into place when the difference between men and women becomes the issue. The ability of human beings to generate meaning will be placed in jeopardy as long as the question of who has the authority to initiate the process remains undecidable. In order to resolve this matter Rousseau must repeat the very mistake he diagnosed in the *Essay on the Origins of Language;* women must in effect "play giant," figuratively representing an innate and irreducible difference, so that the generic concept, "man," may prevail. Rousseau demands of women that they act as the custodians of culture by standing in for nature, allowing men to initiate the rules of a game which can't in fact be played at all unless they (the women) consent to pretend that it is not a game, but simply the natural and inevitable condition of things.

The subterfuge being recommended here is nearly identical to one discussed by Paul de Man in his recent account of the *Social Contract.*[30] Citing an early draft of this text, de Man takes a phrase omitted from the final version ("secretly:" *en secret)* as an indication of Rousseau's hesitancy about admitting, openly, the covert operations by which social "justice" must be maintained: " 'Why is the general will always right, and why do all citizens constantly desire the well-being of each, if it were not for the fact that no-one exists who does not (secretly) appropriate the term *each* and think of himself when he votes for all?' "[31] De Man speaks of a theft which occurs here, when any individual appropriates a particular application ("I") from the generality ("tous") of the contractual text. Interestingly, in the *Letter to d'Alembert,* Rousseau speaks in nearly the same terms of an equally deceitful, but symmetrically reversed, procedure that is habitually indulged in by immoral members of the audience in a theater:

What better treaty could he make, than to oblige the entire world to be just, except himself, so that each one will faithfully give him what they owe him, and he gives back nothing in return to anyone? No doubt he loves virtue, but he loves it in others, because

29. Rousseau, ibid. p. 506.
30. *Allegories of Reading* (New Haven and London: Yale University Press, 1979), pp. 246–77.
31. Cited in de Man, ibid. p. 269.

he expects to profit by it; he doesn't want it for himself, because it might cost him something. What then does he see in the spectacle? Precisely what he would like to find everywhere; lessons of virtue for the general public, from whom he excepts himself, and people who sacrifice everything to their duty, while none of these demands are made of him. [140]

The theater functions like a travesty of the social contract, as the audience *(le méchant)* wickedly returns the goods that were stolen in the other text, exempting him (or, as it turns out, her) self from the general public "lessons of virtue" which the play goes on uselessly delivering: "See what becomes of all the fine sentiments and brilliant maxims which are so emphatically displayed; they are relegated forever to the stage *(la scène)*, so that we can see virtue as a theatrical trick, fine for public entertainment, but insane if it were seriously transferred to actual social life" (142). The theater is, in effect, the social contract openly making a spectacle of itself; and because she is paid to do just this, an actress constitutes a particularly grave threat to the public welfare: she is "always the first to parody her role and destroy her own work" (196). Rousseau cannot merely dismiss the theater (and women) as secondary elements that might get out of hand; he views them as rival institutions whose priorities are, in principle, at odds with those that properly govern Geneva: "the effect . . . which changes good into evil, and evil into good, resulting from the very existence of the theatrical spectacle, is constant and real; recurring every day, it will drag everything along with it" (174). It is this "spectacle," this subterfuge in the social contract openly displayed in the theater as self-mockery, against which Rousseau seeks to protect his native republic in the *Letter to d'Alembert.*

To say, then, that Rousseau assigns women "second place" in his socio-political theory does not quite accurately convey the crucial yet ambivalent status they in fact acquire in this text, which continues to sound the alarm against them, and against the theater, as equivalent sources of an uncanny power. The very same power is attributed, in the *Social Contract,* to the legislative branch of government—the chief agent of the subterfuge required to maintain the workings of justice. Rousseau's lawgiver preserves the authority vested in the general will by referring it back to a God—an act of blasphemy, according to de Man, since the *Social Contract* cannot lay claim to any such divine inspiration.[32] Woman, in the *Letter to d'Alembert,* allows man the same primary, initiatory but totally contrived authority to which theater-goers pay lip-service as long as the show goes on. The script for this deadly drama is essentially the same in both texts. One particularly striking episode, in the *Social Contract,* bears the title "On the Death of the Body Politic."[33] Here, just

32. Ibid. p. 274–75.
33. Rousseau, op. cit. pp. 297–8. Subsequent references to the *Social Contract* will be included in the body of the text.

as he anatomizes the state (dividing it into "legislative" and "executive" forces), Rousseau also predicts its inevitable decay: "the body politic, like a man's body, begins to die at the moment of its birth and carries within it the causes of its own corruption." As an artificial body, however, it outlasts individual men, and this longevity is located in the legislative branch:

The legislative power is the heart of the state, the executive is the brain, which makes all the other parts move. The brain can suffer a paralytic stroke while the individual still goes on breathing. Even an imbecile is alive; but as soon as the heart ceases to function, the animal is dead.

If the religious foundation Rousseau attempts to give his state turns out, as de Man says, to be blasphemous, this organic foundation is equally disastrous biologically. Elsewhere the legislative "heart" which mindlessly keeps the state going is said to "reanimate or supplement" its laws by appealing to "morals, customs, and especially public opinion . . . which always secretly concern the great legislator" (272). Legislative secrecy is again invoked in a passage dealing with the very realm which, in the Letter to d'Alembert, was explicitly assigned to women. Woman, like the lawgiver, is the imbecilic guardian of state secrets, the heart which prolongs the life of the political animal, in the absence of conscious, or "executive" control.

If we return now to Laclos' second treatise, we may begin to see a similar pattern emerge. In an important Chapter, "On Beauty," we find Laclos discussing the same issues of revelation and secrecy that preoccupied Rousseau in the Letter to d'Alembert:

From the moment men were united, they lost the capacity for rest (repos). Natural man sleeps as soon as his needs are satisfied; it's not that way with civilized man; he must keep vigil (veiller) at the execution of the social contract; he can't abandon himself to sleep; he sleeps only in the brief periods when he can no longer manage to stay awake. Ceaselessly on the alert against the enterprises of his associates, he watches (il veille), not to act, but to be ready to act if he needs to. [437]

This social restlessness is a more subtle and insidious condition than the tyrant-slave relationship among men and women that Laclos discusses throughout most of the essay. The concept of female "beauty" results from the vigilance imposed by the social contract, and is also its chief antidote. But the specific cost of such wakefulness to women is made clearer in an earlier Chapter, "On Old Age and Death" (418–20). Here Laclos contrasts the peaceful death of primitive men and women to the unquiet end of life in society: "While natural man tranquilly follows the easy and gentle course which ought to lead to his eternal rest, the old man of this century savagely clings to the place destined by nature for his posterity." This social death-agony is the "sad effect of an unruly imagination which ceaselessly transports him from the place he occupies to the place he desires." But if things are bad for old men, they are worse for old women; a man can always find a woman to help deceive him: "he will be the plaything of everyone around him, but he can fail to notice this; he won't be aware of his true situation." An old woman, however, has no such luck; no matter how rich she may be, the greediest of her lovers will be afflicted with impotence: "He loses, in her very arms, all his promised power *(force)*; he lies as if dead between her and her fortune." Here, as in the *Letter to d'Alembert*, an apparently trivial figure of speech ("as if dead") takes on crucial implications. For it is, as always, woman who bears the brunt of the imbalance between literal and figurative meaning at work in this otherwise innocuous cliché. What is only figurative "death" for the man is transferred directly to her, since she must confront, without any imaginative solace, the spectacle of her own unredeemable ugliness, the distasteful sign *(figure:* "face") of human mortality. Beauty, according to Laclos, arises when the natural delight in the body is replaced by society's fixation on the face, (439) and women of every age and station are constantly subject to this ambivalent play between body and *figure,* this restless alternation between nature and culture that is repeatedly evoked in the verb *veiller.*[34] As queen, lover, slave, or pupil, woman is the unwilling guardian of society's bitterest secrets; in order to promote the sleep of the state, she must learn the lessons society would prefer not to teach. Rousseau's legislator has no more onerous task.

As we have seen, the *Letter to d'Alembert* can be read as the other (female) face of the *Social Contract.* Laclos' second treatise on women repeats a lesson to be found in both these texts, and it seems he must also, unavoidably, repeat his own novel even while he attempts to move away from literature into the utilitarian realm of social reform. If we return, now, to *Les Liaisons Dangereuses,* we may be able to locate there the dangerous link between politics and literature that was, for de Tocqueville, the fatal characteristic of all revolutionary thought. For we may view Laclos' novel as a remarkably efficient application of the political and grammatical principles to be found in the *Social Contract.*[35] And we may thus understand why it was impossible for Laclos to write a sequel to his novel, to apply its lesson any further to the case of women.

34. A queen's apparent happiness, for example, is a veritable ordeal of vigilance: "no doubt she will be blessed by her subjects, but let her not hope for a moment of rest; doesn't she have to be constantly alert on behalf of all the others? *(ne faut-il pas qu'elle veille pour tous?)*" (421). In the final chapter, "De la Parure" (On Keeping up Appearances) Laclos advises, "especially avoid late nights *(fuyez surtout les veilles inutiles)*; sleep is more flattering than the deceptive glow of candles" (445). In an early letter from the novel, Valmont taunts Merteuil about Belleroche: "He sleeps tranquilly, while you stay awake *(veiller)* for his pleasure. What more could his slave do?" (37)

35. Paul de Man finds the fatal flaw of the *Social Contract* to lie in the fact that the grammatical logic according to which the text functions collapses the minute a distinct reference or legal application is made, op. cit. pp. 268–70. I am suggesting that Laclos applied the same logic in his novel, which re-enacts the same collapse. Both texts are equally self-propelling and self-defeating.

Let us, first of all, re-examine the implicit sociology of this text. *Les Liaisons Dangereuses* is often classified historically as the portrayal of a decadent aristocracy.[36] But a closer look suggests that we may instead be dealing with an entirely democratic phenomenon, precisely in the Tocquevillian sense.[37] In an important passage, Prévan, the one male character in the book whose erotic expertise rivals that of Valmont, realizes that he can move in on three ostensibly happy couples because they are playing an empty public game: "He soon saw, in effect, that this much-celebrated happiness was, like that of Kings, more to be envied than desired" (165). There is no central source of erotic power in this book, any more than there is of political power; instead the envy that was, for de Tocqueville, the hallmark of a democracy, is at work everywhere.[38] This lack of centrality is what governs the strategy of the book's most effective game-players; it accounts, particularly, for what might be mistaken for feminist leanings in Merteuil herself. Merteuil is certainly no proponent of sisterhood, and her feminism is entirely strategic: it becomes clear that she cannot do without the sexual double standard if she wishes to play the game she does in this otherwise open society. Working within this convention, Merteuil can arrange entirely unforeseen triumphs over opponents like Prévan—who, for his part, triumphs sexually over three male rivals and then turns aside their rage by pointing out that he only did what any of them might have done in his place (168). This episode illuminates the one serious drawback of Merteuil's position: she must either play entirely invisibly (thus failing to rack up a score), or run the risk of destroying the entire game by exposing its principles. Merteuil is in the predicament of a player who has discovered a foolproof method which makes it impossible to lose, and then realizes that if the other players adopted it, the game would be over. She can only console herself temporarily by adopting a dogmatic philosophy about the blindness of the others, and she appears to have chosen, quite early on, the inevitable final Armageddon in preference to the spectacle of perpetual blundering which allows the game to continue.

Perhaps an even more fruitful way of demonstrating how closely *Les Liaisons Dangereuses* duplicates the structure of the *Social Contract* is to

---

36. Readers since Laclos' time have found various ways of isolating this group of libertines from any mainstream to which they might themselves belong; the characters are described as decadent aristocrats, real historical individuals, or marginal members of some sinister *cabal*. Only Baudelaire seems to have regretted their passing. See the reactions provided in Laclos, op. cit. pp. 698–721.

37. The distinction between the powerless aristocrats of de Tocqueville's *ancien régime* and their constitutionally envious counterparts in America is not in any case easy to make. De Tocqueville speaks of the "courtier spirit" afflicting Americans at every social level: *Democracy in America*, trans. George Lawrence, ed. J. P. Mayer (New York: Harper and Row, 1969), pp. 257–9.

38. Ibid. p. 57, pp. 614–45. See also René Girard's account of envy in the novel: *Deceit, Desire and the Novel*, trans. Yvonne Freccero (Baltimore: Johns Hopkins U. Press, 1965). Girard cites de Tocqueville several times in support of his thesis, p. 120; p. 124; pp. 136–38.

consider its peculiar status as a work of pornography. The pathos of this *genre* as a whole is to be essentially disposable; one reads such texts in the service of a sexual aim that is never, unfortunately, achieved on the page. In *Les Liaisons Dangereuses*, however, whatever erotic gratification may occur operates, in principle, exclusively within the text. This is not, technically, an obscene book: its sexual meanings, though always quite explicit, are created by means of a curious kind of figural word-play. For this text refuses to valorize the "proper" or "literal" meaning over the written sign, instead deploying its meanings by what might be termed a collision of opposing proprieties—as when, for instance, Valmont and Merteuil speak of their erotic enterprise in religious terms. (16) These "apostles" of sexuality don't believe in the Gods they invoke any more than Rousseau's legislator does, but it would be wrong to say they "believe" in sex (entitled "Amour") either; neither side of the figural polarity takes precedence over the other. If the religious language advertises itself convincingly as the veil for a fierce sexuality, the process works as well in the opposite direction, releasing an energy that appears to lend some of Merteuil's apparent blasphemies an uncannily literal authority. When she says, "Here am I, like the Divinity, receiving the opposed vows of blind mortals and changing nothing in my immutable decrees" (128), she appears to be speaking without ironic reserve in the only terms strong enough to enable her to say what she needs to. The genuinely dangerous wit of this entire book depends on this scrupulous impartiality, which never chooses between the alternatives brought into play by its figures, and where in fact the ordinary opposition between irony (which wills to mean other than it says) and catachresis (which can't help saying other than it means) becomes impossible to disentangle. This pattern is exemplified especially clearly when Valmont, recounting by hearsay Prévan's remarkable exploit of "scoring" nine times in one night with three different women, expresses some doubt: "Here as you might judge, the history lacks proof; all the impartial Historian can do is point out to the incredulous reader that exalted vanity and imagination can give birth to Prodigies . . ." (168). We have no way of knowing whether he means that the incident was exaggerated by Prévan as he gossiped about it, or whether Prévan's own imaginative exaltation did indeed carry him to such unprecedented heights; we don't even know whether Valmont meant us to take one meaning, or whether he means this double meaning to prevail. If the text appears to place its own impartiality *en abîme* at this point, its more humdrum erotic adventures nevertheless operate according to what is essentially the same mechanism. Explicit erotic "referentiality" (where "referent" refers, specifically, to the genitals) is made possible by means of the documentary *liaisons* among the characters. Merteuil pretends to disparage letter-writing when she warns Valmont against continuing his correspondance with Tourvel, claiming that the act of writing is a poor substitute for the "real thing," but she is only able to assert the official dogma which gives the thing precedence over the word so long as she herself, in writing her letter to Valmont, brings into play the very exchange between letter-writing and sexual activity that she professes to deplore: "It seems to me that what still ought to assure you of success is that she uses up too much energy all at once; I foresee that she will waste her strength defending the word, and won't have any more left to defend the thing *(la chose)"* (71). What is ordinarily an entirely arbitrary gender-distinction appears to receive emphatic motivation in this instance, so that the word denoting Tourvel's female "thing" takes on exemplary status as a genuinely "proper" term—or, at the very least, the perfect (if highly improper) metaphorical representation of such propriety. Such a remarkable feat could, of course, only be achieved by a stroke of the pen.[39] And such effective strokes can only operate within the confines of a designated area (the letter) where Valmont and Tourvel have agreed to allow this passage of meaning to occur by means of the marks they make on the page. In the notorious episode where Emilie's behind becomes a desk *(pupitre)* for Valmont to write on, the trick by which word and thing are made equivalent is possible only because of the dual reading which the letter must have in order to be intelligible: it is presented as the copy of a letter designed to dupe Tourvel, being read by Merteuil, who understands the *duperie.* In all these letters, meanings are activated within the field of forces set in motion by the initial liaison between Valmont and Merteuil. Merteuil celebrates the occasion when this contract was made, in a figure which perfectly illustrates how this text, as a document, perpetually signs, seals and delivers its sexual messages: "The happy Chevalier lifted me up, and my pardon was sealed *(scellé)* on the same ottoman where you and I sealed *(scellâmes)* our eternal rupture." (37)

As pornography, then, this text can with justice be termed a Utopia, which works as well, and as long, as we could expect of any text that was built on the Rousseauian contractual-grammatical model. Rousseau's contract does not, however, survive the "happy instant" of its own formulation,[40] and, as Paul de Man has pointed out, it cannot successfully apply its governing principles to particular cases without going into auto-destruct. This problem is particularly well illustrated in a key passage from the *Social Contract,* where Rousseau

---

39. For a similar figural analysis of Laclos' erotic writing, see Thomas Fries, "The Impossible Object: the Feminine, the Narrative (Laclos' *Liaisons Dangereuses* and Kleist's *Marquise von O . . .*)," *Modern Language Notes,* v. 91 (Baltimore: Johns Hopkins U. Press 1979), pp. 1296–1326. Fries sets out to dismantle the "phallocentrism" of Laclos' text: "the phallus becomes central only in discourse." (p. 1313) I find Laclos' text more provocatively decentered from the start; Merteuil's (or Tourvel's) *chose* has the same dubious and exclusively textual status as the phallus. Fries and I are nevertheless essentially in agreement, as is evident in his discussion of the "dialogic balance" of male and female aspects of the text, and the impossibility of assigning surrogate authorship either to Valmont or to Merteuil (pp. 1313–15).

40. Rousseau, op. cit. p. 247.

addresses himself to the question of how the otherwise empty formulas of the State are to be embodied:

> In order that the social pact should not just be an empty formula, it tacitly imposes this guarantee *(engagement)* which alone can enforce the others, that whoever refuses to obey the general will will be constrained to do so by the entire (social) body *(par tout le corps)*; which signifies nothing more than that one forces him to be free; for this is the condition which, giving each citizen to his own country *(patrie)*, safeguards him from all personal dependence—condition which makes the artifice and the play *(jeu)* of the political machine . . . [246]

This description of a perfectly self-perpetuating machine, operating by the play of its own internal constraints and freedoms, also wills itself to be a description of an organic whole—a "body," and this body is invoked as evidence that what was a mere abstract formula has indeed been "applied." This application, as practised on each individual member, can be described in two ways: we can see the individual function as a focal point where the opposing forces of freedom and constraint intersect, or we can watch the individual disappear as a vanishing-point, somewhere where the movement of a will *(volonté)* and the inertia of a body *(tout le corps)* must inevitably collide. In either case—whether it functions on greased wheels or by internal combustion—the machine goes on working, replenishing its energies by means of its individual members.

We can regard *Les Liaisons Dangereuses* as an exemplary pedagogical text, implacably hammering home this same lesson—copying it out on Emilie's behind, or teaching it to the class dunce, Cécile, in the form of an assignment in dictation.[41] Insofar as the novel has a plot, it is exclusively a plot of indoctrination, the unfolding of a foregone conclusion: when Tourvel, the last hold-out, has been forcibly liberated, the lesson is over. This text, like the *Social Contract*, has essentially nothing to teach (or inculcate) other than its own design. The lesson Merteuil is bent on teaching Tourvel is the lesson of her own complicity in this process, which requires her to admit that she has not merely succumbed to Valmont as he wished her to, but succumbed—totally, in principle, and without reserve—to the entire collective machinery in which she is as thoroughly implicated as anyone else—even the despised Emilie.

The *Social Contract* documents a Law as unavoidable as it is unheedable; at the end of *Les Liaisons Dangereuses*, a quarrel breaks out over who will be delegated to ratify this document on behalf of the entire social body. Understandably, no-one wants the job. Laclos appointed a woman (Merteuil); she, in turn, tried to demonstrate how anyone can do it. This is how it's done: you simply sign on by signing off—*Ce n'est pas ma faute.*

41. The lesson is effective: Cécile, as a "machine à plaisir" (251) can be regarded as the ultimate imbecilic embodiment of the Social Contract.

Textual Pedagogy

BARBARA JOHNSON

Teaching Ignorance:
L'Ecole des Femmes

The teaching of ignorance is probably not what the majority of pedagogues have in mind. It may, indeed, be a structurally impossible task. For how can a teacher teach a student not to know, without at the same time informing him of what it is he is supposed to be ignorant of? This, at any rate, is the problem faced by the would-be Professor, Arnolphe, in Molière's play *L'Ecole des femmes*.

I. NEGATIVE PEDAGOGY

In the opening lines of the play, Arnolphe is explaining to his friend Chrysalde his pedagogical method for turning an innocent young girl into a faithful wife. He has picked out a docile four-year-old, paid off her mother, and kept her locked up and ignorant ever since.

> I'm rich enough, I think, to have felt free
> To have my wife owe everything to me.
> From her dependency has come submission;
> She cannot flaunt her wealth or her position. . . .
> In a small convent, undisturbed by man,
> I had her raised according to my plan,
> Which was to have them try as best they could
> To keep her ignorant and therefore good.
> Thank God, the outcome answered my intent,
> And now she has grown up so innocent
> That I bless Heaven for having been so kind
> As to give me just the wife I had in mind.[1]

Young Agnes, in other words, has sprung fully disarmed from the brow of Arnolphe. But the middle-aged protector's belief that his charge's total ignorance of the world will ensure her fidelity to him is soon undercut by the arrival on the scene of young Horace, the son of an old friend of Arnolphe's. Horace gaily recounts to the older man the tale of his encounter with a young

1. *The School for Wives*, I,i. In quoting from *L'Ecole des Femmes* in English, I have generally followed the Donald Frame translation (*Tartuffe and Other Plays by Molière*, New York: The New American Library, 1967). Passages in which I have modified the translation will be marked "T.M." All translations of French texts other than *L'Ecole des femmes* are my own.

girl whom he has spotted on the balcony of a house in which some jealous old tyrant has tried to imprison her. Not realizing that his confidant is his foe, Horace keeps Arnolphe informed of the progress of his love, and for the rest of the play Arnolphe is condemned to hear from the mouth of his young rival the detailed account of the failure of his own desperate attempts to forestall the completion of his ward's education. In the seemingly gratuitous ending, the long-absent fathers of the two young people return to the city with the intention of joining their children in marriage, only to learn, much to their satisfaction, that this is the very plan their children have already conceived. Arnolphe, his dreams of domestic bliss thus dashed, leaves the stage in speechless frustration.

This *School for Wives* could thus be aptly re-named "the portrait of an anti-teacher." Not only does Arnolphe intend that his student learn nothing, but even in this negative pedagogy, he fails. His methods are unsound, his lessons backfire, and his classroom is, at the end of the play, silent and empty. The pedagogical model presented to us by the play is apparently designed to be roundly disavowed. Indeed, perhaps the delight with which we literature teachers view the play arises out of the ease with which we can dissociate ourselves from Professor Arnolphe. Yet our delight is perhaps not without discomfort: this image of the ridiculousness of age, power, and authority is painted upon a figure whose *role* is after all similar to our own. For Molière, too, it seems that Arnolphe was mainly designed as an object of disavowal— precisely because the middle-aged suitor was also, secretly, an object of repressed identification. In 1662, at the age of forty, Molière himself had married the charming but spoiled twenty-year-old sister or daughter of his lifelong companion or mistress, having doted on the girl since birth. In the context of what would seem to be a hyperbolic representation of denial, our concentration on the ridiculousness of the desire to possess and repress may therefore perhaps be blinding us to the ways in which Arnolphe's aims and strategies may not be so different from our own.

What, then, are Arnolphe's pedagogical imperatives? In the first scene of the play, Arnolphe is presented to us not as a teacher but as a critic. The object of his criticism is the rampant spread of cuckoldry in the city. It is when his friend Chrysalde warns him that the very outspokenness of his widely published criticism may turn against him that Arnolphe details the pedagogical strategies he has designed to keep his forehead free of decoration.

Chrysalde: My fear for you springs from your mocking scorn,
              Which countless hapless husbands now have borne;
              No lord or rustic past his honeymoon
              Has to your criticism been immune;
              And everywhere you go, your chief delight
              Is in the secrets that you bring to light . . .

Arnolphe:	In sum, when all around lies comedy
	May I not laugh, as spectator, at what I see?
	When fools . . .
Chrysalde:	But he who laughs as loud as you
	Must fear that he'll in turn be laughed at, too.
Arnolphe:	Lord, my friend, please don't be so upset:
	The one who catches *me* is not born yet.
	I know each cunning trick that women use
	Upon their docile men, each subtle ruse,
	And how they exercise their sleight-of-hand.
	And so against this mishap I have planned.
	My plighted wife will, through her innocence,
	Preserve my brow from noisome influence. [I, 1 (TM)]

Universal cuckoldry, in pedagogical terms, can be seen as the tendency of students to seek to learn from more than one teacher. The anxiety of influence Arnolphe expresses here involves the fear that *his* will not be the only school his future wife will attend. In Arnolphe's view of education, then, the sole measure of pedagogical success is to be the only teacher the student listens to.

At the same time, as critic, Arnolphe can only maintain his smug spectator status as long as he *is* his pupil's only teacher. As soon as she begins taking lessons from someone else, Arnolphe's critical detachment from the spectacle of cuckoldry would collapse. It would seem, then, that as soon as there is more than one effective source of authority in a pedagogical system, it is impossible for the teacher-critic to remain masterful, objective, and external to the object of his criticism.

The question of criticism and its exteriority to spectacle is in fact an extremely complex one in the context of Molière's *School for Wives*, not only because the play casts Arnolphe in the role of critic of cuckolds that make a spectacle of themselves but also because the play itself was the object of criticism in no fewer than nine subsequent theatrical productions, two of them by Molière himself. Hardly had the play proven itself to be a success when rival troupes and roving journalists began to attack it both in print and on the stage. Through the existence of these critical comedies, we begin to suspect that not only can *teaching* serve as a source of humor, but there appears to be something funny about criticism as well.

II. AN OBSCENE ARTICLE

The first of Molière's comic defenses of *L'Ecole des femmes*, entitled *Critique de l'Ecole des femmes*, is a mocking representation of his critics. It opens, as do many of today's critical polemics, with a discussion of the fashionable tendency to resort to obscure jargon and far-fetched puns. It soon turns out that among these pretentious neologisms is the strange word "obscénité," which is used by the *précieuse* Climène to denounce the scandalous suggestiveness of some of Agnes' seemingly innocent remarks. The example chosen by Climène takes place in the course of an oral examination administered by Arnolphe to Agnes on the subject of the unauthorized visit of young Horace, about which Arnolphe has just learned.

Arnolphe:	Now, besides all this talk, these tendernesses,
	Didn't he also give you some caresses?
Agnes:	Indeed he did! He took my hands and arms
	And kissed and kissed them with unending charms.
Arnolphe:	Agnes, was there anything else he took?
	(*Seeing her taken aback*)
	Ouf!
Agnes:	Well, he . . .
Arnolphe:	What?
Agnes:	Took . . .
Arnolphe:	Augh!
Agnes:	My . . .[2]
Arnolphe:	Well?
Agnes:	Now look.
	I'm sure you will be angry. I don't dare.
Arnolphe:	No.
Agnes:	Yes.
Arnolphe:	Good lord, no.
Agnes:	Promise me, then, swear.
Arnolphe:	I swear.
Agnes:	He took . . . You'll be mad, I know you.
Arnolphe:	No.
Agnes:	Yes.
Arnolphe:	No, no. Damn it, what an ado!
	What did he take?
Agnes:	He . . .
Arnolphe: (aside)	I'm in agony.
Agnes:	He took my ribbon that you'd given me.
	I couldn't help it, he insisted so.
Arnolphe: (sigh of relief)	All right, the ribbon. But I want to know
	If kiss your arms is all he ever did.
Agnes:	What? Are there other things? [II, 5 (TM)]

The teacher, here, is testing his pupil to make sure that she has not learned anything in his absence. The hesitations of the pupil all seem to the examiner to be signs that she has learned what he does not want her to know. While she only knows *that* she is being censured, he interprets her embarassment to

2. In French: "*Il m'a...pris...le...*"

mean that she knows *what* she is being censured *for*. The further the examination procedes, the closer the examiner comes to telling her what he does not want her to know—telling her, at least, that there are things he is not telling her.

In the discussion of this passage in the *Critique*, Climène views the ellipsis after "he took my . . ."—*il m'a pris le . . .*—as a scandalous allusion, while Uranie defends its innocent literality.

> *Climène:* What! isn't modesty visibly wounded by what Agnes says in the passage we are speaking of?
>
> *Uranie:* Not at all. She doesn't pronounce a single word that is not in itself perfectly decent; and, if you want to hear something else behind it, it's you who are making things dirty, not Agnes, since all she's talking about is a ribbon taken from her.
>
> *Climène:* Oh! ribbon all you want! but that *le* on which she pauses wasn't put there for peanuts. Strange thoughts attach themselves to that *le*. That *le* is a furious scandal, and whatever you may say, the insolence of that *le* is indefensible.
> [Scene iii]

The discussants are thus divided between those with the apparent naiveté of an Agnes and those with the overactive imagination of an Arnolphe. While there is something comical about the desire to censor something that is only perceived by those who wish to censor it, the Agnesian reading is clearly just as inadequate as the Arnolphian. Because the play presents us not only with the suspended *le* but with Arnolphe's alarmed reaction to it, it is not possible for us not to know that strange thoughts can attach themselves to that *le*. Yet what *is* it of Agnes's, in fact, that Arnolphe is afraid Horace might have seized? No *one* obvious word offers itself to complete the thought in Arnolphe's horrified mind as he hears "Il m'a pris le . . ." He took my *what?* Perhaps the truly scandalous effect of this ellipsis lies neither in what it says nor in what it conceals but in the fact that, while searching for something with which to fill the blank, the reader is forced to run mentally up and down the entire female anatomy. Represented both as an absence, a blank, and as a succession of dots, a plurality of small discrete points, female sexuality is both expressed and repressed through this impossibility of summing it up under a single article.

Arnolphe is here up against the problem faced by every parent: it is always either too soon or too late to teach children about sexuality. When the play begins, Arnolphe has been handling Agnes' sex education simply by attempting to insure that no learning will take place. Agnes is seen as a *tabula rasa*—a blank on which nothing is written unless some outside agency comes to write upon it. With the unexpected arrival of a more active tutor, Arnolphe is forced to change his pedagogical strategy. He now attempts to manipulate Agnes' dawning awareness of her own ignorance in such a way as to play up his superior knowledge and to cast doubt on his rival's good faith and on the value of what she has learned.

Arnolphe:	All this, Agnes, comes of your *innocence.*
	What's done is done. I've spoken. No offense.
	I *know* your lover wants but to deceive,
	To win your favor and then laugh and leave.
Agnes:	Oh, no! He told me twenty times and more.
Arnolphe:	*You do not know* what empty oaths he swore.
	But *learn this:* to accept caskets—or candies—
	And listen to the sweet talk of these dandies,
	Languidly acquiesce in their demands,
	And let them stir your heart and kiss your hands,
	This is a mortal sin, one of the worst.
	. . . .
Agnes:	It's all, alas, so pleasant and so sweet!
	I marvel at the joy that all this brings
	And *I had never known* about such things.
Arnolphe:	Yes, there's great pleasure in this tenderness,
	In each nice word and in each sweet caress;
	But these have need of honor's discipline,
	And only marriage can remove the sin. [II, 5]

Arnolphe's challenge here is to give Agnes the impression that for every new thing she learns there is a danger of which she is still ignorant and from which *his* superior wisdom must save her. Yet it is impossible for Arnolphe to cast doubt on the meaning of Horace's pleasurable lessons without at the same time instructing Agnes in the possibility of deception and the manipulation of appearances. Agnes indeed soon proves herself to be a gifted student of the techniques of duplicity.

III. THE INSTITUTIONALIZATION OF IGNORANCE

Satisfied that he has convinced Agnes that he has saved her from the road to perdition, Arnolphe decides to give his bride-to-be a full-fledged lesson in the virtues of wifely ignorance. It is interesting to note that at this point where the paradoxes of teaching ignorance become most explicit, the tyrannical schoolmaster has recourse to the *book* as a pedagogical aid.

   The book Arnolphe assigns to Agnes is a book of Maxims on the Duties of the Married Woman. In typical teacherly fashion, he asks the student to read the book through carefully and promises to explain it to her when she has finished. The book contains a list not of duties but of interdictions: a wife belongs to no one but her husband; she should dress up only for him, receive no visitors but his, accept presents from no man, and never seek to do any writing, to join any feminine social circles, to visit the gambling table, or to go out on walks or picnics. In short, the book for the first time replaces the absence of teaching with the active teaching of the content of ignorance. In place of her former lack of knowledge, the pupil now possesses a knowledge of what she is not supposed to know.

It might perhaps be interesting to ask whether the pedagogical function of the book *in* the play is in any way parallel to the functioning of the play *as* book in its pedagogically-oriented editions. For *The School for Wives*, like the rest of Molière's plays, is published in France in pocket editions copiously annotated for use in the high-school classroom. Molière, indeed, is one of the central devices used by the French school system to teach children to become French. Through these schoolbook editions of French classics, the student absorbs along with the text a certain conception of what his cultural heritage is and what the study of classical texts involves. According to the Bordas edition of *L'Ecole des femmes*, however, this play is a relatively recent addition to the high school curriculum. The first two paragraphs of the discussion of the play are entitled respectively "Une pièce ignorée dans nos classes" ["A play that is unknown in our classrooms"] and "Un chef d'oeuvre pourtant" ["A master-piece nevertheless"]. The editors explain the play's ostracism as follows:

The very theme of this comedy (the fear of cuckoldry), the boldness of the opinions and problems it raises, the salty Gallic vocabulary that comes up in the conversations between Arnolphe and Chrysalde, were all cause for alarm. But isn't this a form of narrow-mindedness that no longer corresponds to our time?[3]

The liberated attitudes of modern editors have thus made it possible to remedy French schoolchildren's ignorance of a play about teaching ignorance. But have all forms of ignorance been thereby dispelled?

What is interesting about this particular play is precisely the fact that the female pupil *in* the play is of the same age as her high-school readers. That this is a play about adult authority and adolescent sexuality seems to be com-pletely glossed over by the editors. It is interesting to follow the techniques of avoidance manifested by the footnotes and commentaries that run the length of the play, sometimes taking up more room on the page than the play itself. Faced with that suggestive little *le* in "il m'a pris le. . .," for example, the editor of the Larousse edition (whose professional title, I note, is "Censeur au lycée de Strasbourg") writes: "A slightly off-colour double-entendre, which many contemporaries reproached Molière for, and which he made the mistake

---

3. *L'Ecole des Femmes*, ed. Pierre Cabanis (Paris: Bordas, 1963), p. 14 (Henceforth referred to as "Bordas.")

of denying in *The Critique of the School for Wives.*"[4] The editor of the Bordas edition, on the other hand, doesn't see what all the fuss is about: "Much ink has been shed over these lines. They have been called scandalous. But all this is just a farcical device. Agnes's words are but a theatrical necessity designed to make us laugh at Arnolphe's stupidity. It is he who, through his questions and frowns, terrifies Agnes, prevents her from answering, and prolongs the suspense. Arnolphe is the one responsible for the ambiguity, which is well suited to his character. The whole scene, about which no one today would think of taking offense, is simply and openly funny, and the whole audience thinks of nothing but laughing" (Bordas, p. 71). Thus, either the ellipsis *il m'a pris le . . .* is an obscenity, or it is a mere joke, a "theatrical necessity." The idea that laughter and obscenity can go together is scrupulously avoided by those who are serving the text up to high school minds.

Yet behind the controversy of Agnes's *le* lies the whole question of female sexuality, which the controversy is in fact designed to occult. The editors' more direct reactions to Agnes's dawning sexuality are of two kinds: they drown it with erudition or they surround it with danger signs. When Agnes first describes her awakening desire, she says to Arnolphe:

> He swore he loved me with a matchless passion
> And said to me, in the most charming fashion,
> Things which I found incomparably sweet
> And every time I hear his voice repeat
> Those things, I tingle deep inside me and I feel
> I don't know what it is from head to heel.
> [Là-dedans remue/Certain je ne sais quoi dont je suis toute émue.]   [II, 5 (TM)]

In the Bordas edition, we find the following note on "je ne sais quoi":

Concerning the frequent use of 'je ne sais quoi' in the language of classicism, there is a very interesting study by Pierre-Henri Simon in his book, *The Garden and the Town*, 1962. This indeterminate expression expresses the irrational and mysterious sides of love, and this is why, according to Mr. Simon, it is the poets and novelists who deal with love that use the expression most frequently. [Bordas, p. 67]

What this note does is to use knowledge provided by Mr. Simon to say "je ne sais quoi" about Agnes's "je ne sais quoi." The sexual component of Agnes's *non-savoir* is being occulted and defused through the asexual notions of irrationality and mystery.

But it is toward Agnes's so-called "pleasure principle" that the editors are most severe. When Agnes asks Arnolphe "How can one chase away what gives such pleasure?" the editors ask, "Is this purely instinctive morality without its dangers?" (Bordas, p. 111). "Can Agnes understand that something pleasant

4. *L'Ecole des Femmes,* ed. Gérard Sablayrolles (Paris: Larousse, 1965), p. 58. (Henceforth referred to as "Larousse.")

might be morally forbidden?" (Larousse, p. 62). Both editors express relief that Agnes has not fallen into the hands of a lover whose intentions are less honorable than Horace's. "Judge Agnes's imprudence," exhorts the Larousse editor. "Show that Molière is also pointing out—for the benefit of the spectator—the danger Agnes would have been in if Horace had not been an honest man" (p. 104). Clearly, an honest man is required to protect unsuspecting girls against the dangers of their own liberation. In warning the young readers against learning too well the sexual lessons that Agnes seems to have learned, the editors of the pedagogically-oriented editions of *The School for Wives* thus unwittingly but inevitably find themselves playing a role similar to that of Arnolphe with respect to their students' sexual education. In repressing the nature of the lesson learned in the book they are presenting, they, too, are in the business of teaching ignorance.

This similarity between the teachers *of* the text and the teacher *in* the text should give us pause. Could it be that the pedagogical enterprise as such is always constitutively a project of teaching ignorance? Are our ways of teaching students to ask *some* questions always correlative with our ways of teaching them *not to ask*—indeed, to be unconscious of—others? Does the educational system exist in order to promulgate knowledge, or is its main function rather to universalize a society's tacit agreement about what it has decided it does not and cannot know? And is there some fundamental correlation between the teaching of ignorance and the question of femininity?

IV. MOLIÈRE'S "FEMINISM"

The question of education and the question of femininity are surprisingly interconnected in the seventeenth century. The burning feminist issue was not yet voting or working, but getting an education equal to a man's. Treatises explaining at length the futility and even the danger of educating women were long the order of the day. As Fénelon wrote in his treatise on the education of women:

Let us now take a look at what a woman needs to know. What are her jobs? She is in charge of her children's upbringing—the boys' up to a certain age and the girls' until they either marry or enter a convent. She must also oversee the conduct, morals, and service of the servants, see to the household expenditures, and make sure all is done economically and honorably. . . .

Women's knowledge, like men's, should be limited to what is useful for their functions; the difference in their tasks should lead to the difference in their studies. It is therefore necessary to restrict women's education to the things we have just mentioned.[5]

5. Fénelon, *De l'éducation des filles* (1687), ch. XI.

Because a woman was always under the protection of her father, her husband, or the church, her education was confined to preparing her for tasks in harmony with these forms of dependency.

It is interesting to recall that the governing purpose behind Arnolphe's pedagogical enterprise was the fear that a learned wife would make him a cuckold. Ignorance, it seemed, was the only way to ensure fidelity. What this implies, paradoxically enough, is that education is an apprenticeship in unfaithfulness. The fear of giving women an education equal to that of men is clearly a fear that educated women will no longer remain faithful to the needs of patriarchal society. Citing the case of Agrippa d'Aubigné, Gustave Fagnier writes in his study of women in the early seventeenth century:

Even though he admired the women who in his time had achieved a scholarly reputation, Agrippa d'Aubigné declared to his daughters, who had consulted him on the question, that a more than ordinary education was, for middle-class girls like themselves, more of a disadvantage than an advantage: the duties of married life and motherhood would take away its profit, for, as he graciously put it, 'when the nightingale has her young, she sings no longer'; then, too, education makes one vain, makes one neglect the household and disdain one's husband, blush at one's poverty, and it introduces discord into the home.[6]

The purpose of *all* education, then, was to foster the harmony of the patriarchal home.

So strong are the mechanisms for preserving the existing hierarchies of sex roles and social classes that the serious struggles of seventeenth-century women to cross the barriers of class and rank and achieve greater power and independence have come down to us through the distorting mirrors of the ridiculousness of *Préciosité*. Yet behind the prudes, the coquettes, and the learned ladies, one can discern an attempt to avoid the bonds of the patriarchal marriage system, to free female sexuality from the constraints of annual childbirth and the double standard, to seek a female identity not exclusively defined in terms of men, and, in a gesture that seems almost post-Saussurian, to free language from its slavishly referential relation to a reality that might somehow thereby itself be escaped. The very extent to which these precious ladies are today not so much forgotten as they are *remembered as ridiculous* is a proof both of their power and of their impotence.[7] While Molière, in other plays, chooses to mock the *précieuses* for their linguistic excesses and their self-delusions, this play in which no *précieuse* actually appears puts its finger

6. Gustave Fagniez, *La Femme et la Société Française dans la Première moitié du XVIIe siècle* (Paris: J. Gamber, 1929), pp. 11–12.

7. For valuable recent analyses of *préciosité* and feminism, see Dorothy Anne Liot Backer, *Precious Women* (New York: Basic Books, 1974); Carolyn C. Lougee, *Le Paradis des Femmes* (Princeton: Princeton University Press, 1976); and Ian Maclean, *Woman Triumphant* (Oxford: Clarendon Press, 1977).

on a much more serious cause for concern. It is precisely when Agnes argues with Arnolphe—clearly and without periphrasis—as *a subject who knows what she wants* that Arnolphe compares her to a *précieuse:* "Just hear how this bitch argues and replies. Damn it! Would a *précieuse* say any more?" [V, 4 (TM)]

It is interesting to note that in the updated Larousse edition of "L'Ecole des Femmes," one of the questions proposed as a discussion topic to the students is: "Was Molière a feminist?" (p. 142). It is even more interesting to note that the answer is already tucked away in the presentational material that precedes the play: "We should recognize that Molière, who, in this play, shows himself to be a feminist, has sided for the education of women and for the liberalization of morals and religion" (p. 18). The assertion of Molière's feminism has indeed become almost a commonplace of academic criticism. As one of the pillars of seventeenth-century studies, Georges Mongrédien, puts it: "It is clear that *L'Ecole des femmes* is a feminist play—as indeed is *Les Précieuses ridicules* in a certain way—that [Molière] is militating for a girl's freedom to choose on the basis of love (Brunetière called it 'nature') . . ."[8]

These notions of freedom of choice, love, and nature are all, of course, names for the granting of greater happiness to women without their acquiring greater power or independence and without any changes being made in the structure of society. By saying that Molière has written a feminist play, the schoolbook editors are not only saving him from the charge of misogyny; they are also offering their students a non-subversive conception of what feminism is: something designed to make women happier with society as it is.

It can easily be seen that although Molière in *L'Ecole des femmes* is taking women's side in advocating their right to marry the man of their choice, he is not really suggesting that anything in the social *structure* be changed. Agnes' newly-discovered sense of her own desire is quickly re-integrated into structures that are in no way disturbed by it. When Agnes takes the independent step of fleeing from Arnolphe to Horace, Horace can think of nothing better to do with her than to entrust her to the father-surrogate Arnolphe, unaware that he is the very rival from whom she has just escaped. Agnes's final liberation from Arnolphe, indeed, occurs only through the fortuitous fact that her long-lost father has arranged with Horace's father that the two young people should marry. The happy ending is decreed by the same kind of paternal authority as that represented by Arnolphe. The liberation of the woman here occurs merely as a change of fathers. Agnes will "belong" to Horace no less surely, although more willingly, than she would have "belonged" to Arnolphe. What has been seen as Molière's feminism is actually a form of benevolent paternalism and not in any sense a plea for the reorganization of the relations

---

8. Georges Mongredien, *La Querelle de l'Ecole des femmes* (Paris: Librairie Marcel Didier, 1971), p. xxviii.

between the sexes. Like all forms of liberalism, it is an attempt to change attitudes rather than structures.

And yet surely a play that so lucidly personifies and ridicules the excesses of patriarchal power cannot *simply* be located *within* phallocentric discourse. Molière's irony would seem to baffle any clear-cut inside/outside categorization. The play consistently undercuts the ideology to which it nevertheless still adheres. Can literature somehow escape or transform power structures by simultaneously espousing and subverting them? The question must be asked of all great literary demystifications: to what structure of authority does the critique of authority belong? This is perhaps *the* feminist question par excellence. For some help in dealing with it, we will now return to the more specifically pedagogical level of our inquiry.

V. HOW AGNES LEARNS

What, then, does Agnes learn in this School for Wives, and what do we learn from her about teaching? Of all the things that Arnolphe wants Agnes *not* to learn, it seems that *writing* is the object of his most violent suspicions. Not only is writing included in the book of don'ts for the married woman, but from the very beginning it is clear that in Arnolphe's mind feminine writing constitutes the husband's royal road to cuckoldry. "A woman who's a writer knows too much," he tells Chrysalde; "I mean that mine shall not be so sublime, and shall not even know what's meant by rhyme." [I,i] In the game of "corbillon," in which each contestant must answer the question "qu'y met-on?" ["what goes into it?"] with something that rhymes with *on*, Arnolphe hopes his wife will answer "une tarte à la crème." Her virginal innocence thus depends on her having absolutely no sense of an ending that rhymes with "on." What Arnolphe wishes to exclude from Agnes's knowledge is play—here, the play of language for its own sake, the possibility that language could function otherwise than in strict obedience to the authority of proper meaning. Agnes indeed demonstrates her ignorance of word play when she answers the go-between's report that she has wounded the heart of young Horace by saying: "Did I drop something on him?" Yet when Arnolphe attempts to stop all commerce between the two young people, Agnes is able to come up with the idea of attaching a secret love letter to the stone she has been instructed by Arnolphe to toss at Horace. How has this naive literal reader so quickly learned the art of sending a double message? What teacher has made her into so skilled a wielder of ambiguity?

According to Horace, fatuously enough, that teacher is "love."

> Love is a great teacher, you must agree,
> Making us what we never thought to be
> And in a moment, under his direction,
> Our character can change its whole complexion.

He breaks down even natural obstacles
And seems to manage sudden miracles. . . .
He makes the dullest soul agile and fit
And gives the most naive its share of wit.
That miracle has happened to Agnes. [III,4]

As an explanation of Agnes' ingenuity in hitting upon the paper and stone device, Horace personifies love as a master teacher. Yet it is not love alone that has made Agnes clever. It is the necessity of complying with the contradictory demands of *two* ardent teachers. As long as the first teacher's power remained absolute and unquestioned, Agnes remained ignorant and unimaginative. Her first acquaintance with her second teacher was not very promising, either. As Agnes describes it:

Out on the balcony to get the air
I saw, under those trees right over there
A most attractive young man passing by
Who bowed most humbly when he caught my eye.
And I, not wishing to be impolite,
Returned a deep bow, as was only right.
Promptly he makes another bow, and then,
I naturally bow to him again;
And since he then goes on to number three,
Without delay he gets a third from me.
He passes by, comes back . . . well, anyhow,
Each time he does he makes another bow,
And I, observing this most carefully,
Returned him every bow he made to me.
The fact is, if the light had not grown dim,
I would have gone on trading bows with him
Because I did not want to yield, and be
Inferior to him in courtesy. [II,5]

If Arnolphe is a teacher of the "do as I say" school, Horace clearly belongs to the school of "do as I do." This opposition between the didactic and the mimetic is in fact the classical polarity into which teaching methods can be divided. From the moment there are two teachers at work, however, they both resort to the method of telling Agnes that she is somehow in the wrong. From Horace she learns of the wound her eyes have inflicted, which she must cure by applying more of the evil as its own remedy. From Arnolphe she learns that she must cleanse the sin of Horace's caresses by marrying. When Arnolphe clarifies the point by indicating that *he* is the one she must marry, she suddenly, for the first time, learns to turn to rhetoric, to find a linguistic substitute, however minimal, for the thought she realizes she must not say.

Agnes: How happy I will be with him!
Arnolphe: With whom?
Agnes: With . . . h'm.
Arnolphe: H'm? h'm is not my taste.
            In choosing a husband you're showing undue haste.   [II, 5 (TM)]

At the end of the scene, Agnes is still protesting the necessity of renouncing such a good-looking man, and Arnolphe, to end the discussion, says: "Je suis maître, je parle: allez, obéissez." "Enough, I am master. I speak, you obey." This, in its simplest terms, is Arnolphe's conception of teaching. His pedagogical aim is to apply and guarantee his own mastery: mastery over language, over knowledge and ignorance, and over the types of outside influence he will or will not permit. In Arnolphe's system, everything is divided between mastery and cuckoldry, between univocal instructions and treacherous ambiguity.

While Arnolphe says "I am your master," Horace says "I am your victim." The position of pseudo-weakness seems to work better than the position of absolute power, but it nevertheless takes the powerful pull of two contradictory systems of demands to shape Agnes into a fully intelligent subject—a writing subject. In learning to manipulate both writing and ambiguity, Agnes marks the destruction of *any* position of absolute mastery. Indeed, when he learns of Agnes' letter, Arnolphe exclaims: "Her writing has just about killed me." [III, 5(TM)]. Let us now look at that letter in order to analyze the way it manifests its discovery of intelligence at the intersection of contradictory lessons.

Je veux vous écrire, et je suis bien en peine par où je m'y prendrai. J'ai des pensées que je désirerais que vous sussiez; mais je ne sais comment faire pour vous les dire, et je me défie de mes paroles. Comme je commence à connaître qu'on m'a toujours tenue dans l'ignorance, j'ai peur de mettre quelque chose qui ne soit pas bien, et d'en dire plus que je ne devrais. En vérité, je ne sais ce que vous m'avez fait, mais je sens que je suis fâchée à mourir de ce qu'on me fait faire contre vous, que j'aurai toutes les peines du monde à me passer de vous, et que je serais bien aise d'être à vous. Peut-être qu'il y a du mal à dire cela; mais enfin je ne puis m'empêcher de le dire, et je voudrais que cela se pût faire sans qu'il y en eût. On me dit fort que tous les jeunes hommes sont des trompeurs, qu'il ne les faut point écouter, et que tout ce que vous me dites n'est que pour m'abuser; mais je vous assure que je n'ai pu encore me figurer cela de vous; et je suis si touchée de vos paroles que je ne saurais croire qu'elles soient menteuses. Dites-moi franchement ce qui en est: car enfin, comme je suis sans malice, vous auriez le plus grand tort du monde si vous me trompiez, et je pense que j'en mourrais de déplaisir. [III,4]

[I want to write you, and I am at a loss how to set about it. I have thoughts that I would like you to know; but I don't know how to go about telling them to you, and I mistrust my own words. As I am beginning to realize that I have always been kept in ignorance, I am afraid of putting down something that may not be right and saying more than I ought. Truly, I don't know what you've done to me; but I feel that I am mortally unhappy over what they're making me do to you, that it will be terribly hard for me to get along without you, and that I would be very glad to be yours. Perhaps it's a bad thing to say that; but anyway I can't help saying it, and I wish it could be done without its being wrong. They keep telling me that all young men are deceivers, that I mustn't listen to them, and that everything you say to me is only to take advantage of me; but I assure you that I have not yet been able to imagine that of you, and I am so touched by your words that I cannot possibly believe they are lies. Tell me frankly what the truth is in all this; for after all, since there is no malice in me, you would be doing a terrible wrong if you deceived me, and I think I would die of sorrow.]

In many ways, this letter shows the simultaneity of liberation and repression. In the play, it is the only passage written in prose. This stylistic change is felt as a liberation from the artifice of verse, but at the same time the letter is not given any line numbers, thus making it impossible to refer to the letter as one refers to the rest of the play. Editorial tradition treats the letter as if it does not count, while by that very exclusion giving the letter a special privilege. The letter is primarily an expression of Agnes' fear of being somehow in the wrong. The desire not to transgress any rule, even a grammatical one, leads to acrobatics of subordination on every level. Agnes' crucial discovery that she might not know what she is still ignorant of is accompanied by a generalized distrust of saying what she means. This love letter is less an expression of love than an inquiry into the conditions under which an expression of love might be possible.

It is interesting to note the ways in which this heavily self-censored letter has been viewed as the very voice of innocent nature. Horace rhapsodizes:

> All that was in her heart, her hand has penned,
> But that in touching terms of kindliness,
> Of simple innocence and tenderness.
> In short, in just the way I'm speaking of,
> Nature expresses the first pangs of love. [III,4]

And the editor of the Larousse edition instructs his students to "analyze the freshness and spontaneity of the feelings expressed in this letter" (p. 80). This tendency to view Agnes' self-censorship as spontaneous and natural would indicate that, for Horace and for the Censor from Strasbourg, the desire not to displease is an innate component of women's nature.

VI. CONTRADICTION, OR THE SUBJECT OF TEACHING

We have thus come to a paradoxical set of conclusions about the nature of the pedagogical process. Learning seems to take place most rapidly when the student must respond to the contradiction between *two* teachers. And what the student learns in the process is both the power of ambiguity and the non-innocence of ignorance. It could be objected, however, that while the efficacy of contradiction-as-teacher may be demonstrable in the burlesque world of tyrannical cuckolds and ingenious ingenues, not every pedagogue is as repressive as an Arnolphe. What if the schema were reversed, for example, and the teacher, instead of saying "I am master," should choose to say "I am ignorant"?

If, as Neil Hertz would have it, the allusion to Socrates is characteristic of "the earnest moment in teachers' imaginings of themselves," it would seem that we have now begun speaking in earnest. It is therefore all the more astonishing to discover the very same conjunction of love, writing, and pedagogical rivalry as the mainspring of the Socratic dialogue itself, as we find it exemplified in Plato's *Phaedrus*, which can indeed be read as one of the most fundamental of Western treatises on teaching.

The dialogue begins on a street in Athens where Socrates runs into the handsome Phaedrus, fresh from a lesson with his master, Lysias. It seems that Lysias has written a speech demonstrating that one should yield rather to a non-lover than to a lover (isn't this precisely what Arnolphe is trying to convince Agnes of?), and that Phaedrus is now heading for the fields in order to practice reciting it. Socrates, contrary to his usual habits, is lured out of the city by the promise of hearing the words of this rival teacher. Inspired by the subject and by the fair interlocutor, Socrates, after hearing Lysias' discourse, launches into two contradictory speeches of his own on love, then goes on to try to teach Phaedrus what effective teaching ought to be. A crux of the Socratic view of teaching is his apparent preference for direct speech over writing. The man who has real knowledge to impart "will not, when he's in earnest, resort to a written form . . ., using words which are unable either to argue in their own defense when attacked or to fulfill the role of a teacher in presenting the truth. . . . Far more noble and splendid is the serious pursuit of the dialectician, who finds a congenial soul and then proceeds with true knowledge to plant and sow in it words which are able to help themselves and help him who planted them; words which will not be unproductive, for they can transmit their seed to other natures and cause the growth of fresh words in them. . . ."[9] What is odd about this law of living dialectical teaching is that Socrates refuses to abide by it in the opening lines of the dialogue. When Phaedrus offers to recite Lysias' speech from memory, Socrates replies, "Good, good, dear boy, if you will start out by showing me what you have under your cloak in your left hand. As a matter of fact, I'd guess that you're clutching the very speech. If that's the case, please realize that though I'm very fond of you, *when we have Lysias right here,* I have no intention of lending you my ears to practice on" (p.5; emphasis mine). While Socrates is profiting from the fact

9. Plato's *Phaedrus*, trans. W. C. Helmbold and W. G. Rabinowitz (Indianapolis: The Library of Liberal Arts, 1956), pp. 70–71.

that Lysias' written words cannot defend themselves aloud, he nevertheless grants them greater authority than he does to Lysias' supposedly more legitimate seed-carrier, Phaedrus himself. The proponent of spoken dialectic has thus been prompted to deny the power of the written word only after he has first been seduced out of himself precisely by the power of the written word. The devaluation of writing that has, according to Jacques Derrida, structured the whole of Western thought can thus be seen as a mere tactical move in a game of pedagogical rivalry.

Before Socrates and Lysias come to look too much like Horace and Arnolphe, it might be well to analyze the two texts with respect to the project—expressly undertaken by both Arnolphe and Socrates—of teaching nothing but ignorance. Up to now we have been viewing the teaching of ignorance in a purely negative light, as a repressive method of instructing the student *not to know*. What Socrates seeks, on the other hand, is to teach the student *that he does not know*. To teach ignorance is, for Socrates, to teach to *un*-know, to become conscious of the fact that what one thinks is knowledge is really an array of received ideas, prejudices, and opinions—a way of *not* knowing that one does not know. "Most people are unaware that they do not know the true nature of the things they discuss; . . . they assume that they do know" (p. 16.) "I am not teaching . . . anything, but all I do is question."[10] "I know only that I am ignorant."

Plato's challenge as a writer and a student was to cast an ignoramus in the role of *sujet supposé savoir*. The philosophical debate over "how far Socrates was serious about his ignorance," as Kierkegaard puts it,[11] arises out of the contradiction between Plato's transferential fantasy of the teacher as subject presumed to know and the content and method of that teacher's teaching, namely, the constant profession of ignorance. Because we see Socrates only through the eyes of Plato's transference, we will never really know whether or not he was "serious" about his ignorance. But the dynamism of the Socratic dialogue in a sense makes the question irrelevant. For if the ideal pedagogical climate, in the *Phaedrus* as well as in the *School for Wives*, is one in which the conflicts and contradictions *between* teachers serve as the springboard for learning, then learning does not result from a personifiable cause. Whether the teacher professes to be in possession of knowledge or of ignorance, the student in effect learns from what the teacher is not in possession of.

To retain the plurality of forces and desires within a structure that would displace the One-ness of individual mastery could perhaps be labeled a feminization of authority. For just as Agnes' *le...* cannot designate any single organ as the graspable center of female sexuality, and just as the existence of

10. Plato's *Meno*, trans. G. M. A. Grube (Indianapolis: Hackett Publishing Co., 1976), p. 15.

11. Søren Kierkegaard, *The Concept of Irony,* trans. Lee M. Capel (Bloomington: Indiana University Press, 1965), p. 285.

more than one sex problematizes the universality of any human subject of knowledge, so contradiction suspends and questions the centering of Western pedagogical paradigms around the single authoritative teacher. In this sense, paradoxically enough, it could be said that Plato's belief in Socrates' pedagogical mastery is an attempt to repress the inherent "feminism" of Socrates' ignorance. And it is out of this repression of Socrates' feminism that Western pedagogy springs. The question of education, in both Molière and Plato, is the question not of how to transmit but of how to *suspend* knowledge. That question can be understood in both a positive and a negative sense. In a negative sense, not knowing results from repression, whether conscious or unconscious. Such negative ignorance may be the necessary by-product—or even the precondition—of any education whatsoever. But positive ignorance, the pursuit of what is forever in the act of escaping, the inhabiting of that space where knowledge becomes the obstacle to knowing—*that* is the pedagogical imperative we can neither fulfill nor disobey.

JAMES CREECH

"Chasing after Advances": Diderot's Article "Encyclopedia"

For Phil Lewis

"Je suis un hors d'oeuvre."
—Diderot, Letter to Sophie Volland

The *Encyclopedia* of Diderot and d'Alembert is a vast pedagogical project whose aim is to teach everything. To do so, it sets out to represent the state of contemporary knowledge globally and systematically. "The goal of an encyclopedia is to assemble the knowledge scattered far and wide on the surface of the earth, to expose its general system to our fellow men with whom we live and to transmit it to those who will follow us, so that . . . our sons, by becoming more educated, might become at the same time more virtuous and happy . . ."[1]. A traditional commentary on this passage reads: "Here in a few lines is the whole program of what was to be called the 'Age of Enlightenment.' Here is the philosopher's confidence in the beneficent effect of expanding knowledge. Here is a hopeful belief in progress through education"[2]. This would certainly seem to be an accurate appraisal.

In *Les Mots et les choses*, Foucault suggests some of the most basic reasons why a philosopher such as Diderot would have been able to feel "confidence" that an encyclopedic representation would fulfill such goals in the "classical age." "The continuum of representation and being, an ontology defined negatively as an absence of nothingness [*absence de néant*], a general representability of being, and being manifested by the presence of representation—all this is a part of the overall configuration of the classical episteme"[3].

1. "Encyclopédie," in *Diderot, Oeuvres Complètes*, ed. Dieckmann, Varloot and Proust (Paris: Hermann, 1975) vol VII, p. 174. All future references will be given in the text.
2. George Havens, *The Age of Ideas* (New York: Henry Holt, 1955), p. 295. Or alternatively, see a similar appreciation in Franco Venturi, *Jeunesse de Diderot* (Paris: Skira, 1939), pp. 260–61. The same passage was recently the object of a quite different evaluation: "In fact, this mission of the *Encyclopedia* does not coincide with its historical role . . . since man's self-concept and action also result from a whole process of denegation that allows the system to function." (Groupe d'Intervention Lettres Nantes, "Lire 'L'Encyclopédie,'" in *Littérature* 42, May 1981, p. 30.) The point of this article, I think, is that the *Encyclopedia* creates its audience as much as it instructs readers, and that the encyclopedic "narratee" turns out upon examination to correspond to a less idealistic model.
3. New York: Random House, 1970, p. 206. All further references are given in the text.

183

The *Encyclopedia* exemplifies the major feature of representation in the classical age in that it is based on the particular status accorded to language. Foucault points out that the work's organization owes nothing to an order believed to be intrinsic to the knowledge that it represents. Rather it is determined by the alphabet, an arbitrary order existing only within language. The text's order is "accommodated within the form of language, within the [representational] space opened up in words themselves" (p. 88). Through that space language has a "relation to the universal" (p. 86) and to being, and can thus determine the organization of a work that attempted to represent the totality of the known[4]. Although modern usage has consacrated the appellation "Encyclopedia," its original name bears witness to a different emphasis which is pertinent in this regard: it is conceived as an "Encyclopedic Dictionary." To be sure, Diderot shared the philosophical confidence of his age in many respects. As he himself claims, "the *Encyclopedia* could only be the endeavor of a philosophical century" (p. 232).

If that is so, the place to look for an elaboration of the relation between optimistic philosophy and this particular work would be at its meta-encyclopedic heart, that is, in its self-definitional article in Volume V that is itself entitled "Encyclopedia" (1755). And yet, in this peculiar text, rather than luxuriating in the epistemological positivity one associates with such a confident epistemology, we find Diderot nail-biting over the difficult conditions of its possibility. The least we can say about this latter problem is that logically it ought to be anterior to any philosophical confidence. Confidence would presume the problem resolved. But this is not the case here: Diderot is both "confident" and at the same time clearly imbued with a sense of the intrinsic impossibility of a true encyclopedia, and of all the hopes for which it is the vehicle.

The very existence of the article bears witness to this point. If we accept the epistemological protocols described by Foucault, we shall still have to wonder to what necessity Diderot was responding when he wrote "Encyclopedia." If the *Encyclopedia* could represent all knowledge and expose its system through the medium of the word, to what imperative was he responding when he added a metadiscursive article whose purpose was to represent the system of the system at another remove—to represent the representation? "Encyclopedia" didactically elaborates the pedagogy of the entire work. It self-consciously teaches how the great Book teaches. On the one hand, it is in the alphabet—in Volume V, under E, between the entries *"Encroué"* and *"Endécagone"*—and like all other terms it can derive its full meaning only by being in its place within that system. But it is also necessarily different from

4. "... Though the being of language had been entirely reduced to its function within representation, representation, on the other hand, had no relation [*rapport*] to the universal except through the intermediary of language" (p. 86).

the system, objectifying and defining it as if from the outside. (In this sense it is fully as pre-liminary as either the "Prospectus" or d'Alembert's "Discours préliminaire.") It is a liminal demarcation of inside and outside, of *représenté* and *représentant*, of spectator and spectacle embedded deeply within the encyclopedic body.

I.

In describing a work that aims to expose the system of knowledge for all time, "Encyclopedia" necessarily comes upon the basic epistemological issue of how to know that we know. Diderot formulates the problem explicitly. "In everything there is an unvarying and common measure, *failing which* we know nothing [*on ne connaît rien*], we can appraise nothing, nor can we define anything. . . ." (p. 206, my emphasis). In fact "measure," and its synonym "model" are two of the text's master terms. They are the focus of a central desideratum.

If we could define (words) according to unchanging nature, and not according to human conventions and prejudices which change continually, such definitions would become seeds for discoveries. Let us observe here again the *continual need* we have of an unvarying and constant model to which our definitions and descriptions might refer, such as the nature of man, of animals or of other beings always extant. All the rest is nothing. . . . [p. 257, my emphasis][5]

Diderot raises this issue of a stable measure relative to all levels of encyclopedic strategy and always in the same way. The first section of the article, for example, deals at length with the question of how to assure the legibility of the work for future generations. Our descendants will be unable to read it at all if the references, the literal meanings of metaphors, the linguistic codes necessary for its understanding are no longer known. Without an assured reference point the *Encyclopedia* will be quickly superannuated. What is required therefore—but once again, not necessarily granted—is "a permanent model" (p. 193), or a "poetics of the genre according to real and thoughtful understanding of the human heart, of the nature of things and of right reason, which are the same in all times" (p. 185).[6]

In terms of vocabulary, where measure equals "definition," the encyclope-

5. Compare to *De la poésie dramatique*, in *Oeuvres Esthétiques*, ed. P. Vernière (Paris: Garnier, 1968), p. 284: "It is certain that there will be no term to our disputes if each person takes himself as a model and judge. There will be as many measures as judges. . . . That suffices, it seems to me, to feel the necessity of seeking a measure, a model [module] outside myself. (. . .) But where to find the unvarying measure that I seek and that I lack?"
6. Diderot defines "poetics of the genre" in this way: "I am taking the term poetics in its most general sense, as a system of given rules one assumes must be followed in whatever genre in order to succeed" (p. 234).

dist must take care to define all root words in Latin or Greek, dead thus unchanging models. In another instance, the use of synonyms, beyond a certain measure that remains to be determined, is deleterious to clarity of meaning. Here the measure must again be determined by the needs of posterity. "Above all, it is posterity that must be kept in mind. There is yet another measure. It is useless to add shades of meaning to words that are not likely to be misunderstood once the language is dead" (p. 208). Or in yet another instance, the encyclopedist needs a stable measure in order to determine the proper length of articles relative to the exact importance or place that their subject matter occupies in the scheme of things. Some articles are too long, some too short in the current work, "but *failing* a common and constant measure, there is no compromise; everything that a science comprehends must at first be included . . ." (p. 214, my emphasis).

Diderot often reiterates that this is at best a "first attempt" (p. 214), necessarily flawed. "If our descendants work on the *Encyclopedia* without interruption, they will be able to bring the organization of its material to some degree of perfection" (p. 214). He anticipates "a great number of editions perfected successively" (p. 215). In yet another formulation he writes, "I am forced to confess that hardly two thirds of an *Encyclopedia* such as ours would be included in a true encyclopedia" (p. 236).

The basic difficulty is clear then: in order for the *Encyclopedia* to fulfill its pedagogical mission for future generations, a stable epistemological measure must be found, but the present generation of encyclopedists does not yet possess the means to derive such a model. Because it is indeed "failing," it remains a desideratum and a projection.

In *The Philosophy of the Enlightenment* [7], Lucien Goldmann characterizes the problem as typical of the situation faced by the essayist—which is his view of Diderot the encyclopedist.

"What matters to the essayist is not the actual process of examining the theoretical basis of particular truths or values. Instead he is concerned with showing that such an examination is both possible and necessary, and, at the same time, that it is both important and impossible to give answers. He is looking for theoretical answers to a series of questions fundamental to human existence which can have no prospect of ever being answered from his point of view. [pp. 45–6]

In Goldmann's view, the essay is a philosphical form insofar as it raises basic issues that are conceptual and abstract, and therefore aiming at general truths. It is a literary form to the degree that, in the first place, it has no means to answer such abstract and conceptual questions, and in the second place, it

7. London: Routledge, 1973, transl. Henry Maas. Further page references will be given in the text.

raises them relative to concrete and particular occasions or events. (One thinks of Montaigne reflecting on a text read or an important experience in his life.) "The true essay thus necessarily inhabits two worlds, and is necessarily ironic: it seems to be talking about particular people and situations, but these are mere 'occasions' for the essayist to raise crucial abstract questions." The *Encyclopedia* is related to the essay form, but is different precisely in that the genre pretends fully to answer the questions it raises. The irony is similar however, because "the encyclopedists realized that this knowledge consti- tuted only a small part of what generations to come would add to the amount hitherto amassed. The progress of knowledge knows no limits" (p. 45).

The ironic point of view is, as always, powerful and persuasive—if for no other reason than that no one wants to miss an irony. It goes far in defining certain givens of the article "Encyclopedia:" Diderot writes an "essay," raising basic and abstract epistemological issues which he and his collaborators cannot resolve, but which must be resolved for the *Encyclopedia* to fulfill the mission it has assigned itself. Yet, the figure of irony that Goldmann privileges through his reading of Diderot's importance to the Enlightenment, while in keeping with the German idealism which Goldmann inherited, does not account for the major operation in "Encyclopedia," which is, as we shall see, governed by a different figure.

II.

The fundamental epistemological principle that consistently emerges in "Encyclopedia"—the "unvarying and common measure, failing which we know nothing"—is indistinguishable from anticipation of its future availabil- ity, or reference back to its past availability in old models such as Greek or Latin. Both operations define such a principle as a prolepsis[8]. Encyclopedic knowledge therefore, because it is not-still or not-yet available, is itself less ironic than it is proleptic. The answer to the fundamental question of a constant epistemological model is not impossible, as Goldmann suggests. Rather it is in referral or deferral, radically forwarded or sent back—all of which is signified in the term *renvoyé*. The complex and laborious set of strategies for deferral must be linked to the work's pedagogical aspirations. But how? The willing learner who is beguiled by the ringing call for a constant point of epistemological reference is repeatedly disappointed to discover upon closer examination that all specific reference points are only virtual. (Diderot even equivocates about the infallibility of Greek—which sometimes must be supplemented by Latin, which is sometimes from unreliable manuscripts, and

8. "Prolepsis" is defined as follows: "1. Figure of grammar consisting in the use of an epithet in which either an anterior or a future state is depicted." (Henri Morier, *Dictionnaire de poétique et de rhétorique* [Paris: P.U.F., 1961].)

so forth.) What kind of instruction is this? What real and empirical knowledge is in fact being represented in "Encyclopedia?"

Even though we may be comfortably ensconced in our skeptical modernity, it is not so easy simply to dismiss the problem of an unchanging epistemological measure by pointing out that it is absent or necessarily ironic. What is more, such measures are not totally in default within the *Encyclopedia*. Or rather, it is their *défaut*—indistinguishable from their *renvoi*—that in a real sense *is* the *Encyclopedia*, its "instruction" and its ideal.

Already at its inception the article "Encyclopedia" is in part conceived as a prosthetic operation, required because of a *défaut* in the *Encyclopedia* that is significant enough to undermine the great hopes of the entire project.

> . . . Familiarity *[connaissance]* with the language is the basis of all these great hopes. They will not be secure unless language is stabilized and transmitted in all its perfection [read: ideality] to posterity, which means that, properly speaking, language was the most important of those objects that encyclopedists should have treated in depth. We realized it too late, and from that oversight, imperfection has sprung up throughout the work. The treatment of language has remained *insufficient [faible]*, . . . and for that reason it ought to be the principal subject in an article in which one is examining one's work impartially, seeking ways of *correcting its defects [défauts]*. I am therefore going to treat the question of language, specially and as I should. [p. 18, my emphasis]

Here at the metadiscursive heart of the *Encyclopedia* is a quick remedial fix of the essential language element in which for the classical "episteme," being and representation are conjoined. Prosthesis is thus an integral part of what is being represented as an encyclopedia. Recognizing a lack and proferring a supplement is therefore, literally, a part of the *Encyclopedia*'s definition of itself. That is what the *Encyclopedia* "is."

What is more, the remedial theory of language that ensues is only a complex of speculations about the future and about how diachronic language will have to be rendered stable in the future through linkage to unchanging referential constants such as nature, the structure of the bocal cavity, dead languages, euphonics, and ultimately to "general and rational grammar" (p. 206). Diderot seems to confirm the reader's response to this linguistic dog chasing its cratylistic tail when he writes: "One can see just how long, difficult and thorny this labor really is" (p. 205). He is implicitly granting a presumed objection by the reader—another form of prolepsis frequent in the article— that the stable linguistic model actually exists in no other guise than anticipation of the final, perfect model. In this instance the radically prospective nature of the model can be detected in the very proliferation of different models, each more unlikely than the other.

Just as the *Encyclopedia* is a permanent anticipation of its epistemological model, the text is itself an anticipation of the object—knowledge—that it is supposed to represent. Diderot explains that only a group can write a successful encyclopedia because only a group could accomplish the task in a reasonably brief period of time. The currency of any knowledge quickly fades. An encyclopedia must fix the totality of knowledge in one moment, like an image of the national mind that will itself become a stable measure by which future progress can be gauged. Quick completion guarantees the integrity of such a moment, the presence to itself of a mind/measure frozen in time. Yet, Diderot himself then proceeds to shatter the very presence and integrity he sought to assure the encyclopedic moment.

... In any work intended for the general instruction of mankind, it is therefore necessary to start by conceiving one's object in the widest possible context, by becoming familiar with the mind of one's nation, by knowing in advance the direction it is going to take, by overtaking it quickly so that instead of leaving your work behind, your work might be in advance of the national mind, which will then come upon it ahead of itself. . . . [p. 186]

Today's knowledge will be the point of comparison to which future generations will look back in order to measure their progress since that moment. But the image of the national mind arrested in the pages of the *Encyclopedia*, in principle, anticipates the mind more than it represents it. The model that is being frozen in time is again something which does not yet exist.

The figure of prolepsis, then, emerges in such disparate moments of the text as to suggest that its effects are general in "Encyclopedia."

The system of *renvois* (references) from article to article is the most ample of these effects. Understanding of a term in its present context is presupposed while at the same time, being recognized as future by virtue of the fact that the term "wants" some further elaboration. The system can produce complex relations. In the article "Encyclopedia," for example—an article that is setting out to define its object as would any other article—there is a *renvoi* to the article entitled "Definition." (Here Foucault looms large for the modern reader.) ". . . A good word-book will never be created without the co-operation of a large number of talents, because definitions of names are no different than definitions of things (See the art. *Définition*) . . ." (p. 177). It is supposed that the reader knows what a "definition" is. Yet at the same time, the *renvoi* makes it obvious that the term is not yet fully understood, that it will be understood only after a future reading of the article "Definition." Once again the supposedly transparent linguistic medium of representation brings with it this proleptic relation of *défaut/renvoi*.

In Diderot's estimation the *renvois* are the "most important part of the encyclopedic order" (p. 221). Knowledge exists as a whole. All its parts are of a piece, existing simultaneously in one arborescent system (p. 227). The problem of representing such a monolithic whole in discrete articles arranged alphabetically was similar to the problem analyzed in the *Lettre sur les sourds et muets:* how can a simultaneous but complex perception or action be

expressed in discourse that is necessarily protracted, incremental and syntactic? With the system of *renvois,* however, a "hieroglyphic" effect is achieved[9].
Both the partial and local integrity of each article of the syntagmatic chain is
assured, and the simultaneous integrity of Knowledge as a whole is signified in
the same process. An organic, integral system is superimposed upon an
arbitrary, alphabetical system[10]. A familiar rhetorical logic transpires, however, in Diderot's language. Temporal becomes spatial prolepsis.

All the sciences encroach on each other: they are continuous limbs branching from the
same trunk. When someone writes a work, he does not enter his subject abruptly, close
himself off rigorously within it, leave it brusquely: he is *compelled to anticipate* upon
terrain neighboring on one side, his conclusions often lead him into another contiguous
area on the opposite side, and through how many other *necessary excursions* within the
body of a work. There is no end [Quelle est la fin] to the forewords, the introductions, the
prefaces, the exordia, the episodes and conclusions. If everything that is off the subject
[hors du sujet] being treated were rigorously culled out, virtually any work would shrink
to a fourth of its original volume. What is accomplished by encyclopedia-style
concatenation, that rigorous circumscription? It demarcates the limits of a subject so
strictly, that only what is essential remains within an article. [p. 227.]

The deprecation of "forewords, introductions and prefaces" is a topos, often
occurring in a preface (in the preface of Hegel's *Logik,* for example), that
betrays an undecidable relation between what is "essential"—book, inside,
work—and what is *hors du sujet*—preface, exteriority, writing[11]. Sooner or
later, however, because of the system of *renvois* every element of this Book at
some point should be enclosed in quotation marks, the way *Encyclopedia* is
here called "Encyclopedia"—exterior and anticipatory, not yet the thing itself.
"Preface" and its synonyms (for example, "Discours préliminaire") are only
different names for the same prolepsis.

But is the *Encyclopedia* not an exception? Precisely, the concatenation of
terms guaranteed by the system of *renvois* is supposed to eliminate such
superfluity. Yet it is Diderot himself who, a few pages later, will write the lines
quoted above: ". . . I am forced to confess that hardly two-thirds of an
Encyclopedia such as ours would be included in a true encyclopedia" (p. 236).
The present version is, again, only an introductory offer, a foretaste of the real
thing, which exists but which exists elsewhere, on the next page, in the next
volume, in another article, in the next century. If there is in this text (returning
to our standard commentary) a "whole program of what was to be called the

9. This is the term Diderot uses in his *Lettre sur les sourds et muets* to describe that aspect of
poetry that overcomes the syntactic and incremental nature of language, permitting a unified
expression of a complex idea. See *Oeuvres Complètes,* Vol. II, p. 169.

10. On the problem of continuity versus contiguity in the encyclopedic order, see Jean
Starobinski, "Remarques sur l'Encyclopédie," *Revue de Métaphysique et de Morale,*
juillet–septembre, 1970, pp. 284–91.

11. See Jacques Derrida, "Hors livre," in *Écriture et la Différence* (Paris: Seuil, 1972).

Age of Enlightenment, . . . a hopeful belief in progress through education,"
that program and that belief are not to be located in any empirical time. The
"essentiality" of the *Encyclopedia*—its status as concept, interiority, Book—is
indistinguishable from the effect of its proleptic reference to the text to come.
The text was what it was (and is what it is) through what it was to be; but the
u-topos of the book to be was (in) the book that it was, not in the real future[12].
Diderot recognizes more than he misprizes that, when someone writes, "he is
compelled to anticipate." And, as more often than we usually acknowledge,
his text contemplates its own effects in the duplicity of the phrase, "Quelle est
la fin des avant-propos?" Indeed, what "purpose" and what "duration" can we
ascribe to the task of anticipating on the definitive representation or the ideal
model to come?

For, to what does a *renvoi* refer but to another *renvoi*, to the very deferral
in function of which the "encyclopedic concatenation" seems to have been
imagined? Diderot is categorical on this point: "The *renvois* in an article are
like those toothing stones ["pierres d'attentes," literally: "stones in waiting"]
that can be seen at the ends of a long wall. . . , and whose crenellation
anticipates similar crenellation and similar toothing stones waiting elsewhere" (p. 230, my emphasis). Moreover, what limits a *renvoi* to a single
reference or destination, to the confines of a single volume or series of
volumes? What assures a reader of Diderot's "Encyclopedia," for example that
he or she will not wind up off the track or on one of those "many other
necessary excursions?" To be "*renvoyé*" is after all to be shown the door, to be
kicked out, perhaps into what Diderot calls the "*dehors du sujet.*" Perhaps
even into Jacques Derrida's essay under the parallel designation of "*Hors
livre,*" which deals precisely with the status of what Diderot above called
"forewords, introductions, prefaces, exordia, episodes and conclusions." Implicitly, then: See "*Hors Livre.*" Diderot refers us to Derrida, anticipates
Derrida. We certainly can follow this *renvoi* to Derrida's essay and find
passages such as this one, which is itself centered around a verb in the *futur
antérieur*: "And if we wanted . . . to know this system in the form of this-
equals-that, we lose just about everything in the waiting: neither pre-face nor
pre-dicate. Toothing stone, corner stone, stumbling block—beginning at the
threshold of dissemination, but also earlier—*will* all *have provided* the
deadfall hindering examination by the petrified reader. So many stones!" And
we find ourselves, perhaps unwittingly, involved in what Derrida goes on to
call a "reconstruction of the textual field beginning with intertextual manoeu-
vres, or with the endless *renvoi* from traces to traces . . ."[13]

12. For a discussion of "utopia" in this text, see: Christie Vance Macdonald, "The Work of the
Text: Diderot's "Encylcopédie,' " *The Eighteenth Century: Theory and Interpretation,* Vol. XXI, no.
2 (spring 1980), pp. 128–44.

13. "Hors livre," n. 24, p. 47 and p. 51, my translation, my emphasis. Further references are in
the text.

But, you may be asking (proleptically, that is), whether there is not at the heart of this lapidary system, lurking, a hidden touchstone, a truly common measure that is more than an anachronistic anticipation, a premature birth? After all, Diderot does write, ". . . I have wanted even the most unimportant objects [in the *Encyclopedia*] secretly to refer to man . . ." (p. 255). Diderot the humanist? Enlightenment theology? Perhaps. This text has been put to such uses, as we saw earlier. (Humanism and theology meld, in the traditional view, as the human center of the work figures, in displaced form, the divine center of the universe[14]). If indeed man is that point of reference to which the most indifferent objects "refer"—*sont rapportés*—we are still left once again to examine the nature and the function of that *rapport*.

Diderot seems to conceive of it visually, spatially, as a relation between man and a kind of mirror.[15] (But as we shall see, it both includes and surpasses the role of the mirror that Richard Rorty placed at the center of modern epistemology.[16]) Referring to man, Diderot asks: "Is there in infinite nature some point from which we might extend, to greater advantage, the immense lines that we propose to send out to all other points? What intense and pleasant reactions will ensue, between nature and man, from man to nature?" (p. 212). The *Encyclopedia* must be made to correspond to the organization of the human intellect, to the flawed features of the human mind rather than to "the absolute perfection of a universal plan" (p. 212). Otherwise we would be faced with the same infinite complexity in reading the text that we already face when we attempt to understand the universe itself. If the Book really represented the universe in its ideal totality, ". . . all the different parts of our knowledge would become just as isolated as they already are; we would lose our grasp of the inductive chain, we would lose sight of the links that precede and those that follow, and soon we would be faced with the same gaps and the same doubts that we face now" (pp. 211–12). That is not the stuff of "intense and pleasant reactions" between man and world.

The world is immensely complex, well beyond our powers of perception, and yet perfectly logical and coherent in itself. Faced with the world we are, like the blind ("we lose sight"), lacking the cognitive access to its perfect system. Only a mirror-like correspondence between the encyclopedia system and the lacunary capacities of its human center would provide that center with an image of itself cured of confusion and weakness. Again, this vast compen-

14. "The authority of the encyclopedic model, analogical unity of man and god, can act by very circuitous means, according to complex mediations. It is moreover a matter of a model and a normative concept: which does not exclude that in the practice of writing . . . some forces remain foreign or contrary to the encyclopedic model and throw it violently into question" ("Hors livre," p. 54).

15. In the *Réfutation d'Helvétius* Diderot will refer to the mind as "this principal organ, . . . this sensate mirror" (*Oeuvres Esthétiques*, p. 612).

16. Richard Rorty, *Philosophy and the Mirror of Nature* (Princeton: Princeton University Press, 1979).

dium of things and knowledge is designed to give humanity a corrected image of itself.

Ariste faces the same difficulty in *De la poésie dramatique* as he sets out to form an ideal model of the philosopher[17]. In both cases, one projects a model of perfection that reflects one's own imperfections, but reversed and thus remedied, mirror-like. Here the *Encyclopedia* is that mirror, linking people and things "by immense lines," but in such a way that the human center no longer experiences its usual inadequacies when faced with the world. The severance between human and world, like blindness, both makes possible and requires figurative, orthopedic representation in the mirror[18].

Given the subject-mirror nature of this *rapport* with our surroundings, what then is its pedagogical function? It is here that we are most irresistibly *renvoyés*—and the *renvoi* is once again *en dehors du sujet:* See "Mirror Stage." For, I believe that Lacan's elaboration of an infant's experience before the mirror in which the "I" is constituted as a prolepsis, permanently chasing after an anticipation of itself, provides the best understanding of the human figuration in the *Encyclopedia.*

III.

The infant before the mirror in Lacan's analysis has no formed ego and is "still sunk in his motor incapacity and nursling dependence"[19]. S/he cannot stand alone and has no mastery over body movements. Like the human figure of "Encyclopedia," the infant is characterized by *insuffisance* (p. 4). But then s/he sees, and recognizes as self, an image in the mirror. "This act . . . immediately rebounds in the case of the child in a series of gestures in which he experiences in play the relation between the movements assumed in the image and the reflected environment, and between this *virtual* complex and the reality it reduplicates—the child's own body, and the persons and things around him" (p. 1, my emphasis). The mirror reflects the child in his or her surroundings at a moment "of an organic insufficiency" (p. 4)—s/he has no motor control. But what the infant gets back from the mirror is an image of the body as a whole, as moving together, and relating as a whole entity to its surroundings. (Lacan invokes the notion of a *Gestalt.*) That image is only a "virtual complex"

17. *Oeuvres Esthétiques*, pp. 283–87. See note 5, above.

18. In any case, it need hardly be said that Diderot has here fallen into a set of epistemological assumptions little related to those we usually associate with the period as represented, for example, by Locke for whom the mirror is not in nature but in the mind: "These simple ideas, when offered to the mind, the understanding can no more refuse to have . . . than a mirror can refuse, alter or obliterate the images or ideas which the objects set before it do therein produce." (*Essay Concerning Human Understanding*, Book II, Chapter I, section 25.)

19. "The Mirror Stage as Formative of the Function of the I as Revealed in Psychoanalytic Experience," in *Ecrits* (New York: Norton, 1977), transl. Alan Sheridan, p. 2. Further references are in the text.

however, because it is the image of a reality that the infant does not yet experience empirically. When the child captures this image of self as a whole, s/he undergoes a "drama whose internal thrust is precipitated from insufficiency to anticipation—and which manufactures for the subject, caught up in the lure of spatial identification, the succession of phantasies that extends from a fragmented body-image to a form of its totality that I shall call orthopedic . . ." (p. 4).

Through this mirror image, the child passes from "insufficiency," not to sufficiency, but to an anticipation of a sufficiency—motor ability and subjective definition—that s/he does not yet enjoy. For Lacan, identification with a proleptic image at the mirror stage is the core of all future identifications, of all future identity[20]. In this way, identity is alienating because it is eternally in anticipation of itself.

Like the infant, the human experience in the encyclopedic mirror stems from the insufficiency that it both remedies and perpetuates at the same time. The orthopedic, ideal image reflected back to us inscribes our epistemological ground, like our "ideal-I," in a permanent relation to our "coming-into-being *[le devenir]*" (p. 2). Therein lies its pedagogical effect. The *Encyclopedia* gives us the confidence we can know everything by teaching us to know our desire in the present and to desire the knowledge that is ours "already" in the future. It is an enormous, Rabelaisian compendium that tries and fails to include knowledge of all things. The object of its lesson is less in the contents of its articles than in this example of its desire.

IV. A LAST LAUGH

But what of the "intense and pleasant reactions [that] will ensue between nature and man, from man to nature?"

In the mirror stage the little human overcomes "motor incapacity" (p. 2) in an experience that Lacan at first calls "a flutter of jubilant activity" (p. 1), and later calls a "jubilant assumption of his specular image" (p. 2). The infant should jubilate while s/he can because the mirror stage terminates in the "identification with the *imago* of the counterpart *[semblable]* and the drama of primordial jealousy" (p. 5). The little apprentice in humanity is still unaware that "desire of the other" is concomitant with a "competition or co-operation of others" that inevitably entails alienation and aggression[21].

One suspects that the reason for Lacan's repeated reference to the infant's jubilation, otherwise unexplained, is to underscore the naiveté of the victim that will then be "pierced" by the ironic blade of one in a position to know. For the ecstatic child is only the first incarnation of the blind idealist, who will

20. See Jane Gallop, *Reading Lacan's "Ecrits"*, Chapter II, forthcoming.
21. I have modified the translation. Future modifications will be indicated in the text.

return a few pages later: "We place no trust in altruistic feeling, *we* who pierce through to reveal *[nous qui perçons à jour]* the aggressivity that underlies the activity of the philanthropist, the idealist, the *pedagogue,* and even the reformer" (p. 7, my emphasis, translation modified). From the idealistic, pedagogical perspective of "Encyclopedia," such a statement invites a certain number of impertinent questions: Who is this "we"? What is its position? What is its interest in piercing the illusions of the naive? Since Lacan is clearly not himself indulging in veiled (altruistic) aggressivity—his aggression is piercingly obvious—how should we characterize his own posture in an article which presumably is also attempting to do something like represent and teach?

To the extent that Lacan's "we" is enunciated from the analyst's position of dominion over the difference between what is said and what is meant, it is the "we" of a master ironist. (But only to that extent.) It is even a royal "we" insofar as, through irony, he may be seeking to remain in a position of overseer, dominating from above the oversights of the naive and the suspicious intentions of the idealist. More than once, Diderot experienced piercing interruptions of his encyclopedic project, as in 1759 when the king's council revoked for the second time the royal privilege to print it. With a little violence to historical verisimilitude one could spin a fantasy in which Lacan would be a metaphor for Louis XV, suspecting pedagogical altruism as a mask for aggression against the crown, or more precisely, against the condition of possibility for what I am calling royal irony. And indeed, in that suspicion Louis and Lacan would have been correct.

Consider Diderot's subtle but explicit critique of at least one aspect of the monarchical order. ". . . Works commanded by sovereigns are never conceived on the basis of their usefulness, but always on the basis of [the king's] personal dignity, which is to say, they embrace the widest possible scope . . ." (p. 182). Diderot reveals a view of kings that is strangely similar to Lacan's view of altruistic pedagogues: kings are not really interested in benefiting others (altruism), but only in the widest possible expansion of their egos (aggression). Any interruption in a royally commissioned project is therefore "deadly" (p. 182) for its successful completion. In its specificity the Royal Ego, the ego as king, does not want to accommodate negativity. That is one of the reasons for which Diderot insists on the intimate link between his conception of the *Encyclopedia* and its composition by a group of individuals motivated—precisely—by a proleptic ideality. In the event that such an individual is interrupted in his project, "he at least gathers together the fragments of his enterprise: he carefully stores materials that can be useful when times are better; he chases after his advances *[il court après ses avances]*. The monarchical spirit disdains such prudence" (p. 183). The sovereign ego disdains relation to its own being as project; the encyclopedists's being is in "chasing after advances," running both ahead of and behind himself because his "advances" represent work already done and work to be done, an image in the mirror. The *Encyclopedia arises* from this interruption of the proleptic future as a differentiating space within the present. It is just this interruption that for a royal project is "deadly."

As part of his anxiety in "Encyclopedia," Diderot tirelessly catalogues the obstacles and inadequacies that would most render his enterprise "ironic" in Goldmann's sense of the term. He spells out the reality principle according to which the "we" represented in the *Encyclopedia* remains an interminable project, an interminable failure in the face of its own *imago*. In the midst of such negativity the more pertinent query, finally, is why Diderot was able to persevere at all. In answering just this question he shows signs of a certain passion, a certain jubilation that is perhaps not unlike that of the infant before the mirror.

. . . We felt rekindled by that thought so sweet and consoling, that men would speak of us, men for whose education and happiness we were sacrificing ourselves, men whom we esteemed and loved even though they had yet to be born, but whose voices we were given to hear through that too voluptuous murmur on the lips of certain of our contemporaries. (. . .) In effect, man is seen by his contemporaries and sees himself just as he is, a bizarre composite of sublime qualities and shameful deficiencies. . . . [But when he dies] there remain only those qualities eternalized in the monuments he has raised to himself or that he owes to public veneration and recognition, honors that his own self-esteem allows him already to enjoy in an anticipated ecstasy *[jouissance]*, ecstasy that is just as pure, just as strong, just as real as any other ecstasy, and in which there can be nothing imaginary except the credentials on which his aspirations are based. Our credentials are forwarded in the present work; posterity will judge them. [pp. 232–33]

The idealist, the pedagogue, the reformer speaks altruistically about his work in which he sacrifices himself now to something to come only later. In terms of present reality, to his contemporaries, he is like the *Encyclopedia* itself, a "bizarre composite of sublime qualities and shameful deficiencies," in which there are many echoes—of the "deficiency of understanding" that the work sets out to remedy, of the early reference to the "treatment of language that has remained insufficient," thus requiring remedial treatment in the article; of Ariste's vicissitudes[22]. But also, he is already what he *will* be, as reflected in what the ironist could only see as an orthopedic mirror. The movement is indeed one of precipitation from insufficiency to identification with an ideal image. But just as Lacan's analysis of the mirror stage neglects the repeated detail of the infants's jubilation at the moment of anticipatory projection (in reality the beginning of his lifelong alienation), an "ironic" reading would neglect to account for the encyclopedist-pedagogue's analogous "jouis-

22. See note 5, above.

sance"[23]. In this moment of ideal fulfillment, does the infant jubilate because s/he is naive, or because s/he knows; in spite of or because of that knowledge? Our reading would anticipate that it is both, that both are necessary precisely in their difference from each other.

Diderot's text opens onto what may be another scene, in which the jealousy and aggressivity of *je* always denied its ideal has for a moment become affirmation and confidence, not of any real future enjoyment of that ideal (which for Diderot is as irreducibly prospective as it is for Lacan), but of the working done in its image. In the working, paradoxically, "there can be nothing imaginary." The work is—good or bad, useful or useless, read or forgotten. The *affairement jubilatoire* in Diderot has prolonged itself in the affair of writing an encyclopedia. In the glassy space between himself and his book, between himself and his measure, there is this future possibility and this past history of a *jouissance* that no measure can know.

23. For an elaboration of *"jouissance"* as a general textual function in Diderot's writing, see my "Diderot and the Pleasure of the Other: Friends, Readers, Posterity," *Eighteenth-Century Studies* XI, No. 4, pp. 439–56.

RICHARD TERDIMAN

Structures of Initiation:
On Semiotic Education and
Its Contradictions in Balzac

"On ne secoue pas le joug de la langue."

—Balzac

The *roman d'éducation* may not yet have taught us all it can. The problematic that it posed a hundred-fifty years ago, and poses still, is worth re-examination. The genre can be read, as I propose to do below, as an early avatar of characteristically modern paradigms of thought; and the prolongation of its ambiguities into our own period—most crucially, in the critical and pedagogical realms which are central to our work as teachers—may help to illuminate some patterns of contemporary intellectual strategy which have systematically refused the contradictions which the *roman d'éducation* long ago defined.

Yet we will find our investigation vexed by a difficulty which does not so much have a source as it does a structure inherent in the problematic of the *roman d'éducation* itself. What looked at first like a dead genre resists our penetration at successive levels of the discourse with which we attempt to surround and invest it. Our entanglement in the problematic takes a characteristically Archimedean twist: it seems that outside of it we have nowhere to stand. To re-read the form and themes, the whole mythic shape, of the novel of education—even to unravel certain of the tangles which its own self-understanding could not penetrate in the early nineteenth century but which with time we can sort out more adequately now—is to involve ourselves, but this time from the *inside*, in precisely those practices of analysis and interpretation which the *roman d'éducation* itself functioned to codify and to propagate. So our position as readers of the form is immediately paradoxical; and the text of our own reading, while it strives to achieve the status of authentic critique, tends to slip back toward recuperation within the protocols of what appeared an obsolete form. The fascination of any attempt to re-read what thus at first seemed distanciable for us resides precisely in this complex and somewhat embarrassing implication of our understanding in its own object. Our attempt to analyse and render readable the paradigms of representation which functioned within the *roman d'éducation* precisely re-enacts these same paradigms. In our responsible, teacherly way, we find that we are writing another novel of education.

This perplexing mutual involution of the subject and object of our discourse is not, however, quite the same thing as that supposed incarceration in circularity—"Thinking about language is impossible without language itself"—which founds familiar contemporary critiques of representation. This is so because the forms of thought which in an investigation of the *roman d'éducation* begin as our object of analysis but seem to end up becoming our means for attaining it are deeply and irreducibly historicized. We can, and indeed we must, examine them in their production within definite historical circumstances, and in the structuration determined by these circumstances. And should we find that they coincide with certain of our own protocols of thinking, no transhistorical impossibility of other paradigms of analysis, or disability of our own, are implied by such coincidence: only the historical subsistence of certain operations of thought, and of the processes of social constitution which have determined them, from the post-Revolutionary period to our own time. Such persistence itself implies a lesson of historical continuity from then to now which is worth remembering. In any case, the formation within which our investigation moves is thus at least potentially established as historical, and the possibility of some authentic differential, dialectical grasp is instituted as thinkable within what at times may have appeared a frustratingly constant re-enactment of the same.

The fundamental tools and operations of such dialectical understanding of the post-Revolutionary social process were being systematized and propagated at precisely the historical moment when the *roman d'éducation*, and realism in general, themselves arose.[1] Already, of course, the paradox alluded to at the outset of my discussion is visible in the structure of such representation. It is a commonplace now to note that the writers who composed these texts, the consciousness out of which they emerged, were in no sense

---

1. A certain number of fictions of the realist period in France exemplify to a high degree what one might imagine as the ideal form of the *roman d'éducation:* in the *Comédie humaine, Le Père Goriot*, the Rubempré cycle, *Louis Lambert* and *Un Début dans la vie;* for Stendhal, *Le Rouge et le noir* and *Lucien Leuwen* would probably serve as the clearest examples. A certain number of texts, from Constant's *Adolphe* to Musset's *confession*, concentrating as they do much more upon the subjective psychological modulations of a love story than upon the exteriorized interchange between a hero and an objective world of social meaning would probably not be usefully included within the category. In the current essay, the use of the term designates much more a tendency to represent as paradigmatic certain personal and social interactions which is present to some degree in nearly every text of this period, than a specific genre or subgenre which might be clearly distinguished from others produced during the same period. In a certain sense, as is well known, that tendency toward depicting the interchange between individual experience and the cultural sphere in which individuality discovers, defines and realises itself—what the French call *formation*, the Germans *Bildung*—is fundamental to the whole project of realist fiction. It is thus a set or protocols for textualization, rather than a specific and exclusively-defined body of texts, which I will designate by the term *roman d'éducation* here.

independent of the process whose production was depicted. As middle-class representation, realism was implicated in, and even threatened to be absorbed by, the structures of bourgeois existence and domination. Authentic contradiction of the post-Revolutionary social real was thus never the object of such representation. What it could establish was rather a situation of distance, of dissidence, of critique which blocked the saturation of the world of discourse by the dominant ideology, and coordinately situated a crucial fragment of the bourgeoisie in a sort of internal emigration within the bourgeois world. This stance of negativity thus founded their imaginative production (and that of their descendents within the critical intelligentsia which we still populate, and which still defines our own existence) as the varied strains of a counter-discourse whose contents and structures subjected the lineaments of the dominant real to a global critique.[2]

The *roman d'éducation* then necessarily exhibits the dissonance arising from its ambiguous existence within realist practice, suspended awkwardly somewhere on a continuum which runs from the approbation of the real to its denunciation, from complicity to contradiction. The interest of the genre arises for us now, however, owing to the conflict within it of two master-discourses which have defined and sustained the self-understanding of post-Revolutionary society, constituted its fundamental imaginative protocols and its underlying ideological system. The first of these is the extraordinary supple and constantly developing capacity for the analysis of generative process which establishes the characteristic rationality of bourgeois production in all realms; the second is that hypostatization of the individual middle-class subject, socially mobile but at the same time radically independent of any generative social logic, alone somehow bracketed from the process of production which middle-class thought conceives as determining all other phenomena in the socio-economic realm.

By applying the protocols which sustain the analysis of production in general to the formation of the self (the constitutive dynamic of the *roman d'éducation*), by elaborating a discourse of socialization and demonstrating the mechanism of cultural reproduction as it forms individuals in concrete historical and social situation, the *roman d'éducation* thus holds two fundamental but contradictory elements of its culture within the same discursive space, and under maximum tension. Given the dissonant structure out of which the text itself is generated, this contradiction is not one which the *roman d'éducation* itself can explicitly confront or theorize. But even in the absence of such overt analysis, the form of the genre comes as close as any representation in the post-Revolutionary period to exploding certain ideological exclusions which otherwise sustain the stability of middle-class con-

2. I have discussed the formation and characteristics of this ambiguous position in a recent article; see "Counter-Humorists: Strategies of Ideological Critique in Marx and Flaubert," *Diacritics*, 9:3 (Fall 1979), 18–32.

sciousness.[3] The stresses, though not named, are deeply inscribed in the form's development; the contradictions proliferate through the *roman d'éducation*, which can neither name nor ignore them. They generate a complex process of ideological formation, undermining any reformulation which is worth examining here.

The function of a text, as Lotman and Piatigorsky usefully define it for our purpose, "is . . . its social role, its capacity to serve certain demands of the community which creates the text."[4] Rarely in cultural history has there been a circuit of such text production more satisfyingly exemplary than the one in which the novels of the realist period in France were generated. As is well known, realism responded to a broadly experienced cultural crisis, in which structural change in virtually every aspect of social relations raced ahead of adequate imaginative expression and consequent ideological mastery of crucial social developments, particularly for the new bourgeois strata whose economic emergence within a social context still dominated by the cultural forms and codes of Ancien Régime France represented an unprecedented and perplexing social fact in this period.[5]

What one might call the conceptual shortfall characterising such situations determines the production of imaginative discourse. Balzac put it with succinct irony in his Preface to the *Livre mystique* (1835):

Si la Société qu'il [l'auteur] a prise pour sujet de son oeuvre . . . était parfaite, il n'y aurait aucune peinture possible, il faudrait chanter un magnifique alleluia social et s'asseoir au banquet pour y achever sa portion congrue.[6]

3. Hegel was more cynical concerning the subversive potential of the corresponding German texts with which he was familiar. He underlined the eventual recuperation of the hero in such texts: "zuletzt bekommt er meistens doch sein Mädchen und irgendeine Stellung, heiratet und wird ein Philister so gut wie die anderen auch" [Still, as a rule he finally finds his girl and some job or other, marries and becomes as much of a philistine as anyone else]; *Vorlesungen über die Aesthetick*, II, in *Werke in zwanzig Bänden*, XIV (Frankfurt: Suhrkamp, 1970), 220. However, the French examples are less reassuring to the dominant ideology, as we shall see.

4. Yuri M. Lotman and A. M. Piatigorsky, "Text and Function" (1968), trans. Ann Shukman, *New Literary History*, 9:2 (Winter 1978), 233.

5. On the production of nineteenth-century realism and its relation to contemporary cultural crisis, the bibliography is large. See particularly the work of Pierre Barbéris, "Mal du siècle ou d'un romantisme de droite à un romantisme de gauche," in *Romantisme et politique 1815–1851* (Paris: A. Colin, 1969), 164–82; his *Balzac et le mal du siècle: Contribution à une physiologie du monde moderne*, 2 vols. (Paris: Gallimard, 1970), particularly vol. I, chs. 1 and 6; vol. II, chs. 7 and 8; and his *Le Monde de Balzac* (Paris: Arthaud, 1973), particularly Part III. The origin of the perception for Western criticism is probably to be found coordinately in Auerbach (see *Mimesis: The Representation of Reality in Western Literature*, trans. Willard R. Trask, Princeton: Princeton Univ. Pr., 1953, ch. 18), and in Lukács (see the 1948 Preface to *Studies in European Realism*, New York: Grosset & Dunlap, 1964). In turn the concept that literature functions to make sense of periods of profound social transition probably came to Lukács from Lenin (see his articles on Tolstoy in *Lenin on Literature and Art*, Moscow: Progress, 1970).

6. "If the society which the author has taken as his subject were perfect, no depiction of it would be possible; one would have to sing a magnificent social hallelujah and sit down at the feast to consume one's appropriate portion." *Comédie humaine*, ed. Marcel Bouteron, XI (Paris: Gallimard-Pléiade, 1954), 266.

The phenomenon which Marx called the "uneven development of material production relative to . . . artistic development"[7] thus identifies the socio-historical basis underlying a pressing imaginative need: a systemic demand for the elaboration of structures and vocabularies which might satisfactorily apprehend, adequately model, the tense conjuncture and the contradictory situation of middle-class experience within it.[8]

The elaborate emotional lexicon of those strains of French romanticism associated with dispossessed aristocracy could thus serve the expressive needs of the nascent bourgeoisie only momentarily. The sense of disorientation within the two groups inevitably diverged in tone and quality. Unlike the aristocratic romantics, the bourgeoisie faced not exile, but an uncomfortable installation; not solitude and powerlessness, but an awkward and chilling intuition of class effectiveness. The romantic *mal du siècle* thus initially furnished lapsed bourgeois liberals in the late Twenties and early Thirties with a language to express their own apparently deteriorating situation, but as time went on increasingly failed to provide an imaginative paradigm corresponding to the particular character of their experience. As the conjuncture evolved, the tonality whose expression bourgeois intellectuals sought to sharpen inflected away from the romantic elegiac, toward a global sense of mistrust, apprehension and insecurity: Stendhal's "soupçon," Balzac's "doute."[9] Coordinately, and in keeping with their class's perception of its emerging role in the socio-economic circuit in process of transformation in the post-Revolutionary period, the sense of dislocation experienced by the members of the middle-class under the early July Monarchy came to be felt not as tragically metaphysical, but as concretely situational. It is in this context that the functionality of the *roman d'éducation*, as the application of middle-class logic of process to the production of contemporary social existence itself, comes into focus.

The social stress of this process of dislocation and of the attempt to master its tensions is figured in the familiar yet still astonishing statistical rates which characterize the first fifty years of the nineteenth century in France, and attempt to take the measure of its changes: the Paris population increased by a factor of 2.6; the proportion of the population of France living in the capital doubled.[10] From 1820 to 1848 the French national income rose by a factor of

7. *Grundrisse: Foundations of the Critique of Political Economy*, trans. Martin Nicolaus (New York: Vintage, 1973), p. 109.

8. On this development, and the relation of mimetic fictions to it, see my "Materialist Imagination: Notes toward a Theory of Literary Strategies," *Helios*, 7:2 (Spring 1980), 29–49.

9. Stendhal: "Le génie poétique est mort, mais le génie du *soupçon* est venu au monde"; *Souvenirs d'égotisme* (1832), ed. Henri Martineau (Paris: Divan, 1950), p. 7. Balzac: "Le XIXᵉ siècle, dont l'auteur essaie de configurer l'immense tableau . . . est en ce moment travaillé par le doute"; Preface to *Le Livre mystique* (1835), p. 266.

10. Pierre Barbéris and Claude Duchet, ed., *Manuel d'histoire littéraire de la France*, Tome IV, 1789–1848, Premier Volume (Paris: Editions sociales, 1972), 314. During the same period, of the

fifty to sixty per cent, the stock of capital doubled, coal consumption increased by a factor of five. By 1840, Paris, though not the largest city, had already become the greatest manufacturing center in the world, with over 400,000 workers employed in industry (by comparison, the entire population of the city forty years previously had been only 547,000).[11] And in a register somewhat different, but relevant to our area of concern here, in the nineteenth century, while only a quarter to a third of French writers were born in Paris, fully one-half of the members of the literary profession died there.[12]

What is evoked by this rapid sampling of demographic evidence (whose overall pattern moreover was as familiar to Balzac himself as it has become to twentieth-century specialists in the period[13]) is an immense internal migration which brought to Paris men and women of all classes having no previous roots in the capital, and which coordinately determined alterations in social status for substantial groups within that population to a degree previously unexperienced. In social terms, these changes in the scale and the character of the urban environment changed nearly everything.

Within the complex evoked by such statistics, but of which they can hardly be said to take adequate measure, the *roman d'éducation* thus both inscribes and attempts to achieve mastery of an unprecedented crisis of socialization. As the theme and the dominant social experience of this period is a massive displacement of individuals and of whole social structures in which their existences are determined and need to be conceptualized, so in response an entire corpus of texts depicting in their complex profusion the signs and status-signals, the employments and amusements, the dangers and the blunders—the entire mapping of a cultural system as intricate and hermetic as that of nineteenth century Paris—arose to initiate successive cohorts of new arrivals. Department stores and display windows, popular newspapers and mass advertising (all Parisian inventions dating from the 1820s and '30s) sought to codify the world of dominant and desirable values for a population prepared by ambition but not by instruction for the complex hierarchizations of the capital. Whence the immediate utility of those curious subgenres providing orientation within this mysterious world of social signs—

regions of the city excluding the northern periphery (where urban settlement was a relatively recent development), the greatest proportional population gain was on the Left Bank of the Seine, whose resonances for the newly arrived provincial projecting a career in the professions or in literature are well known (see the *Manuel*, p. 315). It was about half way through this period that the growth rate of the urban population in France began to exceed that of the rural. See E. J. Hobsbawm, *The Age of Revolution, 1789–1848* (New York: Mentor, 1962), p. 207.

11. Rondo Cameron, *France and the Economic Development of Europe, 1800–1914*, 2nd ed. (Chicago: Rand Mcnally, 1961), pp. 52–53.

12. *Manuel d'histoire littéraire*, p. 305.

13. Louis Chevalier speaks admiringly of the accuracy and breadth of Balzac's demographic knowledge; *Classes laborieuses et classes dangereuses à Paris pendant la première moitié du XIXᵉ siècle* (Paris: Plon, 1958), p. 12.

the *Codes, Tableaux, Dictionnaires, Traités, Monographies, Physiologies* and so on which flourished in the '20s and early '30s.

These novel subgenres of the social text educated those not born to them to an increasingly complex world of hierarchized objects and behaviors. And in its turn the *roman d'éducation* itself could usefully be seen as at once the furthest development of such tendencies, as the dramatization, the mimesis, of their social operation, and as their cognitive metatext, the beginning of what was to prove a long reflection within the culture upon the existence and the functionality of its own new institutions and processes.

Moreover, if we have a *roman d'éducation*, it is in part because the education systemically required in the context of new social realities under early capitalism was not available through any other mechanism. The texts themselves seem to inscribe this absence: it is significant how many of the protagonists in the novels in question here are launched upon their fictional courses precisely at the moment that their institutional schooling terminates or even aborts. And the character of such schooling is presented in the fictions themselves as almost universally vacuous or irrelevant to their later itineraries. One thinks of Lucien Leuwen, kicked out of the Ecole Polytechnique in the first line of his novel; of David Séchard's printing apprenticeship with the Didots in Paris before he returns to Angoulême at the opening of the novel to fail precisely at printing; of the cavalier elision of Rastignac's law studies, more or less consciously passed over in our introduction to him in favor of his "successive initiations" into the complex "human stratifications which make up society";[14] of Raphaël de Valentin's extraordinary autobiography launching the second part (and situating the entire action) of *La Peau de chagrin*, and which he begins by stating that he will skip over his formal education, since it had no bearing on his experience. The tendency is significant: it inscribes the perceived failure of these institutions (France's notoriously deficient system of primary education,[15] her twenty-two universities, even the numerous institutions of higher education, like Polytechnique, founded during the Revolutionary period precisely to respond to the realities of a world in conscious process of transformation) to offer that initiation into the unfamiliar structure of experience which young people newly in the cities, newly confronting transformed relations of production, encountered as a mystery for which they were radically unprepared, and within which it was necessary for them to learn to move.

It thus becomes important to inquire what elements in the textual protocols of the *roman d'éducation* established its functionality—particularly at an historical moment when another primary social text, the one produced within the institutions of formal education which in the modern period we

14. See *Le Père Goriot*, ed. P.-G. Castex (Paris: Garnier, 1963), p. 40.
15. Hobsbawm, p. 227.

have come to expect to find inscribing the fundamental paradigms determining socialization, revealed itself to be crucially deficient. Generally speaking,
the stress within a structure under the kind of tension we have observed here
produces itself under conditions of the sort of historical *déphasage* between
material production and cultural or imaginative development which, as
mentioned, Marx sketched in the *Grundrisse*. An uneven development of
precisely this type, problematizing the self-representation of post-Revolutionary society and the mechanisms by which it understood social meaning to be
generated within it, lies at the heart of the crisis experienced by our middle-
class proto-intelligentsia during the late Restoration and July Monarchy.

In the case of the formerly dominant groups with whose interests
aristocratic values had developed harmoniously over time, organic institutions inculcating and naturalizing such values were well established, and had
long functioned more or less transparently. But members of the new social
strata whose existence has concerned us here experienced a situation intrinsi-
cally more conflicted. On the one hand, as a rising class, they were involuntarily subjected to the assimilation and reproduction of the same systems of
value.[16] But by virtue of their status determined by these values, they were
simultaneously excluded from the traditional initiatory mechanisms. Practically speaking, their most peremptory need was thus to catalogue, master and
institutionalize the knowledge that would enable them to move within a
cultural system in which meaning was signified by counters alien to their
experience and their understanding.

But in epochal transitions of the sort we find inscribed in these developments, the project of historico-cultural innovation rarely operates on the level
of such immediate instrumentality alone. In this regard, Barthes' celebrated
denigration of bourgeois writing in the period before 1848 as an unself-
reflexive and unproblematized practice of representation—a judgment which
has become one of the founding assessments in structuralist and post-structuralist revaluations of our literary history—represses something crucial.[17] It is
true that in the period which concerns us, the profusion of *Physiologies*,
Traités and the like seems indeed to have responded to the sort of instrumental
exigency characterizing the historical moment and the situation of the
middle-class.[18] And on a second level, the fictive itinerary dramatized in the
roman d'éducation surely did serve to provide the cognitive basis for a

16. Hobsbawm (pp. 218–19) puts the constraint clearly: "Rising classes naturally tend to see
the symbols of their wealth and power in terms of what their former superior groups have
established as . . . standards. . . . A culture as profoundly formed by court and aristocracy as the
French would not [suddenly] lose the imprint."
17. "Instrumentality" is Barthes' misprizing term for bourgeois writing in the period prior to
Flaubert; *Le degré zéro de l'écriture* (1953; Paris: Gonthier, 1965), p. 52.
18. Hobsbawm, p. 219, comments on the wide diffusion of such pedagogical texts, along with
manuals of etiquette and gracious living, in our period.

paradigm of socialization which the genre made imaginatively available to members of the newer strata seeking their way in what still remained confusing social territory. But beyond such immediately pragmatic considerations so harmonious with the patterns of middle-class rationality and instrumentality which Barthes deplored, the process of production of these texts simultaneously generated another text, more tentative and diffuse, perhaps, but profoundly innovative and subversive in its implications. This parallel text, whose *critical* bearing our cultural histories have tended to neglect, represents an early but powerful theorization concerning crucial ideological structures of post-Revolutionary life. Moreover its importance of our own cultural history is great. For beyond any immediately practical or purely informational objective, it instituted within our discourse a conceptualizing process that was to lead, at the beginning of our own century, to systematic disengagement of the notion of the sign.[19]

So we need to look again at what was at stake in the *roman d'éducation*. The education which it textualized turns out to be *education into signs:* into an experience of the semiotic which now we see to be crucial in modern relations of production. Such experience today seems so well internalized that one might almost suppose it always was there. But in the early post-Revolutionary period its formation constituted a crisis. It is in this sense that the *roman d'éducation* registered the initiation not only of a young hero, but of a new and conflicted process of socialization, the early staging of penetration into our cultural consciousness by a new paradigm for social life, whose domination has only increased in the intervening one hundred-fifty years.

The *roman d'éducation* must therefore not be seen only in the ungrateful role of precursor within some now obsolescent prehistory of our contemporary scientific knowledge. These texts practiced the sign and the process by which it became problematized within our conceptual discourse. And they initiated the bases for a critique of its functioning, and indeed a reflection upon the conditions under which a notion such as the sign became pertinent, rose into consciousness—concerns moreover significantly absent in certain later versions of semiological theorization. In turn, these aspects of the representation within the *roman d'éducation* provide the relevant response to our earlier interrogation concerning the genre's particular functionality and influence in its own moment. In a society in which signification was in the process of becoming mediate, in which the discourses of social life were losing their transparency and their self-evidence, the *roman d'éducation* offered not only a systematic mapping of the new terrain of meaning, but more fundamentally a powerful reflection on the phenomenon of signification itself.

19. It is evident that no argument concerning the "origin" of the sign is in question here. No more than Saussure, the realists did not "invent" it. What concerns us here is the process by which its concept entered the broad discourse of cultural reflection.

There is no process of institution in social life without a preceding, and determining, destitution. As the transparency characterizing areas of social existence which have not previously been experienced as problematical is lost, the effort to master and renaturalize them in their transformed state attempts, paradoxically, to reproduce a dying innocence through the concerted mobilization of knowledge. By their nature, of course, such strained efforts to recover a period when no special effort was required can never succeed cleanly. The institution of paradigms of consciousness as epochal as the complex we have been examining inscribes this double movement in particularly interesting ways.

For our purposes, it can be said that the process which determined both the thematics and the narrative structure of the *roman d'éducation* proceeded on a double front. Lotman and Uspensky observe that periods of social change generally are characterized by a noticeable intensification in what they term "semiotic behavior."[20] An increasingly acute consciousness of the coded nature of social life tends to arise in all such transitional periods: the diverse practices of the sign (naming and designating, classifying, hierarchizing), as well as the forms of its theorization force themselves into social representation and into conceptual discourse. Nor are such developments ever universally uncontroversial. Critiques were mounted against the penetration of the sign into social consciousness, and against an unanticipated structure of constraints on the forms and performances of social life which the conscious emergence of the semiotic phenomenon seemed to determine. Of course it may seem quixotic to have thought that one might somehow abolish the sign. But in that moment when a culture becomes conscious, creates a model, of itself,[21] the constitutive elements of the model, as happened in our period, can also become the most critical area for any contestation of the new configuration of the world. Let us examine these developments in turn.

For Balzac, signs were everywhere: "Notre civilisation est . . . immense de détails" [Our civilization is pregnant with details].[22] And the codes which such signs compose presented themselves to understanding as clearly determined historical products. For example:

En France, il n'y eut de partis possibles qu'au moment où il exista des intérêts contraires en présence, les révolutions ont commencé par être dans les choses et dans les intérêts avant d'être dans les idées.[23]

20. Yuri M. Lotman and B. A. Uspensky, "On the Semiotic Mechanism of Culture," (1971), trans. George Mihaychuk, *New Literary History*, 9:2 (Winter 1978), 211–12.

21. See Lotman and Uspensky, "On the Semiotic Mechanism," p. 227.

22. Preface to *Une fille d'Eve*, cited by Barbéris, *Monde de Balzac*, p. 104.

23. "In France, parties only became possible from the time when contrary interests confronted each other; the revolutions began in material things and in interests before they occurred in ideas." "Sur la situation du parti royaliste" (1831), cited by Barbéris, *Monde de Balzac*, p. 163. Balzac here curiously anticipates Foucault's analysis in *Les Mots et les choses*. See *The Order of Things: An Archeology of the Human Sciences* (New York: Vintage, 1973), p. 368.

In turn, the consciousness of such historicized realities necessarily gave rise to a science of decoding the social signs we call objects and characters: to a hermeneutics.[24] Bernard Vannier, who has counted, writes that the course of narration in the *Comédie humaine* is interrupted more than five hundred times to provide the description of a character, in order that thus motivated and energized by the meaning coded in the appearance described, the character can participate in the action of the tale.[25] Such appearances then become the text for that exegesis so familiar in Balzac:

Qui n'a pas remarqué que là, comme dans toutes les zones de Paris, il est une façon d'être qui révèle ce que vous êtes, ce que vous faites, d'où vous venez, et ce que vous voulez?[26]

Ces juges vieillis dans la connaissance des dépravations parisiennes . . . avaient les yeux ardemment fixés sur une femme . . . qui ne pouvait être déchiffrée que par eux.

Avez-vous bien saisi les mille détails de cette hutte assise à cinq cents pas de la jolie porte des Aigues? . . . Eh bien, son toit chargé de mousses veloutées, ses poules caquetant, le cochon qui vague, toutes ses poésies champêtres avait un horrible sens.[27]

Barthes' claim, we recall, had been that the discourse of the early realist period failed to grasp language itself as essentially problematized; in his image, realist writing never experienced that "solitude de langage" which marks the crisis of representation that has since occupied us.[28] Foucault was somewhat less categorical in *The Order of Things*. For him the crucial transition occurred somewhat earlier. The passage from the classical to the modern episteme, which he localizes between 1775 and 1825, altered consciousness of the linguistic phenomenon profoundly:

From the nineteenth century, language began to fold in upon itself, to acquire its own particular density, to deploy a history, an objectivity, and laws of its own. (p. 296; cf. p. 221)

In relation to Foucault's hypothesis for localizing the transition, Balzac's perceptions of the constitutive historical and interpretive contingency of language do indeed seem to pose the conditions of possibility for precisely that

24. See Foucault, *The Order of Things*, pp. 297–98.

25. *L'Inscription du corps: pour une sémiotique du portrait balzacien* (Paris: Klincksieck, 1972), p. 15.

26. "Who has not noticed that [at the Opera], as in every part of Paris, there is a mode of being which reveals what you are, what you do, where you come from, and what you want?" *Splendeurs et misères des courtisanes*, ed. Antoine Adam (Paris: Garnier, 1964), p. 6. Subsequent references in the text.

27. "These judges, who had matured in the knowledge of Parisian depravities, were carefully examining a woman who could be deciphered by them alone."

"Have you sufficiently grasped the thousand details of that hovel five hundred paces from the attractive gateway to Les Aigues? Well, its roof covered with velvety moss, its cackling chickens, the pig browsing: all its pastoral poetry carried a horrible meaning." *Les Paysans*, ed. J.-H. Donnard (Paris: Garnier, 1964), p. 51. Subsequent references in the text.

28. *Degré zéro*, p. 52.

objectification of the semiotic which most critics have considered to be the development of a later period than the one which has concerned us here. Moreover, once one begins to look for them, the characteristic traces evidencing the pursuit of such a reflection turn up frequently in Balzac's text. Thus for example we find him acutely conscious of the phenomenon of polysemy in linguistic systems, and of the socio-historical process by which such multiplication of sense occurs:

Les mots sont susceptibles de prendre plusieurs significations, et leur en donner de nouvelles est ce que j'appelle créer. C'est enrichir une langue. Une langue s'appauvrit en gagnant des mots, et s'enrichit en en ayant peu et leur donnant beaucoup de significations.[29]

On another front, in a reflection clearly relevant to what is still one of the controversial areas of contemporary semiotic thinking, one finds Balzac musing, in the divagation on language at the beginning of Louis Lambert, on the vexed problem of the relationship between sound and sense: "N'existe-t-il pas dans le mot vrai une sorte de rectitude fantastique?" [Doesn't the word "vrai" (true) exhibit a kind of fantastic honesty?][30] Yet the age-old myth of some natural and unproblematical relationship between signifier and signified to which Balzac longingly refers seems invoked here, as frequently elsewhere since the Revolutionary period,[31] precisely because its central assumption was coming under increasing pressure within broad areas of social and historical experience. Contingency and facticiousness, rather than transparent naturalness, increasingly appeared to characterize such relations. In that regard, the inflated rhetoric of the passage from Louis Lambert almost seems to transmit a disguised defensiveness, and to denote precisely the uncertainty of its own assertion.

The complex issue of arbitrary relation thus raised by its denial in Balzac's text has been put in a perspective which will be useful for us here in two relatively recent theoretical reflections. In Pour une critique de l'économie politique du signe, Jean Baudrillard argued that any arbitrary relation between discrete signifiers and signifieds is nonetheless inevitably founded by an act of social choice: a specific, concrete system of sociality, an historical conjuncture, are already inscribed in the institution of any sign. In turn, the notion that the parameters of such choices are potentially recoverable in analysis—

29. "Words can take several meanings, and giving them new ones is what I call creating. The process enriches a language. A language is impoverished by taking on new words, but enriched by having few of them but giving them many meanings." Letter to Louis Aimé (April 1844); Correspondance, ed. Roger Pierrot, IV (Paris: Garnier, 1966), 690.

30. Comédie humaine, ed. Marcel Bouteron, X (Paris: Gallimard-Pléiade, 1950), 356.

31. See Michel de Certeau, Dominique Julia and Jacques Revel, Une politique de la langue: La Révolution française et les patois (Paris: Gallimard, 1975), p. 87. The most systematic examination of Balzac's reflections on language, though from a perspective quite different from that taken here, is in Martin Kanes, Balzac's Comedy of Words (Princeton: Princeton Univ. Pr., 1975); see particularly ch. 4.

thereby distinguishing them from purely random or gratuitous connections—
then furnishes one of the central methodological bases for Pierre Bourdieu and
Jean-Claude Passeron in their work on the functioning of educational systems
within culture.[32] It will become evident shortly that such a perception bears
heavily on the paradigms of socialization, and upon that initiation to the
experience of the social sign, which Balzac conceptualizes in the form of the
roman d'éducation.

But we need to pursue a bit further the investigation into Balzac's
problematization of language, and his objectification of the sign, which has
already suggested the presence of a more concerted reflection on his part than
critics have generally assumed. Among the profusion of details which struck
Balzac as characterizing post-Revolutionary culture, and which like others he
sought to catalogue and classify, certain linguistic phenomena have a central
place. Consider the attempt to seize and imitate the variety of dialects and
accents which one finds in the Balzacian text: for example, Nucingen ("*Le
tiaple n'egssisde boinde, dit le baron*"; *Splendeurs*, p. 89); or Père Fourchon in
the celebrated description of the otter-hunt ("Elle ne vous coûtera pas cher, si
elle a du blanc sur le dos, car *eul Souparfait m'disait éque nout Muséon* n'en a
qu'une de ce genre-là"; *Les Paysans*, p. 42).[33] Such divergences from dominant
standard, transparent speech help Balzac to objectify the complex significatory
process of language in its social usage, to figure precisely that meaningful
contingency of semiotic behavior (in terms of historical period, region, class,
work activity, and individual mentality) which constituted the world for him
as a vast coded network awaiting its adequate decipherment. Balzac's texts
thus record an intent consciousness of the most diverse linguistic phenomena
(argots; specialized and obsolete usages curiously subsisting despite historical
change; verbal tics; the sorts of word-games played by the *pensionnaires* at
Madame Vauquer's, and so on) and of a broad range of "non-standard"
communicative situations (overhearing; misunderstanding; ambiguity; deliberate deception) whose variety and frequency in his novels inscribe at the same
time the material complexity and the ultimate systematicity which renders
semiotic interpretation empirically arduous and theoretically possible despite
the difficulty.

The ultimate testing ground for such a construction of the project of

32. Jean Baudrillard, *Pour une critique de l'économie politique du signe* (Paris: Gallimard,
1972), p. 180; Pierre Bourdieu and Jean-Claude Passeron, *Reproduction in Education, Society and
Culture*, trans. Richard Nice (London: Sage, 1977), pp. 8–9. The complex problem of arbitrary
relation has been raised again recently by Jonathan Culler. See his *Ferdinand de Saussure* (New
York: Penguin-Modern Masters, 1977) and the review article by Marie-Laure Ryan, "Is there Life for
Saussure after Structuralism?" *Diacritics*, 9:4 (Winter 1979), 28–44.

33. Of course the otter itself is a fiction, a sign invoked to trick Blondet. No one is more
surprised than Fourchon when his semiotic invention, his imaginary exchange-value, transforms
itself into a real, material otter. Again, the conceptual distance between sign and referent is clearly
marked.

semiotic objectification in the Balzacian text would seem to be those cases, like Fourchon's otter, in which disguise, secrecy, concealment or falsification are present. (Let us recall that Eco designates the possibility of lying as precisely distinguishing the semiotic field.[34]) Such situations, where interpretation of evidence proves difficult or impossible, provide Balzac with a powerful representation both of the structure and of the difficulty of the semiotic phenomenon. Configurations of this kind (one thinks of their centrality in *L'Histoire des Treize* or in *Splendeurs et Misères*, among many other texts) create theoretical models of the interpretive situation which he was striving to conceptualize. And in turn the disguises by which characters overlay their truth with a false representation construct quintessential opportunities for the intervention of the interpretive function which provides much of the energy in the Balzac text—a function whose operation runs through an enormous range, from the stolid explanatory "voici pourquoi" which Proust pastiched so cuttingly, to the brilliant apparition of Vautrin in his guise as ultimate decipherer of the social text.

The Vautrin novels are tales full of mystery, which means they are the paradigmatic *romans d'éducation* in the Balzac canon. The initiator needs someone to initiate; the uninitiated need to know. Whence Rastignac, Rubempré. And Vautrin's power within these texts is signified in part through the staging of competitions in interpretive capacity between him and those other figures whose claim to such capacity is also explicit in the text. A sequence of such incidents provides the interpretive bite in the confrontation in *Splendeurs et Misères* between a series of extraordinary interpreters. The first moment of the process pits the banker Nucingen against the detective-spy Corentin. Their encounter is a combat of readings, and for once Nucingen loses: "Corentin resta pour lui ce qu'est, pour un archéologue, une inscription à laquelle il manque au moins les trois quarts des lettres" [Corentin remained for Nucingen what an inscription lacking three-quarters of its characters would be for an archeologist] (*Splendeurs*, p. 164). In turn Corentin, thus valorized by his triumph over the "loup-cervier," the lynx-like Nucingen, encounters but fails to comprehend the traces of Vautrin: " 'Au profit de qui rançonne-t-on la passion du banquier?' . . . Pour la première fois, les deux artistes en espionnage [Corentin and his associate Contenson] rencontraient donc un texte indéchiffrable. . . ." ["For whose profit was Nucingen's passion being put to ransom?" For the first time, the two brilliant spies thus had met up with an indecipherable text.] (*Splendeurs*, p. 267).

But such suspenseful failures to understand, integral to the social and financial intrigue of this particular novel, really typify a much more universal situation. In the Vautrin novels, in the *roman d'éducation* in general, the profound uncertainty which stresses an individual with the unhappy con-

34. Umberto Eco, *A Theory of Semiotics* (Bloomington: Indiana Univ. Pr., 1976), pp. 6ff.

ing within a crucial code of signs
is a repeated and intense experience. And one is constrained to wonder
whether it does not constitute a significant anticipation of that "solitude du
langage" which for Barthes valorized the textual practice of a later period.

In response Barthes might have argued that the interpretability of such
codes, the continuity of their connection to the referents in the real world the
text projects outside itself, are in no way abolished by the interpretive
difficulties particular individuals may experience in concrete circumstances.
The crisis of interpretation in Balzac would thus seem situational, not
systemic. But as we go on to consider the paradigm of initiation which lies at
the heart of the *roman d'éducation*, we shall see that such initiation, far from
confirming that unproblematic relation between sign and referent which has
been taken as the constitutive protocol of realism, in fact rather opens up an
experience of personal and social alienation *through the operation of the
semiotic system itself*, an experience of the imprisonment in language no less
profound in its implications than those explored later in the century by figures
like Flaubert, Mallarmé, and Nietzsche.

The textual mechanism for exploring these complexities is at the heart,
precisely, of the *roman d'éducation*, since its project is really to gain an
understanding of the manner by which codes and signs in the social world are
constituted, transmitted, and manipulated, and of the consequences of such
social operations. It is in the structure of initiation, in that process by which
significations for the first time objectify and make themselves explicit, that
the sign as a constitutive form and as a comprehensible content of the social
world is most clearly perceived and most adequately conceptualized. Vološinov lays a basis for understanding the mechanism we are examining when he
writes that "every sign . . . is a construct between socially organized persons in
the process of their interaction."[35] The experience of initiation which propa-
gates through the structure of the *roman d'éducation* is precisely the moment
when such *construction* becomes visible: initiation objectifies the sign,
denaturalizes it, forces it to reveal itself for what it is.

The interpenetration of knowledge and power in the social functioning of
any semiotic element then emerges with great clarity.[36] There is no abstract

35. V. N. Vološinov, *Marxism and the Philosophy of Language*, trans. Ladislav Matejka and
I. R. Titunik (New York: Seminar Pr., 1973), p. 21. Authorship of this text is disputed, and on the
authority of Roman Jakobson the French edition attributes it to Mikhail Bakhtin.
36. Vološinov puts this point in a nearly formulaic way: "sign becomes an arena of the class
struggle" (*Marxism and Philosophy of Language*, p. 23). But his insight is less doctrinaire than the
blunt language of this proposition suggests. The social basis of conflict over *meaning* can be traced,
for the Marxist tradition, to the inevitably unequal arrangement within any social configuration for
dividing labor and (since the neolithic period) for distributing surplus. The anthropological basis for
such a notion seems if anything more strongly founded now than it was in Marx's time (see *Capital,
A Critique of Political Economy, Volume One*, trans. Ben Fowkes, Harmondsworth: Penguin, 1976,

content which a sign could inscribe while somehow remaining isolated from the constitutive conflicts of the social process. In that sense, Barthes' strictures against the instrumentality of meaning in the early bourgeois period need to be extended to *all* signification: it never exists "just for itself," and his valorization of the *scriptible* (writable) text comes to seem a curious holdover of romantic ideology.[37]

In consequence we observe initiation as a profoundly self-centered process in the texts which concern us here: no character within them wants to learn simply in order to know; there are no disinterested scholars in this educational system. The bipolar structure formed by the initiator and the pupil thus figures more than a structure of epistemology: it represents a nexus of social determination, and a trajectory of projected social movement.

One of the simplest cases in Balzac is that of Oscar Husson in *Un Début dans la vie*. Instructed successively by his mother, Madame Clapart, by his Uncle Cardot, by his superiors in the law firm where he clerks for a time until he loses money entrusted to him by gambling it away, even later by his former antagonist the Comte de Sérisy, in the end he "arrives," as Balzac puts it in one of his most cynical conclusions:

Oscar est un homme ordinaire, doux, sans prétension, modeste et se tenant toujours, comme son gouvernement, dans un juste milieu. Il n'excite ni l'envie ni le dédain. C'est enfin le bourgeois moderne.[38]

---

pp. 470ff.). This basis is convincingly argued by Marshall Sahlins in *Stone Age Economics* (Chicago: Aldine, 1972). Necessarily such structures include institutionalized systems of ideological-semiological control and regulation (see V. V. Ivanov, "The Science of Semiotics," 1962, trans. Doris Bradbury, *New Literary History*, 9:2, Winter 1978, 200), which are at once assumed as natural by those in power, imitated and internalized by those seeking power, and (at times) contested and denaturalized by those dissatisfied with the structure of power which they sustain. Such a complex of differential relations to the dominant sign system describes perfectly the sort of struggle over meaning, or over the meaningful, to which Vološinov refers. Moreover the existence of such a struggle provides in turn the basis for the historical directionality of evolution in the meaning of signs. The play of forces striving for hegemony over such structures of meaning does not simply describe an abstract *combinatoire*, a neutral and potentially bidirectional or reversible "communications system." Bourdieu and Passeron make this clear when they write, concerning precisely the sort of education paradigm which occupies us here, that "P[edagogic] A[ction] can produce its own specifically symbolic effect only when provided with the social conditions for imposition and inculcation, i.e. the power relations that are not implied in a formal definition of communication" (*Reproduction*, p. 7, cf. pp. 19 and 23). A social and historical materiality resisting any imagined free play of signs is thus inscribed in the very nature of the semiotic process—as indeed in the process of initiation by which meanings are taught and learned—and these can (at least after the fact) become objects of analysis and understanding. On these latter points, see Carol Gould, *Marx's Social Ontology: Individuality and Community in Marx's Theory of Social Reality* (Cambridge: MIT Press, 1978), pp. 29 and 56–68.

37. See Barthes, *S/Z* (Paris: Seuil, 1970), p. 10; and Jonathan Culler, *Structuralist Poetics: Structuralism, Linguistics and the Study of Literature* (Ithaca: Cornell Univ. Pr., 1975), pp. 190–191.

38. "Oscar is an ordinary man, gentle, without pretention, modest, and constantly, like his government, in the center. He attracts neither jealousy nor scorn. He is, in sum, the modern

What is imaged here is that structure of recuperation by the dominant ideology which seems to suggest there is nothing more to the paradigm we have been examining than Hegel's cynical dismissal suggested: a kind of uncritical submission to the essentially enveloping structure of any social system in return for one's share of its rewards (see above, n. 3).

On the level of plot, *Un Début dans la vie* does seem to inscribe consciousness of an unproblematized world, a perhaps complex but nonetheless manipulable structure. Thus, like Oscar, his fellow voyagers in the coach at the beginning of the tale—Georges Marest, Joseph Bridau, Léon de Lora, even the coach-driver Pierrotin, have all advanced nicely by the end of the story. Oscar finishes the novel forgiven by Sérisy despite his grotesque indiscretions, and is installed by the Count, his final initiator, as tax collector in the district of Sérisy's chateau. The plot conclusion thus seems to imagine that if you learn at last, through however painful and halting a process, to read the signs, you will finally come to possess your "appropriate portion" (see above, p. 201) of the world signified.

Yet the locus of dissonance within the representation of these texts bears further investigation. While Oscar "arrives," as we have seen, Balzac sneers. The existence of a contradiction is thus detectable in the realm of tone, if not of action; one almost thinks of the sardonic apotheosis of Homais. The situation in the most powerful of the *romans d'éducation* then profoundly complicates this perception of dissonance. Thus if Rastignac at the conclusion of *Le Père Goriot* projects the possibility of that "arrival"—at a level far beyond what Oscar attains—which has been figured for him in the enticements of Madame de Beauséant and of Vautrin himself, his subsequent story in the *Comédie humaine* resonates much more ambiguously.[39] And more disturbing still, after receiving intense instruction from Madame de Bargeton, from Lousteau, from the members of the Cénacle, and from his continuing, daily tutorial with Vautrin, Lucien de Rubempré graduates by hanging himself in the Conciergerie. Something thus enters the circuit to perturb this structure of accomplishment, of "arrival," even on the level of imagined plot itself; and the perturbation, when analysed will begin to give us access to a strategy of critique of the social semiotic which is only barely perceptible in a story like Oscar Husson's.

What is made visible in these more complex representations of the initiation paradigm is the degree to which the determined practice of the sign binds rather than frees. And this happens *systematically,* producing as narrative figure an irony of a type very old in cultural imagination: the figure of the *trompeur trompé,* of the manipulator manipulated. Two distinct species of ignorance are implied in the process of initiation plotted in such concerted

bourgeois." *Un Début dans la vie* (1842), ed. Guy Robert and Georges Matoré (Geneva: Droz-Textes Littéraires français, 1950), p. 217.

39. See Barbéris, *Balzac et le mal du siècle,* I, 130 and Terdiman, *The Dialectics of Isolation: Self and Society in the French Novel from the Realists to Proust* (New Haven, Yale Univ. Pr., 1976), p. 42.

fashion in these early realist texts. One of these is remediable, but the other is not. All the heroes in these fictions receive instruction concerning the hidden cultural significance of a large number of signs. With practice they learn to understand the code, and even to read that hermetic parallel text which for Vautrin is inscribed like a palimpsest below the apparent surface of the social real: "Il y a deux Histoires: l'Histoire officielle, menteuse, qu'on enseigne . . .; puis l'Histoire secrète. . . ." [There are two Histories: official History, illusory, the one which is taught; and secret History].[40]

But no more than his pupils, despite the acumen in such reading of codes which he claims for himself in the continuation of the same passage, Vautrin is not capable of understanding something essential about the determining mechanism of codes themselves. The techniques of exegesis which he controls more than any other character in these fictions carry social analysis to an astonishingly sophisticated level. But though they enable him to understand signs which no one else can read, they cannot penetrate the regulative structure of the semiotic phenomenon itself. It remains opaque for him and for all the characters in these texts. Against Vautrin, then, one would find it possible to sustain the sort of claim which Barthes urges against early realism in general, that for him the nature of social representation is not truly problematized.

But one cannot sustain this claim against Balzac. In the conclusion of *Un Début dans la vie* it was the introduction of a tonal dissonance which denoted the ambiguity to which the text gives access beneath what would otherwise seem a distinctly positive conclusion. In the Rubempré cycle, the analysis of contradiction has gone further and become more central. What Vautrin cannot perceive as a constitutive failure in his understanding of the structure of his world Balzac has begun to seize. The demonstration is in the shape of the Rubempré story itself, in Vautrin's loss of Lucien. Balzac conceives the *logic* of this failure of control, and with it inscribes a crucial contradiction at the heart of the initiatory paradigm whose representation the *roman d'éducation* was striving to achieve.

The initiation sought by the characters in the texts which have concerned us really figures the distance between two modes of understanding. It traces a myth carrying, within the middle class's experience, and at a crucial moment in its historical development, both the fundamental content of an unrealized need, and the emerging contradiction at its center. The initiation paradigm which Balzac elaborates represents both the ambition to penetrate the sign system, to inhabit it as known territory and manipulate it freely from a secure position at its heart; and the confused projection of the system's transcendence of such control, of its own determinate resistance to such domination.

The *roman d'éducation* comprehends such conflicted consciousness in

40. *Illusions perdues.* ed. Antoine Adam (Paris: Garnier, 1961), p. 709. Subsequent references in the text.

the realm, and within a language, of conjuncturally-specific social control. No individual can achieve stable domination of the sort Vautrin promises within a social structure in which any authority is infinitely mediated by the anarchic process of competing individualisms. And the sign system necessarily inscribes this irrationality irreducible within the social formation (as an ideology of the arbitrary, of some impenetrable randomness or abstraction within the system itself) in its own paradigms of exchange. What lies at the center of the dilemma of initiation perceived in the early post-Revolutionary period is thus that dialectical constitution of a new social configuration, and the contradictory situation of any individual will within it, which persisted uncomfortably remembered at the edge of middle-class consciousness.

Within these texts, the initiation process then has as its referent, and tests the possibility of domination over, a concrete structure of interests and power-relations ("Aujourd'hui, il n'y a plus que des intérêts, répliqua des Lupeaulx. . . ."; "These days, there's nothing left but self-interest," replied des Lupeaulx]; *Splendeurs*, p. 11). But the would-be subject, once initiated, finds himself immersed in the structure of relations over which he sought control, discovers that he is involuntarily speaking the referent *as its own object*. The social system the initiatory process sought to determine in fact thus determines the process even in its seeking; the power over which control was sought turns out to be *power over those who seek power*. There is, within such a hermetic configuration, no exit from the ironic circle which recuperates ambition by having itself engendered it.

This is the significance of ambition as it functions representationally in Balzac's texts. Through the plots engendered out of its inherent diachronicity, it stands as primary means of investigating a system of determination in social existence which had not yet been adequately conceptualized for bourgeois consciousness. Middle-class individuals in the post-Revolutionary period found themselves neither so bound as they had been, nor so free as they thought. The limits of their autonomy, and the mechanisms—no longer primarily legal and political—which mediated such constraints, needed to be more sufficiently understood. André Wurmser, who has carefully studied the manifestations of "ambition" in texts from our period, concluded with a political judgment of its social significance, that "ambition is reactionary."[41] But however accurately perceived in its own terms, this formula fails to seize the overdetermination of such a political vector by the complex structure of the social semiotics in post-Revolutionary existence. Such overdetermination is precisely what the *roman d'éducation* strove at the limit to textualize.

Complex structures of determination are inherently mystificatory: their social functionality and their conscious representation within historical

41. André Wurmser, *La Comédie inhumaine* (Paris: Gallimard, 1970), pp. 167–92, particularly p. 182.

culture necessarily diverge.[42] But mystification is a process, not a state, and for this reason its structures can be more clearly seized in the incipient phase of their constitution and solidification, at that moment when memory of an alternative social consciousness is still effective, and before the colonization of imagination by the new structures proceeds too far. This is the dialectical moment at which the process of such penetration by the new structures can itself be fleetingly thematized in imaginative representation—a moment analogous to that of an individual's early initiation to the post-Revolutionary semiotic phenomenon, when the material reality of the sign and the historical contingency of its operation could be objectified, before its internalization in the middle-class adult (like Husson) rendered the structure frustratingly opaque. This is the privilege of early nineteenth-century realism, and the determining element in its representational force.

In our own time, having proceeded beyond this transition point in the historical constitution of middle-class structures of meaning, in the work of theorists like Althusser, Lacan, Baudrillard among others, the system itself has tended to be conceived as autonomous (Althusser's "theoretical antihu-manism"), the structure of signs as *self*-generating.[43] Such hypostatizations of the structure within which cultural existence and imagination appear bound, though they can appear radicalizations of the dialectic out of which such developments were produced to begin with, in fact seem rather to rigidify it out of history altogether. Rather than maintaining that stance of critique which seems, comparatively, so clear in the *roman d'éducation*, and pursuing definition of the dialectical point from which such a critique could continue to bear against the reality it takes as its object, such reifications appear to capitulate to and to be produced by the penetration of the structures of a

42. The question of such mystification, which founds the problematic of ideology, has constantly preoccupied the Marxist tradition, from Marx's Fourth Thesis on Feuerbach and *The German Ideology* to Althusser and his followers. Fredric Jameson discusses a number of the influential positions on the issue in *Marxism and Form* (Princeton: Princeton Univ. Pr., 1971). The canonical case of a demystificatory critique which inevitably provides a model for all such ideological analyses within the tradition is Marx's penetration of the illusions inherent to the commodity under capitalism *(Capital, Volume One*, Part I, ch. 1, section 4). The structure and assumptions of this analysis and its implications for social knowledge are given a full discussion in G. A. Cohen, *Karl Marx's Theory of History: A Defense* (Princeton: Princeton Univ. Pr., 1978), ch. 9 and Appendix I. The general problematic and its history within post-Marxist sociology of knowledge is clearly outlined in Peter L. Berger and Thomas Luckman, *The Social Construction of Reality* (Garden City, N. Y.: Anchor, 1967). A recent collection of articles bearing on the problem of ideology can be found in *Issues in Marxist Philosophy, Volume III: Epistemology, Science, Ideology*, ed. John Mepham and David-Hillel Rubin (Atlantic Highlands, N.J.: Humanities Pr., 1979). Another useful collection is *Ideology and Cultural Production*, ed. Michèle Barrett, Philip Corrigan, Annette Kuhn and Janet Wolff (London: Croom Helm, 1979).

43. Louis Althusser, *For Marx*, trans. Ben Brewster (New York: Vintage, 1970), p. 229. As a characteristic example of the tendency, consider the lapidary assertion of Baudrillard: "Il n'y a de besoins que parce que le système en a besoin" [Needs exist only because the system needs them]; *Pour une critique*, p. 87.

modern cybernetic capitalism to the deepest levels of social and individual consciousness.

Nonetheless, the force and centrality of these structures (if not their absorption and domination of the entire field of social existence in certain modern theorizations of them) is a clear perception arising significantly in our early nineteenth-century texts, and running forward from them to the contemporary period. And it is one of the elements of continuity, as argued at the outset of this essay, which makes our own relation to those earlier texts in some sense a playing out of their own analytical protocols. For the process of envelopment in the paradigms of social existence which first rendered the sign problematic for a significant and definable social population, and which emerges as a thematized trajectory in the *roman d'éducation,* conceived the structure which links the initiator, his pupil and the semiotic content which is the substance of their transaction as a construct more fundamental than the abstract individualism of the character we (and the texts of the period in question) have known as the "hero." Indeed, it is precisely in this period that the concept of the hero itself became seriously and coordinately problematized, and took on an unmistakable ironic tinge precisely through his determinate insertion in the system of initiation which dominates him as irrefutably as he attempts to dominate it. One need only try to imagine Fabrice del Dongo without Gina, or Lucien without Carlos Herrera, to see how irreducibly derivative such individuality is rendered in these fictions.

It is this dense structuration of individuals within the initiatory situation, and their ultimate domination by the form and substance of relationship itself, that is conveyed in Vautrin's initial conversation with Lucien, as central among the conditions which are to govern any future collaboration between them: "Je ne sais pas quel nom vous donnez à cette instruction sommaire . . .; mais c'est le code de l'ambition. . . . Il n'y a pas de choix. . . . Il faut accepter ce code" [I don't know what name you would give to this rapid lesson; but it is the code of ambition. You have no choice. You have to accept the code] (*Illusions perdues,* pp. 719–20). The irony of such domination by the code is involuntary for Vautrin, but emerges as willed in Balzac's critical consciousness. This is why the tie between Lucien and Carlos, as it develops, vacillates wildly and continuously from the most selfless dedication to the most egotistical possession. Unknown to either, it is the structure of the link itself, and not their wills to create it as they want, nor the language controlled by either of them in defining it, that determines its authentic character. Thus Vautrin to Lucien: "Enfin je me ferai vous!" [In sum, I will become you!] (*Illusions perdues,* p. 719); but only a few moments before: "Vous m'appartenez comme la créature est au créateur" [You belong to me just as the creation belongs to the creator].

The initiatory relationship, which determines the inability of its adherents to penetrate its structure of constraint, induces such slippages between dedication and domination. Neither, however, expresses the real content of the bond—rather, it is the uncertainty of the movement itself which is significant, evidencing the stress that the relation exercises upon those it links. Such vacillation, though it harmonizes with the apparently dependent personality of Lucien, is particularly striking in the case of a figure like Vautrin, who embodies so much of the dialectical tension of early bourgeois consciousness, particularly the contradiction between an ideology of rationality and control, and a critique of the individual and social results of its practice. His evolution, even his celebrated defection to the side of "Order" at the end, bears and uncovers these contraries without hinting any possibility of their harmonization within middle-class production relations. What emerges is a suspicion that there may be no adequate termination for the initiatory structure; its plot, which appeared for a moment resolvable in a story like Oscar Husson's, here reveals itself to stage its own unanticipated undoing, its inexorable miscarriage.

It is a particularly stringent paradox for cultural consciousness to discover that its paradigms of initiation, the protocols which give access to its constitutive sign system, thus issue unexpectedly, on the other side of the process of socialization which they determine, into a *negative* consciousness, the realization of an incapacity to master the reality to which the sign system refers. Initiation then appears to undergo a dialectical flip, and turns up as expulsion.

The logic of Lucien's suicide lies here: not in some depth-psychological "weakness," still less in the stereotypical "femininity" of character which Vautrin repeatedly attributes to him (and which in his final letter he seems to have come to believe), however interesting its analysis might be on other grounds.[44] His suicide means the failure of initiation to *transform* Lucien, to develop in him that power which had been promised, to operate its own transcendence: to inscribe itself as historically *productive*. Lucien says precisely this to Herrera-Vautrin in his last letter: "Vous avez voulu me faire puissant et glorieux, vous m'avez précipité dans les abîmes du suicide, voilà tout" [You wanted to make me powerful and admired, you have dropped me into the abyss of suicide, that's the whole story] (*Splendeurs*, p. 473). And the profound contradiction at the center of the relationship, whose manifestations in Vautrin we have already observed, concentrates itself in the final lines of the letter: "Ne me regrettez pas: mon mépris pour vous était égal à mon admiration" [Don't mourn me: my contempt for you was as great as my admiration].

But the trajectory of initiation thus conceived as overturning its own

44. For example, in an anaylsis of sex-role representation and the distribution of generic signifiers in the early bourgeois period. See my *Dialectics of Isolation*, pp. 50–54.

process really represents a paradigmatic reading of those representations of *disillusionment* so crucial to the self-understanding of nineteenth-century consciousness, and which appear here as the most forceful thematized manifestations of the paradox which inhabits the *roman d'éducation* from the beginning. What thus seems to happen is that fate in these representations takes on a new and more specifically material substructure. The configuration of sociality in the early capitalist world, objectified in the paradigm of initiation to the semiotic which sustains precisely that world at the center of its social existence, is here for the first time plotted as a grave destiny.

This is the cultural structure which Bourdieu and Passeron have attempted to theorize with their notions of "pedagogic authority" and "symbolic violence." If we read *Reproduction in Education, Society and Culture* with our nineteenth-century texts in mind, we will begin to see how the concepts developed in the first part of their work unlock certain of the essential dynamics in the *roman d'éducation.* Their effort in *Reproduction* was to clarify the intrinsic and constitutive relation of compulsion, of constraint, which ideology has necessarily obscured within the pedagogical structure, and which could not be explicitly named or conceptualized in the nineteenth-century texts. Bourdieu and Passeron seek to demystify the "gift" of education, to place it firmly within a social setting which inscribes both the systemic need for semiotic (or what they would call "symbolic") initiation, and the mechanisms of hierarchy and domination by which individuals are submitted to this systemic need without necessarily having chosen to serve it.

Their work (along with Renée Balibar's *Les français fictifs* and her joint study with Dominique Laporte of *Le français national*) might thus be seen as a prolongation in the directions both of theoretical and empirical specificity of Althusser's reflections on ideological apparatuses. Althusser is very clear concerning the conjunctural centrality of the area which has concerned us here: "I believe that I have good reason for thinking that behind the scenes of its political Ideological State Apparatuses . . ., what the bourgeoisie has installed as its number-one, i.e. as its dominant ideological State apparatus, is the educational apparatus. . . ."[45] The *roman d'éducation* perceived this cen-

45. Althusser, "Ideology and Ideological State Apparatuses (Notes toward an Investigation)" (1969), in *Lenin and Philosophy*, trans. Ben Brewster (New York: Monthly Review Pr., 1971), p. 153. Let us recall that central to Althusser's concept of the ISA is that all such apparatuses "contribute . . . to the reproduction of the relations of production" (p. 154), even impose this, but *without* invoking the threat of explicit state repression, of overt violence (pp. 144–45). This perception of the education function (what Bourdieu and Passeron call "pedagogic action") has a long history within the Marxist tradition, beginning as far back as Marx's Third Thesis on Feuerbach (on "educating the educator") and, prior to Althusser, receiving its most powerful development in Gramsci's notion of class hegemony as a mode of domination which not only determines explicitly political behavior, but saturates the entire process of living without overtly exercising violence or coercion—a perception akin to Marcuse's notion of "forms of control" in *One-Dimensional Man* (Boston: Beacon, 1964). On the Gramscian concept of hegemony, see Raymond Williams, *Marxism and Literature* (Oxford: Oxford Univ. Pr., 1977), Part II, ch. 6.

trality at quite an early point in the implantation of capitalism's structures. Its constitutive paradigm, the initiatory relation, already clearly embodies the mystified mechanism of social regulation which still seems essential to advanced capitalist reproduction today. And by objectifying this relation, the genre establishes the conditions of possibility for its critique.

For our purposes, then, Bourdieu's and Passeron's theoretical perception is essential. They argue that any practice of inculcating the meanings which attach to social signifiers—any teaching—tends both to legitimize the social system within which such meanings function, and in return to be legitimized (and even imposed) by the power relations which underlie the system itself (see *Reproduction*, pp. 4–7). While we attend to the content of our instruction, we are fundamentally but imperceptibly modeled by its form; the ideological representation of the world is involuntarily naturalized even through critique of its specific detail (see Althusser, "Ideology," p. 157).

The contradictions which lead to and define the significance of Lucien de Rubempré's suicide in the most important of the *romans d'éducation* are clarified within such a framework. For it exposes the mystification of the original pedagogical transaction between Lucien and Vautrin as irreducible within the structure of their encounter. Lucien is promised the transcendence of social law, but he discovers that the process of initiation which pledges such liberation itself inscribes precisely the structure of power-relations which was to be triumphed over. So Lucien discovers that he has exchanged a more diffuse form of domination during his first stay in Paris (in *Illusions perdues*) for one which during his second period in the capital (in *Splendeurs et misères*) proves immediate, continuous, and intolerably oppressive. In entering into an initiatory relation with Vautrin, he finds he has only tightened what from our perspective we might see as the quintessential modern form of a Hegelian master-slave dialectic which ties the actors within it, a structure all the more perplexing because the violence its configuration determines is radically mystified for both.

This is why Vautrin cannot himself liberate his pupil; both are imprisoned in precisely the relation which was to have freed them. The double-bind is thus absolutely hermetic.[46] Lucien exits out of it the only way he can.

But this text still takes individual destinies seriously, whence the emotional charge of Lucien's suicide and of Vautrin's eulogy. Whence also the

46. Bourdieu and Passeron put the bind in the form of a classical paradox which illuminates the lock-up holding Vautrin and Lucien: "The idea of a P[edagogic] A[ction] exercised without P[edagogic] Au[thority] is a logical contradiction and a sociological impossibility; a PA which aimed to reveal, in its very exercise, its objective reality of violence and thereby to destroy the basis of the agent's PAu, would be self-destructive. The paradox of Epimenides the liar would then appear in a new form: either you believe I'm not lying when I tell you education is violence and my teaching isn't legitimate, so you can't believe me; or you believe I'm lying and my teaching is legitimate, so you still can't believe what I say when I tell you it is violence"; *Reproduction*, p. 12.

shock of recognition which Vautrin's final apostasy causes in us as we realize, in the text's last demystification, the underlying *continuity* of his role throughout: the coming-to-consciousness that not only as *chef de la Police* but *all along*, and particularly as Lucien's instructor-protector, he has enacted precisely and systematically the structural authority, the mode of control, which sustain our modern form of domination: the power to determine meaning, and to order the exchange of signs.

These problems sound much like some which still preoccupy us today, and clear relations tie the problematic central in the *roman d'éducation* to more contemporary concerns. We thus return to that implication of our own ideology and our own practice, as what we now call academics, in the paradigms of social life which began to emerge about a century and a half ago. Whether or not we wish to consider our activity as teachers and critics as solidifying Althusser's ISA's, the element of power and control in our profession, the dialectical stress between our exercise of it (however benign in intention) and those who may be its objects, the tension in our own relation to the institutional structures within which our work is organized—these phenomena render our situation problematical in ways which remain troubling. The notion persists that our practice of instruction, our efforts at criticism, may be involuntarily and systematically reappropriated by a formation against which they nominally direct themselves; that our ministrations license students to access to an existence whose fundamental structures the cultural representations which provide the substance of our teaching have denounced in concert for a hundred fifty years. Our institutions still honor the mythic shape of a certain form of education, indissolubly associated with the dream of social mobility by the middle-class, and in the image of its own rise to power, whose imaginative sources indeed lie in part in the texts which have concerned us here, but whose narratives functioned to impeach the myth itself. Our performance in the academy seems then to reduplicate the shape of this conflicted imaginative experience: we seem still to stage what these texts staged.

There is something unsettling in this reproduction of a pattern which our own investigation instructs us bears crucial contradictions within it. We are unhappily aware that the pedagogical imperative may turn out, in our practice, to have sources, and serve interests, other than those we thought. Such an outcome might not have seemed so surprising within the frankly acquisitive, overtly rapacious structures of early capitalism (and those relatively unmystified structures no doubt represented the conditions of possibility for thematizing the question to begin with). But since that time the need for ideological and structural stabilization has covered over the intersubjective violence underlying the initiation paradigm with the kind of cybernetic anonymity that appears to grant immunity to all economic and social actors today. Yet the scandalous discoveries in the *roman d'éducation* are still known to us, and nothing would suggest that the fundamental dynamic of recuperation by the master-discourse of capitalism is any less present in its advanced form than in its period of primitive consolidation—rather the contrary.

We might recall in this regard Baudrillard's insistence that the arbitrary relation of signifier and signified that constitutes the sign already implies within itself, takes as its condition of possibility, a regulated sociality which stands both as institutional guarantor and as a kind of subterranean referent of the semiotic relation itself. As we have argued, initiation, teaching, offer instruction not only in the discrete content of signs, but in the structure of regulatedness which sustains them, reinforcing the systematicity of the social whole. However this systematicity, like the sign itself, is never abstract, but (as the French say) "oriented": partisan, exploitative, consonant with certain social interests, structures, positions. As such, it constitutes the constraints of a *régime de sens*, of a system governing meaning, whose operation is the more binding on account of its transparency.

An economy like ours, founded on exchange, functions best on the assumption that everyone emerges happy from trading. Exchange-values pass through the system, in the exercise of our rational choice, and to the end of general contentment—or so the system believes on our behalf. And signs, in the position of quintessential exchange-values which has emerged as theirs under advanced capitalism,[47] seem to circulate freely through the universe of social meaning; their transmission seems to carry no responsibility, to implicate no one. A certain liberal ideology of freedom is inscribed in this very insouciance, and the paradise projection some have made of this free play—whether in a fantasy of language's self-reflexive autonomy and of the liberation of the text, or in the homologous fantasy of a corporate economy of such profusion and fluid productivity that no needs need go unsatisfied—seems a vision of the commodity's own utopia, the dream that exchange-value might itself have of its radical domination of all social and imaginative existence.[48] As such, these representations remain enveloped within the hegemonic *régime de sens*, and adjusted to the exchange-economy, which they hypostatize.

Against such projections, one seeks a stance which might recapture the possibility of an authentic critique of such dreams of domination. And although with regard to the nineteenth-century texts which have occupied us here we appear strangely disarmed, seem to have at our disposal only those

47. This relation has been studied in detail, particularly by Baudrillard in *Pour une critique de l'économie politique du signe*, by Jean-Joseph Goux in *Economie et symbolique* (Paris: Seuil, 1972); and by Ferruccio Rossi-Landi in *Linguistics and Economics* (The Hague: Mouton, 1975).
48. My formula imitates certain of Marx's concerning an imputed or imagined language of commodities. See *Capital, Volume One*, p. 176: "If commodities could speak, they would say . . ."

paradigms of analysis which the texts themselves deployed long ago, the problem can be turned around. For us the contradictory structure of Balzacian initiation might stand as a model—perhaps a *scale* model—of more complex figurations of the same operation in our contemporary experience. The structure represents a paradigm of investigation, a protocol of discovery, of the semiological and coordinate socio-economic transactions which link the institution of teaching, and the institutions in which we teach, to functions which are left out of our job- and course-descriptions, but which (often very much despite us) may inscribe themselves secretly within our work, may define its authentic productivity, its real structures of transformation.

The paradigms of the *roman d'éducation* can help us to penetrate our contemporary crisis of comprehension and of representation because it was they that first penetrated the primitive structures whose prolongation into our own period seems now to have undermined our ability to understand. If our grasp on the history which has produced our present seems deadened, they can help to explain the patterns we have internalized in our own initiation to the modern *régime de sens*, which have borne within them the ideological envelopment that makes our thought question its ability to grasp its own material referent, and at times induces it to accept only its own incapacity as object.

Dialectical thought is always dialectical against something, and toward something else. Even to provide a sense of the directionality of the movement which has produced our current impressions of non-movement controverts the stasis in which we seem to find ourselves, the flattened imaginative range of our own period, and that contemporary reification of social relations whose production under capitalism Marx was the first to theorize.

It is fundamental that the interrogation of the sign which still preoccupies us, of the process of its transmission and its exchange, and of the social structures which such processes seem to mediate, emerged in the early nineteenth century in a period of the middle class's conquest and definition of its power. The inscription, even the complicity of the social sign, within a determinate structure of power became mystified as the process of conquest which motivated the interrogation to begin with moved toward later stages of historical consolidation and ideological solidification. The critical bite, the virulence of the early post-Revolutionary analysis of and practice of the sign have thus slowly diminished; today they may strike us as easily assimilable within the apparently seamless ideological protocols of advanced capitalism.

But the emergence of contradictions within the sign inscribed in a complex set of power relations in the period of the *roman d'éducation* permits us now to overcome to some degree more contemporary ideological repression of the problematic which was thus laid bare. The history of these developments, still crucially our history, remains recoverable for us. This is why our investigation of these phenomena reproduces analytical protocols from the genre which has occupied us, why we still find ourselves writing a form of *roman d'éducation* a century and a half after the original example uncovered the necessity of understanding how the pedagogical relation functioned within a modern exchange economy. The key for us is still to reveal the mystified inequality of these exchanges, the disguised productivity secretly inscribed in any transfer of the sign within the determinate system of meaning which still defines its possibility of existence and its ultimate social bearing.

Yet structures are historical, and we cannot expect simply to reproduce them indefinitely. Our situation has unfolded from the one the *roman d'éducation* confronted a hundred-fifty years ago, but under late capitalism it is not now just what it was in the moment of capitalism's incipiency. To be sure, in the circuit which might produce our own text, key elements from the earlier moment persist. As in the realist period, when the sign is discovered as the mystified agent of the domination of others, its alien structure, imposing itself on the possibilities of our own meaning, becomes politically and culturally critical; and such a crisis can then mediate efforts to comprehend the mechanisms producing these alien meanings. But the text we might imagine as our own need not end with the achievement of such comprehension. As a form which lives in history, it might come to inscribe the subversion of these contemporary structures of determination, the projection of alternatives.[49]

Situated as we are at the opposite end of a process of epochal development from the *roman d'éducation* of the realist period, the future which it projected then has become an experience which seems to envelop us now. Vautrin's final recuperation by the overt structures of hegemony in his own time appears to define an early image of our own absorption by structures profoundly more elusive today. We are still living, but how much more painfully, that conceptual shortfall which Marx identified.

Yet as we have observed, such conjunctures are unstable. And it is not unimaginable that a more progressive dynamic lying within the education paradigm, though rarely activated within the period we have investigated here—the capacity to drive present structures beyond themselves, to mediate the institution of change—might at least be released. Within our memory there have already been adumbrations of such movement. Over time, the mechanisms which exercise ideological control, which sustain reproduction of the social formation, have tended to turn ghostly for our consciousness. But though contradictions may be mystified, they are not thereby abolished. The dialectical energy which these mechanisms of control have seemed to absorb

49. The relation between moments of *analysis* of the social configuration which confronts a text and moments of *projection* beyond it is discussed more fully in my "Materialist Imagination."

nonetheless persists within the system, and conserves the potential to force reproduction beyond itself into the production of the new.

Under such conditions, the novel of education will not have outlived its pertinence. In its beginning, deploying analytical tools whose sophistication has not been surpassed, it could devise no tolerable conclusion to the initiatory structure determined within capitalist production relations. But surely history holds the possibility of other plots. And any movement beyond those which the *roman d'éducation* denounced a century and a half ago will require an alternate pedagogic text which could project the paradigms of our initiation to and of the future: a narrative of our learning which would at last assign this ghostly present its historical reality.

ANDREW J. McKENNA

Allodidacticism:
Flaubert 100 Years After

> Et d'enchaîner sur Chamfort, dont la formule qu' "il y a à
> parier que toute idée publique, toute convention reçue est une
> sottise, car elle a convenu au plus grand nombre," contentera à
> coup sûr tous ceux qui pensent échapper à sa loi, c'est-à-dire
> précisément le plus grand nombre.
> —Lacan, *Ecrits*
>
> Vox populi, vox Dei (Sagesse des nations)
> —Flaubert, *Dictionnaire des idées reçues* (epigraph)

Of all the pedagogical figures in French literature—Rabelais, Montaigne, Voltaire, Rousseau—Flaubert's Bouvard and Pécuchet are perhaps the most comical and, as I shall argue, the most disquieting. It is by the conjugation of these qualities that their educational experience, both as learners and teachers, is for our time, most instructive.

Near the term of their encyclopedic foray through Western knowledge, the two autodidacts embark on the task of educating Victor and Victorine, two orphan bastards consigned by the provincial Chavignollais community to reform school and to the convent:

They procured several works relating to Education—and their system was decided upon. It would be necessary to banish all metaphysical ideas and, after the experimental method, follow the lead of Nature. There was no hurry, for the two pupils would have to forget what they had learned. [p. 370]

After this implicit bow to Rousseau, Pestalozzi, Lancaster and others, the second paragraph evokes the Renaissance ideal, according to Rabelais and Montaigne, of training the body along with the mind:

Although they had a solid constitution, Pécuchet wished, like a Spartan, to harden them more, to accustom them to hunger, to thirst, to bad weather, and even that they wear shoes with holes in them to prevent catching colds. [P. 307][1]

One imagines Pécuchet proclaiming the conundrum, *mens sana in corpore sano*. And as one might have expected, "Bouvard s'y opposa." His opposition here is as comical as it is mechanical, recalling the tic-tac of earlier debates

---

1. Gustave Flaubert, *Bouvard et Pécuchet*, ed. Claudine Gothot-Mersch (Gallimard: Folios, 1979), in which my quotes from the *Dictionnaire des idées reçues* are to be found as well; the translations are mine and the page references are to this edition.

between Bouvard and Pécuchet, and exemplifying Flaubert's most consistent tactic in his general strategy of intellectual devastation. To each thesis of Bouvard or Pécuchet the other responds by its equally authoritative antithesis; the resultant impasse goads them to grasp at another branch of the tree of knowledge until "Tout leur a craqué dans les mains" ["Everything has snapped in their hands,]" (p. 414).

The reader may thus feel advised not to take the educational adventure of the two men seriously. After all, they have, as indicated by Flaubert's notes for this tenth chapter of the novel, the last completed in manuscript form, an "idée exagérée de la puissance de l'éducation."[2] On the other hand their experience in its entirety, as it serves as the premise for the novel's conclusion, can lead us to reflect, can educate us, according to the commonplace etymology, on the power of ideas and ideas of power in contemporary history. The issue, as posed by Flaubert's text, and as informed by events of the last hundred years since his death, is nothing less than a choice between a comic or tragic resolution of history itself.

The experiment of Bouvard and Pécuchet in the domain of education, like those essayed in all other fields hitherto, fails, and it fails, in multiple senses of the word, abysmally. The mental obtuseness and vicious conduct of the two orphans conspire with obstacles, to be examined herein, built into the tutorial undertaking, in thwarting the educational aspirations of the two men. As with their earlier ventures in the physical and human sciences, reality proves once again refractory to the constraints of system and the utopia of method. The pedagogical failure of the two "bonhommes" thus deepens the abyss of cognitive nihilism which has already engulfed everything from geology and archeology through history, esthetics and religion. At the same time, Chapter X represents "en abîme" the entire trajectory of epistemological catastrophe that constitutes chapters II through IX, as the two men proceed in quest of foundations for knowledge which forever elude them.[3] This last chapter thus stands in episodic, metonymic relation to the narrative which precedes it; it serves as well as a metaphor for their entire intellectual enterprise.

Their dilemma is everywhere the same. As the two men range pêle-mêle through language, botany, history and religion, with novel, not to say progressive forays into sex education and ecology (pp. 396, 398), their experience is scanned at every turn by the same rhythm of research, essay and failure as in their other scientific ventures comprising chapters II through IX. The inadequacy, the incompletion, the incoherence of each field of study motivates these two researchers to pursue firmer ground in another, then another,

2. Flaubert, *Bouvard et Pécuchet: Edition Critique,* ed. A. Cento (Nizet, 1964), p. 215.
3. This is established by Claudine Gothot-Mersch in her presentation, "Le Roman interminable: Sur la structure circulaire de *Bouvard et Pécuchet,*" at the "Colloque Flaubert" (Collège de France, March 1980) which is to appear shortly with the other papers of the colloquium.

and another, with no end in sight. There is no end in sight because there is no valid, irreducible point of departure; there is no origin which is not arbitrary in its constitution, no foundation whose probing does not reveal an abyss beneath it. Their quest brings to mind a Borgesian archeological dig, which would pulverize each layer of civilization in search of a source buried still deeper in the sand, and become one with it in its disintegration.[4] From on high—"Quel est le but de tout cela?" ["What is the purpose of all that?"]—queries the star gazing Bouvard; and Pécuchet: "Peut-être qu'il n'y a pas de but?" ["Perhaps there is no purpose?"] (p. 139)—as from way down below—"La géologie est trop défectueuse! A peine connaissons-nous quelques endroits de l'Europe. Quant au reste, avec le fond des Océans, on l'ignorera toujours" ["Geology is too defective. We hardly know a few places in Europe. As for the rest, with the bed of the Oceans, we'll always be ignorant,"] (pp. 158–59)—the lesson of defeat is the same, and one wonders about the novelty of our deconstructive criticism, whose tireless errand is to repeat it in the realms of sign and psyche.

Of course we are entitled to say it is not the same thing; it never is—entirely. Proust, I think, enunciates the structural laws of our intellectual passion in speaking generally, as it were indifferently, of passional attachments (I elide references to the affair with Albertine and to the Dreyfus Affair, lest we repeat the error which he describes):

> It is true that the anti- . . . would have replied to me: "But it is not the same thing." But it is never the same thing, any more than it is the same person . . . otherwise, faced with the same phenomenon as before, someone who was a second time taken in by it would have no alternative but to blame his own subjective condition, he could not again believe that the qualities or the defects resided in the object. And so, since the phenomenon, outwardly, is not the same, the intellect has no difficulty in basing upon each set of circumstances a new theory. . . . (And yet, the subjective element that I had observed to exist in . . . vision itself did not imply that an object could not possess real qualities or defects and in no way tended to make reality vanish into pure relativism.)[5]

The possible differences between our nuanced relativism and earlier ones remain to be worked out, genetically and historically, and perhaps too with this cautionary truism in mind: "MEMOIRE. Se plaindre de la sienne—et même se vanter de n'en pas avoir mais rugir si on vous dit que vous n'avez pas de jugement" ["MEMORY. Complain of one's own—and even boast of not having one but roar if you're told you have no judgment,"] (p. 540). For one of the most comically devastating features of *Bouvard et Pécuchet* is its

---

4. Eugenio Donato has covered this ground well, with specific reference to Borges, in " 'A Mere Labyrinth of Letters'/Flaubert and the Quest for Fiction/A Montage," *MLN*, Vol. 89, No. 6 (Dec. 1974).

5. Marcel Proust, *The Past Recaptured*, trans. Andreas Mayor (New York: Vintage, 1971), pp. 165–66.

reduction of Western scepticism, with all its demystificatory pomp fully ripened by Voltaire's time, if not Montaigne's, to the commonplace, the banal:

Science is constituted according to data drawn from a corner of extended space. Perhaps it doesn't agree with all the rest which isn't known, which is much bigger, and which can't be discovered.

One wonders, I say, because, as anyone might observe, we are not Bouvard and Pécuchet; and we know more about space, and the ocean floor, and . . . Yet it behooves us to determine in what ways our scepticism deserves to be distinguished from theirs: not to avoid confusing their levelling and ultimately panic "bêtise" from our own rigorous intelligence of epistemological affairs—if that can be done, for some of the most penetrating readings of this novel of late, I think, are devoted to showing its author as a precursor of our intellectual aporia[6]—but to understand what has transpired since their time, what we have learned and what, as Proust suggests, we have not, so as to boast of a more radical, more informed and more nuanced scepticism. This raises the question of the historicity of deconstruction, of the factors in intellectual, social and political history which determine its emergence in our time, roughly a century after Flaubert. It is a question of which neither its advocates nor its adversaries offer very much in the way of a genetic explanation. It is a question for which there ought to be an answer, if, when we teach Lacan and Derrida and Foucault *et al.*, we suppose we know what we are doing. "HYPOTHESE. Souvent 'dangereuse,' toujours 'hardie' " ["HYPOTHESIS. Often 'dangerous,' always 'bold,' "] (p. 529). It is with the question of difference, as thematized and problematized by deconstructive criticism but not as yet historicized, that we have elected to turn the corner on the scepticism of Bouvard and Pécuchet as of Voltaire and Montaigne. "DOCTRINAIRES. Les mépriser; mais pourquoi? on n'en sait rien" ["DOCTRINAIRES. Despise them; but why? nobody knows,"] (p. 508).

With no end in sight, Flaubert's novel remains appropriately unfinished. It is intended to close, as the scenarios for the conclusion show, with still another "mise en abîme," the letter of Dr. Vaucorbeil recapitulating the adventures of the "deux imbéciles inoffensifs": "En résumant toutes les actions et pensées, elle doit pour le lecteur, être la critique du roman" ["While summarizing all the actions and thoughts, it should be for the reader a critique of the novel"]. And a note adds: "Cette lettre résume et juge B et P et doit rappeler au lecteur tout le livre" ["This letter summarizes and judges B and P

---

6. Consult Françoise Gaillard, "An Unspeakable (Hi)story," *YFS*, no. 59 (1980), the essay by Donato cited in note 4 and, by the same author, "The Museums' Furnace: Notes toward a Contextual Reading of *Bouvard et Pécuchet*" in *Textual Strategies: Perspectives on Post-Structural Criticism*, ed. J. Harari (Cornell, 1979), in which the author of *Bouvard et Pécuchet* is seen as "damningly prophetic."

and should recall to the reader the entire book,"] (p. 443). A representation of the novel as a whole, the letter in turn is destined to representation:

"What are we going to do with it?" No reflections! Let's copy! The page must be filled, the "monument" completed.—equality of all, of good and evil, of Beautiful and ugly, of the insignificant and the characteristic. There is nothing true but phenomena. Exaltation of statistics.

Finish with the prospect of the two old fellows bent over their desk and copying. [p. 443]

It is in terms of this nihilistic vocation to the letter that the full significance of the pedagogical adventure of the two men emerges. This chapter constitutes an indispensable stage in this process of "mise en abîme"—the endless representation of representation—beginning as it does with language study. An unpublished note—"B et P regrettent que les enfants parlent déjà. Sans cela ils feraient des expériences sur l'origine des langues en les isolant" ["B and P are sorry the children speak already. Without that they'd do experiments on the origin of language by isolating them,"] (Cento, p. 222)—reminds us that questions of language ultimately imply questions of origin, that reflection on the one inevitably leads to reflection on the other.

Here, the very hebetude of their pupils allows us to see that the roots of the pedagogical failure on the part of the two men are seeded from well within their enterprise, deriving from a fault or fissure at the heart of the semiological system from which all formal schooling springs. It is the failure of signs to adhere to any logic at their point of origin, as the two men experience in the instruction of the prime matter of our cultural representation, the alphabet:

Bouvard took charge of the girl, Pécuchet of the boy.

Victor made out his letters, but did not succeed in forming syllables. He stammered over them, stopped suddenly and looked idiotic. Victorine asked questions. How come *ch* in "orchestre" has a *q* sound and a *k* sound in archeology? Sometimes two vowels must be joined, other times separated. All that isn't fair. She grew indignant. [p. 371]

The allodidactic experience represents at a more primary level a dilemma encountered in the autodidactic. The two pupils apprehend the confusion and contradiction at the level of the phonemic signifier which their tutors encountered at more elaborate levels of the linguistic articulation. The same incoherence and redundancy reigns in the rules of grammar as in the realm of "idées reçues":

The subject always agrees with the verb, except in the cases where the subject does not agree. [p. 217]
BLONDS. Hotter than brunettes (see *brunettes*).
BRUNETTES. Hotter than blonds (see *blonds*).
DIPLOMA. Sign of knowledge. Proves nothing. [pp. 493, 494, 507]

Victorine's indignation recalls an earlier disillusionment with the signifying system:

Grammarians, it is true, disagree; some see a beauty where others discover a fault. They admit principles whose consequences they reject, proclaim consequences whose principles they refuse, lean on tradition, throw out the masters, and have strange refinements. Ménage instead of *lentilles* and *cassonade* approves *nentilles* and *castonade*. Bouhours *jérarchie* and not *hiérarchie* and M. Chapsal *oeils de la soupe.*

Pécuchet especially was dumbfounded by Génin. How would *z'annetons* be better than *hannetons*, *z'aricots* than *haricots*—and under Louis XIV they pronounced *Roume* and M. de *Lioune* for *Rome* and M. de *Lionne!*

Littré dealt them the final blow in affirming that there never had been correct spelling, and never would be.

They concluded from that that syntax is a fantasy and grammar an illusion. [pp. 217–218]

Their conclusion, we note, springs from a problematic of difference: between written and spoken language, diachrony and synchrony, principles and consequences, such that the elements of signification are ever at a difference from themselves. Once it is scrutinized, the arbitrariness governing the constitution and ordering of the linguistic sign are readily perceived by the unschooled mind, and formal language apprenticeship rightly inspires indignation. Bouvard and Pécuchet have already been frustrated by this arbitrariness, as it emerges in the unbridgeable passage between proper and common nouns in geology:

And then the nomenclature vexed them. Why Devonian, Cambrian, Jurasssic, as if the soils (terres) designated by these words were not anywhere but in Devonshire, near Cambridge and in the Jura? Impossible to make out where you are! [p. 149]

With "ch" and "q" and "k," Victorine perceives a more radical flaw, a split within the signifier. The word or sign does not resemble a thing, nor does it resemble itself.

Victor and Victorine's intellectual conscience remains inviolate to this literal imposture, this semiological scandal, and their tutors will not overcome it by any rational means within the signifying system. Their teachers perform this coup by another, familiar strategy informing the politics of education. Where deduction and induction are fruitless, seduction proves deplorably effective.

They came back to the lessons; and the alphabet blocks, the copy books, the toy printing press, all had failed, when they devised a stratagem.

As Victor was inclined to gourmandise, they showed him the name of a dish: soon he read fluently in the *Cuisinier français*. Victorine being coquettish, a dress would be given her if she wrote to the dressmaker to order it. In less than three weeks, she accomplished this prodigy. It was pandering their faults, a pernicious means but successful. [p. 372]

"Il n'est désir plus naturel que le désir de cognoissance," writes Montaigne, who probably learned it from reading Aristotle rather than from the book of nature. But a knowledge of desire itself seems of more primary importance. Victor's sapience is nourished by his unnatural appetite; Victorine's *libido sciendi* stems causally from her libido, if not from a more metaphysical desire. At any rate, the high-minded aims of education are in question in Flaubert's little apologue, which serves as a parody of enlightened self-interest.

It is largely to the fundamental incoherence in the signifying process, and to the conflict emerging from diverse, incongruous orders of representation, that Bouvard and Pécuchet owe subsequent failures, which proceed in conformity to type. They conform, that is, to the incoherence of their literal, graphological or rather graphillogical archetype. Thus with Victor:

By means of an atlas, Pécuchet explained Europe to him; but dazzled by so many lines and colors, he could no longer find the names. The basins and the mountains did not tally with the countries, the political order muddled the physical.

All that, perhaps, would be clarified by studying History. [p. 381]

The intelligence of Victor is rudimentary, but only the more candid in its perceptions for being so; it understandably balks before such an excess of representation. The geographies of nature and culture, of physis and polis, are heterogenous. The overlay of topography and typography replicates rather than dominates the chaos of the natural. Culture emerges as a second nature, assuming its opacity and disorder, its utter facticity.

The discordant problem of mapping nature and culture is compounded by that of framing. The dilemma of whole versus part, of micro- versus macrocosmic perspectives, presents itself in both geography and history: "They differed in their opinions as to geography. Bouvard thought it more logical to begin with the township. Pécuchet by the world as a whole" (p. 380). Both "*logiques*" are impeccable. "*Logique*" sins against itself, which is the case too with "*pratique*": "It might have been more practical to begin with the village, then the district, the department, the province. But Chavignolles having no chronicles, it was best after all to stick to world history. So much material encumbers it that one should only take its finest flowers" (p. 381).

And so on: through elements of science, whose abstractions surpass the imagination of the pupils; through religion and morality, confounded by the frank carnality of the girl, the nearly pristine brutality of the boy. In the midst of all this, Bouvard and Pécuchet engage in a civic discourse which increasingly absorbs their attention while incurring the unanimous oppobrium of the community. Their political radicalization reminds us of the potentially subversive dimension of education, to which I shall attend via some general reflections on their pedagogical experience.

Granted that *Bouvard et Pécuchet* offers only a caricature, a hyperbolic representation of learning and teaching, it is not any the less radical in its critique of these activities for being so. The mental and moral refractoriness of their pupils constitutes, without any exaggeration in many cases, a notorious impediment to the task of education, as mounting statistics bear out nation-wide. And it is not for any lack of erudition that the two men fail either in their own intellectual aim or in their pedagogical experiment. Flaubert, we know, consumed over 1,500 volumes in preparing their research, and it is his knowledge that they repeat in their quest and that they seek in turn to filter down to their pupils. If anything, they are overeducated, overqualified for the task from that point of view. We cannot charge their failure either to the seeming randomness or incompletion of their instruction. For we can recognize in its very selectivity from an excess of information and overlapping of disciplines the educational construct we designate as an academic curriculum, a choice of data, ideas and methods whose well roundedness, implicit in the name we give it, does not bear up under rigorous scrutiny. The recourse of the autodidacts, for their own enlightenment, to instructional manuals and such like summary compendia anticipates only too well the empire of the "text-book" in contemporary education: that strange and often alienating amalgam of scanty, abridged sources, hasty references and sketchy commentary, replete with such mnemotechnical devices as chapter outlines, indexes, color-coded print, marginal illustrations and rubrics, which informs our educational industry at every level.

Nor can we simply attribute the pedagogical failure of Bouvard and Pécuchet to a "défaut de méthode dans les sciences," as the projected subtitle for Flaubert's novel might suggest. For that phrase is ambiguous by itself; it allows the inference that it is in "les sciences" themselves that method is lacking, rather than in the two autodidacts, who find themselves before contradictory imperatives in education:

It is not an easy dilemma; if one starts from facts, the most simple demands over-complicated reasons, and by posing principles first one begins by the Absolute, by Faith.

What to decide? Combine the two ways of teaching, the rational and the empirical; but a double means towards a single end is the opposite of method. Ah! so much the worse! [p. 383]

It is at least questionable whether any dimension of our academic curricula is immune to this vicious circle, whether any method is but a "pis aller." Flaubert, for his own part, felt that the issue was central to his chapter: "Ça va même très lentement. Mais je *sens* mon chapitre. J'ai peur qu'il ne soit bien rébarbatif. Comment amuser avec des questions de méthode? Quant à la portée philosophique des dites pages, je n'en doute pas" ["It's going very slowly. But I *feel* my chapter. I'm afraid it's quite forbidding. How to amuse with questions of method? As for the philosophical import of said pages, I don't doubt it"].[7] It is largely out of a concern for method that modern science is launched on its stellar career. Flaubert's subtitle recalls handily that of Descartes' autobiographical and resolutely autodidactic essay, *Discours de la méthode pour bien conduire sa raison dans la recherche de la vérité.* This text has been shown by a number of readers—Descartes' rivals in quest of a rationality—to proceed by just such a duplicity as cited by Flaubert. Paul Valéry found occasion to admire the "coup de volonté," the "coup de force," rather than any inherent logic, by which the cogito is constituted. Michel Foucault has pointed to the significant historical coincidence between its constitution and the expulsion of madness into what were to become our mental institutions. Jacques Derrida, elaborating Foucault's reading of the *Méditations,* shows that the cogito in and of itself is more than hospitable to madness, that its rationality flows from an act of faith which is theological in origin.[8] It is meet therefore that the question of the danger Bouvard and Pécuchet pose to the community should turn on the issue of madness, on whose violent expulsion reason depends for its own determination. It is to the local prefect who asks "si Bouvard et Pécuchet n'étaient pas des fous dangereux" that Dr. Vaucorbeil describes them as "deux imbéciles inoffensifs."

The situation of Bouvard and Pécuchet with respect to the community and to community authority is worth examining in all its implications. In a note to chapter X we read: "ils démoralisent les enfants, on vient les leur retirer" (Cento, p. 113). The tutors cannot fail to demoralize their pupils if they seek to anchor their curriculum in rationality, for the foundations of rationality are not in themselves rational.[9] The community, alarmed by their tendencies "au nivellement et à l'immoralité" ["to levelling and to immorality,"] (p. 404), can hardly abide their presence in its midst, and as a consequence of their intrusion into public affairs they are subject to arrest: "On les accuse d'avoir attenté à la Religion, à l'ordre, excité à la Révolte, etc" ["They are accused of having attacked Religion, order, incited to Revolt, etc."] (p. 413), we read in Flaubert's scenario for the conclusion. As they thrust their recently acquired knowledge into civic discourse, Bouvard and Pécuchet assume the status of scapegoats with respect to official values, and their threatened incarceration

7. *Correspondance générale,* (Paris: Conard, 1926–33), Vol. IX, p. 4.

8. Paul Valéry, "Descartes," *Oeuvres complètes* (Gallimard: Pléiade, 1957), vol. I.,p. 807; Michel Foucault, *Histoire de la folie à l'âge classique,* 2nd ed. (Gallimard, 1972), pp. 56–59; Jacques Derrida, "Cogito et histoire de la folie" in *L'Ecriture et la différence* (Seuil, 1966), pp. 90–91.

9. This point is developed by Jacques Derrida in his address on Kant and "Le Conflit des facultés," on the occasion of the centenary of the Columbia University Graduate School (April 1980). My thanks to the author for the loan of the manuscript.

reflects the dynamics of a sacrificial crisis as analyzed by René Girard.[10] It is a crisis of difference, the matrix of value as of meaning itself. Their pedagogical adventure, undertaken as it is "tabula rasa," cannot fail to "saper les bases," even as it occasions their own political radicalization, which is their encounter with the rootlessness of values and institutions. As they do so, we can see a replay of the Enlightenment, with its consequent revolution; with Proust ever in mind, we can see our own demystifications in the offing. What violence do they clear a space for? What violence, however covert, however institutionalized, do we underwrite to fend it off?

When, owing to a local squabble, Bouvard and Pécuchet have their day in court, they utter pronouncements which seem to encapsulate the polemics of Michel Foucault, who has devoted himself to studying the complicity between an arbitrary "Savoir" and an incriminating "Pouvoir":

"Hold on now," cried Pécuchet. "The words contravention, crime and offense are worth nothing. Taking the penalty to classify punishable actions is taking an arbitrary basis. It is as much as saying to citizens: 'Don't worry about the value of your actions. That is only determined by the punishment of the Power Structure! What's more, the Penal Code seems to me an irrational work, without principles. [p. 402]

Codes, principles, rationality, these are what are at stake in the gestation of Western society, in the construction and propagation of its values, and these are what Western society, in its relentless quest for its own foundations, has unceasingly continued to undermine, to "deconstruct." Bouvard and Pécuchet embody the fundamental aspirations of our culture even as they are threatened by exclusion from it. Their protest represents the division of our culture from within; their incrimination the outward projection of its danger—to itself.

One must appreciate, therefore, the rectitude, the implacable logic of the nearly unanimous decision on the part of the community which threatens the expulsion-incarceration of Bouvard and Pécuchet. Pedagogues, intellectuals, descending from the role of scribes to the Heavenly City, are not less a danger to the establishment of its earthly counterpart than they are its assigned guardians and transmitters. The official adversaries of Flaubert in his own time, like those of Baudelaire, are far more consistent and logical in their opposition to the writer than his brilliant admirers in our humanities departments of today. Augustine and Pascal believe as little in the substantial authority of a penal code as Nietzsche.[11] No culture can survive or perdure in the full light of the intuitions shared by Flaubert and his doubles at the projected conclusion of the novel. No education, no acculturation, no order or hierarchy, no structure, primacy or ultimacy are rationally conceivable or

10. René Girard, *La Violence et le sacré* (Grasset, 1972), esp. ch. 2.
11. cf. *Surveiller et punir: Naissance de la prison* (Gallimard, 1975) and *Histoire de la sexualité I: La Volonté de savoir* (Gallimard, 1976).

justifiable in the light of the radical nihilism, rooted in the senselessness of language itself, which radiates throughout the virtually endless pages of Flaubert's novel. Rather culture survives and endures by exclusion, by expulsion, by alienation. Prevalent theories regarding the religious, sacrificial origins of culture can point to the "cultus" from which it springs. They are barbarians to the Greeks who do not speak their language and acknowledge their gods. As a complex of hierarchical differences, culture marks off as utterly and otherwise different—sacred, mad or "bête"—groups or individuals which threaten to dissolve its differenciations. (Jean-Louis Bouttes writes ingeniously of the fated meeting between Bouvard and Pécuchet and Zarathustra.[12]) This expulsion hangs over anyone who, since at least the time of Socrates, questions the inarticulate substantiality of its valuations from within. This properly sacrificial destiny is especially legible in the historical experience of French writers: from the time of the mythically outlawed Villon and of Rabelais, who was vilified by both Protestant and Catholic opponents (and whose encomium Flaubert composed in the youthful time of his aspiration to be a "démoralisateur" [Corr. I, 41]), to the time of Baudelaire, who subversively dialectized good and evil, and of Flaubert himself, justly tried for the immorality of Madame Bovary (and justly acquitted, for its profound immorality escaped its readers of his day, and is only appearing in our time[13]).

The incarceration of the two men is only forestalled, according to Flaubert's scenario, by the offhand diagnosis of madness on the part of Dr. Vaucorbeil: "Vaucorbeil (attracted by the noise) speaks for them, 'They really ought to be hauled off to a madhouse' " (p. 414). This in turn is a fate from which they are preserved perhaps only by their voluntary self-exile in the desert of letters, whereby they end up as they began: "Copier comme autrefois" (p. 414). Thus Bouvard and Pécuchet accomplish the final, pantheistic vow of Flaubert's Saint Antoine— "Etre la matière!"—in a secular, atheistic mode: "être copiste" is to be in the only mode of being which the exhaustion of Western metaphysics has left to man. "Etre copiste" is to be only in the mode of representation, to be ever at a distance and a difference from oneself, of which the letter, as the mark of an absence, is the paradoxical symbol.

The investigations of Derrida suggest that the letter, writing, have emerged at critical junctures in the history of culture—Plato, Rousseau, Saussure—as a theme upon which to focus questions of cultural origins.[14] The importance of writing is paradoxical: its specific privilege within the thematics of culture is that it is not a respecter of persons or of privilege (privus

12. Jean-Louis Bouttes, Le Destructeur de l'intensité (Seuil, 1980), p. 13.

13. cf. Jonathan Culler, Flaubert: The Uses of Uncertainty (Cornell, 1974), esp. ch. 2 on Madame Bovary: "The Perfect Crime."

14. Derrida, De la Grammatologie (Minuit, 1967); "La Pharmacie de Platon," in La Dissémination (Seuil, 1972).

lex), but indifferently accessible to many. It is as such that Plato condemns it in the *Cratylus*. It is as such that it has served as a principal means of secularization and democratization in history. It is as such that Flaubert, in one of his rages against modern "bêtise," is prepared to condemn it to oblivion: "If the emperor tomorrow suppressed the printing press, I'd journey to Paris on my knees and I'd go kiss his ass as a sign of gratitude. That's how tired I am of printing and of the abuse it's put to," (*Corr.*, III, 261).

Flaubert himself longed for a preponderant vocal power, of the kind to which Ioakannan, as if inspired by the Holy Spirit, gives vent in "Hérodias." To this oratorical force the writer contrasts the mindless repetitition of his century which will later be incarnate in Félicité's parrot in "Un Coeur Simple": "Je sens pourtant que je ne dois pas mourir sans avoir fait rugir quelque part un style comme je l'entends dans ma tête et qui pourra bien dominer la voix des perroquets et des cigales ["I feel nonetheless that I should not die without having found somewhere a way to roar out a style as I hear it in my head and which could dominate the voice of the parrots and cicadas,"] (*Corr.*, II, 440). This contrast provokes in turn an allusion to letters, and to *Don Quijote*, the novel whose antithetical doubles represent the opposition between bookish versus oral culture: "We take our country on the soles of our feet and we carry in our hearts without knowing it the dust of these dead ancestors. As for me personally, I would do a demonstration of that as simple as A + B. It's the same in literature. I rediscover all my origins in the book which I knew by heart before I could read, *Don Quijote*. . . . ibid.). In Flaubert's time, this antithesis collapses, this difference is erased by the advance towards universal literacy, of which the widely read Homais is the paragon. In *Bouvard et Pécuchet*, the theme of writing emerges in conjunction with the theme of the double, as if by way of demonstrating that the dissolution of meaning to which they are destined by their research brings on a dissolution of identity. Thus Flaubert's notes read:

> Their intrinsic difference must be perceived in spite of their union until the end where they become in the joy of Copy and in the community of passion the same man, down to resembling each other physically one and the same being doubled. [Cento, p. 4]

It is as a difference which is in itself insignificant that writing plays a role in Flaubert's critique of modern culture. It is as such, with Derrida and others, that it resurges at the epicenter of cultural debate today, as the symbol of a crisis on a world becoming totally, globally Western, a world in which cultural difference is on the wane. "L'humanité s'installe dans la monoculture," writes Claude Lévi-Strauss, whose *Tristes Tropiques* repeats the gesture of Plato, Rousseau and Saussure in condemning writing.[15]

For Derrida as for Lévi-Strauss, writing is the mark of a violence suggest-

15. Claude Lévy-Strauss, *Tristes Tropiques* (Plon, 1955), p. 39.

ing a tyrannical rather than contractual order in the organization of culture. Our contemporary impasse concerning origins should not blind us to the concrete possibility of an ultimate violence, wrought by a technology which descends from writing and which owes its development unequivocally to our Western, writerly culture. On page one of the issue of *Le Monde* (April 25, 1980) containing a special section commemorating the hundredth anniversary of the death of Flaubert, a French deputy calculates that the nuclear capability worldwide is adequate to put two tons of dynamite under the feet of every one of its inhabitants. It is in terms of this possibility that the conclusion of *Bouvard et Pécuchet*, even as it concerns pedagogical imperatives, is fraught with significance.

The two autodidacts do not embark explicitly on the quest for the origins of culture, but in the concluding scenario we do find them prognosticating about its end. "Our studies give us the right to speak," (p. 410), they decide in announcing a program of adult education. It appears from Flaubert's notes for this episode that the author first contemplated a unified perspective: "They arrive at contemporary Socialism which is Cosmopolitanism, and absolute levelling—Auto-idolatry of humanity, the Dogma of progress; without defining it," (Cento, p. 70). "*Autolâtrie,*" as the logical destiny of man in a desacralized universe, is how Flaubert, judging by his correspondence, views the future of humanity (*Corr.*, II, 208). As a seeming divine capacity for destruction accrues to man, it is a view worth serious consideration. But it is when, in an effort to define progress, Flaubert outlines "leurs deux prosopo-pées sur l'humanité," that his text offers a most telling reading of our situation, as well as a comic lesson in reading.

When Pécuchet views the future of humanity "*en noir,*" Bouvard views the same "*en beau.*" For the former, modern man is "amoindri et devenu une machine" ["diminished and become a machine"], while for the latter he is "en progrès." The one foretells:

Final anarchy of the human race (Buchner, I.II)
Impossibility of peace.
Barbarism through excess of individualism, and the rage of Science.

There will no longer be any ideal, religion or morality.
America will have conquered the earth. [pp. 411–12]

This view is balanced in perfect equilibrium by the other's positive expectation that

Europe will be regenerated by Asia, the law of history being that civilization goes from East to West—role of China—the two humanities will be finally fused.

Disappearance of evil by the disappearance of need. Philosophy will be a religion. [p. 412]

Of course one can dismiss this text as still another exercise in intellectual futility, a parody of "world historical swashbuckling" (the phrase is Kierkegaard's) already in vogue in Flaubert's time. Still the text betrays an uncanny pertinence to contemporary ideological conflict, in which rival eschatologies, East and West, Communist and Capitalist, identify their cause with the future of humanity as the stakes at large.

One is tempted to suggest, according to an open-minded, liberal view of affairs, that the future lies somewhere in between, and furthermore that a modicum of common sense and generous effort would inflect matters along a hopeful, positive course, the right course—which political left and political right each identify as their proper course, the course proper to their aspirations for mankind. Such a view has ever been the Western one, which has prided itself on its optimism and good will towards mankind, and which has sought, with unprecedented missionary zeal, to educate the world in the wisdom of its liberalism. Such a view would not fail to claim its identity in the optimistic, progressive role assigned to the East, and thereby operate a change of signs, a Sino-American exchange in this instance. But this about-face or reversal of signs leaves intact the Manichean dualism of Flaubert's text, its tic-tac automatism. Rather it is necessary to abstract altogether from the historical and political referents in order to perceive the relevance of Flaubert's schema for contemporary history.

For to confide in the substantial pertinence of these rival prognostications is to succumb to the veritable folly which their symmetrical juxtaposition is designed to reveal. It is to underwrite or subscribe to a difference, to a difference in substance or to the substance of a difference, which only resides in the tension between the opposing stances. These in turn do not reflect an ideological stalemate, a static impasse of opposing views. They are antithetical valuations of a single destiny, ambi-valenced assessments of a single future, whose law of becoming is perhaps best expressed in Pécuchet's third hypothesis:

Three hypotheses. Pantheist radicalism will break all ties with the past, and an inhuman despotism will follow; 2° if theist absolutism triumphs, the liberalism with which humanity has been imbued since the Reformation succumbs, everything is overturned; 3° if the convulsions which exist since 89 continue, without and between two issues, these oscillations will blow us away by their own forces. [p. 411]

The oscillatory hypothesis does not reconcile or synthesize the thesis and antithesis preceeding it; it summarizes the law of their interaction. The violent outcome of the opposition represented by Bouvard and Pécuchet is thus enfolded within the logic of one of its terms, this asymmetry being the essential dynamic of a binary structure which, as such, is perfectly blind to its own rigorous symmetry.

Ideological conflict corresponds less to political, historical or socio-economic realities than to the structural laws of binary opposition which govern language, which is, as Saussure reminds us, a form not a substance. According to these laws, the sign derives its meaning or value in terms of its difference from other signs; its value is negative, oppositive, relative; words signify not by any meaning proper to them, not by any substance in them but by their difference from other words in the lexicon. It follows from this that East and West cannot significantly oppose each other until or unless they speak the same language; they are never so likely to clash as when they are competing under the same ensign, never so likely to differ as when they resemble each other. "It is then," writes Vincent Descombes, "the same song on both sides" (he is speaking of the French national anthem, of the "sang impur" whose spilling it acclaims):

> Symmetry turns a thing around an axis, and presents it thereby as *vis-à-vis*, as an adversary, in the spatial sense of the word. It thereby opposes the thing to itself, the same to the same, and it is in that identity of adversaries that we must find *adversity* in the second sense, no longer only spatial: *hostility*. It is symmetry, that is the absence of any difference other than that of rotation in space by which the same can see itself in the other, which is the ground of enmity ["le fond de l'inimitié"].[16]

It is the comic revelation of this identity in difference which we find in Flaubert's formula, "un même et un seul être en partie double."

These same laws of language govern the composition of *Bouvard et Pécuchet* from its inception, that is from the very first appearance of the two men on the scene of literature in Chapter I of the novel:

> Two men appeared.
>
> One came from the Bastille, the other from the Jardin des Plantes. The taller, in a linen suit, walked with his hat cocked back, his waistcoat unbuttoned and his tie in hand. The shorter, his body enveloped in a brown frock-coat, held his head low beneath a pointed cap.
>
> When they reached the middle of the boulevard, they sat down at the same time on the same bench. [p. 51]

16. Vincent Descombes, *L'Inconscient malgré lui* (Minuit, 1977), p. 38. Consider too this passage. "We just said: . . . good understanding reigns with someone like ourself and bad with someone unlike. But we have to correct all that, because there is only hostility with someone like ourself (ourself seen in the other) . . . There is violence when there are two adversaries, and there is adversity when each of the two has lost the possibility of identifying the other with a trait which would set him apart, not from the others, but rather from oneself, such that neither of the two can any longer address himself to the other. Each loses in the same stroke the possibility of setting himself apart from the other, each can only henceforth identify himself with the other, finding himself constantly where he looks for the other. In this relation of adversity reigns the *imaginary*, since one finds, where one seeks another, the *image* of oneself, as in a mirror" (p. 39). Descombes' reading of the processes of enunciation, via Aristotle and Lacan, accounts handsomely for the mechanics of ideological conflict as well as for the "*dédoublements*" and "scissions périodiques" which generate intellectual debate.

"L'un, l'autre, le plus grand, le plus petit," East, West, thema, anathema: negative, oppositive, relative. Bouvard and Pécuchet, these complementary non-entities drawn from the democratic herd and whose difference is in so many senses only nominal *(bos/pecus)*, are shortly to be identified as copyists. They are in fact copies of each other, positive and negative representations of each other. They are *"repoussoirs,"* as Flaubert says of Jules and Henry of the first *Education sentimentale (Corr.,* II, 344), like concave and convex, like "B" and "P" themselves, the latter being but an unvoiced repetition of the former, its phonemic negative, its literal, mute representation, its specular double in every sense. With these two individuals as with the ideological confrontation they configurate, we are dealing with a phony opposition which rings hollow even as we pronounce it, and of which the letter is the unsubstantial trace, the arbitrary, violent mark.

It is the vocation of B and P, as we may now spuriously identify them, to lettering, to *"la Copie,"* that reduces their *"différence intrinsèque"* to "un même et un seul être en partie double." The projected resolution of Flaubert's novel conforms to the law of relativity, according to which matter-as-energy is ever at a distance from itself. This is the law which governs everything in our universe from the movement of atoms to the determination of signs, where it goes by the name of *"dissémination," "différance."*[17] It is a law, the opposition of same to same, of the thing to itself within itself, which emerges, as if providentially, as cultural differences erode worldwide. In a world left entirely to its own all-too-human devices, difference is nowhere without and everywhere within, as humanity lines itself up "en partie double" for an intraspecific contest without parallel in the animal kingdom.

17. Relativity is our physics and our metaphysics, as a comparison of Derrida's "La Dissémination," in the volume by that name (op. cit.) and his "La Différance," in *Marges de la Philosophie* (Minuit, 1972), with Einstein's *Relativity: The Special and the General Theory* will show. The theory which designates the same as dynamically different from itself accounts for the metaphysical character of our Western compulsion to overcome metaphysics. Freud's "Uncanny," which designates the familiar as unfamiliar, the homely as alien, sinister, conforms to this law, even as it applies to both the non-reference and the shocking relevance to contemporary history of B and P's prognostics. The differing of matter from itself is cited in passing as an instance of the paradoxical "logique du scandale" which Shoshana Felman shows operating in the debate between continental and Anglo-American approaches to philosophical discourse. *(Le Scandale du corps parlant: Don Juan avec Austin ou la séduction en deux langues* [Seuil, 1980], p. 212). This scandalous logic characterizes in turn the argument formulated by Barbara Johnson concerning "la crise" in Mallarmé, which consists in the dysfunctioning of the notion of crisis as it would be expected to apply to the (non)difference: *vers"* vs. *"prose" (Défigurations du langage poétique: La Seconde Révolution baudelairienne* [Flammarion, 1979], pp. 161–211—the second revolution is patently Einsteinian). Relativity might have been cited, à propos all theory, by Descombes as an analogue to the "scissiparité inséparable de sa position de discours" (op. cit., p. 166); it explains the emergence of the unconscious *"malgré lui"* because of the illusory presence of mind we invest in the self. An Aristotelian might see relatively as the formal and material cause of Girard's apprehension of a properly religious, sacrificial crisis which is at its most virulent in a thoroughly desacralized world. In the event of global nuclear fission, its application, relative to the human species, would be definitive, absolute.

Homo sum et nihil humani alieno puto. But what is proper to humanity is the double part it plays against itself, unto possible annihiliation. This is a prospect that might not have disappointed Flaubert, who reads the progress of mankind as "paganisme, christianisme, muflisme" (*Corr.*, VI, 202). But Flaubert's works also suggest, in a specifically educational context, a means of averting the prospect—if anything like a pedagogical imperative can do so.

The first, lamentable appearance of Charles Bovary on the scene of literature is situated in a class of students engaged in the study of Latin, a dead language known only through writing, studied only in books. *Pensums* are distributed to punish the disorderly mockery which greets the appearance of Charles, who for all his ineffectual innocence does not escape the punitive assignment of self-mockery: "Quant à vous, le *nouveau*, vous me copierez vingt fois le verbe *ridiculus sum*" ["As for you, the *new boy*, you will copy out twenty times the verb *ridiculus sum*"[18]]. The inaugural thematics of copy, repetition, "bêtise," doubtless speak for themselves at this stage. The structural dynamics of this scene, as it is narrated by an anonymous "nous," come more fully to light by contrast with its specular reversal in the opening pages of *Mémoires d'un fou.* Here we find a volatile first-person narrator exclaiming with febrile rancor against his schoomates:

I still see myself, seated on a class bench, absorbed by my dreams of the future; thinking what a child's imagination can dream of the most sublime, while that pedant of a teacher made fun of my Latin verse, while my snickering schoolmates looked at me. The imbeciles! Them, to laugh at me! They, so weak, so common, so narrow minded; I whose spirit was drowning in the limits of creation, who was lost in all the worlds of poetry, who felt greater than them all, who enjoyed infinite pleasures and who had heavenly ecstasies before all the intimate revelations of my soul. [I, 223]

Of course Charles, who is last seen by *"nous"* as "cherchant tous les mots dans le dictionnaire et se donnant beaucoup de mal" ["looking for every word in the dictionary knocking himself out,"] (I, 576), is different from this character, whose Latin phrasing doubtless exceeds the classical measure expected by his professor. They are not the same, unless we allow that Flaubert has reversed the perspective, from strident first-person narrator vaunting his victimized singularity to the anonymous, impassive *"nous,"* in order to portray himself as incongruously other, to see himself as others might see him. For it is clear that the beginning of *Mémoires d'un fou* and of *Madame Bovary* compose the same scene "en partie double." The "eux-moi" opposition of *Mémoires* is a tragic or romantic modality of the double, of which the later *"nous"* is an ambiguous, evasive stage. In the *"sottisier"* to be compiled by Bouvard and Pécuchet, the reader would find the pride of his intellectual culture held up to ridicule, such that no one could utter a statement without fear of falling victim to (self-)

18. Flaubert, *Madame Bovary* in *Oeuvres complètes* (Seuil: "Intégrale," 1964), Vol. I, p. 575, in which my quotes from *Mémoires d'un fou* are to be found as well.

mockery, without fear of evidencing his own *"bêtise"* (*Corr.*, III, 67): this is perhaps the definitive stage. All, *"eux," "moi," "nous,"* are summoned to copy, *"comme autrefois,"* the *pensum* assigned to *"*le *nouveau,"* until it is learned by heart, learned as one's very inmost truth, as access to the only possible presence of humanity to itself, the syllables of a dead language: *ridiculus sum.*

JACQUES DERRIDA

All Ears: Nietzsche's Otobiography

[The following excerpt is taken from a lecture delivered by Derrida at the University of Virginia in 1977. The lecture deals with institutions, signatures, and the authorities and authorizations that link them. Having discussed a number of texts, from the American Declaration of Independence to the autobiographical elements in the writings of Friedrich Nietzsche, Derrida moves to the question of the "perversion" of Nietzsche's writings by Nazi theories of culture. The focus of Derrida's analysis is a number of passages from *On the Future of Our Educational Institutions* (a series of lectures delivered in 1872 but never published by Nietzsche) in which Nietzsche deplores the degeneration of German culture and the disfigurement of the mother tongue, and describes—in typically problematic Nietzschean rhetoric—the conditions for a possible cultural and educational renewal. It is with the following remarks that Derrida concludes his lecture.—Ed.]

> For there are human beings who lack everything, except one thing of which they have too much—human beings who are nothing but a big eye or a big mouth or a big belly or anything at all that is big. Inverse cripples I call them.
>
> "And when I came out of my solitude and crossed over this bridge for the first time I did not trust my eyes and looked and looked again, and said at last, 'An ear! An ear as big as a man!' I looked still more closely—and indeed, underneath the ear something was moving, something pitifully small and wretched and slender. And, no doubt of it, the tremendous ear was attached to a small, thin stalk—but this stalk was a human being! If one used a magnifying glass one could even recognize a tiny envious face; also, that a bloated little soul was dangling from the stalk. The people, however, told me that this great ear was not only a human being, but a great one, a genius. But I never believed the people when they spoke of great men; and I maintained my belief that it was an inverse cripple who had too little of everything and too much of one thing."
>
> When Zarathustra had spoken thus to the hunchback and to those whose mouthpiece and advocate the hunchback was, he turned to his disciples in profound dismay and said: "Verily, my friends, I walk among men as among the fragments and limbs of men. This is what is terrible for my eyes, that I find man in ruins and scattered as over a battlefield or a butcher-field. And when my eyes flee from the now to the past, they always find the same: fragments and limbs and dreadful accidents—but no human beings."
>
> —*Thus Spoke Zarathustra*

245

Is there anything "within" Nietzsche's oeuvre that can help us understand its double interpretation and the so-called perversion of the text? The Fifth Lecture tells us that there must be something uncanny [*unheimlich*] about repression [*Unterdrückung*] when it is brought about by the force of the least degenerate needs. Why *unheimlich*? This is another form of the same question.

Uncanny is the ear: what it is—double; what it can become—large or small; what it can make or let happen [*faire ou laisser faire*] (we can say "let," since the ear is the most obliging, the most open organ, as Freud points out, the only one the infant cannot close); and the way in which it can be pricked or lent. It is to that ear that I will pretend to address myself, in order to conclude, here and now, by speaking, as promised, of "academic freedom." Mine and yours.

When Nietzsche, lecturing in the University, appears to be recommending linguistic training as an antidote to the kind of "academic freedom" that leaves students and teachers free to pursue their own thoughts and programs, it is not in order to oppose constraint to freedom. The silhouette of a constraint far more ferocious and unbending takes shape behind "academic freedom" in the concealed and disguised form of letting things take their course [*laisser-faire*]. Through the agency of "academic freedom," the State controls all. The State: that is the great accused in this trial, and Hegel, the great thinker of the State, stands as the guilty party's proper name. In fact, the autonomy of the university, as of those inhabiting it—students and professors—is a ruse of the State, "the most perfect ethical organism" (Hegel cited by Nietzsche). The State wants to attract docile and unquestioning functionaries to its cause. To accomplish this, it imposes tight controls as well as rigorous constraints which these functionaries believe they have initiated auto-nomously. The Lectures can thus be read as a modern critique of the cultural machinery of State and of that fundamental system of State constituted, even as recently as the advent of a fully industrialized society, by the educational system. And if nowadays it appears that this system is being partly replaced by or associated with the mass media, this makes Nietzsche's critique of journalism—and Nietzsche never dissociates journalism from the educational system—all the more compelling. Of course, he implements this critique from a perspective that would make any Marxist analysis of this machinery, including its organizing concept of "ideology," appear as another symptom of degeneracy, as a new form of subjection to the Hegelian State. But all such issues—the question of *the* Marxist concepts of the State, the nature of Nietzsche's opposition to socialism and democracy (*The Twilight of Idols* says that "Science is part of democracy"), or the functioning of the opposition science/ideology—must of course be looked at more closely and from both points of view. Elsewhere we shall pursue the development of this critique of the State in the *Nachlass*-fragments and in *Zarathustra* ("On the New Idol": "State? What is that? Well, then, open your ears to me. For now I shall speak to you about the death of peoples. The State is the name of the coldest of all cold monsters. Coldly it tells lies, too; and this lie crawls out of its mouth: 'I, the State, am the people.' That is a lie! . . . Confusion of tongues of good and evil: this sign I give you as the sign of the State. Verily, this sign signifies the will to death! Verily, it beckons to the preachers of death . . . 'On earth there is nothing greater than I: the ordering finger of God am I—thus roars the monster. And it is not only the long-eared *(Langeohrte)* and shortsighted who sink to their knees! . . . State I call it where all drink poison, the good and the wicked; . . . State, where the slow suicide of all is called 'life.' ")[1]

The State not only bears the paternal sign and figure of death, but it also wants to pass for the mother; or, in other words, for life, the people, the womb of things themselves. In *Von grossen Ereignissen* a hypocritical dog, likened to the Church, claims that his voice emanates from the "belly of things."

The hypocritical dog speaks to your ear through his educational systems that are acoustic or acroamatic machines. Your ears enlarge. You turn into "long-eared asses." And this occurs when, rather than listening to and obeying the best master and the best of leaders with small, finely tuned ears, you think yourselves free and autonomous with regard to the State, and when you open thus your great ear tubes *(pavillons)* to the State without knowing that it is already contaminated by reactive and degenerate forces. Having become all ears to this dog—the dog of the phonograph—you transform yourself into a high fidelity receiver. And the ear (your ear which is also the ear of the other) begins to occupy in your body the same disproportionate place as in the "inverse cripple" *(umgekehrte Krüppel)*.

Is this our situation? Is it a question of the same ear—the one you are lending me or that I lend myself in speaking, in other words, a borrowed ear? Or rather, do we hear, do we already hear each other with another ear?

The ear offers no response.

Even here, who hears whom? Who, for instance, listened to Nietzsche when in the "Fifth Lecture" he lent his voice to the philosopher of his fiction to describe—for instance—this very situation *(scène)*?

"Permit me to measure this autonomy *(Selbstständigkeit)* of yours by the standard of this culture *(Bildung)*, and to consider your university solely as a cultural institution *(Bildungsinstitution)*. When a foreigner wants to understand our university system, he first asks earnestly: 'how is the student connected with *(hängt zusammen)* the university?' We answer 'By the ear, as a listener.' The foreigner is taken aback: 'Only by the ear?' he repeats, 'Only by the ear,' we again reply. The student listens. The student is autonomous, i.e., not dependent upon the educational institution when he speaks, when he sees,

1. Trans. Walter Kaufmann, in *The Portable Nietzsche* (New York; Viking, 1968), pp. 160–62.

when he walks, when he enjoys the company of his companions, when he engages in artistic activity: in short, when he *lives*. Quite often, the student writes as he listens; and it is only in these rare moments that he dangles by the umbilical cord of the university *(an der Nabelschnur der Universität hängt)*."[2]

Dream this umbilicus: it holds you by the ear, but by the ear which dictates to you what you presently write when you write according to that mode called "taking notes." In fact the mother—the bad or false one whom the teacher, in his capacity qua functionary of the State, can only simulate—yes, the mother dictates to you precisely that which, passing through your ear, moves along the cord as far as your stenography. This in turn links you, like a leash in the form of an umbilical cord, to the paternal belly of the State. Your pen is its pen; you hold its teleprinter as you hold those ballpoints in the post office which are attached to chains. And all the motions are induced through the body of the father representing *(figurant)* the *alma mater*. How can an umbilical cord create a link to this cold monster that is a dead father—or the State. This is what is *unheimlich*.

We should be attentive to this: the *omphalos* of which Nietzsche makes you dream resembles both an ear and a mouth. Containing invaginated folds and involuted orificiality, the *omphalos* maintains its center at the base of a cavity. This cavity remains, however, invisible, restless and sensitive—to all waves, whether coming from the outside or not, whether emitted or received, and always transmitted by the trajectory of dim circumvolutions.

The person transmitting the discourse which you teleprint in this situation does not himself produce it; indeed, he barely emits it. He reads it. Just as you are ears that transcribe, the master is a mouth that reads; and what you transcribe amounts to what he deciphers of a text that precedes him—and from which he is suspended by the same umbilical cord. Here is what transpires: I read, ". . . it is only in these rare moments that he dangles by the umbilical cord of the university. He himself may choose what he is to listen to; he is not bound to believe what he hears; he may close his ears if he does not care to listen. This is the acroamatic method of teaching." Abstraction itself: the ear can be closed and contact can be suspended because the *omphalos* of a disjointed body rejoins a dissociated segment *(morceau)* of the father. As for the professor, who is he? What does he do? Look, listen: "As for the professor, he speaks to these listening students. Whatever else he may think or do is cut off from the student's perception by an immense gap. The professor often reads while speaking. As a rule he prefers to have as many listeners as possible; in the worst of cases he contents himself with just a few, and rarely with just one. One speaking mouth, with many ears, and half as many writing hands—there

2. *On the Future of Our Educational Institutions*, trans. J. M. Kennedy (Edinburgh: T. N. Foulis, 1910). (In this and the following quotations, I have often modified Kennedy's translation in order to bring it closer to the German original.—Trans.)

you have, to all appearances, the external academic apparatus *(äusserliche akademische Apparat);* there you have the university culture-machine *(Bildungsmachine)* in action. As for what remains, the proprietor of this one mouth is severed from and independent of the owners of the many ears; and this double autonomy is enthusiastically loaned and lauded under the heading of 'academic freedom.' And of what is left, one can say—so that freedom is still accrued—more or less what one wants, as the other may hear more or less what he wants. . . Except that, behind both of them the State stands at a measured distance with all the intentness of an overseer. It stands there now and then reminding professors and students that it, the State, is the aim, the goal, the be-all and end-all *(Zweck, Ziel und Inbegriff),* of this curious speaking and hearing procedure." End of quote. I have just read, and you have just heard, a fragment of a discourse lent to or cited by Nietzsche and placed in the mouth of an ironic philosopher ("The philosopher laughed, not altogether good-naturedly" before holding the discourse that was just recorded). This philosopher is old; he resigned from the university, hardened and disappointed. He is not speaking at noon, but in the afternoon, at midnight. And he has just protested the unexpected arrival of a flock, a horde, a swarm *(Schwarm)* of students. What is your objection to students? they ask him. At first he offers no response. Then, after a pause: "So, my friend, even at midnight, even on top of a solitary mountain, we shall not be alone; and you yourself are bringing a pack *(Schar)* of mischief-making students along with you, although you well know that I am only too glad to be cut off from *hoc genus omne.* I don't quite understand you, my distant friend . . . in this place where, in a memorable hour, I once came upon you as you sat in majestic solitude *(feierlich vereinsamt),* and where we would earnestly deliberate with each other like knights of a new order. Let those who can understand us listen to us; but why should you bring with you a throng of people who don't understand us! I no longer recognize you, my distant friend!"

"We did not think it proper to interrupt him during his disheartened lament: and when in melancholy he receded into silence, we did not dare tell him how greatly this distrustful repudiation of students distressed us."

The temptation is strong. I am referring to that temptation which leads *all* of us to recognize *ourselves* in the program of this very situation or in the partition of this very piece. I could demonstrate this further if the academic allotment of lecture-time did not prohibit it. Yes, to recognize *ourselves, all* of us, in these places, and within the walls of an institution whose collapse is heralded by the old philosopher of midnight ("Constructed upon clay foundations of the current *Gymnasien*-culture, on a crumbling groundwork, your edifice would prove awry and unsteady if a whirlwind were to swirl up").

But even if we yielded to the temptation of recognizing ourselves, all of us, and no matter how well we demonstrated it, what indeed would we recognize but all of *us*, ourselves, a century later? I would say in French "*nous tous,*" not "*nous toutes*"—all of us men, not all of us women. For such is the profound complicity linking the protagonists in this situation or scene; such is the contract that masterminds all, even their conflicts: woman, if I have read correctly, never appears. Neither to engage in study nor to teach. She appears at no point on the umbilical cord. The great "cripple," perhaps. No women—and I would not want to extract from this remark the supplement of seduction that figures as part of all courses today: the vulgar sleight of hand related to what I propose to call "gynegogy."

No women, then, if I have read correctly. With the notable exception of the mother, of course. But this makes up part of the system, for the mother is the faceless, unfigurable figure of a *figurante.* She creates a place for all the figures by losing herself in the background, like an anonymous persona. All returns to her—and, in the first place, life—all addresses and destines itself to her. She survives—on the condition of remaining in the background.

Translated by Avital Ronell

Contributors

James Creech teaches French at Miami University (Ohio). He has just completed a book on *Representation and Difference in the Writing of Denis Diderot*.

Joan DeJean, whose work has focused primarily on seventeenth-century French literature, teaches French at Princeton University. Her most recent book is *Libertine Strategies: Freedom and the Novel in Seventeenth Century France*.

Paul de Man teaches French and comparative literature at Yale University. He is the author of *Blindness and Insight: Essays in the Rhetoric of Contemporary Criticism* and *Allegories of Reading: Figural Language in Rousseau, Nietzsche, Rilke, and Proust*.

Jacques Derrida teaches philosophy at the Ecole Normale Supérieure in Paris. Many of his best known works, including *Of Grammatology, Writing and Difference,* and *Dissemination,* have been translated into English. His most recent work is *La Carte Postale: de Socrate à Freud et au-delà*.

Shoshana Felman teaches French at Yale University. She is author of *La "Folie" dans l'oeuvre romanesque de Stendhal, La Folie et la chose littéraire,* and *Le Scandale du corps parlant: Don Juan avec Austin, ou la séduction en deux langues* (the latter two forthcoming in English).

Christophe Gallier, currently in Paris, is a student in the Film/French Program at the University of Iowa.

Jane Gallop teaches French at Miami University (Ohio). She is the author of *Intersections: A Reading of Sade with Bataille, Blanchot, and Klossowski* and *Feminism and Psychoanalysis: The Daughter's Seduction*.

Barbara Guetti teaches literature and the humanities at Simon's Rock of Bard College in Great Barrington, Mass. She has previously published on Rousseau, and is currently working on a series of articles examining the efforts of novelists, critics, and philosophers to explain or defend the practice of fiction.

Neil Hertz teaches English at Cornell University. He has published essays on Longinus, Wordsworth, Flaubert, George Eliot, and Freud.

Barbara Johnson teaches French and comparative literature at Yale University. She is author of *Défigurations du langage poétique* and *The Critical Difference*, as well as translator of Jacques Derrida's *Dissemination*.

Jean-François Lyotard, of the philosophy department at the University of Paris at Vincennes (now at St. Denis), has written numerous books, including *Des dispositifs pulsionnels, Dérives à partir de Marx et Freud, Economie libidinale, La Condition postmoderne,* and *Au Juste.*

Andrew McKenna teaches French at Loyola University of Chicago. He has published essays on Baudelaire, Flaubert, Rimbaud, Borges, and contemporary literary criticism.

Angela Moger teaches French and literature at Sarah Lawrence College. She has recently completed an extended study of frame narrative.

Avital Ronell is currently holder of an Alexander von Humboldt-Stiftung Grant, and is working on a book on Goethe.

Michael Ryan teaches English at the University of Virginia, and is author of the forthcoming *Marxism and Deconstruction: A Critical Articulation.*

Richard Terdiman teaches French and comparative literature at the University of California at San Diego. His essay (on Balzac) is drawn from a larger project on nineteenth-century "counter-discourses."

Steven Ungar teaches French and comparative literature at the University of Iowa. "The Professor of Desire" is drawn from his forthcoming book on Roland Barthes.

YALE FRENCH STUDIES, 315 William L. Harkness Hall
Yale University, New Haven, Connecticut 06520

The following issues are still available through the Yale French Studies Office:

19/20 Contemporary Art	$2.50	
23 Humor	$2.50	
32 Paris in Literature	$2.50	
33 Shakespeare	$2.50	
35 Sade	$2.50	
38 The Classical Line	$2.50	
39 Literature and Revolution	$3.50	
40 Literature and Society: 18th Century	$2.50	
41 Game, Play, Literature	$2.50	
42 Zola	$2.50	
43 The Child's Part	$2.50	
44 Paul Valéry	$2.50	
45 Language as Action	$2.50	
46 From Stage to Street	$2.50	
47 Image & Symbol in the Renaissance	$2.50	
49 Science, Language, & the Perspective Mind	$2.50	
50 Intoxication and Literature	$2.50	

52 Graphesis: Perspectives in Literature & Philosophy	$3.50	
53 African Literature	$2.50	
54 Mallarmé	$3.00	
55/56 Literature & Psychoanalysis	$6.00	
57 Locus: Space, Landscape, Decor	$5.00	
58 In Memory of Jacques Ehrmann	$5.00	
59 Rethinking History	$5.00	
60 Cinema/Sound	$5.00	
61 Toward a Theory of Description	$5.00	
62 Feminist Readings: French Texts/American Contexts	$5.00	

Add for postage & handling

United States	$ .50	Foreign countries (including Canada)	$1.50
Each additional issue	$ .30	Each additional issue	$ .75

The following issues are now available through:
Kraus Reprint Company, Route 100, Millwood, N.Y. 10546

1 Critical Bibliography of Existentialism	17 The Art of the Cinema
2 Modern Poets	18 Passion & the Intellect, or Malraux
3 Criticism & Creation	21 Poetry Since the Liberation
4 Literature & Ideas	22 French Education
5 The Modern Theatre	24 Midnight Novelists
6 France and World Literature	25 Albert Camus
7 André Gide	26 The Myth of Napoleon
8 What's Novel in the Novel	27 Women Writers
9 Symbolism	28 Rousseau
10 French-American Literature Relationships	29 The New Dramatists
11 Eros, Variations. . .	30 Sartre
12 God & the Writer	31 Surrealism
13 Romanticism Revisited	34 Proust
14 Motley: Today's French Theater	48 French Freud
15 Social & Political France	51 Approaches to Medieval Romance
16 Foray through Existentialism	

36/37 Structuralism has been reprinted by Doubleday as an Anchor Book.

YALE FRENCH STUDIES is also available through: Xerox University Microfilms, 300 North Zeeb Road, Ann Arbor, MI 48106